INTRODUCTION

Within seven months of the conclusion of the 1954 Geneva Conference, the historical office of the Joint Chiefs of Staff completed this historical narrative of JCS involvement in the development of US policy on Indochina. The title's reference to the Indochina "Incident," which perforce strikes us now as odd, must have seemed more appropriate then. After the Geneva decision to partition Vietnam, US military strategists did not want to commit to South Vietnam any more resources than were necessary for that country's internal security. They believed that the United States would carry any future major fighting in the area directly to what they saw as the most likely source of trouble—the People's Republic of China. "If at all possible," the authors note, "United States strategists wished to avoid becoming involved deeply in the militarily unimportant area of Southeast Asia." Thus the JCS historians in 1954-55 could write the story of American aid to the unsuccessful French effort in Indochina as the history of an incident; the rest of the play would be acted out, it appeared, on a larger stage.

This is not to say that the authors were unaware of the significance of French rule for the Vietnamese people. The narrative begins with a brief but vivid description of the severe economic and social effects of a harsh French colonialism. Read with the hindsight of a quarter century, the sure condemnatory tone provokes a feeling of irony—others one day would bitterly accuse the critics' nation of darker crimes against the same people. Foreshadowing the theme of the volume, the authors couple their critique of French colonialism with a sketch of the history of Vietnamese political parties that spotlights the Indochinese Communist Party. Ho Chi Minh they limn as strictly an agent of international communism. This setting of the scene prepares the reader for the book's central assumption: the United States had to assist France in Indochina because the alternative was too grim to contemplate.

As the authors relate, with only minor exaggeration, President Franklin D. Roosevelt's attitude toward Indochina constituted American policy until April 1945. Once the American landings in North Africa had been completed in November 1942, the president stopped proclaiming that the United States would assist in the restoration of the French Empire. Sufficient evidence now has been unearthed to show that Roosevelt did not shift ground in anger over French resistance to the invasion, but rather because there was no longer an immediate military reason to placate a nation whose decadence, he believed, had caused it to crumble before German attacks and Japanese pressures in 1940.

Roosevelt and the Joint Chiefs of Staff agreed in the fall of 1943 that the United States should not meet a Free French request for military supplies for use against the Japanese in Indochina. But the reasons of the president and his military advisors for concurring were significantly different. Besides his anti-French feelings, Roosevelt was politically and ideologically loath to support the restoration of a colonial regime (and, it may be added, still entertained the hope that Chiang Kai-shek's China would join with the United States as a post-colonial stabilizing force in Asia after the war). The Joint Chiefs naturally thought in military terms: French efforts to wrest control of Indochina from the Japanese would be militarily insignificant and would contribute virtually nothing to the war effort. In August 1944 the JCS were of the same mind, opposing any French participation in regular military operations in the area. They were sympathetic, however, to the establishment in Adm. Louis Mountbatten's Southeast Asia Command (SEAC) of a French military mission to engage in planning for clandestine operations in Indochina. When American officials in SEAC recognized this mission, Roosevelt in October angrily withdrew the recognition as an unwarranted political decision. He made clear that he wanted nothing done that could be interpreted as an American commitment to help the French regain Indochina.

According to the authors, the state department and the Joint Chiefs rigidly adhered to Roosevelt's dictum until the president relaxed it in March 1945. Recent research has qualified this statement. While high civilian and military officials may have heeded the presidential warning, Roosevelt himself in January 1945 quietly and informally gave the British approval for Mountbatten to employ the French in clandestine operations. Moreover, American commanders in China had been cooperating on intelligence matters with the French in Indochina since 1943. Immediate tactical concerns, combined with irregular policy guidance from Washington, led the men on the ground to use the means at hand to accomplish their missions. Roosevelt's "hands-off" order of October 1944, followed by his unannounced modification of it in January, sowed confusion in the Far Eastern theaters.

The Japanese overthrow in March 1945 of the Vichy French administration in Indochina brought an official relaxation of Roosevelt's policy. He approved aid to the French as long as it did not interfere with planned military operations. The JCS historians speculate that Roosevelt primarily sought to gain some leverage against any British-French coalition designed to reinstate colonial regimes. They also point out that Roosevelt and the Joint Chiefs feared that exclusive British aid to the French might strengthen SEAC's position in its jurisdictional squabble with the China theater over Indochina. But other pressures contributed heavily to the softening of the president's stand toward the French in the early months of 1945. Chiang's regime was demonstrating that it lacked the strength to play the role of a stabilizing postwar big power. The increasing potency of Free French forces, on the other hand, demanded some recognition. Many state department officials were strongly in favor of a restoration of the French pressure in Indochina because they feared chaos would result otherwise. Members of the JCS privately had expressed sympathy for a French return.

At the end of the war, the Truman administration passively accepted the restoration of French sovereignty in Indochina. The authors note that there were two alternatives to this policy: active assistance to the French or the establishment of an international trusteeship over Indochina. Aid to the French, they observe, would have been unacceptable to the American public for ideological reasons and because it would have tied up US forces scheduled to come home. The other alternative, opposed by the British and the French, virtually had been precluded by a provision of the United Nations Charter that would have required French consent for a trusteeship.

Correct so far as it goes, this analysis fails to mention the important role of the American military establishment in the emasculation of the trusteeship concept; nor does it place the Truman administration's decision in the context of Soviet-American relations. Roosevelt, who had favored a trusteeship plan, had been erratic in actively supporting and developing it. The war and navy departments and the JCS consistently opposed the idea because they feared that it would preclude permanent American control over the strategically significant Japanese mandated Mariana, Caroline, and Marshall Islands. This concern over Pacific bases meshed with the fears of state department Europeanists that US support for a UN trusteeship over Indochina would alienate the French and thereby threaten both the establishment of the UN and allied cooperation in Europe. Already, prominent American policymakers had begun to worry about the possibility of Soviet expansion in Europe. As a result of the convergence of these interests, the US acquiesced in a UN charter provision that gave the Security Council, rather than the General Assembly, trusteeship control over strategically important areas, and made trusteeships voluntary on the part of colonial powers.

Discussing the critical period between V-J Day and the eruption of the Franco-Vietnamese war in late 1946, the authors are at pains to refute French charges that the United States was a major source of French difficulties. They stress the efforts of American officials to restrain the involvement of Office of Strategic Services officers with the Viet Minh. This emphasis reflects the predominant attitude at the time both of the events and of the writing. The assumption in 1945 and 1955 was that any aid to Ho Chi Minh was bad policy because he was a communist. Since the subsequent disastrous American involvement in Vietnam, some scholars have asked if the United States could not have obtained a better result by opening a direct channel of communication with Ho. From November 1945 until March 1946, the Viet Minh leader gave abundant signals that he wished some degree of alignment with the West. The history of Chinese-Vietnamese relations should have suggested that a common political ideology — even communism — would not automatically propel a popular Vietnamese leader into a Chinese embrace. And the view of Ho as a loyal agent of Moscow remains as unsubstantiated now as it was in 1945-46. It is well within the realm of possibility that timely diplomatic intervention by the United States could have produced a Franco-Vietnamese solution short of war. Those who, pointing to the ruthless Vietnamese regime of the 1970s and '80s, deride the practicality of this suggestion might do well to ponder how that regime might have been different if it had enjoyed thirty years of peace.

By the late 1940s, with the United States and the Soviet Union solidly in the grip of the cold war, American policymakers saw Indochina as a dilemma: aid to the French might alienate the people of Southeast Asia from the Western powers, but support for full independence for the Vietnamese might lead to a communist state in Indochina. The Truman administration's initial solution was to steer a middle course, recognizing French sovereignty but not supplying the French with arms, and opposing an independent Vietnamese state while calling on the French to allow greater autonomy. A loosening of French control, the United States hoped, would strengthen anticommunist Vietnamese at the expense of the communists. The communist victory in China in 1949 increased the urgency of the situation for American officials, and the state department threw its support behind the former Emperor Bao Dai as a rallying point for noncommunist nationalists. Warnings that Bao Dai was merely a French convenience went unheeded in the face of a dual fear: first, that the need for French support for Western European security precluded any move that would weaken or antagonize France; and second, that Indochinese resources coupled with Chinese power would gravely endanger the entire US security system in the Far East. The United States formally recognized the Bao Dai government in February 1950, shortly after a very belated recognition of Ho Chi Minh's government by the Soviet Union.

While the state department moved toward diplomatic support of Bao Dai, the Joint Chiefs of Staff helped pave the way for military aid to the French. The Connally Amendment to the National Defense Act of 1949 provided $75 million to be spent at the president's discretion in combatting communism in "the general area of China." Clearly, the amendment's supporters intended to earmark the money for the Nationalist Chinese on Formosa. But the JCS, defining the general area of China as including Indochina, Burma, and Thailand, proposed that the United States undertake overt and covert measures to support anticommunist forces and undermine their communist opponents in Southeast Asia. According to the authors, this recommendation, unaccompanied by any military appraisal of US strategic interests in the Far East, laid the groundwork for subsequent policy decisions by the National Security Council. At JCS advice, the NSC revised a December 1949 policy declaration to call for active "support," rather than "encouragement," of Asian countries threatened by communism. President Truman in March 1950 approved the release of $15 million in Connally Amendment funds to finance the beginnings of a military aid program for Indochina. The following month, he approved an NSC policy statement which described Indochina as being under immediate threat and declared it the key area of Southeast Asia for US security interests.

War in Korea shifted the administration's Far Eastern focus at mid-year away from Southeast Asia. As the authors point out, however, the North Korean invasion heightened the concern of the US government about communist advances in the general area of the Far East. President Truman, while initiating American intervention in Korea, also approved a JCS recommendation for increased military aid to Indochina (which meant, of course, nothing more than aid to the French, since they refused to allow the Bao Dai government a role in either the presentation of military requirements or the distribution of US military material).

At the beginning of the Korean War, the Department of Defense was the agency most anxious about Southeast Asia. The degree of this anxiety resulted in part from prodding by the JCS. In the authors' view, the Joint Chiefs "seemed to see more clearly than the State Department the threat to the United States strategic position in the Far East inherent in a Communist Vietnam, and they were more eager to act with the resources at hand in order to salvage it for the free world." JCS concern centered on the future actions of China. In August 1950 the Joint Chiefs tried to convince the NSC that if the Chinese intervened overtly with military force in Indochina, the United States should increase its military aid to the French and mobilize to the extent necessary. The NSC agreed with the expansion of military aid but stipulated that the United States would not allow itself to be provoked by such a Chinese attack into a general war with China. Apparently sharing in a consensus among state and defense department officials that Chinese intervention was more likely in Southeast Asia than in Korea (a belief whose origins merit further study), the Joint Chiefs in October seemed on the verge of urging the use of US troops if absolutely necessary to save Indochina. Then the Chinese struck in Korea, tying down US forces for the foreseeable future.

The authors are on shaky ground when they aver that the Korean War's demands on China probably deterred the Chinese from open military intervention in Indochina. Their assumption is based on intelligence estimates of the military capabilities, rather than the political intentions, of China in the early 1950s. Here the historians seem to reflect the preoccupation of policymakers, during the period under consideration, with the possibility that the Chinese would wage war in Indochina.

Linked to this apprehension was the policymakers' belief that the Soviet Union controlled China's foreign policy. In December 1950 the Joint Chiefs, faced with a powerful Chinese challenge in Korea, recommended against any use of US troops in Indochina; such an action, they feared, probably would result in war first with China, and eventually with the USSR in Western Europe. The JCS warned that the Western powers' strength was insufficient to fight two wars. Other government officials agreed with this line of reasoning.

Believing global war to be a real possibility, the Joint Chiefs wished maximum freedom of action if it came. They resisted movement in 1951 and

'52 toward a possible American-British-French combined command arrangement for Southeast Asia. Pre-established combined commands would only encumber them, the JCS felt, since allied nations could not be expected to make a proportionally sufficient contribution (NATO, designed to defend the allies' homelands, was an exception to the rule). An NSC study of the Southeast Asia situation in February 1952 contemplated joint action with the British and the French to counter any Chinese invasion of Indochina. The Joint Chiefs warned that both Britain and France opposed direct action against China — the British because they feared retaliation against Hong Kong, the French because they did not want their resources diverted from Southeast Asia. And without military measures against China itself, the JCS maintained, the local defense of Indochina could not succeed.

Since mid-1950 the Joint Chiefs had been seeking from the NSC a more definite, stronger policy statement on Indochina. Having dashed cold water on the NSC proposal for combined allied action, the JCS supported unilateral US action if necessary to save Indochina; they pressed, in effect, for a political decision as to whether the United States would go to war with China over Southeast Asia. Several months of discussion and "negotiations" (one may assume the authors chose this term purposefully) ensued between the state and defense departments and the NSC staff. "During this time," the authors laconically note, "the National Security Council decided to give more consideration...to what the United States should do for Indochina in the current situation, that is, in the absence of overt Chinese Communist aggression."

President Truman in June 1952 approved the resultant NSC policy statement, which declared that the primary threat to Southeast Asia lay in the possible weakening of the resolve or the ability of France and the Associated States (Vietnam, Cambodia, and Laos) to continue the struggle. Yet the document proposed, in the event that France no longer seemed prepared to carry the burden, only that the United States oppose a French withdrawal and consult with France and Britain on further measures. As for current policy prescriptions, the NSC pledged to continue support for the French effort while urging France to develop both the national armies and the political independence of the Associated States. At the behest of the Joint Chiefs, the policy statement provided that the United States consider acting unilaterally against China if the British and the French declined to retaliate directly against any Chinese aggression. The new document was a milestone for the JCS, because it allowed them to begin developing specific plans to meet the perceived Chinese threat. However, the statement offered no certainty as to US actions in the event of either Chinese intervention or imminent French collapse.

As the authors observe, there were abundant signs by the end of 1952 that French resolve to continue in Indochina was weakening. Yet the government of neither France nor the United States was willing to face squarely the consequences of this fact. American material aid continued to increase but the French spurned offers of US training assistance for the Vietnamese National Army. French fear of American interference precluded the strengthening of Vietnamese forces that was essential if the French were to succeed. American officials — including those providing intelligence estimates — chose to believe French reassurances that belied the facts.

The Eisenhower administration entered office in 1953 committed to the same single-minded goal as its predecessor in regard to Southeast Asia: stopping communist expansion. Achievement of this aim meant working with and through the French, since the United States was not prepared to assume the task itself.

Early in the year, the French developed a plan for enlargement of the Vietnamese National Army that seemed a step toward the increased responsibility for the Vietnamese that the United States desired. This plan inevitably was accompanied by a request for American money to implement it. The Joint Chiefs endorsed the plan but stressed that it must be coupled with a more aggressive strategy. Indeed, the French assumed a defensive rather than an offensive attitude in Indochina. In the authors' blunt appraisal, the French conducted themselves bravely on the battlefield but lacked "guts" at the planning board, probably partly because of poor support at home. Besides the financial strain of the war on France, which the authors readily acknowledge, a broader perspective would take into account the physical and emotional effects of two world wars on the French nation.

JCS criticisms of the French military approach to the war led to the development of the Navarre Plan in mid-1953. Named after the energetic new French commander in Indochina, this plan for offensive operations met JCS objections on paper but would cost the United States much more in additional aid. Without this further support, the French said, they eventually would have to withdraw from Indochina. American officials believed that the French government then in power probably would be the last one willing to make the exertion necessary for victory, since French public opinion increasingly was turning in favor of a negotiated settlement. If, as some American policymakers expected, such a settlement led to the communization of all Southeast Asia, the United States would be forced to a decision on military intervention.

It was in this atmosphere that the NSC in August predicated its support for the Navarre Plan partly on the willingness of the Joint Chiefs to affirm that the French program held promise of success and could be implemented effectively. The JCS provided the affirmation but emphasized that the plan's success would be contingent upon both vigorous implementation in the field and political support in France. They added that continued US support for the plan should be tied to French willingness to accept American military advice. Within a week of this recommendation, President Eisenhower appointed three new members of the Joint Chiefs, including Adm. Arthur W. Radford as chairman. Receiving reports from Indochina that the French appeared to have no plans for a general offensive until October 1954, the new JCS revised the appraisal of their predecessors. While adding greater reservations, however, they still endorsed the plan. The United States subsequently agreed to support the plan on the conditions that France would carry it out firmly and with dispatch, would take American military advice into account, and would press forward with a program for granting full independence to the three Associated States. In addition, the United States wanted a strict accounting of how its money was spent — something that had been seriously lacking up till then.

By the end of 1953 the United States was sending as much material aid as the French could employ usefully, but General Navarre's plan was in disarray. Despite American warnings of the perils of negotiating from weakness, the French were becoming disposed more and more to a negotiated settlement. Surveying the scene, the American officials assessed the probable consequences of a French defeat. Loss of Indochina almost certainly would lead to communist takeover of the entire region, in the estimation of the ranking intelligence officer on the Joint Staff. The Central Intelligence Agency, although also quite pessimistic, was not as ready to predict the future. In the CIA's assessment, French withdrawal would result in the removal of a significant military barrier to a communist sweep of Southeast Asia; the exposure of the rest of the region to greatly increased external pressures; and a probable increase in the capabilities of local communists. The Joint Staff estimate won out in the NSC, which accepted as policy a further JCS warning that the loss of Southeast Asia eventually might lead to Japan's accommodation with communism.

This dismal outlook prompted the Joint Chiefs to press the Eisenhower administration in January 1954 for a decision as to what the United States would do in the event of French withdrawal. Deputy Secretary of Defense Roger Kyes rebuffed the JCS on what was obviously a pretext — the accuracy of logistical requirements in their presentation of alternative courses of action. Secretary of Defense Charles E. Wilson backed Kyes and in turn was sustained by President Eisenhower. However, Eisenhower overrode Kyes's objections to a proposal, supported by Admiral Radford, to send two hundred US Air Force mechanics to Indochina. The president would not rule out US air and naval intervention, but was opposed to committing ground troops. Beyond that indication of policy he would not go.

In February the United States reluctantly agreed to French demands for discussion of Indochina at the upcoming Geneva Convention. By March the French position in Indochina had so deteriorated that Kyes now approved a JCS recommendation for study of the question of intervention. Shortly thereafter, Eisenhower set several necessary conditions for military intervention: a request for assistance from the Associated States; UN approval and the active participation of other nations; and Congressional assent. Congressional leaders, sounded out by the administration, were skeptical of further Korea-like involvements without major commitments from allies.

Nor would they act without reliable assurances that France was granting the Associated States full independence.

It was now early April and the French garrison at Dienbienphu was in danger of collapse. Gen. Matthew Ridgway, Army Chief of Staff, suggested that the JCS consider direct action against China if the United States intervened. There were no decisive targets in Indochina, Ridgway maintained, and the United States would only dangerously divert its limited military capabilities if it used them there. Although the other Joint Chiefs did not take a stand on Ridgway's proposal at that time, they returned to it in May when the situation had worsened.

Conspicuous by its absence in the JCS historians' account of this tense period in the spring of 1954 is any discussion of the controversial Operation VULTURE. The plan for this operation called for US air strikes, possibly with tactical atomic weapons, on the Viet Minh at Dienbienphu. But the authors cannot be faulted for a sin of omission. They wrote from the official records, which are free of the details of the plan or the debates it engendered within the government. For these facts we have had to rely almost wholly on news accounts and the later — much later — recollections of the participants. It should not be so.

The United States refused French requests to intervene unilaterally. The French refused to consider any intervention by an international coalition because it would lessen their conrol of the situation. Thus Dienbienphu fell on 7 May, the day before the opening of the Geneva Convention.

The Joint Chiefs recommended that at Geneva the United States oppose any Indochina cease-fire not accompanied by a satisfactory political settlement. Given the opportunity of an armistice without such a settlement, the JCS believed, the Viet Minh probably would seek to improve their military position. Both the NSC and the president agreed with this argument, and the recommendation became official policy. As the authors note, the United States actually had little choice but to acquiesce in armistice negotiations, and the talks when they came represented a self-inflicted US defeat.

During the first half of the conference, however, the United States and France continued to discuss the possibility of US military intervention because it suited the interests of both nations to do so. Both viewed the discussions as providing a certain amount of leverage against the communist negotiators. In JCS contingency planning for a possible intervention, the central premise was that the real solution of Far Eastern difficulties lay in the neutralization of China. For obvious political reasons the Joint Chiefs, in detailing how this goal would be accomplished, had to presuppose that China would intervene first. JCS strategy in that case called for a selective atomic offensive against China in addition to the use of conventional weapons and a blockade of the Chinese coast. The Joint Chiefs recommended that these measures be accompanied by the appropriate degree of mobilization in anticipation of a general war that might result. Even absent Chinese intervention, however, the

JCS assumed that an American intervention might result in the covert involvement of Soviet air forces and the use of atomic weapons by both sides. Presciently, the Joint Chiefs in June observed that a determined US intervention in Indochina ultimately would require ground forces and possibly would lead to full US responsibility for the outcome of the war.

Once the Geneva accords partitioning Vietnam were signed in July, the Joint Chiefs were able to face more fully the question of future security arrangements in the Far East. The only significant military power available in the area was in Korea and Formosa, and the cost of developing regional military might in Southeast Asia would be tremendous. Therefore, the JCS envisioned a buildup by each Southeast Asian nation of its own forces for internal security, with any main fighting left to the United States and its more powerful allies. JCS planners assumed that the significant fighting would take place elsewhere; China remained the cynosure as the Joint Chiefs looked to the East.

In their concluding remarks, the authors pose a single question: Why was it that a small and seemingly insignificant insurgent movement was able to defeat a major power of Western Europe? Their answers include the fighting qualities and leadership of the Viet Minh; French intransigence and post-World War II weakness; the US desire to prevent the formation of Marxist dictatorships; and the influence of China, both actual and threatening. One wonders whether the authors, if they were writing today, would attempt to probe the wellsprings of the Viet Minh's fighting qualities — and whether they would ask any more questions.

Terrence J. Gough

NOTE

This volume was originally prepared as a TOP SECRET document for use by the Joint Chiefs of Staff. It was declassified in April 1981 and is now reissued in unclassified form. The text appears as originally written, without addition or reinterpretation. Many of the documents cited in the footnotes have also been declassified, but no attempt has been made to reflect these changes.

20 August 1971

AUTHORITY

This volume has been prepared by historians in the Historical Division of the Joint Secretariat in accordance with professional standards of historiography. Inasmuch as the content of the volume has not been considered by the Joint Chiefs of Staff, it is to be construed as descriptive only and not as constituting the official position of the Joint Chiefs of Staff on any subject.

J. K. BRATTON
Brigadier General, USA
Secretary, JCS

FOREWORD

This study is essentially a reproduction of an earlier study prepared by the Historical Division, Joint Secretariat, entitled "History of the Indochina Incident" and completed on 1 February 1955. In light of current developments in Southeast Asia the subject matter in this study has assumed a timeliness and significance that warrants reissue.

No attempt has been made to bring the study up to date by addition of new material or through any historical reevaluation. Although the conclusions have been rewritten and condensed, no attempt has been made to alter their substance. Some minor editorial and stylistic modifications have been introduced but, in the main, the study conforms to earlier rules of editorial style, format, and JCS usage.

                                        E. H. GIUSTI
                                        Chief, Historical Division
                                        Joint Secretariat, JCS

ACKNOWLEDGEMENTS

The Historical Section, Joint Chiefs of Staff, wishes to express its gratitude to the many persons who aided in the preparation of this study. Without the patient cooperation of those who assisted in obtaining, interpreting, and elaborating upon vital documents, and without the aid of those who imparted information not contained in the records, the task would have been much more difficult to accomplish.

Special appreciation is accorded the following: Rear Admiral George W. Anderson, USN, who made available important documents from the Office of the Chairman, Joint Chiefs of Staff, and opened normally inaccessible channels of information; Lieutenant Colonel John W. Vogt, Jr., USAF, Office of the Special Assistant to the Joint Chiefs of Staff for National Security Affairs, whose knowledge of developments on the NSC and planning level was invaluable; Mr. Paul M. Kearney, Administrative Assistant to the Chairman, Joint Chiefs of Staff, for his special interest in the project and detailed knowledge of pertinent files; Mr. Richard R. Day, and Miss Virginia E. Guinand, all of the Office of the Chairman, Joint Chiefs of Staff; Captain Richard H. Phillips, USN, Deputy Secretary, Joint Chiefs of Staff; Mr. Frederick W. Charles and staff, Research and Records Analysis Section, Joint Chiefs of Staff; Mr. Gordon Causey, Joint Intelligence Group, Joint Chiefs of Staff; Lieutenant Colonel Victor W. Alden, USAF, Office of Military Assistance, Office of the Secretary of Defense, without whose records and explanations the story of American aid to the French in Indochina could not have been developed; Honorable Allen W. Dulles, Director of the Central Intelligence Agency; Colonel Robert W. Fuller, III, USA(Ret), and Mr. John S. Earman, both of the Central Intelligence Agency; Commander Howard S. Hyde, Mr. Charlie A. Baker, and Mr. Henry J. Sandri, also of the Office of Military Assistance, Office of the Secretary of Defense; Mr. Legare Obear, Chief, Loan Division, The Library of Congress; Lieutenant Colonel S. Fred Cummings, USA, General Staff, U.S. Army, Office of the Assistant Chief of Staff, G-3 Operations, and Major Hubert L. St. Onge, USA, General Staff, U.S. Army, Office of the Assistant Chief of Staff, G-2 Intelligence, both of whom served with the Military Assistance Advisory Group in Indochina and generously consented to interviews; Major Jack Doherty, USA, for his authoritative observations on, and analysis of, the logistics system, and Mr. Marion L. Eriese, both of the Office of the Deputy Chief of Staff for Logistics, U.S. Army; and Major Edwin J. Nelson, USA, Office of The Adjutant General.

    This work was a collaborative effort by the Historical Section, Joint Chiefs of Staff, under the direction of Colonel Joseph Dasher, USAF, Executive. The Historical Section consists of the following members, all of whom contributed to the completion of this project: Military Historians - Major Norman E. Cawse-Morgon, USAF, Major William P. Moody, USAF, Captain Ernest Giusti, USMCR, Captain Wilber W. Hoare, USA, Lieutenant(jg) Norman B. Ferris, USNR, and Second Lieutenant Robert M. Utley, USA; Civilian Historians - Mr. Vernon E. Davis and Mr. Samuel A. Tucker; Research Assistants - Mr. Paul K. Wood and Mr. Eugene A. Green; Publications Editor - Miss Julia A. Coppa; Clerical Assistants - Mrs. Pauline S. Butler, Mrs. Janet W. Ball, and Mrs. Celia G. Crown.

1 February 1955

CONTENTS

		Page
INTRODUCTION		
Chapter		xxvii

I	THE NATURE AND CONSEQUENCES OF FRENCH RULE IN INDOCHINA	1
	Economic and Sociological Aspects of French Rule	1
	Rise of Nationalism and Political Parties	7

II	ESTABLISHMENT OF JAPANESE DOMINATION IN INDOCHINA, 1940-1941	13
	Japanese Pressure on the French	13
	U.S. Policy toward France and Japan Concerning Indochina	19

III	AMERICAN POLICY TOWARD INDOCHINA, 1942-1946	23
	Roosevelt Policy	23
	Truman Policy	41
	Immediate Postwar Policy	45

IV	INDOCHINA DURING THE WAR YEARS	55
	Birth and Early Development of the Viet Minh	55
	French Activities in Indochina, January 1943-March 1945	59
	The "Independent" Government of Viet Nam	62
	The Viet Minh Seizes Control	67

V	SIXTEEN MONTHS OF CRISIS, SEPTEMBER 1945-DECEMBER 1946	79
	The British Occupation	79
	The Chinese Occupation	91
	The DRV under the Chinese Occupation	96
	French Charges of U.S. Obstruction in Tonkin	100
	The French Succeed and Fail	101

Chapter		Page
VI	MILITARY AND POLITICAL STALEMATE: GROWING U.S. CONCERN, JANUARY 1947–JUNE 1949	113
	Military Situation in the Spring of 1947	113
	The French Break with the Viet Minh	116
	The Bao Dai Restoration Policy	119
	Culmination of the Bao Dai Solution	125
	American Policy toward Indochina, 1947–1949	131
	Conclusions of the Period Prior to Direct U.S. Involvement	136
VII	ORIGINS OF AMERICAN INVOLVEMENT IN INDOCHINA	139
	U.S. Attitude toward Indochina, June 1949–January 1950	139
	Emergence of a Far Eastern and Indochinese Policy	148
	Beginnings of American Aid	153
	Indochina on the Eve of the Korean War	165
VIII	FROM THE START OF THE KOREAN CONFLICT TO 1 JANUARY 1951	169
	Erskine Report	172
	U.S. Government Acts on Erskine Report	175
	Crisis in Indochina	179
	Letourneau-Juin Mission	180
	Pau Conventions	181
	Vietnamese Army	183
	Change of Command--General de Lattre de Tassigny	184
	MAAG Indochina	185
	Pentalateral Mutual Defense Assistance Pact	188
	Development of U.S. Policy toward Indochina, July-December 1950	189
IX	FROM 1 JANUARY 1951 TO THE DEATH OF GENERAL DE LATTRE ON 11 JANUARY 1952	199
	Military Situation in Indochina Improves	199
	Political Situation in Viet Nam during 1951	201
	Cabinet Crisis in Viet Nam	204

Chapter		Page
	National Army of Viet Nam—A Political Failure	204
	De Lattre-Huu Conflict	208
	First Meeting of the High Council of the French Union, 29-30 November	209
	Viet Minh	210
	Development of American Policy toward Indochina	210
	Singapore Conference	211
	The Pleven Visit	214
	Auriol Visit	217
	The Visit of General de Lattre	217
	First Tripartite Intelligence Conference	221
	Origins of the Tripartite Chiefs of Staff Meeting in January 1952	223
	Progress of Aid to Indochina	225
	ECA Program in Indochina	228
	French Attitude toward the United States Aid Programs	229
X	FROM JANUARY 1952 TO THE END OF THE TRUMAN ADMINISTRATION	233
	The Military Situation in Indochina	233
	Progress of the Fighting in Spring and Summer, 1952	235
	The Autumn Campaign in 1952	235
	The Political Situation in Indochina—No Progress	237
	Development of American Policy toward Indochina	239
	The Washington Chiefs of Staff Conference	240
	The Cooper Statement—An Implied Warning	242
	The Five-Power Ad Hoc Committee	243
	The Development of NSC 124/2	246
	The Joint Chiefs of Staff Act on NSC 124/2	254
	The Five-Power Military Conference on Southeast Asia	255
	The Joint Chiefs of Staff Act on the Five-Power Conference Report	257
	American Public Opinion on Indochina	260

Chapter		Page
	Development of the Aid Program during 1952	261
	The Lisbon Program	262
	The Pleven Proposal	263
	Equipment Shortages in Indochina	263
	French Requests for Additional Aircraft	266
	American Mechanics Go to Indochina	267
	United States Offer to Train Vietnamese Forces	268
	Assessment of MDAP in 1952	269
	The French Home Front Begins to Crack	269
XI	THE EISENHOWER ADMINSTRATION AND THE NAVAREE PLAN	273
	The Main Course of U.S. Policy	273
	The French and Indochinese Political Scenes	295
	Main Features of the U.S. Aid Program	304
	Conclusion	318
XII	SUPPORT FOR THE NAVARRE PLAN, 19 NOVEMBER 1953-14 JANUARY 1954	321
XIII	THE BERLIN CONFERENCE AND ITS AFTERMATH, 15 JANUARY-15 MARCH 1954	345
XIV	PRELUDE TO GENEVA, 15 MARCH-7 MAY 1954	367
XV	THE GENEVA CONFERENCE	397
	French Armistice Proposal and U.S. Reaction	398
	Conditions for American Intervention	411
	French Attempts to Secure Unconditional Intervention	418
	U.S. Military Plans for Intervention	427
	Training of Native Troops	433
	United States Strategy in the Far East	444
	The Viet Minh Terms	454
	Final U.S. Position toward Settlement	461
	Anglo-American Discussions	468
	U.S. Unilateral Declaration on Geneva	475

	Page
CONCLUSIONS	481
APPENDIX I, SUMMARY OF THE AID PROGRAM	485
APPENDIX II, TEXT OF FINAL DECLARATION--GENEVA CONFERENCE	495

INTRODUCTION

The directive furnishing the authority for this study specifies that it should be "a history of the Indochina incident from the beginning."* The Historical Section took this to mean a full survey that would place Dien Bien Phu and the Geneva Conference in a proper historical context.

It was soon noted that the events of the 1950's occurred in an atmosphere charged with acrimony and distrust, in which the motivation of Frenchmen and Indochinese natives sprang as often from passion as from reason. The search for the origin of the emotional attitudes that alone can explain some of the turns in the story led ever backward, until the Section members became convinced that the "beginning" could not be set later than the 1860's, the date of the coming of the French to Indochina. Nevertheless, developments during the nineteenth and early twentieth Century have been treated very briefly.

Investigation also revealed that the beginning of United States involvement in the affairs of Indochina went back farther than had been suspected. Although tenuous at times, the current of American interest in the area runs continuously from the spring of 1940. Moreover, some French accusations of American responsibility for the final outcome in Indochina are based upon shadowy episodes in these earlier days. Hence the account had to deal with a considerable time period. To keep the work within manageable lengths it was necessary to omit many interesting and often illuminating details that were not felt pertinent to the central theme.

The history divides roughly into two parts. The first six chapters provide an explanation of political conditions in Indochina on which any full understanding of the events of the later period must be based. The story of direct U.S. involvement begins with Chapter VII.

────────
*Memo, Exec JCS HS, "History of the 'Indochina Incident,'" 26 Aug 54, confirming telephone instructions by RAdm G. W. Anderson, USN, Executive to the Chairman, Joint Chiefs of Staff.

CHAPTER I

THE NATURE AND CONSEQUENCES OF FRENCH
RULE IN INDOCHINA

Many factors have contributed to the present-day situation in Indochina but, almost without exception, they can be traced back to three fundamental causes: the abuses of the French regime, inflamed Indochinese nationalism, and France's ill-conceived attempt after World War II to reassert the hegemony she had enjoyed in that part of the world since the 1860's.

Her dominion had been won by force, and the threat of force. Viet Nam had once been a single, sovereign Annamese state under its own Emperor. Beginning with Cochinchina, which she turned into a colony, France gradually extended her sway over the rest of the country, and reduced the other two Kys of Annam and Tonkin to the status of protectorates. During the same period, Cambodia was drawn into the French sphere and, by the end of the century, Laos had been added to what was now known as the Indochinese Union. By 1938, less than 40,000 Frenchmen were dominating 24 million subjects, in a land approximately one-third larger than France itself.

Economic and Sociological Aspects of French Rule

Indochina proved to be a rich prize. In the 1930's it was the world's third largest exporter of rice. The country also produced rubber, timber, fish, corn, pepper, cattle, coal, iron, tin, zinc, chrome, phosphates, manganese, tungsten, and bauxite. Industrial development, however, was deliberately kept on a low level to avoid competition with French manufactures. Indochina served French purposes better as a source of raw materials and as a market for French goods.[1]

---

1. Ellen J. Hammer, *The Struggle for Indochina* (1954), p. 15.

French investors and French capital held an especially favored position in the economic life of the country. Land could be purchased only by Frenchmen, or by companies with a majority of French stockholders. Over the years, French metropolitan economic interests received strong governmental support in the form of subsidies, bounties, favorable tariff rates, and state orders. France supplied 53 percent of Indochina's imports, and took 50 percent of her exports. An important factor in French dominance of foreign trade was the policy of carrying on free trade with Indochina, while levying on foreign imports into the colony virtually the same tariffs as on imports into France itself.[2] By 1938, foreign investments in Indochina totaled $384 million, of which more than 95 percent were in French hands.[3]

French economic and political control of the country, following physical occupation, was reinforced by the breakdown of the old Vietnamese social and legal structures. The ancient localism gave way before the pressure of foreign administrative, economic, and public-works systems. Gradually, the autonomy and self-sufficiency of the villages were whittled away. The French made use of the traditional monarchy only to discredit it. They took away its power and put their authority behind venal mandarins and "cais," native foremen on the plantations, in the mines, and in industries.[4]

The alliance of opportunistic mandarin and French bureaucrat produced a state of affairs strikingly similar to conditions in eighteenth-century France that led to the French Revolution. With the passage of time, the number and size of large estates increased and peasant ownership of the land became more and more precarious. The estates were generally acquired by usury, which abounded. Local Chinese and Indians joined the wealthy Vietnamese in battening on the poverty of their countrymen. Eventually, the holdings of this privileged group fell, in turn, into the hands of the all-powerful Bank of Indochina. This

---

2. Lawrence K. Rosinger, "France and the Future of Indochina," Foreign Policy Reports, 15 May 45, p. 55.
3. Hammer, Struggle for Indochina, p. 14.
4. Ibid., p. 67.

economically unhealthy trend was hastened and abetted by the peasants' traditional practice of dividing the land among the children of the family. In overcrowded Tonkin, 62 percent of the peasants owned less than nine-tenths of an acre apiece, and 30 percent owned less than four-tenths. The situation was much the same in Annam. In Cochinchina, the center of French economic activity, conditions were even worse. Landlords normally collected more from usury than from rents. Usury, combined with the French practice of granting extensive concessions in undeveloped land to French companies and rich Vietnamese, led to the rise of an absentee landlord class. The estates were worked by tenant farmers and landless agricultural laborers. Between 60 and 80 percent of all Cochinchinese farmland was tilled by sharecroppers, who generally had to give far more than half their harvest to the landlord, partly as rent, partly as usurious interest.5

As the peasant gradually and reluctantly surrendered the land, he fell prey to other abuses that lowered his standard of living and social status, and heightened his discontent. The labor needs of French planters in south Indochina and of French colonists in New Caledonia and the New Hebrides led to the transportation of thousands of northern Indochinese from their homes to lives of drudgery in alien surroundings. Native agents of southern planters signed penniless Tonkinese and northern Annamese to three-year contracts. Conditions did not match the rosy picture painted by the agents: the laborers were shipped south under armed guard; on the plantations they worked ten hours a day at extremely unhealthy tasks; malaria and beriberi were widespread; in 1927 the death rate on the plantations was four to five times higher than in the rest of Cochinchina. Virginia Thompson said of the native foreman:

> . . . He collects a commission from each meagre salary, he forces the coolie to borrow money from him at fantastically high rates, and he realizes a profit on food and even medical supplies. The worker is a serf to

---

5. Ibid., p. 66.

> this petty creditor and overlord, who in
> addition often subjects him to unfair and
> brutal treatment. . . . Coolies are
> punished by fines and blows; their corres-
> pondence is brutally censored; they are
> cut off from their families and communes.
> Misery and brutality lead to wholesale
> desertions and suicides.[6]

Conditions in the Islands were no better. Ironically, the abuses there were exposed by a French colonist, the Marquis de Montpezat, whose important interests in Tonkin were being threatened by the increasing drain of laborers to the Islands.

> . . . He showed up this twentieth-
> century business as a scandal slave trade,
> and the patriotic motives evoked by its
> sponsors as nothing more than plain prof-
> iteering. The powerful Société des
> Phosphates de l'Oceanie used its influence
> with the administration to procure, through
> the village Notables, more cheap Tonkinese
> labour, so as to save them from having to
> hire the more expensive Chinese. Montpezat,
> in his publicity, spared no detail of the
> terrible conditions, not only on the Islands
> themselves, but on the boats transporting
> the workers. The unhealthy climate, and the
> failure to take any medical care of the sick
> or legal care for the rights of the labourers,
> he also scored. Montpezat became the bane of
> the government's existence, but the facts
> that he brought to light could not be denied,
> notably in proving the administration's
> guilty knowledge of this terrible trade.[7]

The evils of contract labor were equalled, or surpassed, by those of forced labor. Mandatory toil on public works was nothing other than the corvee, against which the French themselves had revolted in the days of Louis XVI. Although this particular form of peonage was legally abolished in Indochina at the turn of the century, it persisted in fact,

---

6. Virginia Thompson, *French Indo-China* (1937), pp. 154-155.
7. Ibid., p. 164.

in one form or another, until 1937. The practice of levying forced labor quotas on the countryside had arisen out of the shortage of free labor for the ambitious French program of public works. Mandarins were indispensable intermediaries for procuring the laborers, and they often used the institution as a means for paying off old scores. The colonial government did not show the same consideration for native customs as had the old Annamite regime. Men were often taken from far more useful work in the fields. Village notables arbitrarily selected their victims, who were perennially the same. These men spent their lives on one <u>corvee</u> after another, without respite or any semblance of <u>family life</u>. The heavy mortality and wholesale desertions were eloquent testimony to the lack of care for the human beings engaged on public projects. It was not unusual that villages would be deserted at the approach of a traveller who might have a permit to requisition labor.[8]

Among the misfortunes of the Indochinese was the government's monopoly on salt, alcohol, and opium, which constituted one of the main sources of revenue for the budget.[9] In addition, French companies and Chinese agents, who paid dearly for licenses to sell the three items, realized enormous profits. The use of opium was not widely practiced in Indochina before the arrival of the French. Thereafter, consumption increased rapidly. In France, opium smoking was a criminal offense; in Indochina, it was a financial prop of the government.[10]

Alcohol was a requirement of Annamese religious rites. Before 1893, the natives had been free to distill it for their own use. After that time, its sale was under government monopoly, and in 1903, a French-controlled company was granted a monopoly on its manufacture. Increased consumption was

---
8. Ibid., p. 162.
9. Charles Robequain, <u>The Economic Development of French Indo-China</u> (1944), p. 155.
10. Thompson, <u>French Indo-China</u>, pp. 184-186.

actively encouraged, while domiciliary searches and bonuses for denunciations were instituted to combat contraband buying and selling.[11]

The *gabelle*, a tax on salt, had been highly unpopular in France under the *ancien regime*. Similar in nature, the salt monopoly in Indochina was the most widely resented form of taxation. Salted fish, together with rice, constituted the major element of Annamese diet. Soon after the government took over the sale and distribution of salt at the end of the nineteenth century, the price trebled. Consumption fell off, with adverse effects upon the health of the natives, to say nothing of their political viewpoint. Speculation and fraud were rampant in the salt industry, and minor reforms in the 1930's did little to relieve popular resentment over the government's salt policies. The monopolies on salt, alcohol, and opium led to a constant struggle between the administration and the masses, with thousands imprisoned yearly for contraband trade in these commodities.[12]

Nevertheless, French rule did bring many genuine benefits to Indochina. The Pasteur Institute, of which the French were justly proud, made important advances in the study and treatment of tropical diseases, and greatly improved sanitation and hygiene. Hospitals and dispensaries were built. The French strengthened and extended the dike system that for centuries past had proved incapable of holding back the waters of the delta areas. Thousands of acres of farmland were reclaimed by drainage and irrigation, and French agricultural experts helped the Indochinese to increase their crop yields. Modern road systems were constructed in and around the cities, and a main highway was laid northward from Saigon to the Chinese border. The French also built the Trans-Indochinese and the Yunnan Railroads, the former paralleling the main highway, the latter linking the interior of south China with the port of Haiphong on the Gulf of Tonkin.

---
11. Ibid., pp. 186-188. Hammer, Struggle for Indochina, p. 69.
12. Thompson, French Indo-China, pp. 184-191.

Rise of Nationalism and Political Parties

There are few better goads toward nationalism than subjection to a foreign power. Before the arrival of the French, the Vietnamese already had a centuries-long history of resistance to Chinese attempts to incorporate, and retain, Vietnam within the confines of the Chinese Empire. On the other hand, Annamese emperors ruled by divine sanction and Confucianist doctrine stressed docility in the face of authority. At first this concept aided the French in establishing themselves in the country. But in pressing their language upon the natives, the French unwittingly opened the way for the discovery by Annamese intellectuals of the historic French revolutionary tradition. Once acquainted with the political liberties of the French people, and impressed by the theories upon which those liberties were based, the Indochinese began to seek similar rights for themselves.

The dissatisfaction of Indochinese intellectuals was heightened by the position they were forced to occupy in their own country. They could not travel among the three Vietnamese regions without permission, and to go abroad they needed a police permit. The few who were allowed to go to France to study were treated there as social equals, but upon their return home they were constrained to revert to being "second-class citizens." Important positions in the government of their own country were closed to them. Even in the few posts available, they received much lower salaries than Frenchmen discharging equivalent tasks. Up to half the members of important councils in Indochina were French, and the Vietnamese members were either appointed by the government or elected under a system of highly restricted suffrage. Moreover, the councils had only advisory power.

Regardless of labels, authority was entirely in the hands of the highly centralized French administration. Policy was laid down in France, sometimes by Parliament, more often by ministerial decree. It was implemented in Indochina by the French bureaucracy, which extended downward from the Governor General, the Resident Superieur of the protectorates, and the Governor of Cochin China, to a network of lesser officials.

Ellen Hammer cites the testimony of a French official who had visited the Philippines in 1925-1926 and had been struck by the fact that "all the services with which travelers came into contact--health, police, customs--were staffed by Filipinos." In Indochina they were all French, not only in 1925 but also in 1940. The French held jobs that white men in other colonies considered below their dignity. As a result, the proportion of French officials to Indochinese was higher than that of European officials to the people of any other southeast Asian dependent area. Many Vietnamese withdrew entirely from public life, in passive resistance to French rule. Others turned to violence and revolution in attempting to expel the French and reestablish imperial Viet Nam, with a corresponding return to ancient doctrine and customs. Each revolt, however, lacking organization, direction, or popular support, was easily put down by the French.[13]

There was an upsurge of nationalistic feeling after the Russo-Japanese War of 1905, which destroyed the myth of white invincibility. World War I also played its part. Over 100,000 Annamites were sent to France as soldiers, farm laborers, and factory workers. Resentment over forced participation in the French war effort, coupled with new ideas, such as that of the political party, was transformed into political action upon their return home.[14]

In the period between world wars, Indochinese nationalism changed direction and grew stronger. Whereas formerly opposition to the French had been centered in the mandarins, who wished to restore the old regime and traditional institutions, there now arose a class of French-educated intellectuals who hoped to take the lead in establishing a modern state along western lines. During the twenties, reform movements sprang up throughout the country.

---

13. Hammer, *Struggle for Indochina*, pp. 72-74. Thompson, *French Indo-China*, p. 455.
14. Thompson, *French Indo-China*, pp. 480-481.

The most important non-Communist political party before World War II was the Viet Nam Quoc Dan Dang (VNQDD), or Nationalist Party, founded in 1927 by a group of young intellectuals who looked to China for aid in ousting the French. By the beginning of 1929, membership exceeded 1,500. Emboldened by their waxing strength, Nationalist Party leaders were instrumental during 1930 in staging a number of anti-French riots and demonstrations, bombings in Hanoi, and raids in various parts of the country. They went too far, however, in inciting the Yen Bay garrison to mutiny and massacre the French officers. French troops ruthlessly quelled the revolt, and the VNQDD leaders who were not executed or imprisoned fled to China.[15] The organization followed the surviving leadership and remained in China until 1945, when it again came to the fore in Vietnamese political life.[16]

Another important political party was the Cao Dai, founded in 1926 in Cochinchina as a religious movement. It professed to look toward Indochinese salvation by uniting Buddhism, Confuciansim, Christianity, Taoism, and Animism. It was organized along the same lines as the Catholic hierarchy, having both a pope and a priesthood. By 1930, it had over a million adherents spread through Cochinchina, south Annam, and Cambodia. Its leaders were highly critical of French rule and strongly nationalistic. From 1934 on, the Cao Dai secretly supported the Japanese pretender to the throne of Annam, and aided the Japanese in policing Cochinchina during the wartime occupation.[17]

The Hoa Hao was also a religious movement, founded just prior to World War II by Huynh Phu So, an "idealistic young leader . . . followed devotedly by many thousands of untutored peasants to whom he quoted ancient prophecies as he preached, somewhat vaguely, independence and social reform."[18]

---

15. State Dept, *Political Alignments of Vietnamese Nationalists*, OIR No. 3708, 1 Oct 49, pp. 21-25.
16. Hammer, *Struggle for Indochina*, pp. 82-84.
17. State Dept, *Biographical Information on Prominent Nationalist Leaders in French Indo-China*, R&A No. 3336, 25 Oct 45, pp. 5-6. Hammer, *Struggle for Indochina*, pp. 51-52, 79.
18. Hammer, *Struggle for Indochina*, p. 52.

The story of the early development of the Communist Party in Indochina is inseparably connected with the life and activity of Nguyen ai Quoc, now known as Ho Chi Minh.

Descendant of an Annamese mandarin family, Ho left home at the age of 19 and worked his way around the world on a French ship. He finally established residence in Paris, where he became interested in Communist teachings. During the Versailles Conference in 1919, he drew up, and introduced, a memorandum of Annamite desiderata. Also while in Paris, he founded the Intercolonial Union of Colored Peoples.[19]

Ho Chi Minh attended the Socialist Party Congress at Tours in 1920. Ideological differences developed, and Ho was among those who split away from the Socialists to establish the French Communist Party. In 1922, he founded a newspaper, in which he denounced French colonial policy, and in October 1923 he went to Moscow as Indochinese delegate to the International Peasant Conference. He remained in the Soviet Union for a year and a half, "studying revolutionary methods and associating with Soviet leaders who esteemed him for his remarkable intelligence."[20]

Ho then went to Canton, ostensibly as a Chinese translator in the Soviet Consultate. His primary mission, however, was evident in his founding, in China, of the Association of Revolutionary Annamite Youth--the first Communist cell for Annamites. He also instructed in the politico-military school of Whampoa, originally established to prepare leaders for a world Communist revolution.[21]

When the Kuomintang turned on the Communists in 1927, Ho fled with Borodin to the Soviet Union, where he was officially given the mission of founding Indochinese Communism.[22] By that time, 250 Annamites had received revolutionary training, and over 200 had returned to Indochina to assume key positions in the Communist movement.[23]

---

19. State Dept, R&A No. 3336, pp. 27-28.
20. Thompson, French Indo-China, p. 490.
21. State Dept, R&A No. 3336, pp. 28-29.
22. Thompson, French Indo-China, p. 491.
23. State Dept, OIR No. 3708, p. 31.

The course of Communism in Indochina did not run smoothly. By 1929, a split in the ranks of the Youth League and the rise of dissident groups led to competition among three separate factions for recognition by the Third Internationale. Moscow understandably showed great reluctance to select any one group for official investiture. Instead, the Soviets called upon Ho Chi Minh, as the only personality capable of the task, to unite the three parties. In this he was successful. Although Moscow gave its blessing and a monthly subsidy of 5,000 francs to the united Indochinese Communist Party, the fact that Ho held in his own hands the key to Soviet support later proved to be a serious weakness.[24] The Party reportedly had over 1,000 members in 1930, but the true index of its strength lay in the estimated 100,000 peasants who followed its leadership.[25]

That same year, however, saw the beginning of a series of events that virtually wrecked the Party. Between May and September, the Communists seized upon the discontent and suffering caused by severe famines to organize a chain of demonstrations and uprisings, several of which reached serious proportions. This activity was undertaken while Ho was apparently out of the country and there is reason to believe that it was without his knowledge and consent. French reaction was swift and effective. The outbreaks were ruthlessly crushed and many Communist leaders were tried publicly as common criminals. As a result, Communist power and influence underwent a sharp decline.[26]

Further misfortunes followed. Ho Chi Minh was arrested by the British in Hongkong. The Party, bereft of its leader, lost touch with the Comintern which, in any event, had been highly critical of the campaign of ineffectual violence. The Indochinese Communist Party was faced with practical disintegration. An attempt at reorganization was smashed by the French police in 1932.[27]

---

25. State Dept, OIR No. 3708, pp. 35-36.
26. Ibid., p. 36. Hammer, Struggle for Indochina, pp. 84-86.
27. Ibid.

Following the release, in 1933, of a number of political prisoners taken during the events mentioned above, the Communist Party slowly began to revive in Indochina. The turning point in its history came at the Macao Conference in 1935. Here, besides reaffirming its adherence to the Comintern, the Party received the order from Moscow to join forces with non-Communists in the fight against Fascism. Henceforth, the Asians were expected to cease opposing their European masters and, instead, campaign for democratic rights so that they could work together with the colonialists to combat the Axis. When the Popular Front collapsed in France in 1938, its Indochinese counterpart, the Democratic Front, did likewise, and the Communist Party went underground. This time, however, the Communists fared better than in 1930-1931. Although the Party was outlawed, and some of its leaders were temporarily at leisure in jail, party organization remained intact, the secret cells were undisturbed and the network of party workers and sympathizers continued loyal.[28]

The political parties accounted for in this chapter are but the more outstanding ones among a bewildering array of groups of every political hue. During the war, and especially during the Japanese occupation, almost all Vietnamese political parties found it necessary to join in coalitions in order to further more effectively the work for independence. And of these coalitions, only the Dong Minh Hoi and the Viet Minh acquired sufficient stature to emerge as potent political entities after the war.

---

28. Hammer, Struggle for Indochina, pp. 90-93.

CHAPTER II

ESTABLISHMENT OF JAPANESE DOMINATION IN INDOCHINA
1940-1941

Japanese plans for the creation of a Greater East Asia Co-Prosperity Sphere relied heavily on possession of Indochina. Rich in rice and raw materials, it was also the natural gateway to all Southeast Asia. In addition, by 1940 the strategic location of Indochina had assumed increasing importance for Japan's prosecution of the long and costly war against China.

By the summer of that year, Japanese forces had driven the armies of Chiang Kai-shek into the interior of south China. Cut off from his coastal ports, Chiang depended for a large part of his supplies upon the Yunnan Railroad and the port of Haiphong. Denial of this supply route was, therefore, an early and important Japanese objective.

Japanese Pressure on the French

With the collapse of the French armies in Europe in the spring of 1940, Japan decided to delay no longer. In April, Japanese aircraft bombarded the Yunnan Railroad, and a strong press and radio campaign was initiated against the "provocations" of French Indochina. Japanese troops stirred along the south China border.

Although they were well aware of the impending storm, there was little the French could do to avert it, for Indochina was woefully weak, both economically and militarily. The French now had cause to regret their mercantile policy of restricting Indochinese manufacturing; the country was almost wholly dependent upon overseas sources for industrial products and munitions. For defense, the French had a widely dispersed army of 50,000 French and native troops, one cruiser, four cutters, a few miscellaneous smaller craft, and no modern aircraft. Munitions and supplies were sufficient for only one month of fighting, at the most.[1]

Yet, though isolated from France, virtually defenseless, and subjected to strong Japanese pressure, the French in Indochina still hoped to protect their sovereignty from Japanese encroachment. They embarked on a desperate and dangerous game of delay and compromise.

On 19 June, two days after Petain had asked Germany for an armistice, Japan demanded of General Georges Catroux, Governor-General of Indochina, that the Yunnan Railroad be closed to shipments of war materials for China. To guarantee that the blockade would be effective, Japan also demanded the right to set up a control commission in Tonkin. Catroux was given 24 hours to reply, or suffer Japanese attack. Although he knew acquiescence would probably result in new demands, Catroux felt he had no choice but to yield.[2]

He hoped that, following his submission, the Japanese would be content to wait a time before demanding new concessions. He planned, in the interim, to carry on negotiations with the head of the control commission, and to use the respite of the rainy season to build up his military strength with the help of France and the United States. But his plan soon went awry. In informal discussion with General Gaku Nishihara, chief of the control commission, Catroux made the mistake of suggesting that Vichy France might grant the Japanese further facilities for carrying on their campaign against southern China, provided Tokyo would guarantee French sovereignty and the territorial integrity of Indochina.[3]

When news of this unauthorized proposal reached France, Petain's Colonial Minister was profoundly distressed. Already dissatisfied with Catroux's bowing to the Japanese

---

1. Direction de la Documentation, Notes Documentaires et Etudes (hereinafter: Notes et Etudes), Rpt of Gen Georges Catroux, "La crise franco-japonnaise de juin 1940," No. 120, 22 Aug 45.
2. Ibid.
3. William L. Langer and S. Everett Gleason, The Undeclared War, 1940-1941 (1953), p. 9.

ultimatum, the Minister urged the French Cabinet to recall him. This was done, and Vice Admiral Jean Decoux was named in his stead.[4]

Decoux relieved his predecessor on 20 July, and less than two weeks later the Japanese presented France with a new list of demands. They asked for transit rights through Indochina for Japanese troops, the right to build airfields, and an economic accord that would tie Indochina's resources to Japan. In desperation the Vichy Government tried to bargain for time. Decoux was ordered to resist a Japanese invasion while Vichy reopened discussions with Japan along the identical lines of Catroux's original suggestion.

Behind this apparent willingness to consider new concessions, however, the French were secretly hoping to strengthen their hand enough to reject Japanese demands. The British were in no position, in the summer of 1940, to support the French in Indochina, which left the United States as the best remaining potential source of aid against Japan.[5]

Even as Vichy was dispatching its conciliatory reply to Japan, another message was on its way to the French Ambassador in Washington, instructing him to inform the United States Government of Tokyo's demands. He was also directed to indicate that "the resistance of the French Government to the Japanese demands would necessarily depend to a large extent on the nature and effectiveness of the support which the American Government would be disposed to give it."[6]

The Ambassador was forced to cable his government that there was "no prospect of active American aid against Japan." James C. Dunn, Political Adviser to the State Department, had informed him that "we have been doing and are doing everything possible within the framework of our established

---

4. Paul Baudouin, *Neuf mois au gouvernement, Avril-Decembre 1940* (Paris, 1948), p. 216.
5. Langer and Gleason, *Undeclared War*, p. 9.
6. Ibid., p. 10.

policies to keep the situation in the Far East stabilized; that we have been progressively taking various steps . . . to exert economic pressure on Japan; that our Fleet is now based on Hawaii, and that the course which we have been following . . . gives a clear indication of our intentions and activities for the future."7

Ambassador Saint-Quentin correctly interpreted this reply to mean that "the United States would not use military or naval force in support of any position which might be taken to resist the Japanese attempted aggression on Indo-China."8

Disappointed in Washington, the French continued to temporize with Japan while they next sought to enlist the aid of their recent conqueror, Germany. Cynically appealing to Nazi racism, they suggested that support in Indochina would ensure an Asian foothold for the white race. Germany, however, while expressing sympathy with France's plight, refused to intervene.9

Japan's threats of military action were becoming stronger, and France could find no outside solution to her predicament. Therefore, on the night of 16 August, the French Cabinet decided to make new concessions, hoping in this way to avoid losing all of Indochina at once. The following day, Paul Baudouin, the French Foreign Minister, notified the American Charge d'Affaires that, "in the absence of any material support from Great Britain and the United States as distinguished from the enunciation of principles," France must yield.10

---

7. (C) Doc A-1, Msg, Dunn to USecState, 6 Aug 40, in (TS) State Dept, Hist Div, Documentary History of United States Policy toward Indochina, 1940-1953, Research Proj No. 354, April 1954 (hereinafter: Doc Hist of US Pol toward Indochina).
8. Ibid., p. 2; Langer and Gleason, Undeclared War, p. 1[?]
9. La Delegation Francaise aupres de la Commission Allemande d'Armistice. Recueil de Documents publie par le Gouvernement Francais, Tome Premier, 29 Juin 1940-29 Septembre 1940, pp. 107-108. Langer and Gleason, Undeclared War, p. 11.
10. Langer and Gleason, Undeclared War, p. 12.

As the result of negotiations carried on in Tokyo, a Franco-Japanese political accord was signed on 29 August. Under the terms of this agreement, Japan recognized the "permanent French interest in Indo-China" and France recognized the "preponderance of Japanese interest in that area."[11]

The French had hoped to gain a brief respite by insisting that the political accord not go into effect until a military agreement had been signed. To their chagrin, on the very next day, General Nishihara handed Decoux the complete text of a military agreement and demanded that it be signed by midnight, 2 September. Decoux rejected the ultimatum and prepared to fight. In the meantime, however, Vichy had appealed directly to the Japanese Government, which disavowed Nishihara.[12]

It had been a close call, and the French sought frantically to escape the closing trap while there was yet time. They approached British, American, and German representatives in turn, seeking material support from Britain and America and, from Germany, permission to send Vichy-owned military equipment to Indochina. Great Britain and the United States contented themselves with remonstrating in Tokyo against any change in the status quo, and Germany refused to release the equipment. On the other hand, the Chinese Ambassador in France had several times proposed that Chinese troops move into Indochina to defend it against the Japanese, but Vichy, suspicious of Chinese motives and also afraid of antagonizing Germany, had rejected the offer.[13]

On 19 September, her patience ended, Japan made it clear that Vichy's dilatory tactics would no longer be tolerated. Three days later a military agreement was signed, granting the Japanese use of three airfields in Tonkin and permission to station 6,000 troops there. The French also agreed to permit the eventual passage of Japanese forces (never to number more than 25,000) through

---
11. Langer and Gleason, *Undeclared War*, p. 13.
12. Ibid.
13. Hammer, *Struggle for Indochina*, p. 21.

Tonkin to Yunnan, and consented, subject to further negotiation, to allow a division of the Kwantung Army to be evacuated through Tonkin.[14] But there was no further negotiation. Elements of the Kwantung Army began to move across the frontier on 23 September and were immediately fired upon by the French. Outnumbered and outgunned, the French were badly beaten; by the twenty-fifth, all resistance ceased. The Japanese proceeded to consolidate their hold by taking over strategic points in the north, but they seemed quite content to leave a framework of French control.

Although free to run the country as before, the French had their work cut out for them. Not only did they have native unrest and rebellion to cope with, but by January 1941, they were also embroiled in an undeclared war with Thailand. On 10 September, Thailand had formally demanded retrocession of territory in Laos and Cambodia, and islands in the Mekong, that the French had taken from them in 1904 and 1907. Vichy rejected the claims and, following border skirmishes, Thailand announced the occupation of three districts in Cambodia on 30 November. After a number of indecisive engagements, the French were soundly defeated on 16 January, but had their revenge the next day, when they sank 40 per cent of the Thai Navy in the Gulf of Siam.[15]

With German help, Japan persuaded Vichy to accept mediation of the dispute, and on 31 January 1941, an armistice was signed aboard a Japanese cruiser in Saigon harbor. The French had little choice; they had been warned to accept Japanese mediation or "face the consequences of Japan's determination to assert leadership in Greater East Asia." On 9 May a compromise peace settlement was signed, whereby Thailand received an estimated 26,970 square miles of territory in western Cambodia and Laos, paying France

---
14. Langer and Gleason, Undeclared War, p. 15.
15. Hammer, Struggle for Indochina, p. 25.

6 million piastres (1.37 million dollars) in compensation. Japan was made guarantor of the execution of the peace terms, and both Indochina and Thailand were bound not to conclude any political, economic, or military agreements with third powers, directed against Japan.[16]

U.S. Policy toward France and Japan Concerning Indochina

The Vichy-Japanese accord of 29 August 1940 brought about a change of attitude in American relations with both signatories. It also set in motion the series of events that led inexorably to Pearl Harbor.

When the United States learned of the accord, and the extent of French concessions to Japanese military demands, patience wore thin. Secretary Hull announced to the French Ambassador that "the French Government cannot imagine our surprise and disappointment when it took this step without any notice whatever to us."[17] His surprise was even greater when Vichy issued a statement on 23 September alleging that the United States had approved of the agreement. An emphatic and public denial was immediately put out by the Secretary.[18]

In the meantime, Ambassador Grew in Tokyo had been instructed to protest to the Japanese Government. The thinly veiled insult he received in reply convinced him of the hopelessness of further temporizing and inspired his now famous "green light" message, advocating much stronger measures.[19] The Administration had had such

---

16. (S) State Dept, Div of Research on the Far East (DRF), SEA Br, "Chronological History of Events in Indochina Since 1940 (Background Paper for Indochina Phase of Geneva Conference, April 1954)," 1 Apr 54 (hereinafter: (S) Geneva Conf Background Paper, Indochina Chronology), pp. 18-19, CCS 092 Asia (6-25-48) sec 60 BP pt 10.
17. Cordell Hull, The Memoirs of Cordell Hull (1948), vol I, p. 904.
18. Ibid., p. 907.
19. Langer and Gleason, Undeclared War, pp. 19-20. Hull, Memoirs, vol I, pp. 906-907.

measures under consideration for some time; it only remained to apply them. On 25 September a loan of 25 million dollars to China was announced and, on the following day, the President brought the export of iron and steel scrap under the licensing system in such a way as to exclude Japan.[20]

In the months that followed, the Vichy Government made repeated attempts to purchase airplanes and munitions for use in Indochina. As Secretary Hull states: "We on our part saw no reason to sell planes to Vichy when at that very moment about one hundred American planes originally destined for France were rusting away at Martinique." Hull offered to get British clearance in order to facilitate shipment of these planes to Indochina. Vichy replied that the German Armistice Commission would not permit movement of the aircraft, but was willing to let arms go from America to Indochina. However, the United States chose to sidestep this obvious trap. In spite of being refused material aid, the Vichy Government, and Pierre Laval himself, were forced to admit that it was American policy in the Far East that was deterring Japan from further encroachment.[21]

The extent to which American policy really acted as a deterrent is debatable. Japan was not ready for southward expansion until she had secured herself against attack by the Soviet Union in the north, and until she was sure that seizure of the Far Eastern possessions of Great Britain, France, and the Netherlands would not be challenged by a presumably victorious Germany. The answer to both problems lay in the Tripartite Pact, signed by Germany, Italy, and Japan on 27 September 1940. Germany, in turn, was allied with the Soviet Union, and Japan relied upon this roundabout relationship to keep the Soviets in check.[22]

The stage was now set for the next move, and it was not long in coming. On 12 July 1941, Baron Kato "regretfully" informed the French Government that Japan felt obliged to send land, sea, and air forces into southern

---

20. Hull, *Memoirs*, vol. I, p. 907.
21. Ibid., pp. 907-908.
22. Langer and Gleason, *Undeclared War*, pp. 21ff.

Indochina. He demanded eight air and two naval bases, the withdrawal of French garrisons from places to be occupied by the Japanese, and freedom of movement in southern Indochina for Japanese forces. If a favorable answer were not forthcoming by 20 July, the Baron explained that the use of force would become necessary.[23]

When Washington learned of the Japanese demands, it instructed Ambassador Leahy to use all his influence to delay a decision as long as possible. Leahy bluntly informed Admiral Darlan that "if Japan was the winner, the Japanese would take over French Indochina; and if the Allies won, we would take it." However, since neither the Americans nor the British held out any prospect of aid, Vichy was helpless. Accession at least meant that French sovereignty would be respected on paper.[24]

Japanese troops occupied the southern portions of Indochina on 21 September and by the twenty-ninth Vichy had formally acquiesced to the use of eight airfields and the naval bases at Saigon and Camranh. No limit was placed on the number of troops to be stationed in the area, and the first contingent consisted of 50,000.[25]

As President Roosevelt expressed it, Japan's daring move posed for the United States an "exceedingly serious problem." The President suggested to Ambassador Nomura that, if the Japanese would withdraw their troops, he would try to obtain a solemn declaration by the United States, Great Britain, China, and the Netherlands to regard Indochina as a "neutralized" country, much like Switzerland, provided Japan made a similar commitment. The alternative, he hinted, might be economic sanctions. Nomura unfortunately transmitted this message to his government in garbled form, stressing the sanctions and almost entirely ignoring the constructive offer. As a consequence, the Japanese continued pouring troops into Indochina.[26]

---
23. Ibid., p. 641.
24. Ibid., pp. 641-644; William D. Leahy, I Was There (1940), p. 44.
25. Langer and Gleason, Undeclared War, pp. 21ff.
26. Ibid., pp. 649-651; Foreign Relations of the United States: Japan. 1931-1941 (1943), vol. II, pp. 527-530.

An executive order freezing all Japanese funds and assets in the United States was issued on 26 July. On the same day, Great Britain and the Dominions denounced their trade treaties with Japan and imposed various financial restrictions. The Netherlands followed suit on 28 July. As one American observer commented: "Japan must move quickly to consummate her conquests in Asia or face economic ruin and defeat."[27]

The Japanese intended to move quickly. A message from Matsuoka to Nomura on 2 July read in part: "Preparations for southward advance shall be reenforced and the policy already decided upon with reference to French Indo-China and Thailand shall be executed."[28] Therefore, when Nomura and Kurusu handed Japan's last-word version of a modus vivendi to Secretary Hull on 20 November, it was, in effect, an ultimatum. It was clear to all that Japan's steadily expanding control over Indochina would cease only at the price of "clearly unacceptable . . . conditions that would have assured Japan domination of the Pacific, placing us in serious danger for decades to come."[29]

On the eve of Pearl Harbor (7 December, Asian time), Japanese troops infiltrated Hanoi and took up key positions throughout the city. The next day Governor-General Decoux was presented with a new ultimatum: do nothing to hinder the activities of the Japanese forces, or else Japan would take over Indochina. Decoux bowed to the inevitable. In recompense, French sovereignty was reconfirmed--for what it was worth--and the French were left in control of their own army and of the administration of the country. As Ellen Hammer observes: "Defeated in Europe in 1940, France was defeated in Asia in 1941. One day the Vietnamese would cite their failure as proof that France had forfeited its right to 'protect' Indochina."[30]

---

27. Wilfred Fleischer in the New York Herald Tribune, 27 Jul 41, quoted by Langer and Gleason, Undeclared War, p. 652.
28. Hull, Memoirs, vol II, p. 1013.
29. Ibid., p. 1069.
30. Hammer, Struggle for Indochina, p. 26.

CHAPTER III

AMERICAN POLICY TOWARD INDOCHINA
1942-1946

Roosevelt Policy

For both military and political reasons, the United States did not challenge Japanese control of Indochina during World War II. Allied strategy called for crushing Germany first, then defeating Japan, and the road to victory over the Japanese did not lead through Indochina. It was assumed by American military planners that victory in the Pacific would mean the end of Japanese control of Indochina--without the necessity of large-scale operations there. Politically, the President made it clear that he did not intend "to get mixed up in any Indochina decision" or "in any military effort toward the liberation of Indochina from the Japanese." Indochina, the President insisted, was "a matter for post-war."[1]

Nevertheless, Indochina was a frequent topic of study and discussion by the President, the State Department, and the Joint Chiefs of Staff during the war. Sometimes this topic arose from French requests for permission to participate in the war against Japan--a euphemism for a French campaign to regain control of Indochina. After March 1945, when the Japanese overthrew the French administration in Indochina, the American Government had to consider the problem of aid to French resistance forces. No less frequently, the subject of Indochina was introduced by the President himself, who held strong views regarding the disposition of Indochina after the war and did not hesitate to express them to such widely differing personalities as his son Elliott, the Joint Chiefs of Staff, the Secretary of State, Churchill, the Generalissimo, General Stilwell, officials of the Turkish and Egyptian Governments, and Stalin.

At first, the President's view was that all French territory should be restored to France after the war. In January 1942 through his Ambassador to Vichy, Admiral William D. Leahy, he assured Petain and Darlan of his

---
1. (S) JCS 1200/2, 11 Jan 45, CCS 370 France (8-5-44) sec 2.

intention to see France, including the French Empire, "reconstituted in the post-war period in accordance with its splendid position in history." Twice in November 1942 the French were assured that America would see that their colonies were returned after the war. On 2 November the President, through Mr. Robert D. Murphy, pledged the reestablishment of French sovereignty "throughout all the territory, metropolitan and colonial, over which flew the French flag in 1939." This pledge was given when American troops were preparing to land in North Africa and the President was seeking to enlist French support, or, at least, to ensure that the French would not oppose the American landings. Then just as American troops hit the beaches, the President himself sent a message to Petain that "the ultimate and greater aim /of the American armies/ is the liberation of France and its Empire from the Axis yoke." Unfortunately, these pledges did not dissuade the French from resisting the American landings. Instead, Petain replied: "We are attacked; we shall defend ourselves; this is the order I am giving."2

After this, the President made no further pledges to restore French sovereignty throughout the Empire, and by the time of the Casablanca Conference of January 1943 he had changed his original view. Whether his change of mind stemmed from anger over French resistance to the American landings in North Africa or from his own strong anti-colonialism is not clear. Whatever the cause, at Casablanca he confided to his son Elliott that he was not sure "we'd be right to return France her colonies at all, ever, without first obtaining in the case of each individual colony some sort of pledge, some sort of statement of just exactly what was planned, in terms of each colony's administration." "The native Indo-Chinese," the President asserted, "have been so flagrantly downtrodden that they thought to themselves: Anything must be better, than to live under French colonial rule!" "Don't think for a moment," the President

---

2. Elliott Roosevelt, ed, F.D.R.: His Personal Letters, 1928-1945 (1950), vol II, pp. 1275-1276. Robert E. Sherwood, Roosevelt and Hopkins (1950), pp. 645-647. (C) Doc A-8, "Extract from Letter of Robert D. Murphy to General Henri Giraud," 2 Nov 42, in (TS) Doc Hist of US Pol toward Indochina.

added, "that Americans would be dying in the Pacific tonight, if it hadn't been for the shortsighted greed of the French and the British and the Dutch." In concluding this discussion with his son, the President pledged that, once the war was won, he would work with all his "might and main to see to it that the United States is not wheedled into the position of accepting any plan that will further France's imperialistic ambitions, or that will aid or abet the British Empire in its imperial ambitions."[3]

At subsequent wartime conferences the President made it clear that he did not want Indochina returned to France. Instead, he favored placing it under an international trusteeship for twenty to twenty-five years to prepare the native population for eventual independence. At Cairo he found the Generalissimo receptive to this idea. At Tehran and Yalta Marshal Stalin was enthusiastic about it. But Churchill was dead set against any action that infringed upon French sovereignty over their colonial empire. As the President explained matters to Stalin, the British opposed establishing an international trusteeship over Indochina because of the implications of such an arrangement to the British Empire. As matters developed, the President never got around to proposing a specific plan for a trusteeship and that idea did not advance beyond the discussion stage.[4]

But, while he lived, the President's attitude toward Indochina constituted American policy. And in the fall of 1943 that policy began to collide with French colonial interests in Indochina. The first collision occurred when the French Committee of National Liberation requested an enormous increase in American arms and equipment for French forces and petitioned for representation on the Pacific War Council.

---

[3]. Elliott Roosevelt, As He Saw It (1946), pp. 114-116.
[4]. (TS) State Dept, Hist Div, "Handbook of Far Eastern Conference Discussions," Research Proj No. 62, Nov 49 (hereinafter: FE Conf Disc), pp. C-4, C-36, C-65, D-7, D-16, D-17, D-20, E-9, E-10, E-24, E-25, E-41. Edward R. Stettinius, Jr., Roosevelt and the Russians (1949), pp. 237-238.

In submitting their new armament program, the French Committee of National Liberation disclosed that it was based in part on aiding the Allied war effort in the Far East and on restoring French sovereignty to all the territories of the Empire. The new program was rejected on both military and political grounds. On 8 November the Joint Chiefs of Staff accepted a Joint Strategic Survey Committee recommendation that, "except for minor readjustments from time to time to utilize trained French personnel, no additional U.S. military assistance and equipment be promised the French beyond that now contemplated." As to French participation in the war against Japan, the Chiefs could not visualize any assistance the French could give. "It most certainly does not appear logical," they stated, "to renovate the French fleet for use in the Pacific at a time when the maintenance of the U.S. and British fleets in that area will tax to the utmost the resources of these countries." As for ground and air forces, the United States and Britain ultimately would have an abundance, "and any assistance which we shall require from the French would be in the nature of token forces for political or psychological reasons rather than for military reasons." Referring to the desire of the French Committee of National Liberation to restore French sovereignty over her colonial empire, the Joint Chiefs of Staff asserted that "the accomplishment of such a purpose is of itself not of direct military interest to the United States and we should not obligate ourselves to furnish military assistance to the French for that purpose." The Chiefs assumed that the defeat of the Axis would restore all French territory, "with possible reservations as to certain sites for naval and air bases."

The Chiefs soon learned that this assumption was false. When they discussed the French rearmament program with the President, the President emphatically agreed that it should not be increased beyond that already contemplated. But he supported his position with a political reason the Chiefs had not taken into account: "we should not commit ourselves to the French to give back to France all her colonies. . . . We should not let our policy regarding this matter give the appearance of a definite commitment." And in listing the territories he felt should not be restored to France, he placed Indochina first.

In the end, the Joint Chiefs of Staff did not even reply to the French request for additional armament. In late December, some two months after the French had submitted their request, they sought to obtain an answer from the War Department. General Marshall was noncommittal. He merely said that the desire of the French to participate in all phases of the operations in their homeland was fully appreciated and that it was planned "to make the fullest possible use of the French forces in this crucial phase of the war."[5]

Meanwhile, the French request for admission to the Pacific War Council had encountered an equally cool reception from the President and the Department of State. On 29 October Under Secretary of State Edward R. Stettinius, Jr., informed the President that the French Committee of National Liberation had informally asked for representation on the Pacific War Council. Stettinius advised the President that the State Department believed this request was based on the Committee's desire to enhance its own prestige, to place itself in a better position to protect French interests in Indochina after Indochina was liberated from the Japanese, and to insure its own eventual control of that colony. If this proposal were accepted, Stettinius pointed out, the Committee's representative would probably take the position that the Committee represented all French interests in the Pacific, including Indochina, and that one objective of the Pacific campaign must be the reconquest of Indochina and its return to France. Therefore, Stettinius recommended that the State Department be authorized to put off replying to the French for an indefinite period. The President approved this recommendation and the State Department merely filed the French request for future reference.

On 13 December, M. Henri Hoppenot, the Delegate of the French Committee of National Liberation, again raised this question with the State Department. Hoppenot pointed out that the British War Office had already accepted a French

---

5. (C) JCS 547, 25 Oct 43; (S dg C) JCS 561, 2 Nov 43; (C) JCS 547/2, 8 Nov 43; (S) Memo, Leahy to Pres, "Rearmament of French Forces," 9 Nov 43. All in CCS 370 France (10-6-43) sec 1. (S) Mns, JCS 121st Mtg, 2 Nov 43, item 11; (S) Mns, JCS 122nd Mtg, 9 Nov 43, item 1; (S) Mns, Mtg, JCS with Pres, 15 Nov 43, item 3. Marcel Vigneras, MS, The Rearmament of the French Forces in World War II (OCMH), Ch XI, pp. 24-25.

military mission to Delhi headed by General Blaizot. This new development, Hoppenot stated, made it even more desirable that parallel collaboration should be established at Washington, by the association of a French representative in the deliberations of the Pacific War Council.

Once more the French did not receive the answer they desired. Instead, they were informed by Assistant Secretary of State Adolf A. Berle, Jr., that their communication had been received and that the question raised therein had been referred to the appropriate authorities of the government. Mr. Berle apparently did not intend to answer either of these French requests any time soon, for he merely forwarded the pertinent correspondence to the Joint Chiefs of Staff for their information. The Chiefs circulated this correspondence, then apparently did not pursue this matter further.[6]

The American Government had, in effect, marked these French requests "file and forget," and for the next few months, as attention focused on opening a second front in Europe, American interest in Indochina lay dormant. Then, in the summer of 1944, when Allied armies had landed in France and the liberation of that nation from Germany appeared imminent, the French renewed and intensified their efforts to obtain American permission to participate in the war against Japan.

In July, Major General M. E. Bethouart, who was visiting Washington on a mission with General de Gaulle, discussed with Admiral Leahy the intention of France to recover Indochina from the Japanese. General Bethouart, of course, asked for American equipment for this purpose. He got nowhere. Instead, Admiral Leahy informed him that "Indo-China could not at that time be included within the sphere of interest of the American Chiefs of Staff."[7]

---
[6]. (R) JCS Info Memo 177, 10 Jan 44, CCS 370 France (10-6-43) sec 2.
[7]. ADM William D. Leahy, *I Was There* (1950), p. 244.

Thus rebuffed by the Americans, the French turned for support to the British, who proved more sympathetic. In July 1944 the French Committee of National Liberation asked the British to obtain American acceptance of French participation in both regular military operations and clandestine activities in Indochina. The French Committee of National Liberation submitted four proposals: (1) that French forces participate in the war against Japan; (2) that they participate in planning the war against Japan; (3) that a French military mission be attached to the headquarters of Lord Louis Mountbatten's Southeast Asia Command (SEAC); and (4) that the French participate in the planning of political warfare in the Far East.

As to French participation in regular military operations against Japan, the British proved no more receptive than the Americans. In submitting these French proposals to the Joint Chiefs of Staff in August, the British Chiefs expressed strong opposition to accepting either French land and air forces or French participation in the planning of military operations. On this point the American and British Chiefs of Staff were in complete accord. There were sound military reasons for their views, which they subsequently listed in rejecting a French offer to form two ground combat divisions for the war against Japan: no operations were contemplated that required a special knowledge of Indochina; because of serious deficiencies in service troops, critical equipment, and shipping, the use of French combat troops would not accelerate operations already planned; deployment and maintenance of French units in the Far East could only be accomplished at the expense of equivalent American and British troops. In short, the British and American Chiefs of Staff believed it would be militarily unsound to use French troops against Japan prior to the defeat of Germany.[8]

But the American and British Governments held sharply divergent views on the question of clandestine operations in Indochina. Eager to undertake such operations, the British firmly supported the proposals of the French

---

8. (C) CCS 644, 5 Aug 44; (C) Rpt by CadC, same subj, "French Participation in the War against Japan," 17 Dec 44; (TS dg C) CCS 644/3, 5 Jan 44. All in CCS 370 France (?-5-44) sec 1.

Committee of National Liberation, and strove for several months to obtain the concurrence of the American Government. Specifically, the British Chiefs of Staff and the British Foreign Office wanted the American Government to agree to have a French military mission accredited to SEAC, where it could effectively assist any clandestine operations undertaken by the British Special Operations Executive (SOE) or by the American Office of Strategic Services (OSS). The British also asked the Americans to accept French participation in the planning of political warfare in the Far East, with the understanding that such participation would be limited to those areas in which the French had a definite interest. Finally, the British wanted the Americans to agree to accept a French <u>Corps Leger D'Intervention</u> of 500 men, already in being in Algiers and designed to operate exclusively in Indochina against Japanese lines of communication.

These proposals threatened to reopen an old controversy over whether Indochina should be in the China Theater or in the Southeast Asia Command. As matters then stood, both the British and the Americans recognized that Indochina was in Generalissimo Chiang Kai-shek's China Theater. But Admiral Lord Louis Mountbatten, Supreme Allied Commander, SEAC, had entered into a "gentlemen's agreement" with Generalissimo Chiang Kai-shek under which both commanders could launch regular military operations in Indochina, when the time came, with theater boundaries to be adjusted according to the advances made by their respective forces. This much of the "gentlemen's agreement" was not in dispute, though it had not been formally ratified by the Combined Chiefs of Staff. But there still existed a difference of interpretation over whether Lord Mountbatten could conduct clandestine or irregular operations in Indochina from SEAC. The British claimed that right under the "gentlemen's agreement." The Americans insisted that this agreement covered only regular military operations. Thus, to agree to the British proposals regarding clandestine activities would be to weaken the China Theater's claim to strategic responsibility for Indochina.

Yet the Joint Chiefs of Staff were sympathetic to the British proposal for clandestine activities. They felt that, since the United States already had recognized Portuguese rights in Timor and Dutch rights in the Netherlands East Indies, it would be proper to recognize, insofar as was consistent with American national policy, French desires concerning Indochina. But in informing the British Chiefs of Staff of their concurrence in the British program, the Joint Chiefs of Staff so qualified their approval that they actually committed neither themselves nor their government. Thus, instead of agreeing to French participation in the planning of political warfare in the Far East, the Chiefs agreed only to French participation in such planning within the limits of the Southeast Asia Command. And they reminded the British Chiefs that Indochina was in the China Theater, rather than in SEAC, and hence was an area of American, rather than British, strategic responsibility. The Chiefs, however, did let the British know that they looked with favor on the establishment of a French military mission at SEAC.

Several weeks later, Lieutenant General Albert C. Wedemeyer, Commanding General, U.S. Army Forces, China Theater, informed the War Department that General Blaizot, with a French military mission, had arrived at SEAC Headquarters, Kandy, Ceylon. The British, Dutch, and French, General Wedemeyer reported, were working closely together to insure the recovery of their political and economic prewar position in the Far East. Toward this end, the Blaizot mission was proposing to infiltrate French parties into Indochina to assist resistance groups carrying out sabotage. Since General Wedemeyer expected to deal with this problem, he asked for United States policy on Indochina. His reply was not long in coming. The President had already been informed through the State Department that General Blaizot's mission had been accorded American approval and recognition at SEAC, and he was very much displeased. Two days after General Wedemeyer asked for instructions, the President informed Admiral Leahy in vigorous terms that he intended to control American policy on Indochina himself:

> With regard to this matter, I wish to make it clear that American approval must not be given to any French military mission being accredited to the South East Asia Command; and that no officer of this Government, military or civilian, may make decisions on political questions with the French military mission or with anyone else.

> I would like further to have it made clear that this Government has made no final decisions on the future of Indo-China, and that we expect to be consulted in advance with regard to any arrangements applicable to the future of Southeast Asia.

The Joint Chiefs of Staff lost no time in communicating the President's policy to General Wedemeyer and to the Commanding General, U.S. Army Forces, India-Burma Theater, and it was strictly adhered to.[9]

Soon after this incident, the British Ambassador to the United States, Lord Halifax, reopened the question of irregular operations into Indochina from SEAC. Specifically, he asked that the American Government agree to the entire program previously advanced by the British Chiefs of Staff and confirm the "gentlemen's agreement" between the Generalissimo and Admiral Mountbatten. Lord Halifax claimed, incidentally, that this agreement covered irregular as well as regular operations. Although the British motives in reviving this question seem to have been primarily political, Lord Halifax stressed the military gains Admiral Mountbatten hoped to achieve through such operations. He emphasized that Indochina lay astride the Japanese land and air reinforcement route to Burma and expressed optimism about the results to be achieved by cooperating with French resistance forces. The French Army and Civil Service in Indochina, according to Lord Halifax, were unquestionably anxious to take part in liberating that area from the Japanese and constituted "virtually a well-organized and ready-made Maquis." All that was necessary to exploit this situation, Lord Halifax emphasized, was the presence in SEAC of French personnel from whom alone the French in Indochina would take orders. In concluding his plea for American approval, Lord Halifax promised that such approval would in no way prejudice the ultimate

---

9. (C) JCS 1013, 22 Aug 44; (C) JCS 1013/1, 28 Aug 44; (C) CCS 644/1, 30 Aug 44; (S) Msg, CG USAFCT (Wedemeyer) to Marshall, CFBX 26367, CM-IN-14501, 15 Nov 44; (TS) Msg, JCS to Sultan & Wedemeyer, WARX 66178, CM-OUT-66178, 21 Nov 44; (TS) Memo, Pres to Leahy, 17 Nov 44. All in same file. (S) Mns, JCS 170th Mtg, 29 Aug 44, item 4. Hull, Memoirs, vol II, p. 1598.

settlement of theater boundaries between the China Theater and SEAC, nor the broader question of French participation in the war against Japan.

Once again the President refused to agree to this program, on the ground that Indochina was a postwar problem with which he was not ready to become involved. "You can tell Halifax," the President informed his Secretary of State, "that I made this very clear to Mr. Churchill. From both the military and civil point of view, action at this time is premature."[10]

The President had made his policy clear, and, until it was slightly relaxed, in March 1945, the State Department and the Joint Chiefs of Staff rigidly adhered to it. Nothing was done during this period that could be interpreted as an American commitment to aid the French regain Indochina. But the position of the Joint Chiefs of Staff and the State Department in following the President's policy was not an easy one. For while the President had freely expressed his views on Indochina to Churchill, Stalin, and to numerous others, he had studiously avoided discussing them with the French. And the French, by submitting numerous proposals to the Joint Chiefs of Staff, sought to discover what the President's policy was. Such proposals the Joint Chiefs of Staff had to treat with the utmost caution to avoid revealing American policy. In these circumstances, they answered as many as they could of these proposals the same way--with a generous "thank you" for bringing them up, a polite rejection of whatever was proposed, and a promise to reconsider the matter should conditions change.

But this simple formula for answering French requests had its limitations, and in February 1945 the Chiefs were forced to abandon it. This came about when Admiral Fenard

---

10. (S) JCS 1200, 16 Dec 44, CCS 370 France (8-5-44) sec 1. (S) JCS 1200/2, 11 Jan 45, same file, sec 2. (U) Doc A-16, Memo, Stettinius to Pres, 27 Dec 44; (U) Doc A-17, "Extract from Stettinius Diary," nd. Both in (TS) Doc Hist of US Pol toward Indochina.

submitted a proposal so clearly involving American national policy that the Joint Chiefs of Staff decided to refer all such requests to higher authority. Admiral Fenard reported that General Wedemeyer had recently approached the French military attache in Chungking to ascertain the attitude of French resistance forces in Indochina toward possible Allied operations there. The French Government, said Admiral Fenard, was eager to bring to bear its maximum strength in support of Allied forces everywhere, but it needed to know Allied intentions concerning Indochina before making any commitments for the use of French resistance forces. Also, there were several conditions the French Government considered essential to effective cooperation between Allied and French resistance forces: (1) French resistance forces could be called to action only on French orders; (2) regular French forces from without Indochina must be employed; (3) the French Government must be kept informed of contemplated operations; and (4) the Allied assault must be in sufficient force to warrant calling the resistance forces to arms, without risk of premature suppression by the enemy.

It quickly became apparent that General Wedemeyer had neither contemplated a major operation in Indochina nor played fast and loose with the President's policy, as Admiral Fenard's statement seemed to indicate. In late November 1944 General Wedemeyer had, at the request of the Generalissimo, sought to determine the French attitude toward a possible Chinese advance into Indochina to forestall a Japanese drive on Kunming. He had held one informal discussion with the French military attache at Chungking, then dropped the matter. But he had learned, through this discussion, that the French were fearful of Chinese ambitions and suspicious of American plans for postwar disposition of Indochina. And this suspicion of American intentions was doubtless the reason for the barrage of requests the French had been submitting to the Joint Chiefs of Staff.

At least the Joint Staff Planners thought so. In reviewing Admiral Fenard's request, the Planners made the following observation:

> The various proposals submitted by the French, their timing and the agencies to which they are

submitted, indicate a definite pattern of French effort to obtain under the guise of military considerations an expression of U.S. policy with respect to Indochina. Any reply, no matter how noncommittal, furnishes the French with some information either directly or by inference with respect to our national policy. When considered together, the various replies, each of little significance in itself, indicate trends from which the French can make definite deductions and can take action accordingly to jeopardize the U.S. position.

The Planners had some further incisive comments to make. The British, they said, were actively assisting the French in Indochina by clandestine operations from SEAC. Such assistance was of little military value, but its political significance was considerable. By this acquiescing in French desires rather than in American policy toward Indochina, the British were seeking to create a situation whereby Indochina should logically be considered in a British rather than an American sphere of strategic interest. As for the views of the French Government concerning cooperation between the Allies and French resistance forces, most of them were unacceptable. Thus any reply to Admiral Fenard based on purely military considerations would furnish the French with further indication of American policy and support the British contention that Indochina belonged in a British sphere of responsibility. Therefore, the planners recommended, and the Chiefs agreed, that Admiral Fenard's proposal be referred to the State-War-Navy Coordinating Committee (SWNCC). And, until the heads of state had reached a decision on the future of Indochina and communicated that decision to the French, the Chiefs would review all similar requests from the military viewpoint and pass them on to SWNCC.[11]

The State-War-Navy Coordinating Committee at once began a study of Admiral Fenard's proposal, and the SWNCC Subcommittee for the Far East drafted as non-committal a

---
11. (S) JPS 599/D, 19 Jan 45, CCS 370 France (8-5-44) sec 2. (S) JCS 1200/6, 15 Feb 45; (TS) Memo, JCS Secy to SecWar and SecNav, 22 Feb 45. Both in same file, sec 3.

reply as Admiral Fenard had yet received. But this one was never sent, for spectacular events had overtaken this study and invested the problem of aid to Indochina with an aura of urgency it had hitherto lacked.

On 9 March 1945 the Japanese overthrew the French administration in Indochina, interning many French officials and waging ruthless warfare against those members of the underground who resisted. This dramatic turn of events spurred the French to an all-out effort to obtain immediate American aid. On 12 March the French Ambassador to the United States asked the American Government to intervene through the Joint Chiefs of Staff to obtain CCS approval of aid to French resistants. On the same day Major General A. M. Brossin de Saint-Didier, Chief of the French Military Mission to the United States, submitted the following requests to the Combined Chiefs of Staff: (1) that all possible information be furnished the French relative to this Japanese aggression; (2) that Allied air forces bomb the Japanese and drop arms and ammunition to the resistants; (3) that American ground forces nearest the Sino-Indochinese frontier render active support; and (4) that General Blaizot, Chief of the French Military Mission at SEAC, be accredited to the headquarters of the commander of the theater of operations concerned, to assist in coordinating whatever steps were taken to aid the resistants. Additionally, General de Saint-Didier reminded the Combined Chiefs of Staff of previous French offers to employ regular French troops in the war against Japan.[12]

In these circumstances, the President began to relax his policy somewhat. The day after General de Saint-Didier asked for American aid, Admiral Leahy informed the Joint Chiefs of Staff that the President did not object to according General Blaizot a status that would enable him to be of help "in such efforts as we can make towards assisting the French forces now in Indo-China." Three days later Admiral Leahy and General Marshall agreed that General Blaizot could talk to the China Command on the

---

12. (S) SWNCC 35/4, 15 Mar 45; (TS) SWNCC 35/2/D, 14 Mar 45; (C) CCS 644/16, 13 Mar 45. All in same file.

single subject of relief for the French underground. They also agreed that Admiral Fenard could confer with General Wedemeyer, who happened to be in Washington on a mission concerning China. General Wedemeyer did discuss the Indochina crisis with Admiral Fenard and also with the President himself. On 19 March General Wedemeyer sent the following message to General Chennault, announcing a new departure in American policy: "Admiral Fenard reports 14th Air Force loaded and ready to aid French resistance, but unable to move without permission from Washington. Informal statement of new attitude US Government is to help French provided such aid does not interfere with planned operations. The 14th Air Force may undertake operations against the Japanese in Indo-China to assist the French within the limitations imposed by the above policy."[13]

This deviation in the President's policy did not mean a return to his original view that all French possessions should be restored after the war. Nor did it herald the approach of vast American armies marching to liberate Indochina. The President instructed General Wedemeyer to give the French only such support as would be required in direct operations against the Japanese. And he urged the general to "watch carefully to prevent British and French political activities in that area"--as if the General could! As to military operations in support of French resistance forces, the only Americans entering Indochina under this policy were members of the OSS, whose mission was to gather intelligence and furnish arms to those fighting the Japanese.[14]

---

13. (TS) Memo, McFarland to Marshall, King, Arnold, "French liaison in Southeast Asia," 13 Mar 45; (S) Memo, Leahy to Marshall, King, Arnold, McFarland, 15 Mar 45; (S) Memo, Col McCarthy to Leahy, 16 Mar 45. All in same file. (S) Msg, Wedemeyer to Chennault, WARX 55402, MAPLE 52, 19 Mar 45, Msg file "MAPLE," 06104-2-E, vol III, DRB AGO.
14. (TS) Msg, Wedemeyer to Marshall, CFB 38169, CM-IN-27033, 28 May 45, CCS 385 Chinese Theater (12-29-44). (S) Memo, LTC Paul L.E. Helliwell (Ch SI OSS CT) to Strategic Services Officer, CT, "OSS Activities in French Indo-China," 10 Apr 45, "French Indochina, File No. 93-1, Operations and General Information." CIA Archives.

No American in a position of responsibility seriously entertained the idea of employing American ground forces to aid the resistants. In the first place, there was just one battalion of American combat troops in that vicinity. And even had more powerful American combat forces been available, their use in support of the French underground almost certainly would have been precluded by the strategy adopted for winning the war against Japan. As the Joint Chiefs of Staff viewed the problem of aid to the French underground, Indochina, though flanking Allied positions in China and Burma, was of relatively minor military significance at that particular time. Furthermore, activities of resistance groups in Indochina would not be of substantial military benefit to the United States. And, finally, any lasting commitment of American resources to aid the French could only be at the expense of operations in China and in the Pacific, requirements the United States was already being severely strained to meet.

Why, then, did the President and his military advisors decide to give the French underground any help at all? This, unfortunately, is a question the available records do not wholly answer. But they do furnish some clues. From the evidence at hand, it seems very likely that the President and the Joint Chiefs of Staff were seeking to prevent the British from stealing a march in the jurisdictional squabble over Indochina between SEAC and the China Theater. The Joint Chiefs of Staff believed that unless the United States furnished at least token aid to the French, the British Chiefs might offer to let Admiral Mountbatten render substantial assistance from SEAC. In that event, not only would the matter of Admiral Mountbatten's operations in Indochina be further complicated, but urgently needed American resources might be diverted from China. If, for example, Admiral Mountbatten should employ transport planes to aid the French, his total requirements for SEAC would be increased, and the transfer of planes from the India-Burma to the China Theater might be delayed. Whether the Chiefs communicated this view to the President is not apparent from the records, but it seems most likely that they did.

Such advice from his military advisors doubtless would have been sufficient to persuade the President to give token aid to the French underground. But it seems very probable that he was motivated less by military than by political considerations; that his main reason for aiding the resistants was his own determination to prevent an Anglo-French coalition from exploiting the situation in Indochina in a manner best calculated to restore the <u>status quo ante bellum</u> to Southeast Asia. This interpretation is consistent with the President's many statements on Indochina. It is also supported by his charge to General Wedemeyer to prevent British and French political activities in that area.[15]

One thing is certain: the President did try to prevent the British from obtaining the whip hand in the jurisdictional struggle over Indochina. On 17 March, when the question of American aid to Indochina was still under study, Churchill once again raised the issue of theater responsibility for Indochina. He asked the President to affirm the "gentlemen's agreement" between Admiral Mountbatten and the Generalissimo as applying to "pre-occupational activities" and to agree to a "full and frank exchange of intentions, plans and intelligence between Wedemeyer and Mountbatten." The President countered with the proposal that Churchill agree that "all military operations in Indo-China, regardless of their nature, be coordinated by General Wedemeyer as Chief of Staff to the Generalissimo. . . . This would place on Wedemeyer the normal responsibilities of a theater commander and . . . provide coordination between the extensive Chinese and American operations in Indo-China and any operations by Mountbatten which may be necessary." As to Churchill's proposal for a full exchange of views between Admiral Mountbatten and General Wedemeyer, the President agreed that this was highly desirable.

Not unexpectedly, the Prime Minister refused to accept the President's proposal that General Wedemeyer assume toward Indochina the responsibilities of a theater commander. All Churchill would agree to was that he and the President direct their respective commanders to effect ＿ closest correlation of Allied military interest in that area." And the directive Churchill offered to send Admiral Mountbatten to effect such correlation was carefully phrased to give the commander virtual carte blanche in Indochina.

---

15. (S) JCS 1200/7, 17 Mar 45; (TS) Dec Amending JCS 1200/7, 21 Mar 45. Both in CCS 370 France (8-5-44) sec 3.

Whether President Roosevelt would have accepted Churchill's plan for settling the dispute over Indochina will never be known. For the day after Churchill advanced it, the President died very suddenly at Warm Springs, Georgia, of a cerebral hemorrhage. His successor, President Truman, did not insist that General Wedemeyer be permitted to control all Allied operations in Indochina, no doubt realizing that the British would never consent. Nor did President Truman accept Churchill's proposal that the two heads of state issue joint directives to Admiral Mountbatten and General Wedemeyer. Instead, he preferred to leave such matters to his military advisors. In these circumstances, the British and American Chiefs of Staff directed Admiral Mountbatten and General Wedemeyer to coordinate their activities in Indochina and to refer to their respective Chiefs of Staff any dispute they could not settle themselves. This agreement was probably the best the United States could obtain with the British under conditions then existing. But it fell far short of settling the jurisdictional dispute over Indochina.[16]

Concerning the policy President Roosevelt would have pursued toward Indochina had he lived, one can only speculate. It would appear, however, that before his death he had abandoned the idea of an international trusteeship. To be sure, he had discussed such a trusteeship with Stalin at Yalta, and both had agreed it was desirable. But further than this they did not go. Then, on 3 April, just nine days before his death, the President had approved the release of the following statement by his Secretary of State:

> As to territorial trusteeship, it appeared desirable that the governments represented at Yalta, in consultation with the Chinese

---

16. (TS) Msg, PM to Pres, 17 Mar 45; (TS) Dft Msg, Pres to PM, 21 Mar 45 (pencilled notation indicates it was sent "without substantial change" on 22 Mar 45). Both in OPD 336 TS Case No. 1. (TS) Msg, PM to Pres, 943, 11 Apr 45; (TS) Msg, Pres (Truman) to PM, 4, 14 Apr 45. Both in OPD Exec File 10, bk 63C. (TS) Msg, JCS to Wedemeyer, WARX 69380, CM-OUT-69380, 17 Apr 45; (U) JCS 1315, 13 Apr 45; (TS) Msg, BCOS to SACSEA, COSSEA 240, 19 Apr 45, CM-IN-19827 (21 Apr 45). All in CCS 385 Chinese Theater (12-29-44).

Government and the French Provisional Government, should endeavor to formulate proposals for submission to the San Francisco Conference for a trusteeship structure as a part of the general organization. This trusteeship structure, it was felt, should be defined to permit the placing under it of the territories taken from the enemy in this war, as might be agreed upon at a later date, <u>and also such territories as might voluntarily be placed under trusteeship.</u>

When this statement was released, General de Gaulle had made it very clear that the government of France expected a proposed Indochina federation to function within the framework of the "French Union." Therefore, the President must have realized when he approved this statement that France would never agree to a trusteeship. And with the strong support the French could count on from the British and the Dutch, the prospect of establishing a trusteeship against the wishes of the French was virtually eliminated.[17]

Truman Policy

The day after President Roosevelt died, members of the State-War-Navy Coordinating Committee began to challenge his policy toward Indochina. They were clearly dissatisfied with it. Speaking for the War Department, Mr. Robert A. Lovett complained that the lack of a clear-cut American policy had seriously embarrassed the military authorities in answering French requests for aid. He also thought the late President's prohibition against discussing American policy toward Indochina should be removed. Mr. H. Freeman Matthews, Chief of the State Department's Division of European Affairs declared that "the time has come when our position must be clarified." Other members of SWNCC strongly agreed, and it was decided that the State Department should seek to obtain from President Truman a precise definition of American policy toward Indochina.

---

17. (TS) JCS 1200/13, 27 Apr 45, CCS 370 France (8-5-44) sec 5.

Mr. Matthews subsequently drafted a memorandum asking President Truman to agree to several changes in the Roosevelt policy, and it was submitted to the Joint Chiefs of Staff for review. The most important of these proposed changes were as follows: (1) the United States should neither oppose the restoration of Indochina to France nor take any action toward French overseas possessions that it was unwilling to take toward those of its other Allies; and (2) French offers to participate in the war against Japan should be accepted as desirable in principle and judged on their military merits. Though the Joint Chiefs of Staff found no objection to the military implications of these proposals, Mr. Matthews' memorandum never reached the President. For there was such a disagreement over it in the State Department that it had to be withdrawn. Nevertheless, this memorandum was important. Not only did it reflect the thinking of Mr. Matthews and the Joint Chiefs of Staff; it also pointed the direction American policy was about to take.[18]

The month of May brought several occasions for French rejoicing. On the seventh, their traditional enemy, Germany, surrendered unconditionally to the Allies. At about the same time, M. Georges Bidault, the French Foreign Minister, received the first genuine assurance since the landings in North Africa that the United States would not oppose the return of Indochina to France. He was perhaps surprised, though, when informed by Mr. Stettinius that the record was "entirely innocent of any official statement of this government questioning, even by implication, French sovereignty over Indo-China." Then, on 19 May, President Truman himself accepted in principle an offer from General de Gaulle of French participation in the war against Japan. After almost two years of submitting such offers, the French had finally had one accepted.

But if M. Bidault experienced a feeling of elation on hearing the President's acceptance, he also had cause for misgivings over the reservations the President

---

18. (UNK) Mns, SWNCC 16th Mtg, 13 Apr 45, item 3. (TS) JCS 1200/13, 27 Apr 45; (TS) JCS 1200/14, 28 Apr 45, dec atchd; (TS) Memo, SWNCC Secy to Mr. Bard & Mr. Lovett, 4 May 45. All in CCS 370 France (8-5-44) sec 5.

attached to it. For the President had accepted only French assistance that synchronized with operations already planned against Japan. And he had emphasized that the extent of such assistance would depend primarily on transport, adding that the problem of transport for the war against Japan involved three times the tonnage required for the war against Germany. Furthermore, the President had stressed that it would be up to General MacArthur to decide how the French military contribution could best be utilized. Clearly, the President's acceptance of French participation in the war against Japan was not a commitment to revise American strategy to help the French regain Indochina.19

When the French followed up this Truman-Bidault conference with an offer to place two divisions "at the entire disposal of the American Command," the difficulties of synchronizing French assistance with American operations soon became apparent. In submitting this offer, General de Saint-Didier estimated that the 9th Colonial Infantry Division would be ready to embark from France by the end of June, the 1st Colonial Infantry Division by the end of July. Their equipment, of course, would have to be furnished by the Americans.

This offer raised some knotty problems for the Joint Chiefs of Staff. When, how, and where should these troops be used? The first of these questions proved the simplest. Owing to the shipping problem, these divisions could not be moved till months after the dates so optimistically advanced by General de Saint-Didier nor committed to action before the spring of 1946. Seeking answers to the other questions, the Chiefs consulted General MacArthur. General MacArthur expressed the greatest admiration for the fighting qualities of French troops, but he did not want them introduced during the initial assault on Japan, lest they greatly weaken it. He advised the Chiefs that, if French troops were furnished him, they should be made available with the "reenforcement echelons." Admiral

---

19. (C) Doc B-1, Msg, Stettinius to Grew, EOC-1608, 8 May 45, in (TS) Doc Hist of US Pol towards Indochina. (TS) SWNCC 35/11, 25 May 45, CCS 370 France (8-5-44) sec 5.

King was less enthusiastic than General MacArthur about the French proposal. He believed that the disadvantages of employing French troops in operations against Japan would actually outweigh the advantages. Therefore, he urged that General de Saint-Didier's offer be referred to the Combined Chiefs of Staff, and he expressed the hope that the British could arrange to use the proffered divisions under British command.

The Combined Chiefs of Staff achieved a partial solution of these problems at the Potsdam Conference, almost two months after the French submitted their offer. On 19 July the Combined Chiefs of Staff informed General de Saint-Didier that his proposal had been accepted in principle, with the understanding that the questions of where and under whose command the French divisions should serve would be settled later. This arrangement reflected the views of the British Chiefs of Staff, who thought the French forces should be employed "in due course" in Indochina and wanted to put off deciding whether they should serve under a British or an American command. The Combined Chiefs of Staff also told General de Saint-Didier that the French were expected to make maximum use of equipment already furnished them under the North African and Metropolitan Rearmament Programs. And, finally, they informed him that, because of shipping and other requirements in the Pacific, the French divisions could not be moved from France for several months nor committed to operations prior to the spring of 1946.

General de Saint-Didier expressed his pleasure over this acceptance of his offer, but objected that to equip French troops with material from the North African and Metropolitan Rearmament Programs would not be satisfactory. For one reason, a large part of this equipment had deteriorated through use in the campaigns in Italy, France, and Germany. Furthermore, the French Army needed it for its mission of occupying Germany. Therefore, General de Saint-Didier urged that General Eisenhower be consulted on this problem, so that further discussions could be held on a "solid basis."

But operations in the Pacific were racing to a climax, and shortly after General de Saint-Didier submitted his request, the war ended. Further American action on the French proposal was suspended when the Combined Chiefs of Staff decided that the French should refer all such problems directly to the British Chiefs of Staff in London.[20]

Immediate Postwar Policy

When Japan surrendered, whatever hopes the French may have had for American aid in regaining Indochina were soon dispelled. At Potsdam the United States had turned its back on that area. Eager to rid themselves of encumbrances to the all-out prosecution of the war against Japan, the Joint Chiefs of Staff had agreed that the Combined Chiefs of Staff should extend Admiral Mountbatten's Southeast Asia Command to include that part of Indochina south of the 16th parallel. Northern Indochina remained in the China Theater, under the responsibility of Generalissimo Chiang Kai-shek. Subsequently, General MacArthur, as Supreme Commander for the Allied Powers, directed all Japanese forces in those two areas of Indochina to surrender to Admiral Mountbatten and the Generalissimo respectively. Thus official responsibility for disarming the Japanese in Indochina fell to the British and the Chinese.[21]

Both the Joint Chiefs of Staff and the State Department were pleased with this arrangement. Engrossed as they were

---

20. (C) JCS 1013/6, 2 Jun 44; (TS) Msg, MacArthur to Marshall, C-17621, CM-IN-1646, 2 Jun 45; (C) JCS 1013/7, 4 Jul 45. All in same file. (S) Mns, JCS 195th Mtg, 16 Jul 45, item 4. (TS) CCS 895, 16 Jul 45; (TS) CCS 895/1, 18 Jul 45; (TS) CCS 895/2, 19 Jul 45; (TS) Memo, CCS Secys to Ch Fr Mil Miss, 19 Jul 45; (TS) CCS 895/3, 6 Aug 45; (S) Memo, CCS Secys to Ch Fr Mil Miss in US, 13 Sep 45. All in same file, sec 6.
21. (TS) CCS 890/1, 17 Jul 45; (TS) Mns, CCS 195th Mtg, 18 Jul 45, item 4; (TS) CCS 900/3, 24 Jul 45. All in TERMINAL, pp. 153-155, 248, 252, 280-282. Supreme Commander for the Allied Powers, Govt Sect, Political Reorientation of Japan, September 1945 to September 1948 (Washington, nd), vol II, p. 442.

with the problems of Japan and Germany, with events in China, and with "bringing the boys home," the Chiefs did not look for additional responsibility in Indochina. And if they had, they probably would have met with objections from the State Department. For American policy toward Indochina, as described by Mr. Dean Acheson, was neither to oppose the restoration of French control nor to assist it by force. Moreover, Mr. Acheson said, American willingness to see French control reestablished assumed that French claims to the support of the people of Indochina were "borne out by events."22

The French soon learned that the United States would not be a party to those events. When Admiral Fenard asked the Joint Chiefs of Staff about arrangements for the Japanese surrender in Indochina, he was referred to Admiral Mountbatten and to Generalissimo Chiang Kai-shek. He was told, however, that "the United States supports French presence in connection with Japanese surrenders" in both northern and southern Indochina. When Admiral Fenard asked the Combined Chiefs of Staff to transport to Indochina the French forces previously offered for employment against Japan, the Joint Chiefs of Staff eagerly accepted a British proposal that the French send all such requests directly to the British Chiefs of Staff in London. And when the French Military Mission to the United States asked the Combined Chiefs of Staff to transport by plane from China to Indochina General Alessandri and his detachment of 5,000 men, it was the American Chiefs who drafted the memo denying this request. "The movement of French forces from China into French Indo-China," the Chiefs asserted, "is a matter for consideration by the Chinese and French governments." Besides, American aircraft were "fully committed to other urgent tasks and cannot be diverted at this time from the accomplishment of those duties." This explanation was fully acceptable to

---

22. (C) Doc B-3, Msg, Acheson to AmEmb Chungking, 1622, 5 Oct 45. in (TS) Doc Hist of US Pol toward Indochina.

the British Chiefs, who amended the memorandum, however, to indicate that British aircraft also were unable to fly in General Alessandri and his men.[23]

Special precautions were taken to avoid American involvement in either British or Chinese occupation policy. In the Chinese zone, American liaison teams were attached to Chinese forces, but their role was to assist in the supply and movement of Chinese troops. OSS personnel also were present in the Chinese zone. Indeed, some of them had been there since March 1945, when the United States decided to aid the French resistance forces. But during the occupation they were under strict orders to disassociate themselves from the French and to remain aloof from Sino-French-Annamese relations, lest they place the United States "right in the middle." Their role during the occupation was limited to aiding prisoners of war and internees. Nor were these directives to be taken lightly. When General Wedemeyer heard that members of the OSS had interceded in Franco-Annamese disputes, he ordered all uniformed OSS personnel withdrawn from the Chinese zone of occupation.[24]

Even before Japan surrendered, the United States had begun to consider how to avoid involvement in British

---

23. (U) JCS 1475, 17 Aug 45, CCS 387 Japan (2-7-45) sec 2. (C) CCS 903, Memo from Ch Fr Nav Miss in US, "French Participation in Surrender of Japanese Forces in Indochina," 16 Aug 45; (C) CCS 903/1, 19 Aug 45; (C) CCS 903/2, 6 Sep 45; (S) Memo, CCS Secys to Ch Fr Mil Miss in US, 7 Sep 45. All in CCS 370 (4-25-45). (C) CCS 644/35, 28 Aug 45; (C) CCS 644/36, 11 Sep 45; (S) Memo, Cornwall-Jones to McFarland, "Transportation of French Forces from China to Tonkin," 13 Sep 45. All in CCS 370 France (8-5-44) sec 6.

24. (S) Msg, Wedemeyer to CO, OSSCT, OFBX, 24 Aug 45, (S) Msg, Davis to Heppner, NR 889, 1 Sep 45; (S) Msg, Indiv & Swift to Mims, Nr 6849, 9 Sep 45. All in "FIC 93a-1," CIA Archives. (S) Msg, Wedemeyer to CO, OSS, CFB 11209, 10 Oct 45; (UNK) Ltr, Col W. R. Peers to CGUSFCT, "SSU Personnel in FIC," 2 Nov 45. Both in "FIC 93a-3," CIA Archives.

occupation policies. On 11 August the American Consul at Colombo, Mr. Calvin H. Oakes, informed the State Department that British members of the Southeast Asia Command seemed perturbed because the war might end before they could mount an operation considered important to British prestige. Mr. Oakes also stated that if an appreciable length of time should elapse between the end of the war and the beginning of this operation, it would appear that the British were substituting their own occupation for a Japanese occupation. In these circumstances, he wondered if the State Department wanted to continue American participation in SEAC after the Japanese surrendered.

On this question the State Department and the Joint Chiefs of Staff took different positions. The Assistant Secretary of State believed the United States should participate in SEAC at least until American consulates were established in Thailand and in other important listening posts within the area of the Southeast Asia Command. The Chiefs demurred. They felt that, since the United States had already withdrawn all its combat forces from SEAC and would not participate further in SEAC operations, continued American participation on a reduced basis would be ineffective and American influence "practically nil." Moreover, the Chiefs believed that the required American consulates could be established without maintaining the Allied character of SEAC. Therefore, they recommended that official American representation give way immediately to an American liaison section at, but independent of, Lord Mountbatten's headquarters.

On 14 September the State-War-Navy Coordinating Committee informed the Joint Chiefs of Staff that it approved their recommendations but wanted to delay American withdrawal until Lord Mountbatten had reached a military agreement with the Thai Government. Here matters rested for another month. Then on 15 October the State-War-Navy Coordinating Committee asked the Chiefs to notify the British immediately of their intentions to withdraw from SEAC. "Prompt action in this connection is particularly necessary," SWNCC stated, "in order that the implication of United States participation in Southeast Asia Command policies and activities in the Netherlands East Indies and Indo-China may be eliminated immediately."

On 1 November 1945 official American representation at SEAC gave way to a section having liaison functions only. But whether the implication of American participation in SEAC policies was entirely eliminated was a moot point. For, out of deference to a British request to avoid publicity, the Chiefs did not publicize their withdrawal until January 1946.[25]

The United States observed a strict "hands off" attitude toward British and Chinese occupation policies until late December 1945, when the British Chiefs of Staff served notice that British forces would be withdrawn from Indochina. They informed the Joint Chiefs of Staff that the British withdrawal would be substantially completed by the end of January 1946, at which time most of the Japanese would have been disarmed. It might be necessary, however, to leave behind one brigade to guard disarmed Japanese in the Cap St. Jacques area until French forces were able to assume that task. In any event, the British wanted the Joint Chiefs of Staff to agree that when the Commander of the 20th Indian Division withdrew, all of southern Indochina, with the possible exception of the Cap St. Jacques region would be removed from Admiral Mountbatten's responsibility. The British did not specify who would finish repatriating the Japanese, but, by references to the buildup of French forces in Indochina, they left the impression that the French would assume that responsibility.

From the attitude taken by the Joint Chiefs of Staff and by the State-War-Navy Coordinating Committee toward this proposal, it would seem that the United States had not decided whether it wanted French sovereignty restored

---

25. (TS) SWNCC 177, 23 Aug 45; (C) JCS 1494, 29 Aug 45. Both in CCS 092 Thailand (1-4-45) sec 1. (C) JCS 1494/1, 4 Sep 45; (C) JCS 1949/2, 14 Sep 45; (C) JCS 1494/3, 17 Oct 45. All in same file, sec 2. (R) CCS 930, 15 Oct 45; (TS) Memo, Cornwall-Jones to McFarland, 19 Nov 45; (TS) SM-4593, 5 Dec 45; (S) Memo, Cornwall-Jones to McFarland, 7 Dec 45; (C) CCS 930/2, 12 Mar 46; (TS) Msg, CGIBT to War Dept, CRA 6078, CM-IN-3751, 17 Mar 46. All in CCS 323.361 (6-19-43) sec 2.

to Indochina. On 28 January the Chiefs informed the State-War-Navy Coordinating Committee that to transfer to the French the responsibility for repatriating the Japanese in Southern Indochina would in effect admit France to a coequal status with the other Allied powers in enforcing the surrender terms. In that event, the terms of General Order No. 1 for the surrender of Japanese military forces might have to be renegotiated at the government level. Moreover, the French might seize such an opportunity to demand the return of all of Indochina to their control. From the military viewpoint, the Chiefs preferred that the British remain in Indochina until the last Japanese had been disarmed and evacuated. This position was approved by the State-War-Navy Coordinating Committee, and on 1 February the Chiefs asked the British to retain control of Indochina until the last Japanese had been repatriated. Otherwise, the Chiefs stated, it might be necessary to renegotiate the terms of General Order No. 1.

The British Chiefs rejected this request. In their reply they said: "On the British side at any rate, it has always been the intention that the French and the Dutch should resume responsibility for their own territories as soon as they are in a position to do so and it is felt that the resumption of this control cannot possibly await the repatriation of all the Japanese, which may take some three years to complete." But the British were willing to compromise. As an interim measure, Lord Mountbatten would transfer to the French full responsibility for southern Indochina but continue to represent the Allied powers there for the limited purpose of repatriating the Japanese. This arrangement, the British Chiefs pointed out, would eliminate any necessity for the French commander to deal directly with General MacArthur.

The Joint Chiefs of Staff promptly accepted the British proposal.[26] Indeed, they could hardly have done otherwise, for they had been informed by General Wedemeyer that

---

26. (S) CCS 644/38, 21 Dec 45; (TS) JCS 1200/16, 17 Jan 45; (TS) SWNCC 35/13/D, 29 Jan 46. All in CCS 370 France (8-5-44) sec 6. (S) CCS 644/39, 1 Feb 46; (S) CCS 644/40, 22 Feb 46; (S) JCS 1200/17, 26 Feb 46; (S) CCS 644/41, 27 Feb 46. All in same file, sec 7.

the Chinese also were preparing to withdraw from Indochina. Subsequently, General de Saint-Didier asked the Combined Chiefs of Staff to approve a Franco-Chinese military agreement by which French troops would relieve Chinese forces in northern Indochina by 31 March 1946. Simultaneously, the French Embassy raised this question with the State Department.

Taking the position that such an agreement was a matter for the French and the Chinese Governments, the State Department and the Joint Chiefs of Staff approved this arrangement. Accordingly, the Chiefs drafted the reply which the Combined Chiefs of Staff forwarded to General de Saint-Didier. On 3 April the Combined Chiefs of Staff informed him that they accepted the Franco-Chinese agreement. Since their acceptance would bring all of Indochina under French control, they asked that the French military commander assume responsibility for disarming and evacuating the Japanese from northern Indochina. As to southern Indochina, Admiral Mountbatten would be directed to make the necessary arrangements to transfer his responsibility there to the French commander.

On 8 May the British Chiefs informed the Joint Chiefs of Staff that Lord Mountbatten had arranged for the French to assume the task of disarming and evacuating the Japanese from southern Indochina. The time set for this official transfer of responsibility was 13 May 1946 at 2400.[27]

---

27. (S) Msg, Wedemeyer to JCS, CFB-24359, CM-IN-5928, 27 Feb 46; (U) Memo, Fr MA, in US to CCS, "Replacement by the French of Chinese Troops Occupying Northern Indo-China," 12 Mar 46; (U) SWN-4017, Memo, SWNCC Secy to JCS Secy, "Relief of Chinese Forces in Northern Indo-China by French Forces," 14 Mar 46, w/encls; (S) JCS 1200/18, 21 Mar 46; (S) CCS 951/1, 3 Apr 46; (S) Memo, CCS Secys to Fr MA, "Relief by French Forces of Chinese Troops Occupying North Indo-China," 3 Apr 46; (S) CCS 951/3, Memo by RECOS, "Transfer of Responsibility to the French Authorities for Disarmament and Repatriation of Japanese from French Indo-China," 8 May 46. All in same file.

Thus did the British and the American Governments come to recognize French authority over all Indochina. Whether the French could persuade the natives to accept it remained to be seen.

In reviewing American policy toward Indochina from Pearl Harbor to the end of the British and Chinese occupations, several questions naturally arise: Did either President Roosevelt's or President Truman's wartime policy delay the restoration of French sovereignty? Did America's immediate postwar policy delay that restoration? What might the United States have done, that it did not do, to bring peace to Indochina?

President Roosevelt, to be sure, did not help the French reestablish their control. From Casablanca to Yalta he spoke of placing Indochina under a trusteeship. But shortly before his death, he apparently abandoned that idea. In any event, it would be difficult to show that his policy postponed the restoration of French control. It must be remembered not only that the President died before VE Day, but that the Combined Chiefs of Staff believed it militarily unsound to employ French troops against the Japanese prior to the defeat of Germany. Furthermore, those who shaped America's Pacific strategy did not contemplate a campaign to liberate Indochina, either before the President's death or after.

It would be even more difficult to show that President Truman's wartime policy postponed the return of the French to Indochina. Indeed, Mr. Truman showed more sympathy than his predecessor toward French desires. He did not object to the restoration of French control, and he accepted in principle French participation in the war against Japan, leaving it to his military advisors to decide what contribution the French should make. For military reasons, neither General MacArthur nor the Joint Chiefs of Staff were eager to use French troops in the assault on Japan. And though the Chiefs seemed inclined to agree that French troops might eventually serve under British command in a campaign to liberate Indochina, the war ended before French troops could be committed.

When Japan surrendered, there were three obvious policies the United States might have pursued toward Indochina: (1) help restore it to the French; (2) help the Indochinese toward eventual independence by establishing a trusteeship; or (3) observe a "hands-off" attitude. Accepting the first would have entailed the use of American troops or resources. And the American public undoubtedly would have complained about aiding French imperialism and delaying the demobilization of American servicemen. The second policy had virtually been precluded by a provision of the United Nations Charter that would have required French consent to the establishment of a trusteeship. The United States chose the third course, and left the solution to the Indochina problem to the French, Indochinese, British, and Chinese.

Possibly, an international trusteeship might have brought better results than the restoration of French rule. But such a solution was strongly opposed by the French and British, and even President Roosevelt did not advance the idea with sufficient vigor to obtain its acceptance. Nor can anyone say for certain that it would have worked. In retrospect, then, it appears, that given the situation from Pearl Harbor to the return of French rule, the United States followed the course that at the time seemed most suited to its own interests.

CHAPTER IV

INDOCHINA DURING THE WAR YEARS

Birth and Early Development of the Viet Minh

In the spring of 1941 a group of Vietnamese nationalists meeting in South China founded the Viet Minh League. Little fanfare attended the birth of the League, and the event went largely unnoticed by the statesmen and soldiers of the western world. Initially the Viet Minh League seemed to be only another of the myriad national groupings that functioned ineffectually outside their homelands. Yet, in little more than a decade it was to become the vehicle of Communist domination over approximately half of Viet Nam.

For years Vietnamese revolutionaries had sought sanctuary in South China whenever the French police began to breathe too heavily on their necks. With the outbreak of the war these dissident elements were soon augmented by a new flow of Indochinese nationalists over the border. Though often pledged to different parties, these newcomers shared a common goal. They aimed at the explusion of both the Japanese and the French from Indochina, and the creation of an independent Viet Nam. Rightly they reasoned that their closest and most promising source of aid was China, for the Kuomintang had an important stake in Indochina. In the prewar years China had permitted French economic penetration of Yunnan in return for access to the Gulf of Tonkin. Then in the hour of China's greatest need the French had closed the Yunnan Railroad to Chinese supplies. Also, Indochina had become an important base of Japanese operations against South China. "It became a matter of direct military concern to the Chinese National Government to strike a blow against the Japanese in this area. The utilization of Vietnamese for espionage purposes and the creation of a local military force against the Japanese became a military necessity. The remnants of the nationalist parties and groups in exile began to reform their ranks and vie for support from the Chinese."[1]

---
1. SD OIR No. 3708, p. 58.

The Viet Minh was conceived by Vietnamese Communists, and from the start the League was dominated and directed by the members of the Indochinese Communist Party. Under the leadership of Ho Chi Minh, the Party, in a classical Communist tactic, planned and worked for a united front to which parties and groups of virtually every political shade could adhere. To win these adherents the Communists played upon the nationalistic feelings of the exiles. Shrewdly, the members of the Party soft-pedaled orthodox Communism, and emphasized independence and its benefits. They were well aware, however, that the independence of Indochina would have to wait until after the war. And any help they might give during the struggle to the Allies would strengthen their case. In the meantime they could as part of the Viet Minh improve their organization, increase their numbers, and strengthen their military elements. The Viet Minh, therefore, made collaboration with the Allied nations in the war against Japan a cardinal tenet of its policy.

Before long, however, the Viet Minh ran into serious trouble with the Chiang Kai-shek government. Ever distrustful of Communists, the Kuomintang was displeased that Ho Chi Minh and his followers dominated the Viet Minh. To restore the balance of leadership in the Indochinese Nationalist movement the Chinese decided to sponsor and support a rival league, a league whose parties and leadership might be more easily persuaded that the future of Indochina was indissolubly linked with China's future.[2]

In April 1942 the Chinese arrested Ho Chi Minh as a "French Spy," and in October of the same year the Viet Nam Revolutionary League (Dong Minh Hoi) was founded under the aegis of Chinese Marshal Chang Fa-Kuei. Most of the leadership of this new League was provided by the VNQDD, or the Viet Nam Nationalist Party, which was strongly pro-Chinese. "The program of the Dong Minh Hoi was modeled broadly on that of the Chinese Kuomintang . . . . It sought the liberation of Indochina from the French and the Japanese and envisaged close cooperation between Vietnam and China. Organizationally, the Dong Minh Hoi was set up as a paramilitary formation to work in close

---
2. Ibid., pp. 60-63.

liaison with the Chinese Nationalist Army. It also maintained an espionage network in northern Tonkin centering on Moncay, Hanoi, and Haiphong."[3]

The Viet Minh League, despite Chinese hostility towards its leadership, lost no time in affiliating with the new League, but the Viet Minh preserved its extensive and separate organization. The Chinese permitted the Viet Minh this autonomy in their own interest, for they soon discovered that "only the Viet Minh had a network of cells throughout the Vietnamese lands, which it had inherited from the Communist Party and its affiliates."[4]

In June of 1943 the Chinese went a step farther. Marshal Chang Fa-Kuei released Ho Chi Minh from prison so that he might improve the espionage activities of the Viet Minh and other political groups in Indochina. As the most prominent leader of the Viet Minh, Ho Chi Minh was made a member of the Central Committee of the Dong Minh Hoi, but his main efforts were devoted almost exclusively to strengthening the ranks and organization of the Viet Minh in Indochina. The Viet Minh, as well as the other affiliates of the Dong Minh Hoi received a monthly stipend, military equipment, and military training from the Chinese, who before very long had cause to regret aid given to Ho Chi Minh and his followers.[5]

Though the Dong Minh Hoi was, theoretically, a working coalition, in fact the Viet Minh never merged its organization with the others. Indeed, Viet Minh and the Dong Minh Hoi waged an under-the-surface but constant struggle for leadership of the nationalist movement, for mass support in Indochina, and for Chinese and American aid. This friction ran counter to Chinese plans, and in March 1944 the Kuomintang made another effort to redistribute the balance of power.

Under Chinese auspices a nationalist congress was convoked at Liuchow, in March 1944, and a republican government for the future state of Viet Nam was selected.

---
3. Ibid., p. 63.
4. Hammer, Struggle for Indochina, p. 96.
5. SD OIR No. 3708, pp. 61-63.

Ho Chi Minh was to be one of several ministers, and the Viet Minh one of several forces in the new government. However, the creation of this provisional government increased rather than decreased the power and prestige of Ho Chi Minh and his followers.[6] The Viet Minh had the only well-knit organization functioning in Indochina, and it used the organization to convince the population that the Viet Minh alone spoke in the name of the united revolutionary parties and the new government; that the Viet Minh alone was capable of leading the fight for independence; and that Ho Chi Minh was the great champion of their cause. By August 1944 the Viet Minh claimed a membership of 220,000 in Tonkin alone. French sources, however, credited the League with only 50,000 followers.[7]

Inevitably, the growing strength of the Viet Minh re-aroused the Chinese distrust and fear of Viet Minh intentions. Relations between the two grew steadily worse, so the Viet Minh tried to get American support. "It offered the Allies co-operation in the war and asked in return that the great powers, particularly the United States, give the Vietnamese military support and recognize their eventual independence under the Atlantic Charter."[8] No such support or recognition was granted but the Viet Minh did succeed in establishing relations with American Office of Strategic Services (OSS) groups and French resistance elements.[9]

Meanwhile in northern Tonkin a new and formidable figure began to emerge, Vo Nguyen Giap, the leader of Viet Minh guerrilla forces. A Doctor of Law and a member of the Indochinese Communist Party, Giap fled to China with the outbreak of war. At Yenan, the Chinese Communist capital, he studied guerrilla tactics and learned his lessons well. Returning to his homeland in 1943, Giap became chief of all Viet Minh clandestine activity. In his activities Giap combined persuasion with terrorism, converting and recruiting the Indochinese who were susceptible to persuasion and terrorizing those who were not.

---
6. Philippe Devillers, *Histoire du Viet-Nam de 1940-1952* (Paris, 1952), p. 109.
7. (S) Geneva Conf Background Paper, Indochina Chronology, p. 24.
8. Hammer, *Struggle for Indochina*, p. 97.
9. SD OIR No. 3708, p. 61.

In addition to espionage and the harassment of the Japanese, Giap's guerrillas also helped American aviators shot down in Indochina to reach safety in South China. But his main efforts were always directed toward building up the strength and military capabilities of his force.[10]

By the end of 1944 Giap had built up a force of approximately 10,000 hardy guerrillas that kept the Vichy French and Japanese detachments in border areas in an almost constant state of alert. The force Giap created during this period was the nucleus of the Viet Minh army that would in the fall of 1950 drive the French out of their strong border positions, and in the spring of 1954 defeat a strong French force in pitched battle at Dien Bien Phu.

French Activities in Indochina, January 1943-March 1945

During World War II while Ho Chi Minh and Giap prepared for the struggle that would follow the fall of Japan, the French made preparations of their own.

From the beginning the Free French never lost sight of Indochina's importance to France. During the war de Gaulle and his advisers devoted a great deal of time and effort to charting the future of Indochina as part of the French Empire. They worked unceasingly to secure United States agreement for French participation in the war against Japan, hoping thereby to bring Indochina back into the fold of the French Empire. At the same time they watched jealously for any indication of Allied designs on their Far Eastern territory and were not reluctant to state their own plans for the future of Indochina.

On 7 December 1943, for example, the French Committee of National Liberation announced:

> . . . France solemnly repudiates every act and every cession of territory that may have been accomplished in complete disregard of her rights and of her interests. . . .

---
10. Jean Sainteny, *Histoire d'une Paix Manquee* (Paris, 1953), p. 243.

> . . . France will not fail to remember the proud and loyal attitude of the Indo-Chinese peoples, the resistance which by our side they opposed to Japan and to Siam, the faithful bonds which tied them to the French community.
>
> To these people who have been able to assert both their national feeling and their responsibility, the French mean to give a new political status by which, within the French community and within the framework of the federal organization, the franchises of the different countries of the Union will be reshaped and established on a wider scope; a status whose institutions will have a more liberal character without losing the features of Indo-Chinese traditions and civilization, and whereby at last, all Indo-Chinese citizens will have access to every position and every public office of the state.
>
> With this reform of the political status, there will be a recasting of the economic status of the Union which, based on a system of autonomy concerned with customs and taxes, will ensure its own prosperity and contribute to that of the neighboring countries as well.[11]

The Free French did not, however, limit themselves merely to making proclamations. They organized a resistance movement in Indochina that eventually included the French military forces and a substantial part of the civilian Frenchmen of the country. In the end Admiral Decoux himself took his orders from de Gaulle.

After the fall of France few Frenchmen chose to risk open adherence to de Gaulle. But as the fortunes of the Allies and Free French rose, more and more joined the ranks of de Gaulle supporters. In 1943 de Gaulle established a Free French mission in Calcutta and another in Kunming with the task of "maintaining a discreet contact between our French comrades who remained in Indochina and Free France."[12] A year later de Gaulle officially appointed General Mordant to lead the resistance movement.

---

11. "French Committee's Statement on Indochina," The United Nations Review, vol. IV, 15 Jan 44, p. 16.

12. Sainteny, Histoire d'une Paix Manquee, p. 21. (Translated by author.)

And Admiral Decoux, after consulting with de Gaulle's government, established a new Council with General Mordant as Vice President.

The French mission in Kunming received little encouragement or help from the Americans and Chinese, who reflected the cautious attitude of their governments toward the future of Indochina. In Calcutta, however, it was quite a different story. The British were more than willing to help France regain its prewar positions in Indochina. Although Indochina was in the China Theater of Operations, the British were soon dropping agents, arms, and equipment into Tonkin, Laos, Cochinchina, and Annam.[13]

Unfortunately for the French, the Japanese were well abreast of the resistance movement's progress. The secret of the movement was no secret at all. The resistance was common talk among the white men in Indochina, and in Saigon every Frenchman knew that Mordant was the head of the movement. Some of the air drops fell into Japanese hands and Indochinese agents in Japanese employ provided a steady flow of information. But the Japanese chose to bide their time.

Meanwhile the French, who had their own intelligence sources, began to receive reports that the Japanese, too, were planning a showdown. And in January 1945 General Mordant drew up a plan of operations for use in the event of a Japanese attack on French forces. This plan called for a gradual withdrawal of the French Army from the population centers to the mountain regions of Tonkin and Laos where guerrilla operations would be carried out against the Japanese. In January the plan was approved by the French Government in Paris, and the deployment of troops was initiated according to plan.[14]

Meanwhile the Japanese had begun to suspect that Indochina would soon be invaded by an American amphibious assault. And they feared that unless they disposed of the French Army, Japanese troops would be attacked from the front and rear simultaneously. French troop movements and increased aerial activity seemed to indicate an attack in the very near future. The Japanese decided, therefore, to strike first.

---

13. Devillers, *Histoire du Viet-Nam*, p. 121.
14. Ibid.

In the evening of 9 March the Japanese demanded that Admiral Decoux place all French armed forces in Indochina under Japanese command. Any delay would be interpreted as a refusal. That night the Japanese troops, already deployed, attacked the dispersed French forces. In less than twenty-four hours the French Army of Indochina was destroyed as an effective military force. A handful of small units escaped to the mountains of Laos, and a few thousand men, under Generals Sabatier and Alessandri, made their way to South China but most of the French troops were rounded up by the Japanese and interned. General Mordant himself was captured and Admiral Decoux was taken into "protective custody."

The "Independent" Government of Viet Nam

With considerable forethought the Japanese had prepared the overthrow of the French, politically as well as militarily. In anticipation of the 9 March coup they had encouraged the pro-Japanese nationalist parties to give up their underground activities and prepare to take over the government of Viet Nam. The Japanese protected the leaders of these parties from arrest by the French authorities and permitted them to organize their followers. Thus, on 9 March the Japanese had two coalitions of parties as well as several other unaffiliated parties ready to organize a native regime friendly to Japan. One of the party groups was the Viet Nam Restoration League, which soon absorbed the other organizations as affiliates and became the dominant group of the coalition.[15]

The Japanese lost no time in setting up a friendly Vietnamese government. Too few in number and unequipped to take over the whole government apparatus, they were forced to rely on the Vietnamese for the maintenance of services, utilities, and civil administration. On the day after the coup, 10 March, they announced that the country was "free" and proclaimed Bao Dai as Emperor of Viet Nam.

Bao Dai was the direct descendant of a famous prince of Annam who in the eighteenth century unified Cochinchina, Tonkin, and Annam into a single country of Viet Nam, and ascended the throne as Emperor.

---

15. SD OIR No. 3708, pp. 53-54.

However, by 1925, the year Bao Dai took the throne, the powers and prerogatives of the royal house had been gradually whittled away until the Emperor served merely as a French-supported figurehead. Bao Dai's imperial government at Hue possessed no real authority in Annam, and not even the semblance of authority in Tonkin and Cochinchina. The Emperor seemed content to while away his days in Hue indulging his sybaritic tastes and co-operating wholeheartedly with the French administration.[16] When, however, in March 1945, the Japanese promised him the chance to reunite Viet Nam, he revealed his patriotism and manifested a good deal of energy and skill.

Later Bao Dai was to explain that the French themselves had ended their protectorate over Viet Nam by their failure to defend the country from the Japanese. "I could have accepted it /Independence/ or refused it. But in the latter case they would have imposed their administration; also I chose what would save my people from the worst. And then they gave us our independence which was the first thing."[17]

Bao Dai cooperated as fully with the Japanese as he had with the French, but within the narrow limits of authority permitted him by the Japanese, he attempted to unite and govern Viet Nam.

On 11 March Bao Dai issued an imperial proclamation in which he abrogated the French-Annamese Treaty of 1886, pronounced Viet Nam an independent country, and pledged the adherence of Viet Nam to the Japanese bloc of Greater East Asia.[18]

---

16. Hammer, Struggle for Indochina, p. 46.
17. Le Monde, 23 Feb 46. (Translated by author.)
18. Devillers, Histoire du Viet-Nam, p. 125.

From the beginning, however, it was apparent to Bao Dai and his supporters that government by fiat could not endure long. It was essential that the new regime have a broad base of national support. To rally this support, Bao Dai tried to win further Japanese concessions to Vietnamese nationalism, hoping to organize a government that would be more representative of the seething political forces of the country. On both scores he had but little success.

Annam was ostensibly independent but the status of Tonkin and Cochinchina remained unresolved for several months, although in both parts of the country, as in Annam, Vietnamese functionaries took over the administration in the lower echelons. Supposedly, the Imperial Court was to appoint resident superiors to govern in Tonkin and Cochinchina. In fact, however, the Japanese kept control in their own hands. Like the French, the Japanese governed Cochinchina as a colony, merely replacing the French officials at the top of the administration with their own functionaries. Only when they saw clearly that their dream of a Greater East Asia was no longer realizable did the Japanese permit Viet Nam to incorporate Tonkin. They surrendered Cochinchina even more reluctantly, waiting until 8 August before they permitted Bao Dai to issue an imperial edict officially joining Cochinchina to Viet Nam.[19]

On 10 March the members of the existing Imperial Cabinet were all representatives of the mandarinate. It was obvious to all, including Bao Dai and the Cabinet itself, that the government was not representative of the political forces of the country. Bao Dai knew that without the support of these political forces and the popular will they reflected, a stable government for Viet Nam was not feasible. He tried repeatedly, therefore, to broaden the representation in the government. In his effort to engage important and popular political figures for a new government, Bao Dai several times attempted to secure the services of Ngo Dinh Diem as Prime Minister.

Ngo Dinh Diem was a Catholic mandarin of high reputation. In 1933, at the age of 32, Diem had served as Minister of Interior and secretary of a government reform

---

19. SD OIR No. 3708, pp. 55-56.

commission, but he had resigned from the government after only a few months, saying "that he was no longer able to take part in this comedy" of government.[20] Diem's importance stemmed from the high esteem in which he was held throughout Viet Nam. His integrity and ability, widely known, and his sincere devotion to the cause of independence and unity for Viet Nam were recognized even by the Japanese. In addition, Diem represented the support of conservative Catholic elements whose participation in the government was much to be desired.

During the war Diem had been antagonized by Admiral Decoux, and along with other nationalists had turned to the Japanese for support. At the time of Bao Dai's overtures he was living under Japanese protection in Saigon. Diem knew that there was little substance to the Japanese promises of independence and unity, and he remained deaf to Bao Dai's pleadings.

Finally, Bao Dai dared delay no longer, and on 17 April he appointed Tra Trong Kim as Prime Minister. Kim was a respected scholar, a prominent Freemason, and a nationalist, but he was subservient to the Japanese and a man of limited political ability. Under Kim the government was composed largely of pro-Japanese nationalists who wanted to make the most of their new independence. They hoped to create a functioning government that would survive the Japanese control of the country and greet the Allies as an independent and stable government.

The Kim government was supported by several nationalist groups, of which the Greater Viet Nam Nationalist Association (Dai Viet) and the Viet Nam Restoration League were the most important. The Dai Viet, a wartime creation, was a hodgepodge of intellectuals, Boy Scouts, students, and extremist patriots. The Viet Nam Restoration League was a much older party, tracing its origin to before World War I. The League had a long history of friendly relations with the Japanese and opposition to the French.[21]

---

20. Devillers, *Histoire du Viet-Nam*, p. 126. (Translated by author.)
21. SD OIR No. 3708, p. 54; Hammer, *Struggle for Indochina*, pp. 48, 49.

The members of the Kim government tried to govern well, but the heavy hand of Japanese control, lack of wide public support, a disrupted economy, famine, and their own limitations all contributed to their failure. A few concessions were granted by the Japanese, but the government's inability to bring Cochinchina under its rule, as well as its apparent subservience to the Japanese, prevented it from gaining strong support among the mass of the people. It had little support even among the mandarinate, and it was opposed by influential elements--for example, Diem and his followers.[22]

As the weeks passed a sense of impotence grew among members of the government. They saw the end of the war approaching, and they realized that when peace came they would be regarded as collaborators. They showed less and less initiative at a time when the internal situation required the utmost efforts of the government. When French rule ended and the new government of Viet Nam was organized, the mass of the people did not realize the independence carried with it serious responsibilities. The countryside thought of the change mostly in terms of no more taxes, no more requisitions, no more control. Even the ranks of government employees were not immune to a certain "live and let live" attitude. As a result the government soon found that it possessed little or no authority outside of the principal towns, and in certain provinces an administrative vacuum existed.[23]

Adding to the woes of the government, spring brought famine to Tonkin and Annam. Hundreds of thousands died. Rioting and lawlessness became widespread. Discontent infected all ranks of the population. By August the government held only the trappings of authority donated by the Japanese.

More and more the Vietnamese turned ears and eyes toward the northern frontier. They heard that the Viet Minh was already ensconced in the northern provinces; that the Viet Minh had a powerful army and a patriotic leadership; that collaborators would be hanged; and, of the greatest importance, that the Viet Minh was the ally

---

22. (S) Geneva Conf Background Paper, Indochina Chronology, p. 26.

23. Devillers, *Histoire du Viet-Nam*, p. 128.

of the United States, China, and the USSR. There was little truth and much fiction in these stories. Nevertheless, the stage was being set for Viet Minh's rise to power. It did not keep its audience waiting long.

The Viet Minh Seizes Control

In the early months of 1945, while Giap strove to expand, equip, and train his military formations, Ho Chi Minh was already at war on the political front. Under his inspiration and guidance a comprehensive postwar program was drawn up and publicized by the Viet-Minh--the only group to do so. The Viet Minh promised the Vietnamese a republican constitution that would guarantee democratic rights and privileges, an end of French taxes, a national economy without colonial influence, industrialization, and improved agriculture. Along with all these pledges, it promised, would come a program of social legislation undreamed of by the mass of the people--the 8-hour day, unemployment insurance, a minimum wage, aid to large families, increased medical facilities, and educational and intellectual stimulation in all ranks of Vietnamese life. But as long as the French governed, these were only empty promises. However, once the Japanese had neatly disposed of the French, the Viet Minh laid down a program of action and stepped up its activity.[24]

The Viet Minh bitterly attacked the Tran Trong Kim government as a Japanese puppet regime, and in the tone of a directive appealed to the people, exhorting them to organize processions, demonstrations, and strikes against the Japanese; to hold back rice and pay no taxes; to destroy communications, transportation facilities, ammunition dumps, and foodstores; and to launch surprise assaults against isolated outposts and small patrols.[25]

In April the Viet Minh called a military conference to map out the strategy and organization for a national revolt. A general staff of the army was appointed, and Giap was named its chief. Thereafter, Viet Minh forces increased their harassment of the Japanese but they never risked a pitched battle. They contented themselves with hit and run raids against numerically inferior Japanese

---
24. Hammer, Struggle for Indochina, p. 98.
25. Ibid., p. 99.

units and the destruction of Japanese communications facilities and supplies. Their greatest "battle" was an assault by approximately 500 Viet Minh troops against a post manned by forty Japanese soldiers. After a 24-hour combat they broke off the fight, leaving behind eight dead Japanese.[26] Nevertheless, as Japanese commitments to the south increased, Giap's guerrillas were able to move out of their mountain lairs in force and gradually extend their hold on the border provinces.

In May, with the French Army no longer a factor in its military considerations, the Viet Minh was strong enough to organize a "liberated" zone of Tonkin.[27] This zone, made up of six northern provinces, Cao Bang, Lang Son, Ha Giang, Bac An, Tuyen Quang, and Thai Nguyen, formed a substantial part of Tonkin. In the eyes of the population Viet Minh control over such a large area was a considerable achievement, and the stock of the Viet Minh went up accordingly. Emboldened by its success, "Viet Minh Central Headquarters," under Ho Chi Minh's leadership, called a National Congress for Viet Nam but "transportation difficulties," or perhaps the Japanese, forced its postponement.

In the spring the Japanese made some effort to seek out and destroy Viet Minh units in the north, but by summer they needed all their forces to control key cities and villages, the main lines of communications, and the more vulnerable parts of the coast. As a result the Viet Minh guerrillas and innumerable agents were soon operating throughout the Tonkin delta area and as far south as Annam.[28]

Constantly in evidence were certain skills the Viet Minh had acquired from the Communist Party--skillful agitation, excellent organizational ability, and successful infiltration of the opposition. Agents cleverly

---
26. Devillers, *Histoire du Viet-Nam*, p. 133.
27. (S) Geneva Conf Background Paper, Indochina Chronology, p. 27.
28. Devillers, *Histoire du Viet-Nam*, p. 135.

created and exploited disorder and discontent, steadily increasing the ranks of Viet Minh adherents. They organized revolutionary committees and provincial organizations with allegiance to the national central committee. They infiltrated the pro-Japanese parties and the very highest ranks of the Kim government. And by July the Viet Minh had sympathizers even among the members of the Cabinet.[29]

Wherever members of the Viet Minh found an audience they dinned into its ears the claim that their organization was part of the Allied coalition, that the Allies supported the Viet Minh, and that victory would soon be theirs. Actually, however, they knew that the future of Indochina was still far from decided. They knew, too, that even if the Viet Minh succeeded in replacing the Kim government, it would have to contend with an aroused Free France, jealous of its overseas empire and eager to reassert its hegemony over Indochina. The Free French had already made it abundantly clear that France had no thought of permitting Indochina to go its own way.

Earlier, when the Japanese had toppled the Decoux regime, the French Provisional Government had hastened to state its plans for Indochina lest any nation or group doubt France's firm intention of re-acquiring the territory. On 12 March the Minister of Colonies in an address before the Provisional Consultative Assembly said: "We firmly hope that the sometimes touching loyalty of which the people of Indochina have given proof, and the courage and patriotism manifested by the French there, will quickly find their reward." At the moment Indochina was still in the grip of the enemy. "But," said the Minister, "soon our flag will float anew over Hanoi, Hue, and Saigon as at Strasbourg and Metz."[30]

Less than two weeks later the French Government announced a postwar plan for Indochina, to go into effect as soon as possible after the end of the war. The Indochinese Union would be replaced by an Indochinese

---

29. Ibid. Hammer, Struggle for Indochina, p. 100.
30. Notes et Etudes, "L'Indochine française delivrée," No. 115, 17 Aug 45, pp. 1-2. (Translated by author.)

Federation composed of five semi-independent states united under the French flag. This Federation was to constitute with France and the other members of the old French Empire a French Union whose interests would be represented abroad by France. Within this Union, Indochina would enjoy autonomy; nationals of the Indochinese Federation would be at the same time Indochinese citizens and citizens of the French Union. This double citizenship would entitle them to all federal posts in Indochina and in the Union, on the sole ground of merit and without discrimination of race, religion, or national origin.

Indochina would have its own federal government, presided over by a Governor-General, and composed of Ministers responsible to him. These Ministers would be selected from among the Indochinese as well as the French residents, and a State Council composed of the outstanding members of the Federation would assist the Governor-General in preparing the laws and regulations of the Federation. A representative body chosen in accordance with the mode of election best suited to each of the States of the Federation, and in which French interests would be represented, would vote on the imposition of all taxation, approve the federal budget, and discuss the bills. Freedom of thought and creed, liberty of the press, right of association and meetings, and, generally speaking, all domestic liberties would constitute the basis of all Indochinese laws.[31]

In prewar Indochina this declaration would probably have exceeded the fondest hopes of Vietnamese nationalists, including Ho Chi Minh, but by the summer of 1945 it was not enough. The proposed reforms were still cast in the traditional French mold. The Governor-General was in essence the "High Commissioner." He was to retain control, flanked by ministers appointed by and responsible to him. A Council would assist him in preparing the laws and regulations of the Federation. The "representative body" would vote on taxes, approve the federal budget, and discuss the bills, but there its powers ended. Tonkin, Annam, and Cochinchina would remain separate.

---

31. (S) Geneva Conf Background Paper, Indochina Chronology, p. 21.

In July the Viet Minh made several attempts to meet with Jean Sainteny, chief of the French mission in Kunming, but without success. The only French-Viet Minh contact worthy of note during this period came about through the good offices of the OSS. Using OSS channels the Viet Minh sent a message to the mission in Kunming listing certain reforms which it wanted instituted in the "political future of French Indochina." The Viet Minh asked that:

1) a parliament be elected by universal suffrage to govern the country and a French governor act as President until independence was assured.

2) independence be given to Indochina in a minimum of five years and a maximum of ten.

3) the natural resources of the country be returned to it inhabitants after fair compensation was made to the present holders; France continuing to benefit from economic concessions.

4) all the liberties described by the United Nations be assured to the Indochinese people.

5) the sale of opium be forbidden.[32]

The Viet Minh's request was carefully studied by Inspector of Colonies de Raymond, his deputy, Leon Pignon, General Alessandri, and M. Sainteny. In brief, the French representatives were bound by the already announced government policies which were incompatible with conditions set forth by the Viet Minh and the limitations of their authority. In their response, therefore, they were unable to offer the Viet Minh much hope that the French Government would look upon the five conditions with favor. Actually, an encouraging reply would probably have come as a surprise to the Viet Minh.

In the beginning of summer, 1945, OSS activity in Indochina increased sharply. By the middle of July several OSS teams, supplied by airdrops, were operating in Tonkin where they organized and directed guerrilla action against

---
32. Sainteny, *Histoire d'une Paix Manquee*, p. 57. (Translated by author.)

the Japanese. These teams also provided military and political intelligence to OSS headquarters in Kunming. The July and August reports of the head of one of the teams are revealing. He had been in close contact with a Dr. Hoo and a Mr. Van (actually Ho Chi Minh and Giap) for a period of almost two months. Both Ho Chi Minh and Giap had strongly manifested their hostility to the French. At Ho's insistence the head of the team had been compelled to send a French officer attached to his group back to China. He also reported that Ho "would welcome a million Americans to come /to Indochina/ but not any French," for Ho considered the return of any French an "opening wedge." Yet the Viet Minh knew that the French would return eventually. When they did the Viet Minh would insist that complete independence be given to Indochina after a specified number of years. According to the report, the Viet Minh also realized that Indochina would need outside technical help. The Viet Minh would especially welcome United States aid.[33] Clearly, the Viet Minh was looking ahead, but as it planned and prepared for the future, it was overtaken by events.

When it came, the collapse of Japan was so quick that it scrambled the Viet Minh timetable. On 26 July Great Britain, the United States, and China called upon the Japanese Government to surrender unconditionally. And on 6 August the first atomic bomb was dropped on Japan. Rightly the Viet Minh surmised the surrender of Japan was now a matter of days. The Viet Minh knew that its preparations still left much to be desired--in the north it wanted more time to train its troops and to organize a larger following among the broad mass of the population; in the south the Viet Minh had no military formations worthy of the name and less than moderate public support. Nevertheless, the Viet Minh realized that the decisive moment to seize power had arrived. On 7 August Giap's guerrilla formations became the Viet Nam Army of Liberation, and at Viet Minh headquarters Military Order No. 1 was issued. It announced that "The hour has struck for a general offensive on all fronts." In rapid order the command was issued to march on Hanoi. A country-wide insurrection was launched, and a National Congress was hastily convened.[34]

---

33. (S) Thomas Rpts, Jul-Aug 45, FIC file 93a-3, SI Projects, CIA.
34. Devillers, *Histoire du Viet-Nam*, p. 135. (Translated by author.)

The so-called National Congress convened by the Viet Minh met in the "liberated" province of Thai Nguyen on 14 August, the day that President Truman announced that Japan had accepted unconditional surrender. At this gathering the Viet Minh laid down a clear-cut program which bore on the following points:

    a) to disarm the Japs before the entry of Allied forces into Indochina;

    b) to wrest the power from the hands of the enemy;

    c) to be in a position of authority when receiving the Allied Forces.[35]

The National Congress also set up an executive organ, the People's Liberation Committee, to assume power in Hanoi as the official government of Viet Nam. Ho Chi Minh was unanimously elected President. The Committee was composed of fourteen members--six belonged to the Indochinese Communist Party, six to other parties of the Viet Minh League, and two were members of the Viet Nam Democratic Party. But it was dominated by the six Communists, one of whom was Giap. Though the Committee had a wide popular support in the north it fell far short of representing the whole nationalist movement. In truth, there existed considerable opposition to the high-handed People's Liberation Committee and its monopoly of the center stage. In Tonkin bitter fighting broke out between Giap's troops and the military formations of the Nationalist Socialist Party and the Viet Nam Nationalist Party. In Annam, too, sporadic clashes occurred between Viet Minh units and other nationalists. Nevertheless, the Viet Minh succeeded in temporarily composing its differences with these local groups and soon established itself as the main stream of the nationalist movement.[36]

Meanwhile, as Giap's men approached Hanoi, the Japanese showed that they had no intention of opposing the Viet Minh. As far as they were concerned, the war and their dream of the Co-Prosperity Sphere were over. Better, they reasoned, that Indochina should fall to Asians, even if they were

---
    35. SD OIR No. 3708, p. 66.
    36. (S) Geneva Conf Background Paper, Indochina Chronology, p. 27.

not of the pro-Japanese camp, than to Japan's conquerors.
At least it would be in keeping with Japan's historic
task--the liberation of Asia from white imperialism.
Isolated cases of fighting between Japanese and Viet
Minh units did occur but these clashes were minor. In
the main the Japanese held to a benevolent neutrality.
They did, however, turn a considerable amount of arms and
material over to the native forces and they posed no obstacle to the Viet Minh's seizure of public facilities
and property. It is doubtful that the Viet Minh could
have come to power without at least the passive acquiescence of the Japanese.[37]

Even before Giap's formations entered Hanoi, the
city passed into the hands of the Viet Minh. Large demonstrations took place in Hanoi on 17-18 August, and for
the first time Viet Minh adherents began to harangue the
crowds openly, the imperial flag was lowered and the red
flag with a gold star was raised in its place, and processions moved through the streets carrying Viet Minh
banners and shouting Viet Minh slogans. On 19 August,
Giap's men reached Hanoi where they were immediately
joined by the local militia. On 20 August, the Viet
Minh became master of the city without opposition. In
the next few days the Viet Minh extended its grip over
most of the Tonkin countryside, using the revolutionary
committees and the youth groups trained by the French
and the Kim government to good advantage.[38]

In the meantime, in Hue, Bao Dai was preparing to
surrender the seal of national power to the Viet Minh.
He saw on every side the evidences of the Viet Minh's
superior power. The Kim government had already resigned
on 15 August and Hue itself had a revolutionary committee.
At first Bao Dai attempted to maintain his position as
Emperor. On 20 August he sent messages to the Allies,
including France, pleading that they recognize the independence of Viet Nam, and on 22 August he invited the
Viet Minh to form a new government. Bao Dai heard nothing
from the Allies, and from the Viet Minh came only messages
urging his abdication. Even among his personal counsellors

---

37. Devillers, *Histoire du Viet-Nam*, pp. 136-137;
Hammer, *Struggle for Indochina*, p. 101.
38. SD CIR No. 3705, p. 66; Devillers, *Histoire du Viet-Nam*, pp. 136-137.

were those who advised him to give up his throne. By 24 August Bao Dai felt there was no other course open to him; he wired to the Viet Minh in Hanoi that he was ready to abdicate and that the revolutionary government should send its representative to Hue for the transfer of legal power.[39]

The Viet Minh took Bao Dai at his word. On 25 August a delegation, headed by the Communist Vice President of the People's Liberation Committee, Tran Huy Lieu, arrived in Hue. That evening, without incident and in a friendly atmosphere, Bao Dai handed Tran Huy Lieu the two traditional symbols of rule, the gold seal and the gold sword with the ruby-encrusted handle. In return, Lieu pinned a red insignia with a gold star to the tunic of the former Emperor.[40]

In his abdication address, Bao Dai stated: "We ask all parties and groups, all classes of society as well as the Royal Family to unite and support without reservation the Democratic Government in order to consolidate national independence. . . . Henceforth we shall be happy to be a free citizen in an independent country. We shall allow no one to abuse our name or the name of the Royal Family in order to sow dissent among our compatriots."[41] As Citizen Vinh Thuy, Bao Dai now became Supreme Commander of the new government.

Hanoi became the new capital and Ho Chi Minh reorganized the People's Liberation Committee into the "Provisional Government" of Viet Nam. It was a ministerial government with a more moderate composition, but Ho remained President and the largest representation was given to the Communists who filled posts in the new cabinet. Of the remaining posts, three were filled by other Viet Minh adherents, three by the Democrats, three by independents, and one by a Catholic representative.[42] Ho Chi Minh took for himself the portfolio of Minister of Foreign Affairs, and Giap became Minister of Interior.

---

39. Devillers, *Histoire du Viet-Nam*, p. 139.
40. Hammer, *Struggle for Indochina*, p. 104.
41. Devillers, *Histoire du Viet-Nam*, pp. 139-140. (Translated by author.)
42. (S) Geneva Conf Background Paper, Indochina Chronology, pp. 27-28.

On 2 September, Ho Chi Minh solemnly announced the birth and independence of the Democratic Republic of Viet Nam (DRV). The new government was now master of Tonkin and Annam, but in Cochinchina it was quite a different story.

In the south the defeat of Japan produced an immediate upsurge of activity by all the nationalist organizations. The Viet Minh did not represent a large enough body of the population to dominate the nationalist movement. It controlled Saigon, but little more; it was compelled, therefore, to vie for power with many rival organizations. Each of these organizations had armed elements, and each was thus able to impose its control on those areas where it was strongest. For example, the Cao Dai and the Hoa Hao attempted to set up unitary religious states. The militant wing of the Cao Dai maintained the seat of its order in the city of Tay-Ninh, and the Hoa Hao set up an independent state in Can-Tho. All the parties and groups wanted independence, although each aimed for an independence modeled after its own conception.[43]

Since, however, no party or group was strong enough to impose its will on the others, each was forced to compromise its aims. On 14 August a United National Front was established, composed of the formerly pro-Japanese parties and Trotskyists. The National Independence Party, the Cao Dai, elements of the Hoa Hao, and the Trotskyists of "the struggle" group formed the most important elements of the front. Under the influence of the intransigent Trotskyists the United National Front favored a policy of resistance to all foreign powers, including the Allies. In contrast, the Communist-dominated Viet Minh was inclined toward a policy of negotiation with the Allies and friendly relations with foreigners. It, too, however, proclaimed its readiness to fight "foreign imperialism."[44]

The formation of the United National Front gave the members of the Viet Minh good cause to fear that they might soon find themselves confronted by a coalition of nationalist parties, strong enough to control the political future of Cochinchina. They reacted to this threat by appealing to all nationalist parties to compose their differences in order to meet the Allies as a unified body,

---
43. SD OIR No. 3708, p. 68.
44. Ibid.

76

with a common policy. The Viet Minh called a meeting in Saigon of all political groups on 25 August. The United National Front participated in this meeting, but unity was difficult to achieve. The Viet Minh and the United National Front found themselves far apart in their attitudes toward the Allies and the conduct of the struggle to maintain the independence of Viet Nam. Nevertheless, the Viet Minh's argument that in unity there is strength was strong enough to achieve a superficial unification, and a Provisional Executive Committee of Southern Viet Nam was formed. But the Committee was dominated by the Indochinese Communist Party, and it was not representative of the general nationalist movement. It considered itself as the southern adjunct of the Ho Chi Minh government in the north.[45]

As such the Provisional Executive Committee could hardly hope to unite the widely diversified political elements in the south. All parties knew that unification was a short-range affair. In effect, all parties were observing a short period of truce. In the interim they would try to rally more supporters, to increase their military strength, and to plan for the struggle that was certain to break out shortly. The truce was even shorter than they expected.

---

45. Ibid.

CHAPTER V

SIXTEEN MONTHS OF CRISIS
SEPTEMBER 1945-DECEMBER 1946

The months from September 1945 to December 1946 were a period of increasing turmoil in Indochina. The occupation forces of Great Britain and China came and went. The Viet Minh became the spokesman and principal force of the Vietnamese nationalist movement. The French returned to Indochina in force, and clearly indicated their intention to remain. The French and Viet Minh alternated negotiations with charges and counter charges of bad faith. They spilled each other's blood, and it was often impossible to distinguish the victim from the aggressor. By the end of 1946 one thing, at least, was clear--Vietnamese were prepared to fight and die to assure the independence of Viet Nam. But it soon became equally clear that Frenchmen were prepared to fight and die to preserve the French Empire.

The British Occupation

At the end of World War II the South East Asia Command's area of responsibility was increased to include Indochina south of the 16th parallel. Consequently, after the defeat of Japan, the occupation of southern Indochina fell within the province of Admiral Lord Louis Mountbatten, Supreme Allied Commander, South East Asia. In its occupation planning SEAC assigned Indochina the lowest priority. Malaya, Hongkong, Siam, and Java all ranked before Indochina, for it was assumed that the French would take over occupation of the country at the earliest possible moment. Since, however, the end of the war found the French unprepared to carry out the occupation, SEAC assumed more of the task than it had originally contemplated.

As stated on 14 August the SEAC objective in Indochina was "to introduce a force into French Indo-China south of 16 degrees north in order to control the Japanese Southern Army headquarters, to concentrate and evacuate Allied prisoners of war and internees and to disarm Japanese forces." "The eventual re-occupation of FIC is a matter for the French. . . . As far as possible all matters affecting the civil population should be dealt with through the French representatives . . . who should be given every assistance necessary."1

On paper the occupation of Indochina seemed to be a routine matter of no great moment. The Japanese had only to be rounded up and disarmed, and Allied prisoners of war and internees taken care of. The French would soon be available to handle the more complicated and nettlesome problems of civil administration. And, as far as the British knew, the "liberated" native population would be friendly. But it was not very long before the British were disabused of these notions.

The British advance mission that arrived in Saigon on 6 September immediately found itself beset by problems beyond its competence and means. Saigon was full of conflicting groups that might at any moment turn the city into an arena of bloodshed. Only the Japanese possessed enough strength to control the situation, but, for reasons of their own, they preserved only a semblance of order. The Vietnamese independence demonstrations of 2 September had culminated in unorganized attacks on French homes. Each day brought new incidents. And try as it might the Committee of the South could not control the extremists in the ranks of the nationalist parties. The French returned the hatred of the Vietnamese in equal measure, but for the time being they were weak, and dared not react against the Vietnamese. Their hour of vengeance would come later.2

As their first task the members of the British Mission tried to restore order in Saigon. They directed the Japanese to increase the police forces in the city to seven battalions, and they ordered the disarmament of the Vietnamese. Tran Van Giau, the Communist-Viet Minh head of the Committee of the South, was willing to comply, for he still hoped to convince the Allies that the Vietnamese were capable of governing themselves, an important qualification of independence. Thus when Japanese headquarters issued a directive ordering general disarmament,

---
1. (TS) HQ SACSEA, War Diary, vol 85, par 2, 1-2 Sep 45; ibid., par 10.
2. Devillers, *Histoire du Viet-Nam*, pp. 154-155.

Giau supported the order. He called upon the population to obey the directive, and pleaded for the people's confidence. "In the interest of our country," he said, "we call on all to . . . not let themselves be led astray by people who would betray our country. It is only in this spirit that we can facilitate our relations with the Allied representatives."[3]

Giau's appeal, coupled with the rumor that the British planned to bring back French rule, brought the Trotskyists and elements of the Hoa Hao and Cao Dai out into open opposition to the Viet Minh. In the countryside para-military formations of the Hoa Hao and Cao Dai clashed with Viet Minh units while in the city the Trotskyists ordered the population not to give up its arms, and incited the people against the British troops who were expected momentarily.[4]

As soon as British troops appeared in Saigon the Trotskyists issued a manifesto accusing the Committee of the South of treason. The Viet Minh's reaction was swift and deadly. In the name of the Committee of the South Viet Minh police arrested the entire Central Committee of the international Trotskyist movement. The result was a violent conflict between Trotskyists of all shades and the Viet Minh. But it was an uneven contest, and a short one. The Viet Minh were by far the stronger faction. They killed the leaders of the Trotskyists, and dozens of the hierarchy. In the end the Viet Minh succeeded in destroying the Trotskyists as an important element in the nationalist movement.[5]

While the Viet Minh were acting against the Trotskyist organizations on the one hand, on the other they were trying to appease other discontented political groups. Viet Minh places in the Committee of the South were reduced from six to four and the membership of other groups increased from three to nine. Tran Van Giau stepped down from the Presidency of the Committee, and an independent took his post.

---
3. Hammer, *Struggle for Indochina*, p. 109.
4. SD OIR No. 3708, pp. 72-73; Devillers, *Histoire du Viet-Nam*, p. 156.
5. SD OIR No. 3708, p. 73; Hammer, *Struggle for Indochina*, p. 110.

But the fighting between the Viet Minh and other nationalist groups left deep scars. This conflict largely explains both the later inability of the Viet Minh to maintain order under the British occupation and the gradual weakening of the Vietnamese nationalist position in the south.[6]

The First Allied Occupation Forces, consisting of one battalion of Indian troops from the British 20th Division and one company of the French 5th Colonial Infantry, arrived in Saigon by plane on 12 September. British Major-General Douglas D. Gracey, the Commander of the occupation force, landed the next day. He found the situation little improved from what it had been at the time of the British mission's arrival. Tension remained high between the Vietnamese and the French, and sporadic warfare was going on between the Viet Minh and other nationalist groups. Though General Gracey's primary duty was to disarm the Japanese, his troops were so few that he felt compelled to use Japanese troops to maintain order "as they were the one safeguard against lawlessness and disorder, until the French troops should come, if British forces were not to become involved."[7]

The French, however, now felt much more secure. Without incident they took over from the Japanese control of the port, the arsenal, and other key points. Their success increased their aggressiveness, and, with the memory of their recent terror still fresh in their minds, they urged the French authorities to take repressive measures against the Vietnamese. At this time the highest French official in southern Indochina was Jean Cedile, a colonial administrator, and the delegate of the High Commissioner of France for South Indochina, Admiral Georges Thierry d'Argenlieu. Cedile had parachuted into the country three weeks earlier with the firm intention of negotiating with the Vietnamese. According to instructions from his government Cedile was to re-establish order, re-assert French sovereignty, and prepare for the future regime envisioned by the Declaration of 24 March. In his view the first two conditions were necessary to achieve the third, but under the circumstances there was little hope that order

---
6. SD OIR No. 3708, p. 72; Devillers, *Histoire du Viet-Nam*, p. 156.
7. (TS) HQ SACSEA, War Diary, vol 90.

and French sovereignty would be established in the near future. He decided, therefore to go to General Gracey and enlist his help "in safeguarding French lives and property."8

General Gracey hesitated, for he found himself in an extremely awkward position. His instructions did not authorize him to intervene in Franco-Vietnamese matters, and the political advisors he had been promised were not yet available. Nevertheless the British Commander felt that "although the situation was not serious," some action ought to be taken to curb Vietnamese nationalists before serious violence occurred. First he ordered the Japanese to take measures to maintain order between the French and Vietnamese. But half-hearted Japanese measures failed to have the desired effect, and when the Viet Minh leaders admitted that they were powerless to control all elements of the population, he took matters into his own hands.9

On 20 September General Gracey issued a proclamation affirming his responsibility for the maintenance of law and order in all of Indochina south of the 16th parallel. In the next twenty-four hours he ordered the Vietnamese press shut down, banned all public gatherings and the carrying of arms, directed that all Vietnamese police be confined to barracks, and all troops remain in their present location, proclaimed martial law and a curfew, and announced that sabotage and looting would be punishable by death.10

Even after these stern measures had been ordered, there was still a slim chance that the Viet Minh at least might bow to the British Commander's authority. But the French, abetted by General Gracey, made a peaceful solution to the problem impossible. On the 22nd the British took over from the Viet Minh control of the central prison and released the French parachutists who had been confined there since the Japanese coup of 9 March. The same day Cedile went to General Gracey and secured

---
8. Devillers, *Histoire du Viet-Nam*, pp. 156-158.
9. (UNK) Pers Msg, Gracey to SAC, 211500Z Sep 45, in (TS) HQ SACSEA, War Diary; Devillers, *Histoire du Viet-Nam*, p. 158.
10. Ibid., pp. 158-159.

his permission to rearm 1,400 French troops "to lighten the task" of the overburdened British-Indian force. That night French soldiers descended on the city and occupied the public buildings against virtually no opposition. In the early morning hours they moved on the city hall, the seat of the Committee of the South, but forewarned, the members of the Committee escaped the French net. By dawn the French controlled the city.[11]

The pendulum now swung the other way as Frenchmen set out to pay back the debt of Vietnamese violence and terror. "'The behavior of the French citizens during the morning of Sunday, 23 September, absolutely ensured that counter-measures would be taken by the Annamites. The more emotional of the French citizens . . . unfortunately took this opportunity of taking what reprisals they could. Annamites were arrested for no other reason than that they were Annamites; their treatment after arrest, though not actively brutal, was unnecessarily violent.'"[12]

The situation was getting out of hand on the 23rd when the French authorities tried to apply the brakes. Cedile still hoped to negotiate with the Vietnamese nationalists and he feared the reaction of foreign newsmen, present in Saigon, to the French coup. More important he feared the reaction of General Gracey, who was certain to be displeased, and the results of that displeasure. Cedile moved about the city urging peace and moderation on the French population, but matters had gone too far.

General Gracey had good cause to be angry, for the French, like the Viet Minh, failed to maintain order. In his own words Frenchmen were engaged in "exacting revenge from any Annamite that they could get their hands on or arresting them without charge and beating

---

11. (S) Geneva Conf Background Paper, Indochina Chronology, p. 28; Devillers, *Histoire du Viet-Nam*, p. 159.
12. Supreme Allied Command, Southeast Asia, Commission No. 1, Saigon, *Political History of French Indochina South of 16 Degrees, 13 September-11 October 1945*. Quoted by George Sheldon in an unpublished manuscript, and quoted by Hammer, *Struggle for Indochina*, p. 117.

84

them on the flimsiest pretext."[13] Gracey ordered the French troops to return to their barracks and surrender their arms. Further, he announced that it was his firm intention to treat breaches of law and order by Frenchmen under his proclamations of 20 and 21 September. Cedile agreed fully with General Gracey, and issued a stern warning to French civilians. Unfortunately, the damage had already been done.

As soon as the shock of the French coup had worn off, the Viet Minh struck back. On 24 September several dozen Frenchmen disappeared in the port area, never to be heard from again. The central power station was attacked and electric service cut off. Armed Viet Minh bands invaded the city proper and took the center of Saigon under fire. That night, under the eyes of indifferent Japanese guards, several hundred Vietnamese infiltrated a French suburb of the city and massacred over 150 French men, women, and children before the French and British authorities could intervene. Arms were now hastily reissued to the French troops, but it was too late. Giau ordered a general strike, the interdiction of the main thoroughfares, and the evacuation of the city by the Vietnamese population. Saigon, he promised, would be reduced to ashes.[14]

General Gracey divided the city into sectors held by Anglo-Indian, French, and Japanese troops. Civilians were either barricaded in their homes or herded together to make their protection easier. All waited for a large scale Viet Minh attack. But the Viet Minh were too weak and disorganized to launch such an attack, and in the next few days, General Gracey was able to stabilize the situation in the city. It was in this period that Lieutenant Colonel A. Peter Dewey, head of the OSS detachment in southern Indochina, was ambushed and killed in the outskirts of the city by Vietnamese of undetermined political affiliation. Other American officers and some newspapermen were besieged for several hours before a contingent of Gurkhas came to their relief.[15]

---

13. (TS) HQ SACSEA, War Diary, vol 89, 25 Sep 45.
14. (S) Geneva Conf Background Paper, Indochina Chronology, p. 28; Devillers, *Histoire du Viet-Nam*, p. 160.
15. (S) Geneva Conf Background Paper, Indochina Chronology, p. 29.

In the last days of September, General Gracey's problem was still a serious one. He had only about 2,500 British-Indian troops, and the French troops available created problems instead of solving them. Also available in Saigon, however, were approximately 5,000 Japanese, and had the British Commander been able to rely on this force he would have had little trouble in coping with the Viet Minh. Indeed, had the Japanese cooperated with General Gracey from the beginning, the establishment and preservation of order probably would not have been a problem. Instead the Japanese often betrayed their sympathy for the nationalist movement. There was little doubt that they would have preferred to see the Vietnamese victorious in a struggle between "white imperialism" and "Asiatic nationalism." As early as 14 September Admiral Mountbatten had warned General Gracey that there were "strong indications . . . Japanese providing Annamites with arms . . . ." In the next two weeks the British confirmed several instances of Japanese turning arms over to Vietnamese. Some elements of the conquered army went even farther. There were cases of Japanese troops making common cause with Vietnamese units against the Allied forces. In other cases, while acting as escorts or guards, they permitted Allied personnel to be killed and wounded, and in one instance Japanese soldiers opened fire on troops of the occupation force.[16]

Repeatedly General Gracey warned the Japanese that they were expected to cooperate fully in maintaining order, and repeatedly violations of his orders occurred. Finally, on 27 September with the city virtually besieged by the Viet Minh, General Gracey threatened to treat the Japanese as war criminals unless they mended their ways, but the Japanese chief of staff replied that his men feared Vietnamese reprisals after they were disarmed. Then, with a straight face, he offered to mediate between the British and French and the Vietnamese.[17]

Adding to British woes in this period, news of the French coup and General Gracey's apparent support of the act had, in the meantime, spread outside Indochina. The

---

16. (TS) HQ SACSEA, War Diary, vol 88, 14 Sep; vol 90, 27 Sep; vol 91, 1 Oct.
17. Ibid., vol 90, 27 Sep; Devillers, *Histoire du Viet-Nam*, p. 161.

first press reaction was unfavorable, and the British could now expect strong public criticism of their position in Indochina. Nevertheless, Admiral Mountbatten quickly came to the defense of his subordinate. He wired the British Chiefs of Staff that, in his opinion, General Gracey had acted "with courage and determination in an extremely difficult situation." Had General Gracey acted otherwise, continued Admiral Mountbatten, "the safety of the small British force and the French population in Indochina might have been risked."[18]

In the next few days a steady stream of accusations poured from the DRV radio station in Hanoi. The Ho Chi Minh government announced to the world that Gracey's command was guilty of acts of "barbarism," and that responsibility for any future bloodshed in southern Indochina would rest squarely on British shoulders. Even more galling to the British was the DRV charge that "the main reason for the unfair and inhuman attitude of the /occupation force/ . . . is her /sic/ interest in seeing the French oppress Indochina as a screen for British oppression of other countries."[19]

In varying degrees the British were now assailed by the press of several countries, but the strongest criticism came from India. The British were particularly sensitive to criticism from this quarter, for General Gracey's command was composed primarily of Indian Gurkhas. From India Lord Wavell, the British Viceroy, tried to forestall Indian criticism of the use to which the Gurkhas were being put. He wired Admiral Mountbatten that the Indian division should be withdrawn "the sooner . . . the better." Unfortunately Admiral Mountbatten had no replacement available. He was compelled not only to leave the original force in Indochina, but to augment it during the fall with the remaining elements of the 20th Division.[20]

When the Indian reaction came, it was a bitter one. Pandit Nehru issued a statement in which he declared, "We have watched British intervention /in Indochina/ with growing anger, shame and helplessness that Indian

---

18. (TS) HQ SACSEA, War Diary, vol 89, 24 Sep.
19. Ibid., vol 90, 26 Sep; vol 91, 2 Oct.
20. Ibid., vol 90, 26 Sep; vol 94, 29 Oct.

troops should thus be used for doing Britain's dirty work against our friends who are fighting the same fight as we."[21]

At the end of September matters in Saigon took a turn for the better. An Anglo-French convoy dropped anchor in Saigon and landed French reinforcements. The balance of power now shifted definitely into the hands of the British and French. The Viet Minh recognized this fact, for on 1 October a number of Viet Minh leaders called upon General Gracey with proposals for peace.[22] General Gracey informed the delegation that his sole mission was to disarm Japanese, but he insisted that the Viet Minh put a stop to terrorist activity. The delegation countered with the proposition that only by reinstating the DRV government with all of its former powers, could peace be established. To attain this result the Viet Minh were willing to negotiate with the French provided the British would arbitrate. General Gracey agreed and arranged with the Viet Minh for a truce to commence the following evening. It was also arranged that French and Viet Minh representatives would meet on the morning of 3 October with a member of the British staff acting as observer.

At this initial meeting the French laid down the prerequisites for satisfactory conversations. The Viet Minh would have to return all hostages, agree to a mutual exchange of prisoners, and retrieve for occupation authorities the body of Colonel Dewey, the murdered American officer. The Vietnamese accepted these conditions, and the conference concluded on a note of harmony that prompted General Gracey's opinion that "undoubted progress" had been made.[23]

---
21. NY Times, 31 Dec 45.
22. (TS) HQ SACSEA, War Diary, vol 91, 1 Oct. The new Anglo-French supremacy also became apparent to the Japanese. Early in October General Gracey's headquarters reported that although "some Japanese are assisting the revolutionaries . . . /the Japanese commander/ has condemned them as traitors to the Emperor, and the bulk of the Japanese forces are carrying out defensive talks in accordance with General Gracey's orders." Ibid., vol 93, 24 Oct.
23. Ibid., vol 91, 3 Oct.

General Gracey's optimism, however, was premature. Three days later the Viet Minh leaders returned to admit failure. They had been unable to uncover evidence pointing to the whereabouts of the missing French hostages or to locate the body of Colonel Dewey. The French replied that this admission was proof of native incapacity to govern effectively, but they were assured that efforts to meet the French demands would be redoubled.[24]

The Viet Minh returned on 9 October, but hardly had the meeting commenced when news arrived of a Vietnamese attack on a British-held airfield. "Considerably taken aback," the Viet Minh delegation left immediately to try to end the fighting. The attack on the airfield was followed next day by an even more serious incident. British troops were fired upon from ambush, and four soldiers were killed. These actions terminated the short-lived truce and led General Gracey to warn the Vietnamese that they "now must take full consequences for any armed action against any Allied or Japanese forces."[25] And Gracey's threat was not an empty one. His small army had recently been strengthened by reinforcements of French soldiers under General Leclerc.

The reconquest of Indochina was now begun.

With Tonkin and most of Laos still under Chinese occupation, the French were primarily concerned during the autumn of 1945 with establishing their supremacy south of the sixteenth parallel. While French soldiers were steadily arriving in Saigon preparatory to "pacifying" Cochinchina, French and British troops had already made progress in bringing Cambodia back under French influence. The Cambodian monarch had remained loyal to France, and his subjects, most of whom were lacking in political consciousness, had followed his example. Nevertheless, Son Ngoc Thanh, an ardent nationalist, had maneuvered himself into the post of Prime Minister. After the Japanese capitulation, he secured a quantity of Japanese arms and contested the French advance. The Japanese watched from the sidelines and "made no attempt whatsoever to quell the disturbance."[26] On 10 October,

---
24. Ibid., 6 Oct.
25. Ibid., vol 92, 11 Oct.
26. Ibid., vol 89, 20-25 Sep.

however, an Anglo-French force seized the capital of Pnom Penh. Thanh was captured and sent to Saigon, while his followers either scattered into Thailand or went underground. General Alessandri and King Norodom Sihanouk began negotiations looking to a French-Cambodian agreement, and Prince Monireth formed a government committed to a pro-French policy. On 22 October the King announced that Cambodia desired unreserved collaboration with France.[27]

Although British troops had participated in the conquest of Cambodia and were stationed in Cochinchina, by early November French authority was rapidly supplanting British influence. England and France had signed an agreement on 9 October that recognized France's paramount rights in Indochina and turned over civil administration of Indochina south of the 16th parallel to French authorities.[28] To organize the administration, the new French High Commissioner, Georges Thierry d'Argenlieu, arrived in Saigon on 31 October. A strange combination of Carmelite monk and Admiral of the French Navy, d'Argenlieu was an unyielding imperialist. Whatever his intentions when he arrived in Indochina, he soon became the most prominent exponent of force as a solution of the Indochinese problem.

Admiral d'Argenlieu was immediately confronted with the problem of assuming control of Saigon and a small surrounding perimeter from the British and then spreading that control effectively throughout Cochinchina. He made it plain from the beginning that his primary concern lay not in a peaceful adjustment of differences with the Viet Minh, but in the rapid re-establishment of French sovereignty.[29] This inflexible attitude was bound to heighten the conflict with the Vietnamese. The French were soon faced with increased guerrilla opposition. Led by Tran Van Giau, once an advocate of peaceful negotiation, the Viet Minh organized a resistance movement that bitterly fought the French advance into Cochinchina.[30]

---

27. (S) Geneva Conf Background Paper, Indochina Chronology, p. 30.
28. Ibid., p. 29.
29. Hammer, Struggle for Indochina, pp. 122-123.
30. Ibid.

The Viet Minh were outnumbered and ill-equipped, but they proved stiff opposition. They conducted a scorched earth campaign that sorely harassed General Leclerc's army. Leclerc's forces repeatedly encountered burned villages, mined roads, and demolished bridges in the course of its pursuit of the rebels. Although the General had virtually reconquered Cochinchina by the end of November, he soon discovered that establishing effective control was quite another matter. An estimated 100,000 men would be required to stamp out guerrilla resistance and consolidate French military gains. These forces the French simply did not possess; and the British division, having fulfilled its mission, was soon to be withdrawn.

Nevertheless, the French by late December felt themselves able to hold their gains until sufficiently strong to assert their authority throughout Indochina. French reinforcements continued to debark in Saigon, with more promised shortly. Already General Leclerc's command numbered 21,500 French soldiers.[31] The Japanese were no longer a difficult problem for the French, most of them having been disarmed and assembled near Saigon to await repatriation. Admiral d'Argenlieu faced the year 1946 with rebellious guerrillas in Cochinchina and an entrenched DRV government backed by an unfriendly Chinese army in Viet Nam and northern Laos. His success or failure in coping with these obstacles would, in a large measure, determine the future of Indochina.

The Chinese Occupation

While the French and the Viet Minh waged war, in Cochinchina, in Tonkin they preserved an uneasy peace. The Viet Minh, guided by the experienced hand of Ho Chi Minh, was firmly in power. The new DRV government was backed by Giap's military forces, a coalition of Vietnamese political parties, and substantial public support. The French on the other hand had only a few officials in Tonkin. Remnants of the French army defeated by the Japanese in March remained in the Hanoi Citadel under Viet Minh guard, and General Alessandri had failed to secure Chinese permission or American and British help to move his 5,000 troops into Tonkin. In northern Indochina, as in the south, the decisive factor was the occupation force. But in the north, the occupation force was pro-Vietnamese.

---

31. (TS) Encl, "Present Situation in French Indo-China," to (TS) CCS 644/38, 21 Dec 45, CCS 370 (8-5-44) sec 6.

Soon after the Japanese capitulation of 16 August, M. Sainteny and a small party of his staff succeeded in reaching Hanoi along with an American OSS group, headed by Major Archimedes Patti. The Americans were well received by the Viet Minh and the Japanese, but the Frenchmen were confined in the Governor-General's palace. The first few days after M. Sainteny's arrival were crucial for the future of French sovereignty over northern Indochina. Bao Dai's regime was passing from the scene. Giap's army was marching on Hanoi. Within the city itself the Viet Minh were in the process of taking over the administration of Hanoi. Next they would extend their control over most of Tonkin and Annam. The commissioner for north Indochina appointed by Admiral d'Argenlieu had been captured by the Viet Minh, and was being held incommunicado. There was no one to represent France in the north except M. Sainteny, and he lacked credentials. The Japanese doubted his authority, and refused to deal with him. Repeatedly, M. Sainteny appealed by radio to French authorities in Calcutta and Kunming for the powers he needed to deal with the Japanese, but his superiors seemed to have no inkling of the urgency of the situation. They would not replace him, and they would not give him authority to speak for France. On 2 September M. Sainteny, still without powers, looked on while crowds of Vietnamese marched through the streets of Hanoi celebrating "the independence of Viet Nam."[32]

Although the Viet Minh declared itself against violence to Frenchmen, and did try to keep a tight rein on extremists, occasional attacks against French civilians took place. The anti-French feeling among the Vietnamese was as great in Hanoi as it was in Saigon, and the French population of the northern city also lived in daily fear of Vietnamese pillaging and attack. If the French population hoped for relief from the Chinese occupation they were soon disappointed.

The Chinese occupation of northern Indochina began at the end of August. Four Chinese armies, 180,000 men, marched into Viet Nam and spread out over the land. On 18 September Lieutenant General Lu Han, the commander of

---

32. Sainteny, *Histoire d'une Paix Manquee*, pp. 91-96; Hammer, *Struggle for Indochina*, pp. 130-131.

the occupation force, arrived in Hanoi. He was soon joined by Brigadier General Philip E. Gallagher, head of the American mission attached to General Lu Han's command, General Alessandri, and Leon Pignon.

From the beginning General Lu Han made no secret of his hostility toward the French. He ejected M. Sainteny, who had just been appointed French Commissioner for North Indochina, from the Governor-General's palace, and left him to seek quarters elsewhere. As one of their first acts, the Chinese set about dismantling the French military fortifications along the Sino-Vietnamese border. At the Japanese surrender ceremonies the French flag did not fly among those of the Allies, and as a result General Alessandri walked out on the gatherings. General Lu Han refused to recognize M. Sainteny's authority, and stated in the Chinese press of Hanoi that China was bringing independence to Indochina. The Chinese pointedly ignored French requests for permission to move soldiers and civil administrators into Tonkin, and every Frenchman entering the occupied area was searched. Vietnamese were permitted to keep their weapons, but all Frenchmen were disarmed. Control of most public buildings, public services, communications, and the whole structure of administration was in the hands of the DRV, and the Chinese were content to see it rest there.[33]

The French knew that General Lu Han was hostile to them, but they did not know to what extent he reflected the policy of the Chinese Nationalist Government. Actually General Lu Han was, in general, carrying out the policy of his government. Behind the obvious Chinese hostility lay a long history. For many years the Chinese had nursed a deep resentment of French territorial and economic concessions in China. While Frenchmen enjoyed special rights in China, Chinese in Indochina lived in special communities under close French supervision, under administrative restrictions, and under heavier taxes than those levied on other foreigners. Also fresh in Chinese minds was the comparatively recent closing of the Yunnan-Haiphong railroad.[34] The Chinese had learned the hard way

---

33. (S) Geneva Conf Background Paper, Indochina Chronology, p. 28; Sainteny, Histoire d'une Paix Manquee, pp. 123-124; Hammer, Struggle for Indochina, pp. 130-134.
34. Cf. Ch. II.

that this railroad was a vital trade outlet from southwest China to the seas.[35]

Other and older reasons lay behind the Chinese intransigence. The Chinese army that marched into Indochina marched into a country once ruled by China. The people and the civilization of the country were very much like those of China. For many years the Chinese had given sanctuary to the political exiles who fled across the border, and the Kuomintang government had long encouraged and supported the nationalist movement in Indochina. Moreover, Chinese dreams of dominating the country through the installation of an independent, but pro-Chinese, government of Indochina were not quite dead.

Yet with all these reasons to oppose the return of the French to Indochina, the Chinese were open to persuasion. Despite their unfeigned hostility to the French, the Chinese were willing to turn northern Indochina over to the French, but the price they were preparing to ask for their cooperation was high, very high. The Chinese felt that the greater the French fear of losing northern Indochina the higher the price France would be willing to pay. The greater the insecurity of Frenchmen in Tonkin the greater would be the urgency to come to terms with China. To this end the Chinese tried to keep the French and the Viet Minh at swords point, for a French-Vietnamese conciliation would weaken China's bargaining position. They succeeded admirably.

Agreement between the French and the Viet Minh would have been difficult even under a completely neutral occupation force, for the two were far apart in their demands. In northern Indochina the Viet Minh were strong and the French weak, but the French wanted to negotiate as if the reverse were true. In brief, the DRV was "determined to mobilize all its courage, strength and wealth to preserve this liberty and independence," while the French refused to budge from the policy laid down in the declaration of 24 March. In the fall of 1945, therefore, the meetings between the leaders of the DRV and French officials produced no tangible result.[36]

---
35. Hammer, *Struggle for Indochina*, pp. 135-136.
36. (TS) HQ SACSEA, War Diary, vol 89, 21 Sep; Hammer, *Struggle for Indochina*, p. 148.

French inflexibility in dealings with the DRV was undoubtedly reinforced by the hope that, with the end of the Chinese occupation, France would be able to move into northern Indochina in sufficient strength to redress the balance of power. Should this hope be realized France would then be in a position to force the Viet Minh to accept French terms. As they were well aware, however, first the Chinese would have to be paid off.[37]

A first installment on the purchase price had already been paid. On 18 August France had returned to China the Kwangchowwan territory, leased to the French in 1898. Chiang Kai-shek had promptly disavowed any territorial ambitions in Indochina, but then went on to say that it was his "hope that Indochina would emerge to independence."[38] The French made no public response to the Generalissimo's statement, but their private reaction is not difficult to imagine.

Two months later Admiral d'Argenlieu was in Chungking to discuss "the affirmation of French political rights in Indochina" and the future status of the French-owned railroad connecting Yunnan with the port of Haiphong. The Admiral balked at the Chinese demands, however, and no concrete agreement emerged from the negotiations.[39]

It was not until matters in Tonkin took a turn for the worse that the French renewed negotiations with Chungking. In January 1946 Viet Minh and Chinese hostility reached a high pitch. French sources cite fifty-four Vietnamese and thirty-three Chinese acts of aggression committed against Frenchmen during that month alone. In six cases Frenchmen were killed. Reluctantly the French decided to reopen negotiations with the Chinese. Hat in hand, they again made the pilgrimage to Chungking. On 28 February France and China signed a treaty providing for the relief before 31 March of Chinese forces stationed in Indochina by the French Army, and Chinese recognition of French sovereignty over Indochina. According to the terms of the agreement France gave up her concessions at Shanghai, Tientsin, Hankow, and Canton, and all extraterritorial rights in China. She also guaranteed that

---

37. Devillers, *Histoire du Viet-Nam*, pp. 205-206.
38. *Notes et Etudes*, No. 555, 24 Feb 47; *NY Times*, 25 Aug 45.
39. Ibid., 14 Oct 45.

Chinese goods shipped over the Yunnan-Haiphong Railroad would be exempt from customs and transit duties, and that a free zone would be set up for Chinese merchandise reaching Haiphong. Those portions of the railroad lying in Yunnan would be turned over to China. Finally, France agreed to special privileged treatment of Chinese residents in Indochina.[40]

With this treaty the French assured themselves entry into Tonkin, but the question was could they stay there, for the Viet Minh had, in the meantime, weathered a serious crisis of its own, and emerged virtually unscathed.

The DRV under the Chinese Occupation

When the Chinese marched into Tonkin in September 1945, they brought with them the exiled leaders of the Dong Minh Hoi and VNQDD movements. The exiles counted heavily upon Chinese assistance to re-establish themselves as a political force in Indochina. As the Chinese army moved through Tonkin on its way to Hanoi, it stopped along the way to remove the Viet Minh representatives from positions of authority, installing in their places members of the Dong Minh Hoi or VNQDD. These two parties, along with elements from the Dai Viet movement, soon controlled the northernmost provinces in Tonkin, living off the land and tribute collected from the population. They fought intermittently among themselves and with troops sent by the Viet Minh in an attempt to subdue them.[41]

Among General Lu Han's first efforts after his arrival in Hanoi was his attempt to introduce the Dong Minh Hoi and VNQDD into the Viet Minh government. Nguyen Hai Than, leader of the Dong Minh Hoi, stated publicly that the Chinese would not tolerate the presence of Ho Chi Minh at the head of the government for long, and demanded a place in the Provisional Government for his party and the VNQDD. He was confident of the support of Siao Wen, heading the Political Secret Service of

---

40. (S) Geneva Conf Background Paper, Indochina Chronology, p. 33; Notes et Etudes, No. 555, 28 Feb 47.
41. Devillers, Histoire du Viet-Nam, p. 193; SD OIR No. 3708, p. 67.

the Chinese Occupation Army, whose primary mission was to bring the Vietnamese nationalist movement under Chinese control.[42]

In the face of constant pressure from the Chinese, the Dong Minh Hoi and VNQDD, Ho Chi Minh decided to make whatever political concessions were necessary to maintain power in the hands of the Viet Minh. His first act along these lines was to initial a pact with a dissident segment of the Dong Minh Hoi "as a prelude to unity." The two contracting parties vowed to "defend the liberty and independence of the Democratic Republic of Viet Nam /against/ the aggressive attempts of the colonial French. . . ."[43]

Another tactic used by Ho Chi Minh was to minimize the role of the Indochinese Communist Party in the Provisional Government. On 11 November, both to placate the Chinese and as a protest against the French Communists who had failed to support Indochinese aspirations toward independence, the Indochinese Communist Party formally dissolved itself. The rank and file of the party, who had never been communists in the classical sense, drifted away to join other groups, but Ho Chi Minh reorganized the Communist hard core into a number of Marxist "study groups." The leadership of these "study groups," including such militant Communists as Vo Nguyen Giap and Tran Van Giau, continued to exercise considerable influence in the Viet Minh government.[44]

Probably the most popular Viet Minh move of all had been their promise to hold elections for a National Assembly at the end of the year. Siao Wen, realizing that these elections would only confirm the popularity of the Viet Minh, tried to get the elections cancelled, but with no success. He was only able to get them postponed for two weeks, until 6 January 1946.[45] On 23 December the Viet Minh announced that, whatever the

---

42. Devillers, *Histoire du Viet-Nam*, pp. 193-194.
43. SD OIR No. 3708, p. 77.
44. Ibid., p. 92.
45. Devillers, *Histoire du Viet-Nam*, p. 200.

result of the voting, the Dong Minh Hoi would receive twenty and the VNQDD fifty seats in the projected National Assembly.[46] It was hoped that this would satisfy the appetite of these two parties long enough for the Viet Minh to consolidate its power in the country.

Meanwhile, the Viet Minh faced other problems. The Chinese occupation created an economic dilemma for the DRV, as well as a political one. Unlike the British and French forces in the south, the Chinese lived almost entirely off the country, constituting a severe drain on the resources of Tonkin and Annam, already depleted to the danger point during the floods, famine and drought experienced earlier in the year.

When French authorities in Cochinchina offered during October to send shiploads of rice to Haiphong in exchange for coal to meet Saigon's urgent need for fuel, the Viet Minh refused their offer.[47] Instead, Ho Chi Minh's regime instituted an intensive food production campaign, patterned on the "soviet" system. Although the claims made by the Viet Minh of amazing increases in crop yield cannot be substantiated, there is no question but that the famine expected in 1946 was averted largely due to the Viet Minh food production program.[48]

The Viet Minh regime's hold on the country was increased not only by its successful battle against famine, but also by certain basic alterations that it made in the administration of local government. The mandarinate and councils of village notables who had governed in the hinterland of Indochina as long as anyone could remember were replaced by so-called "people's committees," theoretically chosen by the local inhabitants but actually by the Viet Minh. Other measures, such as an intensive propaganda campaign, the organization and indoctrination of youth groups, the banning of prostitution and gambling, and the prohibition of the

---
[46]. SD OIR No. 3708, p. 77.
[47]. (TS) Msg, SACSEA to REAR SACSEA, SAC 25924, TOO 200551Z, in (TS) HQ SACSEA, War Diary, vol 93, 16-24 Oct.
[48]. Hammer, *Struggle for Indochina*, pp. 145-146.

use of alcohol and opium, helped to gain the support of most of Tonkin and northern Annam for the Viet Minh. In lieu of unpopular French taxes, the Viet Minh promulgated a system of "voluntary contributions" and "popular subscriptions" which seemed to insure the government an income adequate to its needs.[49]

As the year 1945 came to an end, the Viet Minh continued to control the Provisional Government of Viet Nam in spite of all the Dong Minh Hoi and VNQDD could do, yielding on specific issues only when necessary to placate the Chinese. While the pro-Chinese parties seemed content to battle among themselves for tribute exacted from an unwilling population in the provinces under their control, the Viet Minh concentrated on building up good will through propaganda and reforms of various kinds. The determining factor in the struggle for power among the nationalist factions was to be the January elections.

On 6 January 1946, the DRV government held the long awaited elections for a National Assembly, openly in Tonkin and Annam, and clandestinely in parts of Cochinchina. The elections themselves were no more than could be expected from a country unfamiliar with the parliamentary system. Discrepancies were common. But there was no mistaking the general sentiment in favor of independence and in support of Ho Chi Minh, who was said to have received ninety-eight percent of the vote.[50]

Apparently, the results of the election so impressed Siao Wen that he promptly threw his support to the Viet Minh, hoping thereby to bring them under Chinese influence and prevent them from reaching an understanding with the French. It was clear to the leaders of the Dong Minh Hoi and the VNQDD that they had lost the battle for political supremacy; therefore they were happy for the opportunity during February to merge with the Viet Minh in a united government. Nguyen Hai Than, head of the Dong Minh Hoi, became Vice President under Ho Chi Minh, and VNQDD members took over the Ministries of Foreign Affairs, Economy, and Social Welfare. In

---

49. Ibid., pp. 141-143.
50. (S) Geneva Conf Background Paper, Indochina Chronology, p. 32.

addition, Ho Chi Minh also dropped, temporarily, two leading Communists from the Cabinet--Vo Nguyen Giap (Interior) and Tran Huy Lieu (Propaganda).51 This seemed to satisfy all concerned, and a united DRV, backed by the Chinese, turned to face the threat of French invasion.

French Charges of U.S. Obstruction in Tonkin

The failure of the French to reassert their sovereignty over Tonkin in these early postwar days gave rise to strong French criticism of American army officers and OSS personnel in northern Indochina. These officers were charged with inciting the Viet Minh to oppose the return of the French during the early phase of the Chinese occupation. Actually, these Americans were so few in number and remained in Tonkin so short a time that it would have been difficult for them to have altered appreciably the eventual outcome. The one officer whose exploits were questionable, the head of the American OSS mission, was transferred as soon as word of his activities reached his superiors.

Nonetheless, some French sources have used the presence of these officers to charge the United States with being in large measure responsible for French difficulties. The United States, motivated by what Sainteny termed an "infantile anticolonialism," was alleged to have urged Ho Chi Minh to resist France and establish an American type of democracy. The United States, they have asserted, had other interests in Indochina too. It harbored an uncommon interest in the port of Haiphong and the strategic routes into south China, and it wished to promote American business interests in order to make Indochina an economic satellite of the United States.

There is no foundation for these charges. As has been seen, the American attitude was neither to assist or oppose the re-establishment of French authority in Indochina. The United States even insisted that Britain and China accept the Japanese surrender in Indochina. The small number of American officers in

---

51. Hammer, *Struggle for Indochina*, p. 144.

Tonkin were under strict injunction to remain aloof from internal affairs and were promptly withdrawn when OSS involvement became apparent to General Wedemeyer. High American officials in 1945, far from wishing to substitute the United States for France in Indochina, went out of their way to maintain a strict neutrality in Indochinese affairs.

The French Succeed and Fail

The year 1946 was one of political maneuvering between the French and Viet Minh. Moderate elements of both sides wished to compromise, but their differences were so pronounced that compromise proved a virtual impossibility. Divergent views appeared on the point of reconciliation as conference followed conference, but extremist elements on both sides blocked more than an illusory settlement. The negotiations of 1946 appeared promising on the surface, but actually they were merely agreements to agree. Although seeming harmony prevailed on the diplomatic front, there was vicious guerrilla fighting in the back country. More ominous yet, both France and the Viet Minh embarked upon a program of military expansion. Should a decision by force become necessary, both intended to be ready. By the end of the year, all negotiations having failed, the future of Indochina was entrusted to the French and Viet Minh armies.

The early months of 1946 saw the gradual spread of French civil and military authority throughout most of Indochina. In Cochinchina British forces turned over the administration to French authorities in February and evacuated Saigon. The new French High Commissioner, Admiral d'Argenlieu, quickly suppressed the weak southern arm of the DRV and re-established French rule; but the activities of nationalist guerrilla bands confined actual French authority to the cities and a few key towns of Cochinchina.

French rule in Cambodia had been reimposed during the autumn of 1945. The French military had crushed resistance bands in Cambodia, and King Norodom Sihanouk, by hurriedly switching his allegiance from Japan to France, managed to save his monarchy. French-Cambodian relations were put upon a more secure footing by an agreement concluded on 7 January 1946 that brought Cambodia into the Indochinese federation. Locally, Cambodia was to be ruled by French-advised administrators, and in internal affairs of federal concern France and Cambodia would exercise joint responsibility. Foreign relations were to be conducted exclusively by France. The reconquest of Laos had been delayed by the Chinese occupation, but French troops entered Laos in March 1946. On 27 August 1946 a similar arrangement was concluded with Laos, where King Sisavong Vong followed the example of his fellow monarch and swore loyalty to France.[52]

With French control tightening upon Cochinchina, Cambodia and Laos, the immediate problem facing the French in early 1946 was to secure entry into Tonkin. Ho Chi Minh's DRV government at Hanoi, backed by a hostile Chinese occupation army, effectively controlled northern Indochina and barred the returning French. The Sino-French treaty of 28 February 1946 eliminated a major obstacle, leaving the French to overcome the final and higher hurdle of Viet Minh opposition. Negotiations begun in January by Sainteny dragged through February and into March.

While Sainteny and Ho Chi Minh were maneuvering in Hanoi, the Viet Minh had been attempting to improve its bargaining position by clothing the DRV in the trappings of popular support. In January elections for a National Assembly had been held openly in Tonkin and Annam and clandestinely in Cochinchina. The extent to which these elections can be considered as an expression of popular will, however, is open to serious question. Before the elections the DRV assigned blocs of Assembly seats to the Dong Minh Hoi and Viet Nam Nationalist Party, and after the election it claimed a suspiciously large vote

---

52. SD OIR No. 4303, 10 Mar 47, pp. 14-15.

for an area whose inhabitants were largely ignorant of the idea of popular representation.[53]

Even as the first session of the National Assembly convened in Hanoi on 2 March, the French were nearing agreement in principle with the DRV. On 6 March 1946 an accord was signed by Vo Nguyen Giap for the DRV government and General Raoul Salan for France. The so-called March 6 Accord formed the basis for the negotiations between France and the DRV during the remainder of 1946. It represented a major concession in principle by both France and the Viet Minh.

The French attained their major aim of securing entry into Tonkin, where the DRV pledged its followers to receive French forces "in a friendly way." France would supplant the Chinese occupation army with a mixed Franco-Vietnamese army under French command. This army was limited by the terms of the agreement to 25,000 soldiers, of which 10,000 were to be Vietnamese. France promised to withdraw one-fifth of its troops each year and at the end of a five year period terminate its occupation.[54]

Although the Viet Minh leaders had conceded an important point, they had gained what in their estimation was an equally important concession in return. France in the March 6 Accord acknowledged the DRV as the legitimate government of Viet Nam and recognized it as a free state in the Indochinese federation of the French Union. According to the agreement, Viet Nam was now to have an indigenous government, parliament, and army, and

---

53. (S) Geneva Conf Background Paper, Indochina Chronology, p. 32. In assigning blocs of Assembly seats to the Dong Minh Hoi and Viet Nam Nationalist Party, Ho Chi Minh was following the policy of strengthening his regime by attempting to win the allegiance of non-Viet Minh nationalists. Some nationalist leaders refused to cooperate with Ho. Such was Ngo Dinh Diem, whom the Viet Minh held captive in the Tonkinese mountains in an effort to coerce him into supporting the DRV. When Diem remained intractable, Ho at length released him. Hammer, Struggle for Indochina, pp. 149-150.

54. Notes et Etudes, "Accord annexe a la Convention preliminaire du 6 mars 1946," No. 548, 15 Feb 47.

the right to conduct its own finances, concessions that would have exceeded the fondest dreams of prewar nationalists.55

The March 6 Accord also called for a referendum to be held in Cochinchina to determine whether its inhabitants desired union with the DRV. This provision laid the basis for a dispute that became the principal issue preventing a settlement between France and the Viet Minh during 1946. The DRV had always contended the Cochinchina was an integral part of Viet Nam. The ties between the two areas were geographic, ethnic, cultural, and economic; and according to the DRV these ties should be completed by bringing about the political union of Cochinchina with the rest of Viet Nam. French colonial officials, however, were extremely reluctant to yield so important an area. French authority was much more firmly entrenched in Cochinchina than elsewhere in Indochina Cochinchina had a long tradition of French rule; it was of great economic value to France; and Saigon had long been the center of French colonial power in the Far East. Now, in the view of many Frenchmen, they were being asked to yield the seat of their power to what many of them considered a group of nationalistic adventurers in Tonkin. Nevertheless, French negotiators at Hanoi, in the interests of conciliation, agreed to submit the question to popular vote in Cochinchina and abide by the results. France's failure to carry out this promise was a major factor in the breakdown of subsequent negotiations.

France found an excuse for postponing the referendum in the continued opposition of resistance groups in Cochinchina. Conditions outside the cities had become so chaotic that French authorities claimed that elections were not possible until order had been restored. The DRV was convinced that a referendum would demonstrate an overwhelming native desire for unification with Viet Nam, and it urged the Cochinchinese nationalists to stop contesting French authority so that elections might be held. But French colonial officials stepped up their campaign of encouraging autonomist and separatist tendencies, and the guerrilla opposition broke out anew.56

---
55. Ibid., "Convention preliminaire franco-vietnamienne du 6 mars 1946," No. 548, 15 Feb 47.
56. SD OIR No. 3708, pp. 79-80.

If the French faced open hostilities in Cochinchina, the Viet Minh were hardly better off in Tonkin. In the opinion of many Viet Minh adherents, Ho Chi Minh had gone too far in his attempt to compromise with France. Only by placing his full prestige behind the agreement of 6 March had he secured its grudging acceptance by the bulk of the nationalist movement. Yet even Ho's great prestige could not silence all of the opposition in the diversified political alignment that composed the DRV. Certain elements of the Dong Minh Hoi and Viet Nam Nationalist Party, angered by Ho's "pro-French" policies, had demonstrated their hostility by spreading terror through the Tonkin countryside. The growing DRV army, together with the French troops that marched into Tonkin pursuant to the March 6 Accord, organized a campaign to crush the dissidents. The Franco-Viet Minh military forces within a short time eliminated most of the organized resistance and drove the leaders into China, where they organized a "Nationalist Front." The Front was designed to serve as a nucleus for disaffected nationalists.[57]

Against this backdrop of civil strife in Tonkin and Cochinchina the first step in implementing the March 6 Accord was taken. The Accord had specified that further discussion would be held in the near future to define more precisely its terms and to arrive at means for carrying out its principles. Accordingly, French and DRV negotiators gathered at Dalat on 19 April, but three weeks of discussion failed to establish agreement on more than minor educational and cultural matters. Even a mixed armistice commission, organized to attempt a solution of the Cochinchinese fighting, found itself unable to agree and disbanded after several fruitless sessions. Nevertheless, the Dalat Conference ended with the participants believing that a basis for future compromise had been reached.[58]

The Dalat Conference having failed to resolve the issues preventing settlement, a second conference was scheduled for July, this time at Fontainebleau, France. The agenda for the Fontainebleau meeting would include all of the problems vital to better relations between France and the Viet Minh. To be discussed were such

---

57. Ibid., p. 78.
58. (S) Geneva Conf Background Paper, Indochina Chronology, p. 34.

items as foreign relations, the composition of the Indochinese federation, the Cochinchinese problem, economic questions, and finally the all important issue of a treaty to define the relationship between the two countries.59 Ho Chi Minh departed for France late in May, but even before his arrival an event was in the making in Cochinchina that would wreck the Fontainebleau Conference.

Since his arrival in Saigon as High Commissioner, Admiral d'Argenlieu had been earnestly seeking to prevent the union of Cochinchina with the DRV. As early as February he had erected a "Provisional Consultative Council" in Cochinchina that could rule should the occasion to do so arise. At the same time, French officials had encouraged separatist tendencies in every way possible and had attempted to foster the impression that the people of Cochinchina in fact desired an autonomous and separate regime. The DRV had protested the French actions and insistently demanded that the promised referendum be held. The French answer came on 1 June. Admiral d'Argenlieu announced the creation of the "Autonomous Republic of Cochinchina" as a member of the Indochinese federation of the French Union. Immediately thereafter he sponsored a provisional government under the presidency of Dr. Nguyen Van Thinh. The Admiral's action resulted in an increased tempo of guerrilla resistance to French authority that revealed the close ties between the Committee of the South and the DRV government at Hanoi.60

The developments in Cochinchina did not improve the disposition of the Viet Minh delegation arriving at Fontainebleau. Since the referendum question was included on the Fontainebleau agenda, Admiral d'Argenlieu's move must have impressed them as an act of singularly bad faith and certainly did not augur well for the negotiations. But the Admiral was not finished yet. The Fontainebleau Conference had been in session only

---
59. Ibid, p. 36
60. Ibid., (S) State Dept, Brief on Issues in Dispute between France and Vietnam, OIR No. 4303, 10 Mar 47, p. 9.

three weeks when he called a second Dalat Conference, without representatives of the DRV government, to discuss federalization of the Indochinese states. He recognized as participants in the meeting Cochinchina and Annam, whose future status was even then under consideration at Fontainebleau. The DRV delegation, with considerable justification, regarded the second Dalat Conference as a serious violation of the March 6 Accord and refused to continue the Fontainebleau talks.[61]

Undaunted by the repercussions of their gathering, the representatives at Dalat continued their discussions. They agreed at length upon a blueprint for federalization that would have effectively subordinated Indochina to French control, and they concluded by denouncing the DRV delegation at Fontainebleau as unrepresentative of the Vietnamese people. In the final analysis, the only accomplishment of the Dalat Convention was to destroy hope of an agreement at Fontainebleau.[62]

Ho Chi Minh, however, refused to abandon his pursuit of a settlement. Hoping to salvage something from the wreckage of Fontainebleau, he remained in France when the DRV delegation departed for Hanoi. On 14 September Ho and Marius Moutet, Minister of Overseas France, signed a provisional modus vivendi. The modus vivendi was designed to continue in effect the policy established by the March 6 Accord until a new meeting could be held in January 1947. It reaffirmed the principle of referendum and provided for (a) reciprocal democratic rights for citizens of one country in the territory of the other; (b) reciprocal property rights and restoration of seized French property; (c) establishment of a single currency unit for Indochina by tying the piastre to the franc; (d) a customs union, free trade, coordinated transportation and communication; and (e) a Franco-Vietnamese armistice commission for Cochinchina.[63]

---

61. (S) Geneva Conf Background Paper, Indochina Chronology, p. 36.
62. Ibid., p. 37.
63. Notes et Etudes, "Modus vivendi Franco-Vietnamien du 14 septembre 1946," No. 548, 15 Feb 47.

Ho Chi Minh regarded the modus vivendi as "better than nothing," but it actually solved none of the burning questions that were disrupting French-Vietnamese relations. The agreement fell far short of Viet Minh aspirations, and some of the more extreme elements bitterly attacked Ho for conceding too much to France. Handbills disseminated in Hanoi by Ho's opponents suggested that his long residence overseas had made him a foreign slave. On the other hand, French colonial officials in Indochina were none too happy with the concessions made by the Paris government. Mutual distrust thus destroyed any chance that the modus vivendi might effect even a temporary solution, and after the Haiphong incident in December both sides freely violated the terms of the agreement.[64]

The repeated breakdown of negotiations, the ineffectual modus vivendi, the erection of the autonomous regime in Cochinchina, and continued guerrilla fighting throughout Indochina, set the stage for the convening of the second session of the DRV National Assembly in October. Since the March session of the Assembly, the DRV had been energetically engaged in consolidating its hold on Viet Nam and increasing its popular support. In the absence of Ho Chi Minh, these efforts were carried out primarily by Giap. Following Bao Dai's departure into voluntary exile the preceding April, Giap had inaugurated a campaign to eliminate opposition either through repression or absorption. To facilitate this process, he had built a relatively strong Vietnamese army. Giap also instituted a number of social welfare measures that, incidentally or designedly, strengthened the DRV among the people. The National Assembly that met in October to draft a constitution was supposed by many to be another indication of the DRV's resolve to become a democratic state.

---

64. Ibid., Hammer, Struggle for Indochina, pp. 177, 181-182; (U) Institut franco-suisse d'Etudes coloniales, France and Viet-Nam, The Franco-Vietnamese Conflict According to Official Documents (Geneva, Aug 47), pp. 41-42 (hereinafter: France and Viet-Nam). The latter source is an extremely biased French account of the origins of the Indochinese conflict and contains the French viewpoint on violations of the modus vivendi.

Although questionable as an expression of popular will, the Assembly nonetheless was broadly representative of the dominant political groupings. Several instances of Viet Minh intimidation of non-Viet Minh assemblymen occurred, but the body succeeded in producing a constitution nevertheless. The document that resulted incorporated many features of western democracy, including such ideals as freedom of the press, assembly, inviolability of person, and ministerial responsibility. Since almost immediately war broke out between France and the Viet Minh, the DRV government was never put to the test of proving that the high sounding phrases of the constitution were not empty words. Two facts, however, were significant. After its adjournment, the National Assembly was not called again until 1953; and the government that assumed power on 3 November registered an increase in Communist Cabinet representation from three to five ministries. Thus the guiding or controlling hand of avowed Communists was now much more apparent in DRV policy--a reflection of the dangerous deterioration of relations with France.[65]

Clearly, any further deterioration of Franco-Viet Minh relations would almost certainly bring war. That deterioration was not long in coming. Again the locus of conflict was Cochinchina, where the President of Cochinchina, Dr. Thinh, found himself facing an almost impossible political tangle. French colonial officials in Saigon supported the Cochinchina Autonomous Republic, while the Paris Government dealt with the DRV within the framework of the _modus vivendi_, which reaffirmed the principle of referendum. Confronted with this anomalous situation, and harassed by French and native political intrigue, Thinh committed suicide on 10 November. Although the Cochinchina Assembly elected a new President, Cao Daist Le Van Hoach, the developments in Cochinchina put an increased strain on relations between French authorities and the DRV. All that was needed to touch off a full-scale war was an incident.[66]

---

65. SD OIR No. 3708, pp. 82-83.
66. (S) Geneva Conf Background Paper, Indochina Chronology, p. 39.

That incident came in the form of two clashes between French and Viet Minh troops on 20 November. A French War Crimes investigating team journeyed to Lang Son to disinter the remains of some French officers allegedly killed by the Japanese the preceding year. On its return trip to Hanoi the team was fired upon by Viet Minh troops and nine Frenchmen were killed. Each side accused the other of provoking the skirmish.[67]

This incident was of minor significance compared with the armed encounter in Haiphong the same day. The Haiphong incident was the culmination of a lengthy customs dispute. A French patrol craft seized a Chinese junk running contraband and was fired upon by DRV troops on the shore. Fighting spread to the city of Haiphong. General Morliere, commanding the French troops in northern Indochina, and Hoang Huu Nam, the DRV Under Secretary of State, immediately intervened and by 22 November had restored peace to the city. Upon learning of the situation in Haiphong, Admiral d'Argenlieu, who was then in Paris, cabled General Valluy in Saigon to instruct General Morliere to reply with force. Morliere protested that order had been restored and the situation was under control. General Valluy then bypassed Morliere and wired Colonel Debes, commanding the French garrison in Haiphong, to "make yourself completely master of Haiphong by all means at your disposal and bring the Vietnamese Army to surrender." On 23 November Colonel Debes moved to carry out these instructions. Encountering resistance, he called upon the French fleet in Haiphong Harbor for naval and air support. The resulting bombardment killed an estimated six thousand residents of Haiphong. After five days of street fighting, French troops established absolute supremacy in the city.[68]

The Haiphong incident dealt a mortal blow to any hope of settling the differences between France and the DRV. During the ensuing few weeks, rumors were rife among the Vietnamese that the next blow would fall on Hanoi. Frenchmen and Vietnamese were killed in the

---

67. Hammer, *Struggle for Indochina*, p. 182; *France and Viet-Nam*, pp. 43-44.
68. (S) Geneva Conf Background Paper, Indochina Chronology, p. 40; Hammer, *Struggle for Indochina*, pp. 180-182.

streets of the city, and ~~Viet Minh riflemen sniped at~~
Frenchmen from the windows of the public buildings. Vo
Nguyen Giap, the Viet Minh Commander-in-Chief, concentrated upon preparing native armies throughout Indochina
for war; Ho Chi Minh, on the other hand, seemed to be
making every effort to avert war through conciliation.
Both France and the DRV, determined not to be taken off
guard should the other attack, repeatedly violated the
provisions of the modus vivendi. On 19 December General
Morliere ordered the Viet Minh militia to surrender its
arms, and that night Vo Nguyen Giap struck. The Viet
Minh cut off Hanoi's water and electricity and launched
a full scale assault upon the French garrison, and in
the process killed a number of French civilians. After
twenty-four hours of hard fighting, French troops
succeeded in expelling the Viet Minh and restoring
order to the city. Giap immediately called for a general
offensive against the French throughout Indochina.
French garrisons were attacked simultaneously at Phu
Lang Thuong, Bao Ninh, and Nam Dinh in North Viet Nam,
at Hue and Tourane in Central Viet Nam, and two days
later at outposts in Cochinchina.[69]

The eight year war had begun.

---

69. (S) Geneva Conf Background Paper, Indochina
Chronology, p. 41; Hammer, Struggle for Indochina,
pp. 186-187; France and Viet-Nam, pp. 50-52.

CHAPTER VI

MILITARY AND POLITICAL STALEMATE: GROWING U.S. CONCERN, JANUARY 1947-JUNE 1949

In Indochina, the two and one-half years between January 1947 and June 1949 formed a pattern of guerrilla war and diplomatic maneuver. On the military front France fought an indecisive war of attrition with the Viet Minh, while on the political front the French Government struggled to create a central Indochinese government that would capture the imagination and loyalty of the Vietnamese. The vital first step in the creation of this new regime was to persuade Bao Dai to return to his homeland at the head of an anti-Viet Minh government. Unfortunately, negotiations with Bao Dai dragged on for almost two years before a formula acceptable to both the ex-Emperor and France was found. All the while the war continued; the Viet Minh held its own, but France slowly expended more men, money, and materiel than she could afford.

At the start of the period United States policymakers, preoccupied by the growing threat of the Soviet Union, paid little more than routine attention to the problem of Indochina. Gradually, however, United States interest increased until in the summer of 1948 the United States adopted a position of tentative support of the Bao Dai solution. As French reluctance to make real concessions to Vietnamese nationalist aspirations became manifest, United States interest grew into concern. And with this concern came the first United States consideration of more active support of the Bao Dai restoration movement, and of the general French position in Indochina.

Military Situation in the Spring of 1947

The outbreak of war in late 1946 had tended to unify the various parties in the Viet Minh-controlled DRV in united opposition to France. The Viet Minh had long been under attack from other nationalist parties and extremist elements within the coalition, all of whom strongly opposed Ho Chi Minh's apparent willingness to compromise with the French. In early 1947, however, the DRV concentrated its activities on the conduct of military action, procurement of supplies, control of the flood program in Tonkin, and coordination of the nationwide educational program. All DRV parties now joined in the non-controversial policy of supporting the war and in a common effort to achieve social and economic progress, thus increasing the unity of the coalition.

To bring the various parties even more closely together, the DRV government was twice reshuffled, giving the appearance of more equal representation to all political forces in the nationalist alliance, but in fact the Communists and Viet Minh representatives continued to dominate the government.[1]

During the first five months of 1947, Ho Chi Minh's attempts to reach a peaceful settlement through negotiation gradually ceased in the face of French intransigence. Although the French Premier declared his willingness to submit the unity of Cochinchina to a popular referendum, he insisted that all previous agreements had been made null and void by the Viet Minh attack in December. Firmly adhering to this view, the French Government rejected a Vietnamese proposal for an armistice based on the accord of 6 March; it also rebuffed a peace appeal by Ho Chi Minh on 20 February, calling for an end to the war, independence, and unity within the French Union.[2]

This diplomatic impasse found its reflection in the military situation. From February on it became increasingly clear that the war had reached a stalemate. In the early weeks of the conflict the French had regained control over the major cities of the Tonkin Delta and had lifted the siege of Hue. Elsewhere, except for the principal highway from Haiphong to Hanoi, the road system and most of the countryside were in the possession of the Viet Minh forces. The fighting had spread from Tonkin southward into Cochinchina, and aggressive bands of nationalist guerrillas appeared from time to time on the outskirts of Saigon to harass the numerically superior French forces.[3]

---

1. SD OIR No. 3708, pp. 86-89.
2. (S) SD OIR No. 4303, pp. 10-11.
3. Ibid., pp. 13-14.

Early in 1947 the Viet Minh commanded a force of approximately 150,000 troops, but the units of this force were still basically guerrilla formations. Only about one-third of the troops were organized and equipped with weapons at least the size of small arms. Their heavier weapons included about 50 artillery pieces, 650 automatic weapons, and 150 mortars.[4]

The bulk of the Viet Minh Army was concentrated in Tonkin, but Giap was also able to control most of Annam's long coastline against relatively weak French opposition. In Cochinchina, the lack of unity among the nationalist forces and the preponderance of French military strength restricted the Viet Minh to ineffective guerrilla activity. In the north, however, Giap's larger, better equipped, and better organized units were more successful, and by 7 February they had inflicted 1,855 casualties on the French.[5]

Matched against the Viet Minh Army were some 100,000 of the best trained and best equipped regular troops at the disposal of the French.[6] According to one source, these troops were supported not only by armament brought along with them from France, but also by more than $77,040,000 worth of army equipment turned over to French authorities in Indochina by Great Britain. It was alleged that the British sold this equipment to France so that General Leclerc "could pursue operations against the Viet Minh and Ho Chi Minh." This materiel was reported to be sufficient to equip completely one light division, one infantry brigade, and the major part of any army corps composed of two divisions, as well as an airborne division of 16,000 men, and assorted antiaircraft, engineer, and parachutist units.[7]

When the question was raised in the House of Commons, the British Secretary of State for Foreign Affairs asserted,

---

4. (S) War Dept, Intel Div, WDGS, *Intelligence Review*, No. 65, 15 May 47, pp. 51, 54-56.
5. *NY Times*, 8 Feb 47, p. 6.
6. (S) War Dept, Intel Div, WDGS, *Intelligence Review*, No. 62, 24 Apr 47, pp. 26-27, 36-37.
7. *NY Herald-Tribune*, 10 Mar 47, p. 3.

in a carefully worded statement, that "No aid specifically designed for Indo-China has been given to the French armed forces."8

It is not clear whether or not the equipment referred to was provided by the British; the most accurate guess would probably be that it was actually captured Japanese equipment turned over to the French during the British occupation of south Indochina.9

Whether or not the French received aid from the British, they still found Indochina an expensive proposition. The French budget for 1947 called for the expenditure of 25 million dollars to support the campaign in Indochina during the first three months of the year. Although desperate efforts were being made in Paris to trim other budgetary expenses, there was little protest, except by the Communists, against the government's proposals to increase military spending for Indochina.10

The French Break with the Viet Minh

In March, while French forces battled the Viet Minh in Indochina, French legislators fought each other on the floor of the National Assembly in a series of spirited debates on Indochina policy. On three separate occasions, the Communist delegates walked out of the chamber after sharp verbal clashes. Once, blows were exchanged.

A Communist deputy, Pierre Cot, accused the government of instructing French troops to use the accord of 6 March 1946 as a lever to bring about a coup d'etat. He stated that the day of colonialism was over and that the only practical policy was one of free collaboration and association with the Indochinese people.11

---

8. House of Commons, Parliamentary Debates, vol. 435, 24 Mar 47, p. 827.
9. (TS) HQ SACSEA War Diaries, "Draft Civil Affairs Agreement - French Indo-China," vol. 87, 11 Sep 45, DRB AGO.
10. NY Herald-Tribune, 10 Mar 47, p. 3.
11. Journal Officiel, Assem Nat, pp. 869-871.

In rebuttal, Premier Ramadier took the position that the French constitution of October 1946 invalidated several provisions of the 6 March Accord.[12] He made no promise of negotiation or peace in Indochina, saying only that:

> We have done everything possible, conceded everything reasonable; it did not work. One of these days there will be some representatives of the Annamite people with whom we can talk reason. If it is desired, France will not oppose union of the three countries nor refuse to admit the independence of Viet Nam within the French Union.[13]

At the end of the debate on Indochina, the Premier received a vote of confidence from the Assembly. The delegates approved his position on Indochina by a vote of 410-0, with 195 abstaining. The results of the balloting appeared to indicate that French Communists were not seriously concerned with the struggle for independence in Viet Nam except as it served their own ends. Although the Communist deputies withheld their votes, their fellow party members in the cabinet voted with the majority in support of the war. Also, the Communist Vice-Premier, Marcel Thorez, put his signature on a directive ordering military action against the Viet Minh in accordance with the Premier's recommendations.[14]

Throughout April and May, the French continued to adhere to an extremely inflexible policy toward Indochina; consequently there was little progress toward a settlement. In March, Admiral d'Argenlieu, who had been the subject of increasing criticism, was replaced by Emile Bollaert, Radical-Socialist parliamentarian and politician. M. Bollaert arrived in Saigon on 1 April and immediately set to work to implement Premier Ramadier's policy. He announced in May that "France will remain in Indochina and Indochina will remain within the French Union. That is the first axiom of our policy. . . . we do not admit that any group has a monopoly on representing the Vietnamese people."[15]

---

12. Ibid., p. 905.
13. Ibid., p. 29.(Translated by author.)
14. Hammer, Struggle for Indochina, pp. 199-200.
15. Ibid., p. 209.

This assertion was the first important indication that the French were considering doing business with someone other than Ho Chi Minh in their search for a solution to the Indochinese problem. This idea was soon to become the keystone of French policy, but in April there were several items holding a higher place on M. Bollaert's agenda. First, agreements had to be negotiated with Cambodia and Laos, in order to draw them more closely into the French sphere and reduce the possibility that they would join with Viet Nam at some future time to oppose the French.

On 6 May, by means of a document patterned on the French Constitution of 1946, Cambodia changed from an absolute to a constitutional monarchy. The new government included a Cabinet responsible to an elected bicameral legislature, the functions of the upper house being mostly advisory. Division of power among three branches of government--executive, legislative, and judicial--provided a system of checks and balances. All power emanated from the King; his authority, however, had to be exercised in accordance with the Constitution, and each of his acts, except those pertaining to palace matters, had to be signed by the Prime Minister and one other member of the Cabinet.[16]

On 11 May, a Laotian constitution, similar to that of Cambodia, was promulgated. Despite the complete newness of a representative government in the country, the document was seemingly assured of strong popular support owing to its approval by a "highly respected" monarch.[17]

The DRV still continued to press the French for a settlement. As early as February, Ho Chi Minh stated the terms on which he proposed to base all future negotiations when he said, "we want unity and independence within the French Union. . . . /then/ we will respect the economic and cultural interests of France in this land."[18]

---

16. (S) Geneva Conf Background Paper, Indochina Chronology, pp. 43-44.
17. Ibid., p. 44.
18. NY Times, 27 Feb 47, p. 4.

On 19 April 1947, the DRV Minister of Foreign Affairs sent a proposal for "the immediate ending of hostilities and the opening of negotiations for the pacific settlement of the conflict" to the French Government. In reply, the French drew up a series of clearly unacceptable demands and sent Paul Mus, M. Bollaert's personal counselor, to contact the DRV leaders.[19] He was directed to request the Vietnamese forces to:

    1. Cease immediately all hostile acts, terrorism and propaganda.
    2. Deliver over the greater part of their armament.
    3. Allow free circulation of French troops throughout Viet Minh territory.
    4. Surrender hostages, prisoners and deserters.[20]

The nature of these demands made it a foregone conclusion that the Mus mission would fail. It was hardly correct to claim, as did the Minister of Overseas France, that the mission failed only because of the clause in the French demands concerning the handing over of foreigners in the ranks of the Viet Minh.[21]

So far M. Bollaert had accomplished little more than his predecessor. Considerable revision of French policy was long overdue.

The Bao Dai Restoration Policy

The failure of the Mus mission in early May convinced the French that further talks with Ho Chi Minh would serve no purpose. They decided, therefore, to encourage and assist the formation of an anti-Viet Minh government for Indochina.

French emissaries had been in touch with Bao Dai in Hongkong as early as March, but he had declined thus far

---

    19. (S) Geneva Conf Background Paper, Indochina Chronology, p. 43.
    20. Devillers, Histoire du Viet-Nam, pp. 389-390. (Translated by author.)
    21. Journal Officiel, Assem Nat, p. 1569.

to commit himself to any particular course of action. Indications were, however, that the ex-Emperor realized the strength of his position, and that he would demand concessions similar to those insisted upon by Ho Chi Minh. It was M. Bollaert's task to outmaneuver Bao Dai, and to bring him to agreement on terms favorable to the French.

Conveniently, a number of Vietnamese nationalists appeared, who were willing to work with Bao Dai to create a new central government under French auspices. Among these nationalists were the exiled leaders of the VNQDD and Dong Minh Hoi who, after losing control of the nationalist movement to the Viet Minh in 1945, had fled to China where they had established a "National Union Front" under Chinese sponsorship. This group of Bao Dai supporters was soon augmented by the Cao Dai, the Hoa Hao, and a number of mandarins and monarchists in Annam.[22]

These political elements constituted a core around which Bao Dai could form an anti-Viet Minh government; the French saw to it that a steady procession of nationalist leaders called upon the former Emperor to keep this idea firmly planted in his mind. In response to this barrage of attention, Bao Dai gravitated toward a position of alignment with the National Union Front, twice rejecting Viet Minh suggestions that he negotiate with the French in the name of the DRV.[23]

On 5 July 1947, Bao Dai finally broke his long silence, declaring that:

> If all Vietnamese place their confidence in me, and if through my presence I can contribute to reestablishing good relations among our people and France, I will be happy to come back to Indochina. I am neither for the Viet Minh nor against it. I belong to no party. . . . Peace will return quickly if the French are only ready to admit that the spirit of our people is not the same today as it was ten years ago.[24]

---

22. Hammer, Struggle for Indochina, pp. 209-211.
23. Ibid., pp. 209, 217.
24. Devillers, Histoire du Viet-Nam, p. 399. (Translated by author.)

In the meantime, M. Bollaert was busy preparing the way for Bao Dai's return to Indochina. During May, he presided over the installation in Saigon and Hue of two "Provisional Administrative and Social Committees." These two groups worked closely with the French to rally Indochinese public opinion behind the Bao Dai restoration movement. The committee at Saigon demanded the unification of Viet Nam, the admittance of a free and independent Viet Nam to the French Union, and the creation of a central national government disassociated from the DRV.[25]

Even with French support it was clear that Bao Dai's only hope for lasting success lay in securing from France the two major concessions that Ho Chi Minh had failed to obtain. Conscious of this, Bao said in September: "I want first of all to get independence and unity for you."[26] As the French subsequently learned, he did not intend to compromise on these terms.

Meanwhile, in a last bold attempt to come to terms with the DRV, the French High Commissioner planned a striking departure from his government's recent policy of intractability toward Ho Chi Minh. M. Bollaert decided to direct a conciliatory speech to the DRV on 15 August, the day on which India and Pakistan received their independence. He intended to offer Ho Chi Minh a cease fire, and French recognition of an independent Viet Nam within the French Union. But before he could make his speech, M. Bollaert was summoned to France for consultation, presumably because news of the content of his address had reached the French Government.

When Bollaert arrived in Paris, the French Cabinet was called into session and the MRP members made clear their firm opposition to taking any action from which Ho Chi Minh might profit. It would be the Viet Minh which would be strengthened, not Bao Dai, if there were to be a truce in Viet Nam, they reasoned, and therefore France could not afford peace.[27]

---

25. (S) Geneva Conf Background Paper, Indochina Chronology, pp. 44-45.
26. Hammer, *Struggle for Indochina*, p. 214.
27. Ibid., pp. 212-213.

M. Bollaert finally gave his speech on 10 September, but it bore little resemblance to the original. No mention was made of either a truce or independence for Viet Nam, and the address included the condition that all of the proposals put forth by the High Commissioner would have to be accepted without alteration. It stipulated that:

    a. The Indo-Chinese people must agree to remain in the French Union. . . . On the other hand, France will not interfere in the three disputed States' /Cochinchina, Annam, Tonkin/ decision to join in a Vietnamese Federation or remain aloof.
    b. France is prepared to surrender direct and indirect administration to a qualified Government.
    c. The French will retain control over foreign relations, although the Indo-Chinese States are expected to participate in the representation of the Union . . . .
    d. The French Republic will ensure the coordination of the military resources to be pooled by all members of the French Union (including Viet Nam) for the defense of the Union as a whole.
    e. Collaboration among the several States in such general problems as customs, currency, immigration policy, and in economic development will proceed under the aegis of the French High Commissioner.
    f. The High Commissioner will further guarantee the protection of French interests in Indo-China and will oppose any interference by one State in the internal affairs of another.
    g. The French pledge themselves not to take reprisals against the Vietnamese, and all prisoners will be exchanged under conditions of reciprocity.[28]

As expected, Ho Chi Minh rejected these terms. It appears probable that the French offer had been purposely vague and unacceptable in order to provide an excuse for resuming military operations the following month. The rainy season was rapidly drawing to a close, and good fighting weather was expected.[29]

---
28. (S) War Dept, Intel Div, WDGS, *Intelligence Review*, No. 83, 18 Sep 47, pp. 13-15.
29. Ibid.

From October 1947 to the beginning of 1948, a lull occurred in the French-Bao Dai conversations while the French military forces attempted to "liquidate" the DRV, and thus clear the way for Bao Dai's return. Although the French Minister of War had estimated that it would require a force of at least 500,000 men to take back the areas controlled by the Viet Minh,[30] not more than 60,000 French troops were utilized during the fall campaign. The objectives of this drive were to close the China frontier, cut DRV lines of communication, kill or capture the DRV leaders, and destroy, as far as possible, their regular army.[31]

The French succeeded in cutting the principal supply route between Tonkin and China, but traffic continued to move freely across other parts of the border. And, although they captured large stocks of DRV military supplies and seized two broadcasting stations, shortages of manpower and supplies soon forced the French to withdraw from many of the areas they had occupied. "None of the principal DRV leaders were killed or captured /and/ . . . DRV political and military resistance to the French remained basically unimpaired."[32]

The unsuccessful fall offensive cost the French heavily. It was reported that France spent more than $33,613,446 (4 billion francs) monthly on Indochina during this period, and lost over 600 men a month in combat.[33]

Even before military operations had ceased, Bao Dai and M. Bollaert resumed negotiations. On 8 December, aboard a French cruiser in D'Along Bay, they initiated a secret protocol, in which Bao Dai tentatively agreed to return to Indochina as soon as France sanctioned a united Viet Nam. The following were reported to be the terms of agreement:

---

30. Hammer, Struggle for Indochina, p. 207.
31. (S) Geneva Conf Background Paper, Indochina Chronology, p. 47.
32. Ibid.
33. William C. Bullitt, "The Saddest War," Life Magazine, 29 Dec 47, pp. 64-66.

(1) Viet Nam, which will include Tonkin, Annam, and Cochin-China, will be granted "independence" within the French Union; (2) Viet Nam will have an "independent" army, which will, however, be "available for defense of any part of the French Union"; (3) foreign relations are to be conducted by France, with Viet Namese included in the French Foreign Service; and (4) there will be common customs and integration of transportation facilities in the several states of Viet Nam.[34]

The D'Along Bay Agreement did not measure up to the expectation of Bao Dai's supporters in Hongkong and Viet Nam. They urged him to disavow it and seek more favorable terms.[35] Soon thereafter, taking the position that he had approved the protocol only in the capacity of a private individual, Bao Dai renounced the agreement.[36]

The French, however, were not yet ready to give up hope of reaching an agreement. On 23 December 1947, the French Cabinet announced that it had instructed M. Bollaert "to carry on, outside the Ho Chi Minh government, all activities and negotiations necessary for the restoration of peace and freedom in the Vietnamese countries."[37] By thus making the Bao Dai restoration solution the official policy of France, the French Government enhanced Bao Dai's bargaining position. But M. Bollaert, during several interviews with Bao Dai in January, refused to compromise on his terms of 8 December. The main point of disagreement was that while both Bao Dai and the French agreed that he was to return to head a provisional government in Viet Nam, they differed on procedure. Bao Dai insisted upon unity and independence prior to his return, whereas the French wanted him to return immediately as head of a nationalist government with which they could then negotiate regarding the manner in which unity and independence would be realized.[38]

---

34. (C) Dept Army, Intel Div, GSUSA, *Intelligence Review*, No. 97, 1 Jan 48, p. 26.
35. (S) Geneva Conf Background Paper, Indochina Chronology, p. 47.
36. Hammer, *Struggle for Indochina*, p. 215.
37. Ibid., p. 216.
38. (S) Geneva Conf Background Paper, Indochina Chronology, p. 49.

Following Bao Dai's return to Hongkong in March 1948, a growing coolness became apparent in his relations with the French. While Bao Dai doubted French assurances that they would no longer attempt to negotiate with Ho Chi Minh, the French for their part suspected that the former Emperor was engaged in undercover dealings with the Viet Minh.[39] Another factor contributing to Bao Dai's suspicion of French intentions was the announcement on 4 March 1948 of a Thai Federation in upper Tonkin, founded under French auspices. This step appeared to indicate a French desire to weaken any Vietnamese government which might come to power by setting up French-controlled political subdivisions under the pretense of protecting minority rights. There was a precedent for such a French policy in Admiral d'Argenlieu's recognition of the Cochinchinese Republic during the Fontainebleau Conference and, later, the establishment of a separate Moi state in southern Annam.

Culmination of the Bao Dai Solution

As the year 1948 unfolded, Bao Dai remained adamant in his refusal to return to Indochina without official French recognition of Vietnamese independence and unity. This the French were not prepared to grant. Reluctantly they turned to General Nguyen Van Xuan, President of the Provisional Government of South Viet Nam (Cochinchina), to form a provisional government for Viet Nam.

Plans for the establishment of such a government were formulated in consultation with Bao Dai and differences between the various nationalist elements in opposition to the Viet Minh were gradually resolved. Finally, on 20 May 1948, a number of representatives from Tonkin, Annam, and Cochinchina, "all of whom had been hand-picked by Xuan and approved by the French," met at Saigon as a "Vietnamese Congress" to form a central government for Viet Nam.[40] Bao Dai's approval of General Xuan, expressed in a letter which General Xuan read before the delegates, was sufficient to overcome the remaining opposition to the general's leadership. Without debate, he was

---

39. Ibid.
40. Ibid., p. 50.

designated President of the "Provisional Central Government" of Viet Nam, which was later to supersede the government of Cochinchina. The new government would negotiate with France on the status of Viet Nam, and would be replaced by a permanent government as soon as agreement regarding the powers and responsibilities of the latter was reached.

The weakness of the new government was recognized by all. Powerful elements from among the Cao Dai and Hoa Hao movements refused to lend it their support. Le Van Hoach, ex-President of the defunct Cochinchina Republic rejected an offer of the Vice Presidency. Moreover, administrators of ability were dissuaded by the temporary nature of the new government from joining its ranks; they preferred to wait until Bao Dai returned to Viet Nam before offering their services.

The Xuan regime was formally installed at Hanoi on 6 June. The day before, Bao Dai had met with General Xuan and M. Bollaert at D'Along Bay to seek mutual understanding. Out of this meeting came an agreement wherein the French promised to recognize the unity and independence of Viet Nam within the French Union as a state associated with France.[41] The text of this agreement as reproduced by a French source follows:

> 1. France solemnly recognizes the independence of Viet Nam, whose unity must be freely accomplished. For its part, Viet Nam proclaims its adherence to the French Union in the capacity of a State associated with France. The independence of Viet Nam is limited only by that which its attachment to the French Union imposes upon itself.
> 2. Viet Nam pledges itself to respect the rights and interests of French nationals, constitutionally to ensure respect for democratic principals, and to give priority to French councillors and technicians, for the needs of its internal organization and its economy.

---

[41]. State Dept, "Outline of Basic Treaty Relationships Between France and the Associated States of Indochina," IR No. 5758, 9 Jan 52, pp. 1-2.

3. After the constitution of a provisional
government, the representatives of Viet Nam will
pass with the representatives of the French Republic
various arrangements of a cultural, diplomatic,
military, economic, financial, and technical nature.[42]

It appeared for a while that an acceptable basis for an anti-Viet Minh government had been laid down in the D'Along Bay agreement. But the gift of independence was in fact hedged with qualifications, unity was yet to be accomplished, and the plain fact of the matter was that the French had dealt with a group that did not control the country. Too, Paris seemed reluctant to implement the agreement. Gaston Palewski, de Gaulle's political advisor, said on 7 June that the formation of the Central Provisional Government was "illegal and in violation of the French Constitution."[43] And two days later, M. Coste-Floret, Minister of Overseas France, told the National Assembly that the agreement did not imply French recognition of the unity of Viet Nam, since the status of Cochinchina could be changed only with formal approval of the French Parliament. He went on to state that France would not approve a Vietnamese army, apart from police forces, nor would a separate Vietnamese diplomatic service be tolerated. Vietnamese public opinion "reacted with great discouragement" to these declarations, and the prestige of the Xuan government, never very high, sank even lower.[44]

The D'Along Bay agreement was not ratified by the French National Assembly until 19 August, and then only "in principle." It was under constant attack all the while by a number of influential Frenchmen. One, Georges Bidault, Minister of Foreign Affairs and a leader in the MRP, said that the concessions granted by M. Bollaert were "very dangerous" in view of probable repercussions in French North Africa. He especially condemned the use of the word "independence" in any form.[45] The failure of

---

42. *Journal Officiel, Assem Nat*, 14 Mar 53. (Translated by author.)
43. (S) Geneva Conf Background Paper, Indochina Chronology, p. 51.
44. Ibid.
45. Devillers, *Histoire du Viet-Nam*, p. 422.

the Paris government to implement the agreement speedily cost the French more in terms of Vietnamese popular support than they had gained by signing it in the first place; more and more Vietnamese began to believe further negotiations with the French useless.[46] In view of his failure to persuade Bao Dai to return to Indochina without further concessions, M. Bollaert was recalled to France, and Leon Pignon, formerly French Commissioner in Cambodia, took his place on 20 October 1948.[47]

By the end of 1948, the Xuan government was so obviously a puppet administration that it steadily lost ground in its efforts to win popular support. No Vietnamese of any stature would consent to serve in the administration, and there were rumors of graft and corruption at all levels. It controlled no territory of its own; in fact the governors of north, south, and central Viet Nam felt no responsibility to General Xuan, and in the south, Governor Huu openly defied him. Although the French insistently proclaimed that they had granted independence to Viet Nam, French administrators refused to turn over even the most limited powers to General Xuan. Even in areas where a Vietnamese administration existed, the French retained control of the army, police forces, and the financial structure.[48]

By contrast, Ho Chi Minh's government in its third year of existence controlled the greater part of the countryside. In these areas lived over half the population, producing practically all the food. The DRV aimed at economic self-sufficiency, directing its efforts toward raising the living standards of the peasants. To this end it set up forest factories to manufacture locally items formerly imported, such as textiles and weapons urgently needed by the Viet Minh army. It endeavored to increase food production, and won considerable popularity by lowering land rents as much as 25 per cent.[49]

---

46. (S) Geneva Conf Background Paper, Indochina Chronology, p. 51.
47. Ibid., p. 52.
48. Hammer, Struggle for Indochina, pp. 222, 224, 228-230.
49. Ibid., p. 223.

The DRV continued to pose as a nationalist movement during 1948. Although Communist control was being increasingly tightened, little in the way of Communist inspiration appeared openly in its activities and policies. As yet, it did not reject the Bao Dai restoration plan, appearing instead to entertain the hope that the ex-Emperor could be brought to join Ho Chi Minh in combatting the French.[50]

The military situation showed little change throughout 1948. The French retained control of Saigon, Hanoi, and Haiphong and established small garrisons in Annam, but half-hearted attempts to expand local perimeters met with little success. At the same time, the Viet Minh, gradually stepping up the pace of their activities, harassed the French throughout all of Viet Nam, and the north-south lines of communication were immobilized, owing to the inability of French units to seize and hold them.[51] In view of the growing difficulty of replacing casualties, and troops who had been rotated, the French offered bonuses to all officers and men who extended their service in Indochina beyond two years.[52]

In January and February of 1948, a 12,000-man French task force undertook offensive operations in Cochinchina, the over-all effect of which was to expand French control slightly in the Saigon and Mekong river delta areas.[53] The French also began an offensive in Tonkin during October, as they had the previous year. Their object was to secure communications between Hanoi and outlying garrisons. In this they failed, "owing to low morale, inadequate military transportation facilities, and the replacement of French troops by locally-recruited forces of doubtful loyalty."[54]

---

50. (S) Geneva Conf Background Paper, Indochina Chronology, pp. 52-53.
51. (S) Dept Army, Intel Div, GSUSA, *Intelligence Review*, No. 155, 17 Feb 49, pp. 85-86.
52. (S) Geneva Conf Background Paper, Indochina Chronology, p. 53.
53. (S) Dept Army, Intel Div, GSUSA, *Intelligence Review*, No. 155, 17 Feb 49, pp. 85-86.
54. (S) Geneva Conf Background Paper, Indochina Chronology, p. 53.

Not having achieved appreciable military success, the French once again resumed talks with Bao Dai. There was now a detectable note of haste in the negotiations. A series of Chinese Communist victories seemed to foreshadow the collapse of the Kuomintang and the appearance of a potential Viet Minh ally on the northern border. Since both the French and Bao Dai were still far apart in their demands, a compromise seemed in order if they were to collaborate successfully in creating a government capable of drawing popular support away from Ho Chi Minh.

During the winter of 1948-1949, the French-Bao Dai negotiations made considerable headway and, on 8 March 1949, Bao Dai and President Auriol of France reached a "compromise agreement" at the Elysee Palace in Paris. By means of an exchange of letters, a program for the future of Indochina was agreed upon:

> . . . France recognized the independence of Vietnam within the French Union. In Foreign relations, the government of Vietnam was limited in its independence by its membership in the French Union; internally, Vietnam's autonomy was confirmed, except for certain limitations in the judicial sphere. Vietnam was to have its own national army, and French forces stationed in Vietnam in peacetime were to be confined to designated bases, garrisons, and communication facilities. Vietnam undertook to give priority to French political and technical advisers. It agreed to reciprocal assurances concerning the status and properties of nationals and the freedom of enterprises in both countries, and to similar guarantees with regard to French educational institutions in Vietnam. Vietnam was to enter into a monetary and customs union with the other Indochinese states, and joint institutions were to be created to harmonize the interests of the three states with each other and with those of France.[55]

---

55. Ibid., p. 54; Accords Franco-Vietnamians du 8-Mars 1949 (Imprimerie Francaisa d'Outre-Mar, Saigon), in Dept State Library.

Had the French attitude kept pace with this document, a Bao Dai government would have had at least a fair chance of capturing enough popular support to function effectively. Unfortunately, the "new" French approach was almost indistinguishable from the old. Ex-Premier Ramadier expressed the attitude of a good many Frenchmen when, during March 1949, he said: "We will hold on everywhere, in Indo-China as in Madagascar. Our empire will not be taken away from us, because we represent might and also right."[56]

Until the French Assembly formally declared Cochinchina a part of Viet Nam, the Elysee Agreement was worth nothing. Therefore, on 12 March 1949, the Assembly voted to authorize the creation of a Territorial Assembly of Cochinchina, the sole function of which was to vote union with Viet Nam. This it did on 23 April. A month later the French Assembly ended the colonial status of Cochinchina which, henceforth, was to be "attached to the Associated State of Vietnam."[57]

The way was now open for the Elysee Accord to go into effect. On 14 June, Bao Dai and the French High Commissioner met at a formal ceremony in Saigon to exchange letters in confirmation of the agreement. Bao Dai assumed the position of "Chief of State" of the "Independent State of Viet Nam" and General Xuan's ill-favored government resigned in favor of the new regime. Viet Nam was once again united, but only on paper. Before any real unification could take place, the French and the new State of Viet Nam had still to cope with the Viet Minh.

American Policy toward Indochina, 1947-1949

The war in Indochina posed a dilemma for the makers of American foreign policy. To aid the French might alienate the peoples of Southeast Asia from the Western Powers. To support complete independence for the Vietnamese might lead to a Communist state in Indochina.

---

56. W.L. Briggs, "Vietnam Wins Independence," New Republic, 4 Jul 49, p. 13.
57. (S) Geneva Conf Background Paper, Indochina Chronology, p. 54.

In these circumstances, the State Department sought to steer a middle course. While recognizing French sovereignty the United States refused to supply the French with arms or ammunition to help them assert it. And while opposing an independent Vietnamese state, the United States sought to persuade the French to abandon their "outmoded colonial outlook" and grant the Vietnamese a large measure of autonomy. Such a concession, the State Department hoped, would strengthen the hands of anti-Communist Vietnamese at the expense of the Communists. As a special ad hoc committee of SWNCC stated it:

> Our objective is a prompt, peaceful, and lasting settlement of the present French-Vietnamese dispute providing for the creation of a stable Vietnamese state that will remain in voluntary association with France and will meet the legitimate demands of the Vietnamese for self-government, and be responsive to their fundamental interests. We consider the creation of such a state as the best defense against disintegrative tendencies in Indochina that could lead to a chronic disorder and political extremism, offer opportunities for the extension of Communism, or tempt the intervention of other powers.[58]

Long before the committee set this objective down on paper, the State Department had been finding it difficult to achieve. Four days after the outbreak of hostilities, Under Secretary of State Dean Acheson had invited the French Ambassador to a conference at the State Department. Expressing deep concern over the situation in Indochina, Mr. Acheson made it clear that, while the United States did not wish to mediate the Franco-Vietnamese conflict, it was willing to offer its "good offices" to the French. From every point of view, Mr. Acheson asserted, it was essential that the Indochina question be settled as soon as possible, by conciliatory means.

---

58. (S) Doc B-24, Msg, Marshall to AmEmb Paris, 431, 3 Feb 47, in (TS) Doc Hist of US Pol Toward Indochina. (TS) SWNCC 360/3, Note by Secys, "Policies, Procedures and Costs of Assistance by the United States to Foreign Countries," 3 Oct 47, CCS 092 (8-22-46) sec 7.

Two weeks later, the French officially rejected Mr. Acheson's offer of "good offices." They preferred to handle their problem their own way. The immediate French military objective in Indochina, said M. Lacoste, Minister in the French Embassy, was "to restore order and reopen communications." Once order was restored, the French would try to live up to the accord of 6 March and to the modus vivendi of 15 September 1946. When asked whether he believed the French could restore order "within the foreseeable future," M. Lacoste answered in the affirmative, but "without much evidence of conviction."[59]

Taking into account the instability of the current French Government, the United States did not press the matter further. And when the Chinese proposed joint mediation by the United States, British, and Chinese Governments, the State Department rejected the idea, partly on the ground that any appearance of intervention would provide political ammunition for the French Communists. Throughout the remainder of 1947 the State Department shrank from measures that might embarrass the French Government. While repeating its offer of "good offices," the State Department coupled it with a disclaimer of American intentions to mediate the Franco-Vietnamese conflict and with a frank statement that the United States had no specific solution to propose. Other than urging the French to adopt a more conciliatory attitude toward the Vietnamese and to keep the United States informed of developments, the State Department adhered to the position that the Indochina problem was one for the French and Vietnamese.

Once in 1947 the State Department ventured slightly beyond that position, and with negligible results. In September Secretary of State George C. Marshall informed the American Ambassador to France, Mr. Jefferson Caffery, of his concern over reports that the French were planning to launch an offensive against the Vietnamese in the dry

---

59. (C) Doc B-19, Msg, Byrnes to AmEmb Paris, 6586, 24 Dec 46; (UNK) Doc B-23, Memo, John C. Vincent to Acheson, "French Indochina," 8 Jan 47. Both in (TS) Doc Hist of US Pol Toward Indochina.

season, which would come toward the end of September. "It is obvious," Secretary Marshall said, "that such an offensive, if it took place under these conditions, would have serious effect on public opinion here which would be reflected in a Congress which will be called upon to consider extensive financial aid for western European nations, including France." Secretary Marshall asked Ambassador Caffery to find out whatever he could about this offensive and notify the Department of State. On the following day, Ambassador Caffery reported that he had talked informally with M. Bidault along the lines suggested by Secretary Marshall. M. Bidault "understood" the American point of view, and said that as far as he knew there were no plans for such an offensive. Whether or not M. Bidault was misinformed is uncertain, but early in October the French launched a major military offensive "to annihilate the Viet Minh forces in Tonkin."[60]

By the summer of 1948 the State Department had decided to urge the French toward more decisive action to settle the Indochina conflict, but to avoid applying any pressure that might imperil the French Government. As Secretary of State Marshall viewed the situation, nothing should be left undone that would strengthen the hand of the "truly nationalist groups" in Indochina at the expense of the Communists. In July the French were informed that the United States believed they were faced with two alternatives: either they must promptly and unequivocally approve the union of Cochinchina with the rest of Vietnam and carry out the D'Along Bay Agreement or lose Indochina. As an inducement to earnest effort, the French were informed that, once they put this program

---

60. (S) Doc B-20, Msg, Byrnes to AmCon Hanoi (IC), 25, 31 Dec 46; (S) Doc B-21, Msg, Byrnes to AmEmb Paris, 75, 8 Jan 47; (S) Doc B-22, Msg, Byrnes to AmEmb Paris, 74, 8 Jan 47; (UNK) Doc B-23, Memo, John C. Vincent to Acheson, "French Indochina," 8 Jan 47; (S) Doc B-24, Msg, Marshall to AmEmb Paris, 431, 3 Feb 47; (S) Doc B-25, Msg, Marshall to AmEmb Paris, 1737, 13 May 47; (UNK) Doc B-26, Msg, Marshall to AmEmb Paris, 3433, 11 Sep 47; (S) Doc B-27, Msg, Caffery to SecState, 3715, 12 Sep 47. All in (TS) Doc Hist of US Pol toward Indochina. (S) Geneva Conf Background Paper, Indochina Chronology, p. 47.

into effect, the United States would publicly support it as a "forward looking step" toward solving the Indochina problem and toward fulfilling the aspirations of the Vietnamese. The French were also told that, when these measures were adopted, the United States would reconsider its policy of withholding assistance to Indochina through ECA. But something more than promises was required to obtain action from the French Assembly, and in October Ambassador Caffery reported that he saw little hope of obtaining any positive action toward a solution for Indochina.61

As the war continued the United States drew closer to direct involvement. Alarmed by the Communist victory in China, the State Department looked for ways to avert a Communist Viet Nam. To Mr. Acheson there appeared no alternative to supporting Bao Dai, and in May 1949 he told the American Consul in Saigon that no effort should be spared by the Western Powers or by the non-Communist nations of Asia to assure the success of Bao Dai. At the proper time and under the proper circumstances, said Mr. Acheson, the United States would do its part by extending to Bao Dai official American recognition. And it would do much more. It would provide Bao Dai with military and economic aid. But before these steps were taken, Mr. Acheson wanted both the French and Bao Dai to demonstrate that American assistance was justified. The French should make every possible concession to make the Bao Dai government attractive to the nationalists. Bao Dai should demonstrate his own capacity to conduct his affairs wisely enough to obtain popular support. Otherwise, Mr. Acheson believed, the Bao Dai experiment would be foredoomed to failure.62

---

61. (TS) Doc B-28, Msg, Caffery to SecState, 3621, 10 Jul 48; (TS) Doc B-29, Msg, Marshall to AmEmb Paris, 2637, 14 Jul 48; (S) Doc B-30, Caffery to SecState, 5129, 1 Oct 48. All in (TS) Doc Hist of US Pol Toward Indochina.

62. (S) Doc B-32, Acheson to AmCon Saigon (IC), 77, 10 May 49, in (TS) Doc Hist of US Pol Toward Indochina.

Conclusions of the Period Prior to Direct US Involvement

The history of Indochina from the beginning of World War II to the summer of 1949 is essentially a story of French failure. The period began tragically with the collapse of France before the German onslaught, and the domination of Indochina by Japan. In the years that followed, France strove persistently to regain her position of eminence in the world community of nations. Her desire was strong, but her means remained weak. Furthermore, she labored under a severe handicap. French colonial administrators and bureaucrats of the postwar era seemed generally to have been of poor calibre, and they exhibited most of the failings of the old regime. They were sometimes morally weak, frequently arrogant, and too often blind to the implications of their actions.

Indochina was important to France, not only for its wealth, but also for the sake of prestige and the continued existence of the French Empire. Always in French minds there lurked the spectre of a France divested of her overseas territories. These areas were necessary to the economy of France and, in the French view, a vital attribute of a great power. To many Frenchmen, the loss of Indochina, after the humiliations of World War II, offered an intolerable vista. If France surrendered Indochina to a nationalist movement, where would she draw the line thereafter? In North Africa and Madagascar nationalists had already begun to stir restively.

At the close of the war the French seemed to have almost deliberately ignored the wave of nationalism sweeping over Southeast Asia. They drew comfort and confidence from the recollection that for decades France had succeeded in suppressing the Indochinese nationalist movement. The increased capabilities and fever heat of the postwar movement came as a distinct and unpleasant shock. Yet, despite clear evidence of the sincerity and proportions of the movement, the French clung to their outmoded colonial outlook.

Their strongest opponent, the Viet Minh, started out as a small group of parties under the domination of the Indochinese Communist Party. During the war they represented only a small part of the nationalist movement, and an insignificant number of the Indochinese people. By 1946, the Viet Minh had increased its following and military strength, but it was only one of many forces in Indochina's political life. The allegiance of the majority of the Indochinese people still hung in the balance.

Under the expert guidance of Ho Chi Minh, the Viet Minh did, however, develop excellent leadership, a disciplined and dedicated following, and a military organization far stronger than that of any other Indochinese nationalist group. Then, when the French returned to Indochina, their highhandedness, bad faith, and use of force drove not only politically conscious elements but also the Indochinese peasant and man in the street to make common cause with the Viet Minh against the French. And therein lay an important factor in the success of the Viet Minh.

The French were well aware that the Viet Minh regime posed a serious threat to their plans for Indochina, but they failed to recognize that a French-sponsored substitute for the Viet Minh would have to possess many of the same qualities. Above all they failed to realize that a government sponsored by France would have to offer tangible evidence that Viet Nam was or soon would be unified or independent.

From 1947 to 1949 France fought a costly war against the Viet Minh, and at the same time struggled to create a central government capable of winning the loyalty of the Vietnamese. Unfortunately the government that resulted was jerry-built; it was subservient to the French, and offered the Vietnamese little hope for unity and independence. Instead of gaining public support for the new government, the French maneuver increased the following of the Viet Minh.

By 1949 the French seemed to realize that drastic measures were needed to save Indochina from the Viet Minh. As a result the French came to terms with Bao Dai and pledged themselves to grant Indochina unity and independence.

But time had begun to run out. The growing shadow of the Chinese Communist armies was already darkening

the landscape of northern Indochina and aid for the
sorely pressed Viet Minh was now in the offing. This
prospect filled France and other democratic nations
with unhappy speculation. The hope of keeping Indochina
within the orbit of France by solely French means was
growing steadily fainter. A quick and decisive victory
over the Viet Minh, and the speedy implementation of
the Elysee Agreement might conceivably have redressed
the situation. Unfortunately for France and the western
world, the military stalemate continued, and implementation
of the Elysee Agreement dragged.

CHAPTER VII

ORIGINS OF AMERICAN INVOLVEMENT IN INDOCHINA

The months between the summer of 1949 and the spring of 1950 marked the beginning and early growth of direct United States concern with the war in Indochina. Gradually, American policy planners realized that unless measures were taken to change the course of the conflict France was headed for almost certain defeat. They realized, too, that the defeat of our European ally in Indochina might result in the end of the French Union, the end of the French Empire, and the end of France as a first rate power. This defeat in a sense would also represent a defeat for the United States, for Communist possession of Indochina would increase the power, prestige, and capabilities of the Soviet bloc. More immediately, the power represented by the men, materials, and resources of Indochina, if coupled with that of a Communist China, would gravely endanger the whole American security system in the Far East. Further, as the Japanese proved in World War II, Indochina was the natural gateway for the conquest of Southeast Asia. Obviously, therefore, Indochina was not a single problem that could be isolated and cured by itself; it was a vital part of the whole body politic of Asia. Thus, when early in 1950 the United States decided to help France achieve victory in Indochina, it did so within the framework of an over-all policy for Asia, and with specific objectives in mind.

United States Attitude toward Indochina, June 1949-January 1950

Throughout the last six months of 1949, however, United States policy toward Asia was negative and vague. The defeat of the American-supported Nationalist Chinese armies caused a general United States withdrawal from involvement in the Far East, and until January 1950 no decisive, over-all policy toward Asia was developed. There were, nonetheless, two general objectives apparent in American thinking as applied to all Asian nations. These goals were containment of Communism and encouragement of non-Communist nationalist movements. The former, of 1949, the fort at Dong Khe, lying between Lang Son and Cao Bang on the Tonkinese border, had to be provisioned entirely by air. French Union Forces abandoned a number of scattered strong points in northern Tonkin and concentrated on strengthening and extending the defensive perimeter about Hanoi.6

At the base of the French difficulties still lay the persistent nationalist-colonialist conflict that had prevented a military decision for three years. French efforts to solve the political problem throughout the latter half of 1949 were directed at implementing the Elysee Accords of 8 March 1949. The failure of these Accords to effect a lasting political solution was probably owing to the fact that neither the Vietnamese people nor the sovereign Asian nations believed the new government sufficiently representative of the people or independent of French domination.

As the first step in the erection of a Vietnamese government, Bao Dai was proclaimed Chief of State on 14 June. A week later the government of General Nguyen Van Xuan resigned, but consented to serve temporarily while Bao Dai consolidated his position. Although no constitution was promulgated, two ordinances issued on 1 July defined temporary agencies by which Viet Nam was to be ruled pending the establishment of internal stability. The principal governing institutions, as outlined by the ordinances, were to be the Chief of State, a Cabinet with a Prime Minister, and a Consultative National Council.

The members of the Cabinet were appointed by, and responsible to, the Chief of State. The members of the Consultative National Council were designated by the Chief of State on the basis of their ability to represent regional and national interests and express public opinion. The Council was supposed to develop gradually into a more representative organ, and it was anticipated that the appointments of the councilors would later be confirmed by popular election. The ordinances also specified that upon the restoration of peace, an elected

---

6. (S) Geneva Conf Background Paper, Indochina Chronology, p. 58.

Constituent Assembly would replace the Consultative National Council and decide upon the future government. For the time being, however, government by executive was established on all levels.[7] The Consultative National Council did not meet until September 1952, and then under a different name. The Constituent Assembly was never convened.

As a result, the form that the Bao Dai government assumed was essentially authoritarian. In addition, the nature and organization of the future government remained extremely vague. The Preamble to Ordinance No. 1 left open the question of whether Viet Nam's political authority would be concentrated in a republic or a constitutional monarchy, a highly centralized or loosely federated regime.

One reason for Bao Dai's failure in succeeding months to unify the country behind his government is thus suggested. While it would not have been realistic to expect a truly representative government, in view of the instability of the internal situation, it was still obvious to all that Bao Dai's source of power lay with the French, and not with the Vietnamese people.

Although the ordinances of 1 July established Bao Dai's regime in fact, specific agreements still had to be concluded to transfer services from the French colonial administration to the Vietnamese Government; and the French National Assembly had to ratify the 8 March Accords to give the entire transaction sanction in law. As the first step in this process, a Joint Commission convened at Saigon in August 1949. The Commission sat for four months, and on 30 December signed twenty-nine specialized conventions by which the French arranged to hand over certain internal administrative services to the Bao Dai government. Although the concessions to native independence were substantial, France still retained predominant interest in such fields as military affairs, press and information, the judiciary and police.[8] With regard to foreign affairs, acceptance of the status of

---

7. (S) NIS 43, Indochina, Ch V, "Political," sec 51, "The Constitutional System," pp. 51-15 - 51-21.
8. (S) Geneva Conf Background Paper, Indochina Chronology, p. 57.

an Associated State within the French Union entailed a limitation on the right of engaging in international relations. The Vietnamese were especially sensitive over the restriction of their right to send diplomatic representatives abroad.

By the agreements of 30 December, the French retained key functions that made Bao Dai extremely vulnerable to charges of being a French puppet. The privileged position that Frenchmen continued to enjoy, both in government and society, did not impress the Vietnamese or their Asian neighbors as a significant reduction in French influence.

Although the French encountered a more troublesome political problem in Viet Nam than in the other two Associated States, they faced similar difficulties in neighboring Laos and Cambodia. Treaties with Laos and Cambodia were signed on 19 July and 8 November 1949, respectively. These agreements closely resembled the Elysee Accords with Viet Nam. Implementing conventions concluded with Laos on 6 February 1950, and with Cambodia on 15 June 1950, transferred sovereignty to the two kingdoms on substantially the same basis as the agreement of 30 December 1949 with Viet Nam. The governing structures that evolved in Laos and Cambodia were more representative than that in Viet Nam. Although the two smaller states were presided over by hereditary monarchs, the National Assemblies were popularly elected and exercised important legislative powers.9

French efforts to translate the 8 March promises into reality were observed with great interest by the United States. Consistent with its twin aims of halting the spread of Communism and encouraging non-Communist nationalist movements, the State Department desired the Bao Dai government to be sufficiently independent of France to win the support of Vietnamese nationalists, as well as the respect and recognition of other Asian countries. Beginning in the summer of 1949, the State Department encouraged the French to interpret the 8 March

---

9. Ibid., pp. 55-57; (S) NIS 43, Indochina, Ch V, "Political," sec 51, "The Constitutional System," pp. 51-6 - 51-15.

Accords liberally enough to achieve these aims. Although American sympathy for Viet Nam's new regime was publicly declared in June 1949, Secretary of State Dean Acheson doubted that the French intended to make the essential concessions. The Secretary felt that the United States could not afford to back a puppet regime; therefore, recognition and aid must be withheld until the French understood the necessity of making the solution attractive to the nationalist elements, and until the Bao Dai regime itself demonstrated a capacity for independent government. Despite their denials, Secretary Acheson feared that French officials in general, and High Commissioner Leon Pignon in particular, regarded the Elysee Agreement as a final concession, whereas the American view was that it was but one step in the evolution of Vietnamese independence.[10]

The United States and Great Britain worked in close cooperation to induce the French to declare their purpose of adjusting the French-Vietnamese relationship in a liberal manner. Indochina was a subject for discussion at tripartite talks held 28 September 1949 between Secretary Acheson and the British and French Foreign Ministers, Ernest Bevin and Robert Schuman. On this and subsequent occasions, Schuman declared his agreement with the American view that the 8 March Accords were but one step in the evolution of the Indochinese problem. But French delay in implementing the Elysee Accords led the United States to doubt the sincerity of this declaration. State Department experts believed France unwilling to make liberal concessions to Vietnamese independence, or to publicize the concessions already made, for fear of causing trouble in North Africa. Schuman was urged to push ratification of the 8 March Accords in the National Assembly, and to place as few restrictions as possible on Vietnamese conduct of their own foreign relations. In particular, the United States and Great Britain wished to see Associated States affairs transferred

---

10. (S) Doc B-32, Msg, Acheson to AmConsul Saigon, 77, 10 May 49; (S) Doc B-33, Msg, Acheson to AmConsul Saigon, 112, 29 Jun 49. Both in (TS) <u>Doc Hist of US Pol Toward Indochina</u>.

from the Department of Overseas Possessions to the Foreign Ministry. Schuman, however, felt that this could not be done until after the Accords were ratified by the National Assembly.[11]

The United States and Great Britain attached great importance to French concessions to Viet Nam in the field of foreign affairs. They felt that unless France made these concessions the Asian nations would refuse to recognize the Bao Dai regime on the grounds that it was not truly independent. Recognition by such sovereign Asian countries as India, Pakistan, Indonesia, and Burma was considered essential to the success of Bao Dai's attempts to strengthen his government. These nations were highly respected in the Far East because they had successfully rid themselves of foreign rule. The United States and Great Britain felt that recognition of Viet Nam by these States might influence wavering Vietnamese intellectuals to back Bao Dai. At the very least, it would improve his standing with the rest of the world. Finally, acceptance of Viet Nam into the community of Asian nations would place the Western Powers in a better position to extend recognition and aid.

Unfortunately, however, the Asian countries did not look with favor upon the Elysee solution. India, whose good will was most desired, regarded Bao Dai as a French puppet, with no genuine popular support. The Indian attitude was not improved by the strained relations with France over continued French rule in Pondichery. Despite British and American prodding, Indian Prime Minister Nehru refused to recognize Viet Nam; and the other Asian nations, with the exception of Thailand, followed his lead. While still urging the Asian countries to reconsider their stand, the State Department, in January 1950, decided to extend diplomatic recognition to Viet

---

11. (S) Doc B-34, Memo of Conv, "Discussion of Various Far Eastern Problems," 14 Sep 49; (TS) Doc B-35, Msg, J. E. Webb, Actg SecState, to AmConsul Saigon, 162, 28 Sep 49. Both in (TS) Doc Hist of US Pol Toward Indochina.

Nam as soon as the French National Assembly should ratify the 8 March Accords, an event anticipated in late January.[12]

After an acrimonious debate, the French National Assembly, by a vote of 396-193, formally approved the 8 March Accords on 29 January 1950. That same day, actually before the Parliamentary vote, United States Ambassador-at-Large Philip C. Jessup, in Saigon, extended the congratulations of the United States to Bao Dai on his assumption of the powers transferred early in January and expressed "confident best wishes for the future of the State of Viet Nam with which it /the United States/ looks forward to establishing a closer relationship: . . ."[13] Formal recognition of Viet Nam, Laos, and Cambodia followed on 7 February. The United States Consulate at Saigon was elevated to Legation status, although Consul Edmund Gullion continued to represent the United States in Viet Nam until Minister Donald R. Heath arrived on 5 July 1950.

Even before ratification of the Elysee Accords, however, the lines of opposition in the Indochinese war had stiffened. American and British efforts to secure world backing for Bao Dai were accompanied by evidence of similar Soviet activities in behalf of the Viet Minh. On 19 January Communist China recognized the DRV as the legitimate government of Viet Nam; the Kremlin followed suit twelve days later. Czechoslovakia, Poland, Rumania, Hungary, Albania, and Yugoslavia subsequently recognized the Viet Minh. Secretary Acheson, commenting on the international diplomatic support that Ho was receiving, declared that "The Soviet acknowledgment of this /the Viet Minh/ movement should remove any illusions as to the 'nationalist' nature of Ho Chi Minh's aims and reveals Ho in his true colors as the mortal enemy of native independence in Indochina."[14]

---

12. (S) Doc B-38, Msg, J. W. Butterworth, Asst SecState (FEA) to Philip Jessup, USAmb-at-Large, Saigon, 25, 20 Jan 50, in (TS) Doc Hist of US Pol Toward Indochina.
13. State Dept Bulletin, 13 Feb 50, p. 244.
14. (U) Doc B-41, State Dept Press Rel No. 104, 1 Feb 50, in (TS) Doc Hist of US Pol Toward Indochina.

American recognition of Bao Dai was accompanied by similar action on the part of England and twenty-five other Western Powers. Indochina thereafter became an increasingly important center of conflict in the diplomacy of the Cold War.

Thus the situation in Indochina, as it stood at the close of 1949, impelled the United States to adopt a positive stand. The Viet Minh was growing stronger; the French were growing weaker. Increasing Chinese activity promised to strengthen the Viet Minh even further, and the possibility of actual Chinese intervention made the future prospects dim indeed. The Bao Dai solution gave scant hope of unifying the Vietnamese in support of the war effort, and it was received with suspicion by most of the Asiatic nations. The French must obviously have help or be expelled from Indochina. Throughout the latter half of 1949, the United States had been reassessing its interests in the Far East, and, by January 1950, it had arrived at an appreciation of the vital role of the Indochinese war in the contest for Southeast Asia.. On this appreciation, plus a realization of France's precarious position, the decision to assist the French was based.

Emergence of a Far Eastern and Indochinese Policy

The decision to help France combat the Viet Minh was the logical outgrowth of a reassessment of American interests in Asia as a whole. This process began in the summer of 1949 in the National Security Council but was given considerable impetus by a bitter dispute in Congress that served to focus public and official attention on Asia. The result was the formulation of an Asian policy that emphasized the Indochinese problem and prescribed a program of assistance to bolster anti-Communist forces in Indochina.

The movement leading to the National Security Council actions on Asia was initiated, in the summer of 1949, by Secretary of Defense Louis Johnson. Secretary Johnson deprecated the "day-to-day, country-by-country approach" of United States policy in Asia. On 10 June 1949 he called upon the staff of the National Security Council to determine exactly how American security was threatened by the current situation in the Far East and to formulate tentative courses of action for consideration by the National Security Council. These courses of action, he emphasized, should be coordinated for the whole region and outline specific objectives to be attained.[15]

While this study progressed behind the scenes, a Congressional battle over the military assistance bill heightened public concern for the Far East and laid the basis for the Indochinese aid program. Although the arms bill was primarily concerned with equipping the projected North Atlantic Treaty armies, a group led by Senator William Knowland sponsored a section to appropriate funds for assisting the Nationalist Chinese armies on Formosa. But the State Department had abandoned the Nationalist cause and Administration forces refused to accept any Asian aid formula that mentioned Chiang Kai-shek or Formosa. Several attempts at compromise failed, but at length a plan was agreed upon by the opposing factions. This resulted in Section 303 of the Mutual Defense Assistance Act, the so-called Connally Amendment, which set aside the sum of 75 million dollars, to be spent at the President's discretion, for combating Communism in "the general area of China."[16]

This money was eventually spent in a manner different than intended by Senator Knowland. On 17 December 1949 the Joint Chiefs of Staff submitted a plan for programming Section 303 funds. The Chiefs defined "the general area of China" as including "not only China proper, but also such areas as Hainan and Formosa, French Indo-China, Burma and Thailand."[17] The Joint Chiefs of Staff thus took the first step in shifting the battle for Asia from China to Southeast Asia. The inclusion of Indochina in "the general area of China" provided the means for an early program of assistance in the French struggle against Ho Chi Minh.

---

15. (TS) NSC 48, 10 Jun 49, CCS 092 Asia (6-25-48) sec 1.
16. NY Times, 25 Aug 49, 9 Sep 49, 11 Sep 49, 13 Sep 49; State Dept Bulletin, 24 Oct 49, p. 605.
17. (TS) JCS 1721/42, 17 Dec 49, CCS 452 China (4-3-45) sec 7, pt 6.

The Joint Chiefs of Staff, in recommending methods for employing the 75 million dollars, did not appraise American strategic interests in the Far East or point out the importance of Southeast Asia and Indochina to the United States. They merely proposed to undertake overt and covert measures to support anti-Communist forces and undermine Communist movements in the countries of Southeast Asia. They had nevertheless laid the groundwork for a series of important policy decisions reached by the National Security Council within the next two months, and created a vehicle by which those decisions could be carried out with dispatch.

The National Security Council study prepared at Secretary Johnson's instigation and considered by the Council on 29 December did warn of the threat to United States security of Communist expansion in the Far East. It reaffirmed that the loss of Asia to Communism would secure for the USSR and deny to the United States a power potential of the first magnitude, a major source of raw materials, and control of coastal and overseas lines of communication. It would also seriously threaten America's defensive island chain. To counter this danger, American objectives in Asia should include the reduction and eventual elimination of Soviet influence and the prevention of any power relationships that might threaten "the peace, national independence or stability of the Asiatic nations." Specifically, it was proposed that the United States provide military assistance and advice to Asian nations threatened by external aggression and internal subversion and use its influence to resolve the colonialist-nationalist conflict in such a manner as to satisfy nationalist demands with minimum strain on the colonial powers.[18]

The Joint Chiefs of Staff, however, believed that the conclusions of the National Security Council report were too general. They desired an integrated policy toward Asia, embodying more concrete courses of action. "The time has come," they declared, "for determination, development, and implementation of definite United States

---

18. (TS) NSC 48/1, 23 Dec 49, CCS 092 Asia (6-25-48) sec 2.

steps in Asia; otherwise, this nation will risk an even greater and more disastrous defeat in the ideological conflict in that area." The Chiefs pointed out that Section 303 of the Mutual Defense Assistance Act provided the means for initiating immediate action in specific areas, and they recommended that a program for spending this money be drafted and executed as a matter of urgency.[19]

In accordance with the advice of the Joint Chiefs of Staff, the National Security Council revised the original report. The resulting policy declaration, NSC 48/2, established more clearly a course of active "support," as distinguished from "encouragement," of Asian countries threatened by Communism. The United States would provide "political, economic, and military assistance and advice where clearly needed to supplement the resistance" of non-Communist governments in the Far East. Authority was given for immediate programming of Section 303 funds, and an ad hoc committee was formed by the Joint Chiefs of Staff to decide how best to spend the money.[20]

That the United States was now resolved to adopt a definite stand in Asia was indicated by Secretary of State Acheson in two public speeches. Before the Washington Press Club and the Commonwealth Club of California, the Secretary declared that the United States was now prepared to grant military and economic assistance to selected Far Eastern countries where it was "the missing component in a problem which might otherwise be solved."[21]

During January and February 1950, it became increasingly apparent that successful solution of the Indochinese problem was an essential precondition to attaining the newly enunciated objectives in Asia. Although this fact had not yet emerged in January, NSC 48/2 recognized the necessity of giving "particular attention" to Indochina by urging the French to remove the barriers

---

19. (TS) JCS 1992/7, 29 Dec 49, same file.
20. (TS) Encl B, NSC 48/2, 30 Dec 49, to (TS) JCS 1992/3, 5 Jan 50, same file, sec 3.
21. (U) State Dept Bulletin, 23 Jan 50, pp. 111-118. Ibid., No. 560, 27 Mar 50, pp. 467-472.

preventing Bao Dai from winning native allegiance. The Joint Chiefs of Staff were more specific. In proposing military aid programs for certain Southeast Asian countries, the Chiefs warned that the situation in Indochina would be greatly complicated should the Chinese Communists come to the aid of the Viet Minh. Accordingly, an Asian aid program should give first priority to anti-Communist forces in Indochina. It was recommended that the sum of 15 million dollars be programmed for Indochina from Section 303 funds.[22] The judgment of the Joint Chiefs of Staff indicated a growing conviction that the war in Indochina was among the most critical and immediate concerns to the United States.

The United States officially sanctioned this conviction in late April 1950 when the President approved NSC 64. This paper noted the growing strength of the Viet Minh, the possibility of active Chinese Communist intervention, and the failure to date of French efforts to solve the political problem. The significance of Indochina in US eyes was concisely stated: "It is important to the United States security interests that all practicable measures be taken to prevent further Communist expansion in Southeast Asia. Indochina is the key area of Southeast Asia and is under immediate threat." The Departments of State and Defense were directed to prepare a program embracing "all practicable measures designed to protect United States security interests in Indochina."[23]

By adopting NSC 48/2 the United States, in January 1950, abandoned the uncertain and seemingly confused approach to Asian problems so apparent throughout 1949 and took a definite stand against Communist expansion in the Far East. By adopting NSC 64 the United States, in April 1950, decided that the most direct means of attaining the over-all objective lay in concentrating American efforts on the battle for Indochina. The next

---

22. (TS) JCS 1721/43, 16 Jan 50, CCS 452 China (4-3-45) sec 7, pt 7.
23. (TS) NSC 64, 27 Feb 50, CCS 092 Asia (6-25-48) sec 3. (TS) Memo, ExecSecy NSC to NSC, "The position of the United States with respect to Indochina," 24 Apr 50, same file, sec 4.

step would be to inaugurate a program of assistance aimed at neutralizing the Viet Minh strength and stabilizing the Associated States economies.

Beginnings of American Aid

The principle of extending military and economic aid to threatened Asian countries had been agreed upon by February 1950, and Indochina had been determined the area in most immediate danger. The United States, however, had yet to make specific commitments or enter formal arrangements. It was during the spring of 1950 that the aid machinery was developed and the program of assistance to Indochina actually initiated.

Although the United States had concluded by February that the French would have to be helped in Indochina, negotiations on the subject were actually opened by France. French overtures were inspired by Communist recognition of Ho Chi Minh's government. Paris interpreted the action of Moscow and Peiping as presaging Soviet or Chinese aggression in Indochina and realized that substantial outside assistance was imperative. Accordingly, M. Henri Bonnet, French Ambassador in Washington, presented an aide-memoire to the State Department on 16 February. In this document the French urged the United States to make a public "affirmation of solidarity before the Communist menace" as a warning to China and the USSR and to undertake immediate measures to grant military and economic aid to France and the Associated States in Indochina. They also suggested that the "French and American General Staffs" jointly examine not only French and Vietnamese military requirements but also the military situation in general.[24]

A week later, Alexandre Parodi, Secretary General of the French Foreign Office, further emphasized the need for help. In discussing Indochina with American Ambassador David Bruce and Minister Charles Bohlen, M. Parodi warned that the United States must inaugurate

---

24. (S) App B, Aide-Memoire, Washington, 15 Feb 50, to (TS) JCS 1992/10, 10 Mar 50, same file.

a program of long-term assistance or France might be forced to withdraw from Indochina. French withdrawal was precisely what the United States feared. Since the success of any program of external assistance would be decided by the French determination to remain in Indochina, the United States considered it necessary to obtain a firm French pledge to continue the war. Ambassador Bruce and Mr. Bohlen impressed M. Parodi with this fact in unequivocal terms.[25]

Final decision was reached in March to undertake the Indochinese military assistance program. The Joint Chiefs of Staff, on 16 January, had proposed that 15-million dollars be set aside for Indochina and 10 million dollars for Thailand. The State and Defense Departments approved the recommendations of the Joint Chiefs of Staff on 6 March. Secretary of State Acheson advised the President that "The choice confronting the United States is to support the French in Indochina or to face the extension of communism over the remainder of the continental area of Southeast Asia and possibly farther westward." Accordingly, he recommended that 15 million dollars be reserved from the Section 303 fund to finance the beginnings of a military aid program for Indochina, plus 10 million dollars for Thailand. President Truman approved on 10 March 1950.[26]

The basis for a program of economic aid was slower in developing. In laying the groundwork for specific American programs, it was anticipated that the reports of two surveys and a conference in progress in the Far East would play a major role in determining the form that these programs would assume. Ambassador-at-Large Philip C. Jessup had been visiting various Asian countries

---

25. (S) Doc B-44, Msg, USAmb Paris to SecState, 837, 22 Feb 50, in (TS) Doc Hist of US Pol Toward Indochina.
26. (TS) App A, Memo for Pres, "Allocation of Funds to Provide Military Assistance to Thailand and Indochina under Section 303 of the Mutual Defense Assistance Act," 9 Mar 50, (TS) Ann B to App A, "Military Assistance for Indochina," 9 Mar 50, and (TS) App B, Ltr, Pres to SecState, 10 Mar 50, to (TS) JCS 1721/48, 29 Mar 50, CCS 452 China (4-3-45) sec 7, pt 8.

since December. Dr. Jessup's mission was to analyze the situation in Asia and report his recommendations for an integrated Far Eastern policy. Dr. Robert Allen Griffin headed an economic survey team charged with formulating a co-ordinated economic aid policy for Asia. In addition the Southeast Asian chiefs of diplomatic missions met in Bangkok, Thailand, in February to discuss regional problems and consider prospective economic programs.

The diplomats at the Bangkok conference believed that emphasis should be placed upon Point IV type technical aid in order to increase Asian capacity for self-help, and they agreed that the focal point of the Southeast Asian economic program should be Indochina.[27] The recommendations of Dr. Jessup in March and Dr. Griffin in May coincided substantially with the Bangkok conclusions. Both of these authorities were convinced that only through Indochina could Southeast Asia be saved from Communism, and they believed that small amounts of money properly spent would go far toward achieving this result.[28] As the program subsequently developed, however, the emphasis was on economic projects of immediate benefit to the war effort. Nevertheless, the program, as originally conceived, was based upon the Bangkok conclusions and upon the Griffin and Jessup recommendations.

The decision to undertake an economic program was not made public until 11 May, when Secretary Acheson, at the conclusion of the London Foreign Ministers Conference, announced the American intentions. On 24 May separate notes were delivered to representatives of the Associated States in Saigon and to the President of the French Union in Paris. These notes defined the nature of the proposed assistance. It would, declared the notes, be "complementary to the effort made by the three Associated States and France, without any intention of substitution."[29]

---

27. NY Times, 19 Feb 50; "Matters Considered by Regional Conference of U.S. Envoys in Bangkok," State Dept Bulletin, 27 Mar 50, p. 502.

28. (TS) "Oral Report of Ambassador-at-Large Philip C. Jessup upon his Return from the Far East," 23 Mar 50, in State Dept files; "Administration of Economic Aid to Southeast Asia," State Dept Bulletin, 29 May 50, p. 369.

29. "Economic Aid Program for Vietnam, Laos, and Cambodia," State Dept Bulletin, 12 Jun 50, pp. 977-978.

Mr. Robert Blum was placed in charge of the Special Technical and Economic Mission (STEM) to the Associated States, and he was to begin work even before the bilateral agreements regulating the arrangement were concluded. It was announced in June that 23.5 million dollars, from unexpended China Aid Funds, would be spent in Indochina for Fiscal Year 1951.

In spite of the obvious importance of economic aid in achieving stability, the prospect of military equipment in large quantities had more immediate effect on the political atmosphere of Indochina. The announcement of prospective American assistance created new complexities in French-Vietnamese relations and in Vietnamese domestic politics. Repercussions were felt alike in Paris and Washington and resulted in strained relations between the two capitals that in turn affected the development of the aid program. The French realized that a military assistance program would represent a direct American investment in the Indochinese war and feared that it would be used as a lever for American pressure in the political field. French apprehension was misdirected, however, for it was the Vietnamese who seized upon the pending aid program and attempted to turn it to their own political advantage.

In all discussions with France over the possibilities of American arms aid, the United States continued to emphasize the fact that a political solution was essential to military success. France, however, regarded immediate conclusion of an agreement to furnish military equipment to French troops in Indochina of infinitely greater importance. The French position was summed up in instructions given to Foreign Minister Robert Schuman by the Cabinet before the London Foreign Ministers Conference. M. Schuman was to impress upon Secretary Acheson that, if the United States wanted to save Indochina from Communism, it should quit encouraging Bao Dai to believe he could win greater independence and proceed to the more urgent business of supplying aircraft and arms to French forces in Indochina. France was amazed that the United States insisted upon discussing future Vietnamese independence from France when Vietnamese independence from Communism was at stake.[30]

---

30. NY Times, 4 May 50.

Although Paris circles feared that the United States would insist upon greater French concessions to Bao Dai as a condition for arms aid, the actual American position was that for the present the French had conceded enough--provided they executed the Elysee Accords in good faith. The State Department held that "Bao Dai and Co." were "barely able to discharge responsibilities they are now facing," and tried to convince France that the United States was not arguing for further immediate concessions.[31] The Department did believe, however, that not only must Bao Dai win the allegiance of the Vietnamese people, but the Asiatic countries must be convinced that Viet Nam would evolve into a truly democratic, independent nation. Consistent with this belief, France was insistently pressed to make a public declaration of what had been accomplished by the 8 March adjustment and a public promise of future concessions. France just as insistently refused to make such a statement, protesting that it would encourage the belief that the 8 March settlement had not in fact granted a high degree of independence.[32]

Although Paris entertained a groundless fear that the United States would use the arms program to win Bao Dai more independence, the Bao Dai government itself apparently decided that American generosity might in fact be used to accomplish this purpose. As early as January, Vietnamese actions indicated they intended using the arms program to their own advantage. A list of military and economic requirements for Viet Nam, prepared by Bao Dai's staff without French knowledge, was handed to Ambassador-at-Large Philip Jessup.[33] On 18 March 1950, Charge d'Affairs Gullion warned that "responsible Vietnamese

---

31. (S) Doc B-45, Msg, Acheson to AmEmb Paris, 1363, 29 Mar 50, in (TS) Doc Hist of US Pol Toward Indochina.
32. (S) App C, State Dept, Memo of Conv, "Indochina," 16 Feb 50, to (TS) JCS 1992/10, 10 Mar 50, CCS 092 Asia (6-25-48) sec 3.
33. (S) Memo, Dean Rusk, Asst SecState (FEA), to Maj Gen J. H. Burns, Asst to SecDef (FMA&MA), 20 Mar 50, same file.

believed they held the whiphand on the French and could play us off against them" in an effort to acquire functions not contemplated by the 8 March Accords.[34]

This judgment appeared valid in light of an astute move by the Vietnamese government a week later. Defense Minister Phan Huy Quat outlined to Charge d'Affaires Gullion a plan for equipping the Vietnamese Army without French participation. Quat's plan envisioned an American-equipped Vietnamese Army trained and advised by United States military personnel. Although Mr. Gullion labeled Quat's views "fantastic," he admitted that the Vietnamese attitude raised serious problems.[35] The logical outgrowth of the proposal, of course, would have been an American-controlled Vietnamese Army serving under the operational command of the French Army within a State of the French Union.

Meanwhile, the French had submitted their own list of arms requirements and briefed American military attaches at the Legation in Saigon on their equipment deficiencies. The list was prepared by the French General Staff in Indochina without consultation with officials of Viet Nam. The United States was thus confronted with two separate estimates of arms needs and an exceedingly delicate diplomatic problem.

If the United States decided to deal with the Vietnamese Government in equipping the indigenous army, the French would be highly incensed and probably withhold essential cooperation. But a measure of Vietnamese authority in the direction of their own military affairs was implicit in the 8 March Accords. Therefore, to deal exclusively with the French would not only contradict the American position on the Accords, but also promised to increase Franco-Vietnamese tension and undermine Vietnamese friendship for the United States. The separate

---

34. (S) Msg, Gullion to Acheson, 190, 18 Mar 50, CM-IN-14886, 21 Mar 50, same file.
35. (S) Msg, Gullion to Acheson, 204, 25 Mar 50, CM-IN-15891, 27 Mar 50, same file.

Vietnamese overtures to the United States had already caused friction between High Commissioner Leon Pignon and the Bao Dai government, and led the French to force the resignation of Premier Nguyen Phan Long.

Commissioner Pignon flatly informed the United States that France, and not the Associated States, must control distribution of arms. In M. Pignon's view, the "operations of receiving and distributing important quantities of material involve a series of complex technical problems which only the French military services can resolve at this time." Since the French Commander-in-Chief in Indochina was responsible for the conduct of military operations, he must also direct the distribution of materials. The French lists would be prepared by the French commander, acting in his capacity of Chief of Staff of National Defense for each Associated State, and "There can be no question of changing this established program (procedure)."[36]

The United States was thus faced with the necessity of devising an aid formula that would have minimum adverse effect on the political situation, and the advice of the Joint Chiefs of Staff was sought. Although the Joint Chiefs of Staff recognized the political implications of military aid, they believed that, such was the urgent need for immediate shipment of arms, the aid program should be adapted to the reality of French control of Vietnamese affairs. The requirement estimates drafted by the French General Staff reflected a more realistic appraisal of military needs, and contained more information essential to programming, than the "broadly generalized Bao Dai list." Consequently, deliveries should be made to French authorities, with such Vietnamese participation in reception as the Secretary of State might desire. Although development of a coordinated aid policy for all Southeast Asia was necessary, the Joint Chiefs of Staff believed that Indochina should be given top priority and shipments dispatched with haste. The Chiefs recommended, however, that French

---

36. (S) Informal Trans /Fr/, Aide-Memoire, 11 Apr 50, same file, sec 4.

requests be carefully analyzed and military aid integrated with political and economic programs. This could be accomplished by the creation of a Southeast Asia Aid Committee, composed of representatives of the State and Defense Departments and the Economic Cooperation Administration (ECA), charged with drafting and executing an over-all aid program for Southeast Asia. Although final approval of all requirements would rest with the Chiefs themselves, a military aid group should be established in Indochina to screen French requests and coordinate them with French operational plans.37

The French accorded the American plan a chilly reception. They wanted American arms with no strings attached and on their own terms. Their views indicated a desire that the United States concern itself simply with filling French orders for equipment without attempting to influence types or quantities of material or how it was employed. General Marcel Carpentier, French Commander-in-Chief of Indochina, said that he "would welcome" a United States military mission, but wished it to be as small as possible and a part of the attache group at the American Legation in Saigon. Although he "would welcome" representatives of the Associated States in the receiving and distributing apparatus, only the French High Command "would be equipped /to/ receive and stock American materiel for Indochina." Charge d'Affaires Gullion, however, believed that General Carpentier could be induced to moderate his stand on the size of the military aid mission.38

A formula designed to satisfy Vietnamese demands for participation in the aid program was agreed upon in April. The Vietnamese High Military Committee, a French organ with Vietnamese representatives, would devise the arms programs for submission to the United States. Mixed commissions, including officers of Viet Nam, would then receive and distribute the equipment.

---

37. (TS) JCS 1992/11, 29 Mar 50, same file, sec 3; (TS) JCS 1721/49, 7 Apr 50, CCS 452 China (4-3-45) sec 7, pt 8.
38. (TS) Msg, Gullion to Acheson, UNN, 3 May 50, CM-IN-1262, 5 May 50, CCS 092 Asia (6-25-48) sec 4.

Similar organizations would perform these duties in Laos and Cambodia.[39] Implicit in the arrangement, of course, was French control, and in actual practice the Vietnamese were not admitted to programming conferences until the summer of 1952.

The many problems created by the new character of the Indochinese struggle and the new American role in Far Eastern affairs indicated that Indochina and Southeast Asia would occupy a prominent position on the agenda for the approaching American-British-French Foreign Ministers Conference, scheduled for May 1950.

In preparing for the Foreign Ministers Conference, the State Department faced the knotty problem of formulating a position that would resolve the Franco-Vietnamese conflict over control of the aid program. The Department decided upon a compromise by which the United States, in aid matters, would treat with "the three Associated States and the French as a unified force." Although not stated, this implied French control of all aid. The hard fact was that, although military success depended upon political success, it also depended upon the vigor with which the French prosecuted military operations; and the more political concessions the French made in Indochina, the less they had to fight for. Although not abandoning its desire for a French declaration of future intentions, the United States was led by these considerations to accept an arms program controlled, with a few surface concessions to Vietnamese pride, by France.[40]

The Joint Chiefs of Staff, in light of recent statements by General Carpentier, advised the Secretary of State to "make unmistakable the firm desire of the United States to send a military aid group to Indochina at the earliest possible date . . . ." They linked this to a

---

39. (S) Msg, SecState to USAmb Paris, 1800, 24 Apr 50, CM-IN-19886, 25 Apr 50, same file.
40. (TS) FM D A-2/4a, State Dept Position Paper, "May Foreign Ministers Meeting, Southern Asia," 5 May 50; (S) Encl B, FM D C-3a, State Dept Position Paper, "May Foreign Ministers Meeting, Indochina," 25 Apr 50, to (S) JCS 1992/16, 30 Apr 50. Both in same file.

rejection of the French suggestion made in February that the "French and American General Staffs" proceed to a "joint examination" of the Indochinese military situation, pointing out that the same purpose could be accomplished by consultation between the aid mission and the French High Command in Indochina.[41]

The Foreign Ministers Conference convened in London early in May. Discussions on Indochina were taken up primarily on a bilateral basis between Secretary Acheson and Foreign Minister Schuman. M. Schuman declared that France accepted primary responsibility for holding Indochina against the Communists and promised that she would not withdraw. He pointed out, however, that the continued drain on French resources made it impossible for France to carry on alone in Indochina and at the same time meet her obligations in the defense of Western Europe. Therefore, the United States must reconcile itself to supporting France in the war against the Viet Minh.[42]

Secretary Acheson gave assurances of forthcoming American aid but emphasized that no large sums of money would be available until Congress convened. Although 20 million dollars could probably be programmed before 30 June, he declared, the extent of future support would be up to Congress, which also must reckon with American obligations throughout the world.[43]

The Secretary voiced his concern for Bao Dai's failure to gain prestige at home and abroad but did not press the point. M. Schuman, however, reaffirmed France's intention of granting more autonomy to the Associated States when internal conditions made it safe to do so.

---

41. (TS) Encl A, Dft Memo, JCS to SecDef, to (TS) JCS 1992/15, 30 Apr 50; (S) Encl B, FM D C-3a, State Dept, "May Foreign Ministers Meeting, Indochina," 25 Apr 50, to (S) JCS 1992/16, 30 Apr 50. Both in same file. (TS) JCS 1992/11, 29 Mar 50, same file, sec 3.
42. (S) Doc B-47, Mns (FR), Acheson-Schuman Conversations, 8 May 50, in (TS) Doc Hist of US Pol Toward Indochina.
43. Ibid.

Reflecting French discontent with American interest in Bao Dai, M. Schuman predicted that "If the United States gives France its support in the military field and trusts it for the internal development of its policy, a happy ending will be achieved." He did state, however, that France was now removing all restrictions on the diplomatic representation of the Associated States, and had reached a decision to establish a "Ministry for relations with the Associated States." This new Ministry would be charged with handling Associated States affairs and would be staffed with personnel who thoroughly understood the new status of the Associated States.[44] It was hoped that this would remove the stigma of colonialism inherent in regulation by the Ministry of Overseas Possessions.

The May Foreign Ministers Conference quieted American fears that France would abandon Indochina to the Communists and clarified for France American intentions on military and economic aid. Politically, it marked a further French concession to the independence of the Associated States, even though the public announcement of intention long desired by the United States was still not forthcoming. It also coordinated American, British and French policy on Southeast Asia, although Great Britain, fearing Commonwealth reaction, refused to join in a tripartite declaration of solidarity and collaboration to resist Communism in the region as a whole.

The May Foreign Ministers Conference cleared the way for early inauguration of aid shipments to Indochina. In Washington, machinery was devised to handle a long term, coordinated aid program for Southeast Asia. On the policy level, the Southeast Asia Aid Committee, proposed by the Joint Chiefs of Staff in March, was established. In June its name was changed to the Southeast Asia Aid Policy Committee (SEAAPC) to distinguish it clearly from an operating agency. SEAAPC was charged with coordinating general policy for political, economic, and military assistance to Southeast Asian countries. The Foreign Military Assistance Coordinating Committee (FMACC), an

---

44. Ibid.

interdepartmental organ that supervised world-wide military assistance programs, was still to have final responsibility for policy matters involving military assistance to Southeast Asia. FMACC and SEAAPC would work in close cooperation on military aid policy.[45]

On the operating level, economic assistance would be handled by the Economic Cooperation Administration in Washington, and a Special Technical and Economic Mission in Indochina. Responsibility for the military program was lodged with the Office of Military Assistance (OMA), Department of Defense. A Military Assistance Advisory Group (MAAG) attached to the American Legation in Saigon was to screen French requests and oversee distribution of the material once it arrived. Both OMA and MAAG Indochina would work closely with the Joint Chiefs of Staff and use screening criteria drafted by the Joint Chiefs of Staff.[46]

A special Joint Survey Team, with representatives from the State and Defense Departments, was to be sent to Southeast Asia as soon as practicable. The mission of the Team was to gather information on the internal situation in the various Southeast Asian countries benefiting from the program and to make recommendations regarding specific on-the-spot organization necessary to carry out the program efficiently. Neither the shipment of material nor the formation of MAAG Indochina, however, was to be delayed pending the Survey Team's report.[47] The Secretary of Defense, on the advice of the Joint Chiefs of Staff, appointed Major General Graves B. Erskine, USMC, to head the military section of the Joint Survey Team.[48]

The Joint Chiefs of Staff, early in June, proposed that the 15 million dollars already earmarked for expenditure in Indochina be augmented by an additional

---

45. (TS) Encl, Memo, SecDef to CJCS, "Mutual Defense Assistance Program Implementation for Southeast Asia," 6 Jun 50, to (TS) JCS 1992/18, 8 Jun 50, CCS 092 Asia (6-25-48) sec 4.
46. Ibid.
47. Ibid.
48. (S) Memo, SecDef to JCS, "MDAP Implementation for Southeast Asia," 14 Jun 50, same file, sec 5.

16 million dollars for equipment, supplies, and training. They further advised that, of all Asian aid programs, Indochina should have first priority.[49]

The spring of 1950 thus saw the beginning of a program of military assistance to French and Associated States forces fighting in Indochina and a program of economic aid designed to stabilize the economies of Viet Nam, Laos, and Cambodia. Although the initiation of these programs marked the fulfillment of recommendations made by the Joint Chiefs of Staff as early as the preceding December, it was the logical outgrowth of basic policy decisions reached in January and February, and was expedited by fear of a general disintegration of France's will to continue the war.

Indochina on the Eve of the Korean War

During the first half of 1950, the decisions reached and actions taken by the Western Powers and the Soviet bloc with regard to Indochina lent an international significance to the Indochinese war. The American-led coalition was arrayed behind France to free Indochina, and thereby Southeast Asia, from the threat of Communist subversion and eventual domination. The recognition of Bao Dai's government by the United States and other powers of the free world cleared the way for the American decision to grant military assistance to France and the Associated States. Recognition of the Democratic Republic of Viet Nam by the Communist world presaged similar aid agreements with the Viet Minh. When, in June 1950, the Korean Conflict put a new complexion on the Cold War, a world power alignment had already congealed in Indochina.

Although the prospect of large quantities of American arms encouraged a new determination and hope of success among French and Vietnamese forces, the introduction of Soviet and Chinese Communist equipment to Viet Minh troops vastly improved Ho Chi Minh's ability to wage modern war. By June 1950, intelligence estimates

---
49. (TS) Encl, Dft Memo, JCS to SecDef, to (TS) JCS 1721/55, 12 Jun 50, CCS 452 China (4-3-45) sec 7, pt 10.

indicated that Communist China and the DRV had agreed upon a general plan for Chinese aid and participation in Viet Minh operations. Reinforcing this fact, the intelligence sources discovered that during March 1950 alone Viet Minh forces received from China 52,000 rifles, together with a quantity of automatic weapons, mortars, and artillery pieces. The makings of a major buildup were perceived in the development of a supply corridor from China through northern Tonkin to central Annam. In this region roads were improved, bridges built, concealed supply dumps established, and airfields constructed. Two training camps, which intelligence agencies estimated capable of accommodating twenty to thirty thousand Viet Minh troops, were established in South China. The presence of Soviet training teams at these centers was strongly suspected.[50]

The new Viet Minh strength did not immediately affect the military situation. Although the Viet Minh obviously now possessed new and dangerous capabilities, it was apparently holding them in reserve for the time being. The pressure on the French, however, was undiminished. During the fighting season of 1949-1950, French Union Forces succeeded in clearing and securing the Red River Delta in Tonkin, but on Tonkin's vital northern frontier the French retained only a few scattered and hard-pressed outposts that were supplied with great difficulty.[51]

If the French could anticipate better days to come, they had little to congratulate themselves upon in the current military and political situation. The drain on the financial and manpower resources of France and the Associated States continued. The Vietnamese Army, authorized by the agreements of 30 December 1949, was still no more than a hope for the future. Many of the old political problems remained, with some new ones created by the measure of autonomy granted under the 8 March Accords.

---

50. (TS) JIC 529/1, 16 Aug 50, CCS 092 Asia (6-25-48) sec 5.
51. Ibid.

Bao Dai's success at winning popular support, after some initial progress, had come to a standstill. In January, after six months as his own Premier, Bao Dai appointed Nguyen Phan Long to head the government. Nguyen Phan Long launched a determined campaign to secure the allegiance of the Vietnamese people, but his efforts were unsuccessful. His attempts to orient Viet Nam toward the United States, to the exclusion of France, caused the French to force his dismissal in May 1950. He was succeeded by Tran Van Huu, Governor of South Viet Nam, who adopted a tough policy toward disloyal elements, but failed to better Bao Dai's prestige at home or abroad.[52]

By June 1950 the Indochinese war was on the threshold of transition. The months between the summers of 1949 and 1950 had witnessed what in the French view were generous and concrete measures to satisfy Vietnamese nationalism. These had failed, and the political problem continued to interfere with French military activities. American and Soviet-Chinese interest in the contending forces had focused world attention on the battle for Indochina. The arms shipments already reaching the Viet Minh and soon to reach the French would transform the struggle from a war against guerrilla bands into a modern war of considerable proportions, and make settlement in the near future a virtual impossibility. By their acceptance of external assistance, both France and the Viet Minh were committed to a war without compromise for some time to come. By June 1950 Indochina had become a battleground in world politics.

---

52. Hammer, *Struggle for Indochina*, pp. 272-275.

CHAPTER VIII

FROM THE START OF THE KOREAN CONFLICT TO 1 JANUARY 1951

The outbreak of the Korean Conflict on 24 June 1950 was an event of profound significance for the Indochina problem. Since 1947 the importance of the struggle for Southeast Asia had been largely obscured in the eyes of the United States Government by the overriding necessity to meet the Communist threat in Western Europe. Now, just when the outlines of that struggle were becoming clear they were again overshadowed by a major armed clash in the Far East. From the day that the Communist armies burst across the 38th parallel till the hour of the Armistice, more than three years later, the attention of the American people was focused on Korea. To the American Government, and especially to the Joint Chiefs of Staff, the demands of the Korean battle were more immediately important than those of the war in Indochina. Except for the few weeks in October, 1950, when the Korean fight seemed almost won, there could be no serious consideration of sending Army ground forces to carry out the Truman Doctrine in Southeast Asia. Furthermore, materiel for the MDAP was frequently in short supply, and shipments waiting in West Coast ports were sometimes threatened with diversion to Korea when the situation there turned for the worse. For at least two years the course of the Korean Conflict was one of the major determining factors in American policy toward Indochina.

On the other hand, the forces of the free world fighting in Indochina drew some advantage from the United States reaction to the clash in the Far East. The realization that the Soviet Government was prepared to engage in aggression by satellite heightened American concern for the countries on the periphery of the Iron Curtain. The fact that the attack came in the Far East drew attention to that area. It underlined the threat that Communist possession of certain areas, such as Korea, Indochina, and Indonesia, would offer to the chain of island bases upon which United States defense plans in the Pacific were founded. These factors, reacting upon the thinking of planners in Washington, added to the urgency with which military aid was programmed and shipped to Indochina. And the increased rate of production of military equipment demanded for the Korean Conflict aided, in the end, the support program for Southeast Asia.

Then, too, the fighting in Korea distracted the attention of the Chinese Communists from Indochina. Although United States intelligence estimates in the early months of the Korean Conflict indicated that the Chinese Red Armies had the capabilities of intervening in Southeast Asia and in Korea, at the same time it seems, in the three-dimensioned view of hindsight, that the concentration of Chinese Communist troops, first against Formosa and later in Korea, prevented Peiping from aiding the Viet Minh to the extent that it otherwise might have. That the operations in Korea, which reportedly destroyed much of the trained personnel in the Chinese Communist Armies, must have been a factor in deterring a Chinese invasion of Indochina seems obvious.

On 27 June 1950 President Truman, in announcing the intervention of American armed forces in Korea, also announced that he had "directed acceleration in the furnishing of military assistance to the forces of France and the Associated States in Indochina and the dispatch of a military mission to provide close working relations with those forces."[1] The first result of this policy was the approval of the recommendation of the Joint Chiefs of Staff to increase the MDAP aid programmed for Indochina by 16 million dollars, bringing the total military aid for Indochina from Fiscal Year 1950 funds to 31 million dollars. This amount was allocated among the three United States military services, which had already begun to act on the original 15 million-dollar grant. As of 31 July the Army was scheduled to provide 11.9 millions in equipment, the Navy 15.3 millions, and the Air Force 4.9 millions.[2]

---

1. State Dept Bulletin, 3 Jul 50, p. 5.
2. (S) Memo, Lemnitzer to Burns, "Monthly Status Report - Mutual Defense Assistance Program (to include 31 July 1950)," 5 Aug 50 (hereinafter: MDAP Status Rpt for month of), in Records and Control Office, OASD (ISA).

Although the aid program was somewhat slow at the start, supplies soon began to make their way, by sea and air, to Saigon. On 30 June eight C-47's, loaded with spare parts, arrived in the Indochinese capital. The Director, Office of Military Assistance (OMA), reported that on 31 July Army equipment for twelve Indochinese battalions was afloat, consigned to the High Military Committee of the Army of the French Union. A French aircraft carrier was scheduled to take on forty F6F aircraft in California in September while another French ship was expected to depart the United States in the near future with eighteen LCVP's, six LSSL's and other mixed cargo. The first shipment of infantry equipment arrived in Saigon on 10 August and was delivered to the French supply facilities. This equipment was received without ceremony, because of a delay in arrival.[3]

Further grants of military aid to Indochina were not long in coming. President Truman, on 1 August, asked the Congress for a Fiscal Year 1951 supplemental appropriation of 4 billion dollars for the MDAP. The general appropriations bill, which had already been submitted, was passed on 6 September and included 75 million dollars for "Aid to the General Area of China." Of this amount Indochina was scheduled to receive $25,700,000. Three weeks later the supplemental appropriations bill requested by the President was passed, under the terms of which $107,300,000 was allocated to Indochina. Thus, by 31 October 1950, the total Fiscal Year 1951 program for military aid to Indochina was $133,000,000, this in addition to the $31,000,000 already allotted from Fiscal Year 1950 funds.[4]

---

3. (S) MDAP Status Rpt for month of July 1950, 5 Aug 50; (S) Geneva Conf Background Paper, Indochina Chronology.
4. (S) MDAP Status Rpt for month of October 1950, 31 Oct 50; (TS) JCS 1992/44, 26 Dec 50, CCS 452 China (4-3-45) sec 7 pt 12.

Erskine Report

The Joint State-Defense MDAP Survey Mission for Southeast Asia arrived in Saigon on 15 July. The Mission was headed by Mr. John F. Melby of the Department of State. Major General Graves B. Erskine, USMC, was chief of the military group, which included members from each of the armed services and the United States Coast Guard, the last being included because of the smuggling problem in Indochina. For a period of three weeks members of the Mission talked with French and Indochinese officials, both military and civilian, and observed conditions in the country. Unfortunately, the High Commissioner for Indochina was recalled to Paris during their stay, so that they were unable to hold final talks with him. Also, many of the Indochinese officials were in France attending the Pau Conference. Nevertheless, the members of the Mission believed that they were able to accomplish their aims.

Before leaving Saigon for Singapore on 7 August the Survey Mission submitted a bulky interim report on Indochina to the Foreign Military Assistance Coordinating Committee (FMACC). This report set forth most of the criticisms of French actions in Indochina and the far from optimistic estimates of future prospects that were to be echoed by American representatives in Indochina often in the years that followed. The absolute interdependence of the military, political, and economic problems in the country, the mutual distrust and lack of good faith between French and Indochinese on all levels, the lack of offensive spirit in the French high command, and the correspondingly poor strategical distribution and use of its forces were stressed by General Erskine. Investigations by the Mission, wrote the General, indicated that there were "grounds to doubt that the French authorities have sincerely put forth their best efforts to train and equip a Vietnamese army and thus remove one of the great sources of distrust now existing."

As the Survey Mission saw it, the basic problem in establishing internal security in Indochina and defeating the Viet Minh was winning the cooperation of the people. Military victory was necessary, of course, but it was unlikely to be decisive without a political solution that included concessions on the part of the French and definite plans for eventual independence of Viet Nam. In the words of the report:

> The magnitude of the problem which confronts the French in this respect /Internal security against Communism/ can hardly be overestimated. . . . Many elements which have aligned themselves with the Communists are basically hostile to Communism, but believe that the problem of independence must be solved first and other problems subsequently. It should be noted, parenthetically, that no responsible Vietnamese suggest the desirability of the total withdrawal of French forces at present on the grounds that this would only result in an early Communist victory. Rather, they speak of a timetable for independence and assumption by the French of responsibility for defense against outside attack, leaving internal matters to the Vietnamese. Much public opinion which finds itself in open opposition to the Viet Minh secretly supports the Viet Minh as the group which is having the greatest success in opposing the French. These Vietnamese elements, at the same time, are skeptical of French protestations. The great political problem which confronts the French in Indochina, therefore, is to persuade the Indochinese that they will implement their signed agreements; and at the same time, to persuade that co-operation with the Communists will not, in the end, secure Vietnamese independence, but will represent only another form of subjection to an external force. At the present moment, it may be questionable whether the French can do this in view of the long standing suspicion and deep-seated hatred with which the Indochinese regard the French. . . . It is the opinion of the Mission that unless some agreed political solution can be found, the French will, in time, find themselves eliminated from the scene.[5]

---

5. (TS) FMACC D-33/6, "Report on Indochina," 24 Aug 50 (hereinafter: Erskine Rpt), CCS 092 Asia (6-25-48) BP.

The United States, the Mission believed, should continue to use its influence to obtain implementation in good faith of the political programs agreed upon by the French and Indochinese.

The report went on to the statement, significant for the history of the American effort to hold Indochina against Communism, that the Mission made its recommendations and observations without particular reference to the internal situation in France or to that nation's commitments in NATO. All too often in the succeeding years reports such as this were to be acted upon without real reference to the political situation in metropolitan France. Yet that situation was a morass in which every solution of the basic political problem stated by the Mission faltered. Regardless of the variations of public opinion in France on the Indochina question, the various French governments considered themselves the guardians of the French Empire (officially the French Union) on which rested France's prestige and her position as a great nation. American pressure for concessions to the Indochinese had to be exerted on the French governments through diplomatic channels, for the most part, and had to overcome the natural resistance of those governments to give up part of France's colonial position. And even when a French government was willing to make, and did make, important concessions, their implementation was delayed and resisted by the colonial administrators and the army, the influence of which in French politics should not be underestimated.[6]

---

[6]. It is a commonplace among historians of the Third Republic that while cabinets and legislatures may come and go, the French Government, embodied in the corps of permanent civil servants, remains the same. The power of the army in French government, and even its ability to operate in opposition to the government, is illustrated by l'affaire Boulanger, l'affaire Dreyfus, and the activities of General Mangin in the Rhineland after World War I. It must also be remembered that in regard to colonial affairs the traditions of such men as Marshal Lyautey are still strong in the army.

As to military aid, the Survey Mission found that the existing program was inadequate. General Erskine noted that there had been a considerable increase in Viet Minh offensive capabilities in recent months, as well as a developing threat of invasion by the Chinese Communists in support of Ho Chi Minh. As a result of these developments the French urgently needed more equipment, a list of which they turned over to the Survey Mission on its arrival in Saigon. The Mission viewed the French requests as reasonable but requested that the MAAG, Indochina, the first elements of which had already arrived in the country, screen the list further and furnish its comments to the Mission before that body left the Southeast Asia area. The Mission stated, however, that the materiel requested seemed to be the maximum that the French and Indochinese forces were capable of handling without additional reinforcement.[7]

U.S. Government Acts on Erskine Report

The Indochina Report of the Survey Mission was received in Washington toward the end of August and action on its recommendations began immediately. Prompt consideration was necessary for the Communist threat to Southeast Asia was growing daily. An estimate of the Indochinese situation, submitted to the Joint Chiefs of Staff by the Joint Intelligence Committee on 25 August, confirmed General Erskine's view that Viet Minh capabilities for launching an offensive had grown. Indeed, it went farther to state that the intention of the Viet Minh to make a large-scale attack was established and that their preparations would be sufficiently complete for it to begin on 1 September. A French offensive during the period of good autumn weather would, with the troops and equipment presently available, only postpone the Viet Minh attack since the rebels could retreat across the Chinese border to re-form. The Joint Intelligence Committee did not agree entirely with the Survey Mission's observation on the threat of Chinese Communist invasion. The Committee regarded covert

---

7. (TS) Erskine Rpt.

participation by the Chinese in a Viet Minh offensive as more probable than overt aggression. The Committee's estimate noted, however, that a Communist attack in Indochina in September might reduce United Nations pressure in Korea at a time when the build-up of General MacArthur's forces would be reaching considerable proportions.[8]

The Joint Chiefs of Staff, therefore, were well aware of the urgency of the situation when, on 6 September, the Secretary of Defense requested them to prepare "an interim program of items for immediate supply action based upon the lists of current military requirements" contained in the Erskine Report. This task was turned over to the Ad Hoc Committee on Programs for Military Assistance, which rendered a report on 16 October.[9] In the meantime, however, the French had experienced a severe reverse in Tonkin and were becoming impatient for more military aid. On 12 October the French Minister of Defense, M. Jules Moch, pressed Secretary of Defense George C. Marshall for a schedule of aid to be furnished for Indochina, and especially for quick delivery of a group (thirty) of B-26 light bombers that had been included in the request to the Survey Mission. When asked for their recommendation on furnishing the bombers the Joint Chiefs of Staff replied that while the planes would not materially aid the situation in Indochina their diversion to that country could weaken United States potentialities in Korea and Europe, depending on possible developments in those areas. They therefore recommended against sending the requested aircraft. The Secretaries of State and Defense, however, overruled the Joint Chiefs of Staff and ordered the immediate programming of twenty-one B-26's, the remaining nine to be included in the final Fiscal Year 1951 program for Indochina. In view of the deteriorating situation in Viet Nam these aircraft were to be furnished on a priority ahead of all other MDAP programs and _equal_ to that of

---

8. (TS) JCS 1992/22, 25 Aug 50, CCS 092 **Asia** (6-25-48) sec 5.
9. (TS) Memo, Col Kenneth R. Kreps, USAF, Actg Exec-Secy OSD, to JCS, "Military Assistance to Indo-China," 6 Sep 50; (TS) JCS 1992/32, 16 Oct 50; same file, sec 6.

requirements for the Far East Air Force (FEAF) scheduled to be shipped subsequent to 1 November.[10]

The report of the Ad Hoc Committee on Programs of Military Assistance, rendered to the Joint Chiefs of Staff on 16 October, was approved by them two days later. A program of 133 million dollars worth of equipment was set forth, to be provided as a matter of urgency. Important items in the list included ninety F8F and thirty B-26 aircraft, three PC vessels and other light craft, considerable signal and engineer equipment, with other ground force supplies, and a large amount of ammunition for all three services. The Committee noted, however, that only a small amount of the recommended aid could be shipped within sixty days, and therefore placed its standard of availability at six months. Certain items, such as army general purpose vehicles and SCR 300 radios were in short supply and none could be furnished within that time. Even with this screening, fulfilling the recommended program would occasion deficiencies in essential equipment for United States forces (especially army) then in being and scheduled for activation within the next six months, although precautions had been taken to insure that the equipping of such units would not be seriously hampered.

Because French authorities were in charge of the military campaign in Indochina as well as in control of the native armies, the Ad Hoc Committee recommended, and the Joint Chiefs of Staff agreed, that all military assistance should be delivered to the French with "such participation by the representatives of Vietnam, Laos, and Cambodia as the Secretary of State may deem appropriate." Also, the Joint Chiefs of Staff informed the Secretary of Defense, it was their view that increases in military aid should be provided in accordance with operational plans that were acceptable to the United

---

10. (S) Memo, Kreps to JCS, "Mutual Defense Assistance to Indochina," 12 Oct 50; (TS) Memo, Dir, JS to SecDef, same subj, 13 Oct 50; (TS) Memo, Lemnitzer to John H. Ohly, Actg Dir MDA, State Dept, "Military Assistance to Indo-China," 16 Oct 50; same file.

States and therefore the recommended assistance to Indochina would be subjected to observation and supervision by the MAAG in Saigon.[11]

On 23 October the program set forth by the Joint Chiefs of Staff was approved and the services were directed to expedite its fulfillment. It was assigned a priority immediately below that of the requirements of United States forces in combat or alerted for early movement to the Korean area, and above all military assistance programs other than those in direct support of the Korean effort.[12] The services lost no time in scheduling what deliveries they could. In a message of 26 October the Chief of Staff of the Army instructed General MacArthur to ship to Indochina at the earliest possible date a considerable amount of ordnance spare parts, and signal equipment, some armored cars, one hundred 105-mm howitzers, and a large quantity of ammunition. The Navy began shipping fighter aircraft and additional small vessels, and the Air Force scheduled the first flight of seven B-26's to leave the United States by 1 November. Cargo tonnages shipped to Indochina were low during October and November but increased during December, so that by the end of 1950 a total of 43,400 measurement tons had been sent off, of which over 19,000 measurement tons had been dispatched in the last month.[13]

---

11. (TS) JCS 1992/32, 16 Oct 50, same file.
12. (S) Memo, Lemnitzer to MG R. E. Duff, USA, DepAsst CS, G-3 Army, Capt Howard Orem, USN, Dir Int Aff, DepNav, and Col M. W. Brewster, USAF, P&O Div, DepAF, "Military Assistance to Indo-China," 23 Oct 50, same file, sec 7; (S) MDAP Status Rpt for month of October 1950, 31 Oct 50.
13. (S) Msg, CSA, WAR-95099, to CINCFE, CM-OUT-95099, 26 Oct 50, CCS 092 Asia (6-25-48) sec 7; (S) MDAP Status Rpt for month of November 1950, 7 Dec 50; (S) MDAP Status Rpt for month of December 1950, 12 Jan 51.

Crisis in Indochina

During the latter half of 1950 the military position of the French forces in Indochina was growing constantly worse. The estimates of the Survey Mission and the Joint Intelligence Committee concerning the dangerous increase in Viet Minh offensive capabilities and intentions were borne out in a dramatic fashion in actions along the northeast Tonkin border. On 16 September the rebel forces organized for conventional combat struck at the border post of Dong Khe, erasing two companies of the French Foreign Legion in a two-day battle. As a result the important post at Cao Bang became untenable and its evacuation was ordered. In the first week of October the garrison, consisting of three battalions, left Cao Bang for Thatkhe while a similar force started from Thatkhe to meet and reinforce it. Upon joining, the two groups were smashed by a massive Viet Minh attack and scattered, to straggle back to Thatkhe as best they could. A week later only about one-seventh of the six-battalion force had reached that post, the evacuation of which had already begun.[14]

Although the forces engaged at Cao Bang were small by World War II standards, they were considerable for the Indochina war and the defeat was all but a disaster for the French. Before the year was out they were compelled to abandon all of their northeast border outposts except Moncay, which was near the coast. This withdrawal opened the border and strengthened the communications of the Viet Minh with the Chinese Communists in Southeast China. The rebels thereafter had easier access to the supplies and equipment with which the Chinese had been aiding them for some time. Moreover, they were in a position threatening the rice-rich delta. And not only was the military position of the Viet Minh greatly strengthened and their morale bolstered, but such a triumph as Cao Bang gave them increased prestige among the Indochinese people, the French losing face correspondingly.

---

14. (U) Note handed to State Dept by FrEmb, 14 Oct 50, CCS 092 Asia (6-25-48) sec 6; (TS) Memo by CSA, "Possible Future Action in Indochina," 18 Oct 50, same file, sec 7.

Aside from the purely strategical effects of the autumn Viet Minh campaign, there were important repercussions in other areas. As we have seen, it spurred on the flow of American military aid. It also prompted the French to make certain concessions to Vietnamese nationalism and to speed implementation of some already made. A new strategy was devised, calculated to meet the shift of the Viet Minh from guerrilla to conventional warfare, and a new commander was sent out to make it effective.

Letourneau-Juin Mission

On 17 October General Alphonse-Pierre Juin, French Resident General in Morocco, an officer with long experience in colonial affairs, arrived in Saigon to review the military situation with an eye to changing French strategy and possibly reinforcing the effort in Indochina with additional personnel from the home country. He was accompanied by M. Jean Letourneau, Minister of State for the Associated States in the French Cabinet, whose mission was to assess the political actions required to halt the rapid deterioration of the French position in Indochina. After a week-long survey the two men returned to Paris to report to the French Government.

On the basis of their reports the alarmed French Government took some drastic, necessary, but long-belated actions. In the military sphere, the basic decision was made to pass from a defensive strategy of "pacification" in Indochina to concerted offensive effort to root out and destroy the Viet Minh forces in their own lairs. To accomplish this M. Letourneau was given increased power over the military direction of the war, enabling him to coordinate the activities of the armed service bureaus insofar as they concerned Indochina. And to complement the unification of direction in France, the government decided to unite in the person of General Jean de Lattre de Tassigny the functions of High Commissioner and Commander-in-Chief in Indochina. This step, it was hoped, would eliminate much of the conflict between the French political and military functionaries in that country, a conflict that had contributed greatly to the confusion of aims, the defensive strategy, and the defeatist attitudes of the French forces. The National Assembly backed up these decisions by a strong resolution voted with a large majority.[15]

Pau Conventions

Alongside the military reforms, which were inaugurated in November and December, the French Government made some sweeping political concessions to satisfy the claims of Indochinese nationalism and attract support for the fight against Communism. The twenty-seventh of November saw the signing at Pau, in France, of ten conventions regulating the internal relations of the Associated States and the influence of the French in the Indochinese economy. The Elysee Accords of 8 March 1949 had stipulated that an interstate conference (Conference inter-etats) was to be held between France and the three Indochinese states to determine the scope of joint committees, which were to be erected to govern communications facilities, foreign trade and customs, immigration control, finance, and economic planning. This conference had met on 29 June 1950 and fumbled along for four months with little real progress but with mounting friction and controversy. Not only was the position of the French delegates removed from that of the Associated States, but quarrels developed among the states themselves, the representatives of Laos and Cambodia resenting what they felt to be an attempt by the Vietnamese delegation to dominate them. After the military defeats of October, however, it behooved the French to moderate their position and to compromise. The conference was rapidly and, to some extent, successfully brought to a close with the agreement on the subjects specified, plus conventions regulating the port of Saigon and navigation of the Mekong River. A group of interstate agencies was set up, staffed by personnel of all four countries, to take over the tasks of the "common services" of the former Indochinese Union, which had been administered directly by the French High Commissariat. Agreement on a monetary union and a customs union of the Associated States salvaged to a large extent the economic unity of the peninsula.

---

15. *Journal officiel de la Republique francaise, Debats parlementaires, Assemblee nationale,* 22 Nov 50, pp. 7998-8050.

Although an accord had been reached at Pau, neither the French nor the Indochinese were really satisfied. Frenchmen who felt France's prestige to rest on her empire wailed that too much had been given up. The Indochinese, however, while recognizing the fact that the Pau conventions were an advance from the position of the Elysee agreements, wanted much more independence than the French had been willing to concede. From the standpoint of the Indochinese nationalists, French control was perpetuated by the inclusion of French representatives in the joint agencies and by the guarantees for protecting French interests in the fields of money and banking, foreign investments and exchange, tariff policy and customs control, and certain educational establishments. The port of Saigon and navigation on the Mekong remained under the effective control of Frenchmen. And too many French officials, whom many Indochinese could never regard as anything but colonial exploiters, were to remain in Indochina. The Vietnamese man-in-the-paddy, if he concerned himself about it at all, probably could not discern any difference between the old relationship and the new. For these reasons the Pau conventions, insofar as they were aimed at stimulating native support for a "free and independent Vietnam" and for the fight against Communism, fell short of the mark.[16]

Furthermore, although the Pau conference had its beginning before the autumn attacks of the Viet Minh, the fact that the signing of the conventions came hard on the heels of a series of French defeats gave some Indochinese the impression French concessions were the result of those defeats. Those who already regarded the Viet Minh as the most successful force working for Indochinese independence were undoubtedly strengthened in their belief. The unfortunate sequence of events buttressed the argument that more was to be gained for Vietnamese freedom by permitting the French forces to fall before Communist guns than by supporting an army that, if victorious against Ho Chi Minh, might be used to reassert colonial government.

---

16. Notes et Etudes, "Conventions inter-etats," No. 1.425, 24 Jan 51; Hammer, Struggle for Indochina, pp. 274-281.

Vietnamese Army

In early December the French made yet another concession to Vietnamese nationalism, one intended to bestow on the Emperor Bao Dai the still missing halo of sovereignty and to convince the Indochinese that the French would convey the powers of government to them as rapidly as possible. This was the establishment of an independent national Army of Viet Nam, a step long desired by the Joint Chiefs of Staff and urged on the French by the Department of State in Washington and by Minister Donald Heath in Saigon. The measure was decided upon in principle by the French and Vietnamese Governments in October and about six weeks were spent in discussions at Dalat about the size, organization, and command structure of the army. Finally, on 8 December, the retiring High Commissioner, M. Leon Pignon, signed a military convention with officials of Viet Nam. According to the agreement Bao Dai would be in supreme command of the national army, but responsible to the French High Command in Indochina. French officers and cadres, in Vietnamese uniforms and paid by Viet Nam, would be subject to Bao Dai's command. As a military force, the army was not expected to be effective for at least a year, after which it might be able to take over certain "pacification duties," freeing French units for offensive work in the north.

It was obvious to all concerned that such an army would require heavy support from the MDAP. There was no other source for the necessary armament and supplies. Nevertheless, no American representative was invited to the discussions at Dalat, either to observe or participate. As Mr. Edmund A. Gullion, the Special Assistant for MDAP to the American Minister at Saigon, complained to Washington, this "appeared further to delay implementation of the project."[17]

The outstanding weakness of the sweeping concessions made by the French in the autumn of 1950 lay in the fact

---

17. (S) Msg, Edmund A. Gullion, SpecAsst, MDAP, Saigon, to State Dept, "MDAP Monthly Report No. 3 (October 1950)," 1 Dec 50, G-3 091 Indo China, sec II A, bk I, Case 31; (S) CIA, NIE - 5, 29 Dec 50, p. 2.

that they came too late. Given the perspective of four years it is easy to see that the growing strength of the Viet Minh, the emergent threat of invasion by the Communist Chinese, as well as their increasing ability to support the Viet Minh materially and politically, and the growing distaste in France for the war, did not permit enough time for the measures to have the desired effect. Even before the ink was dry on the new conventions the critical importance of the time factor was apparent to American observers in Indochina. As Minister Heath reported from Saigon, "Had French willingly made two years ago 1950 concessions and had Bao Dai and his government had two years experience under new formula, there would have been radically different IC situation. Basic political question today is whether there is time enough to utilize new political framework to mobilize mass allegiance behind Bao Dai."[18]

Change of Command--General de Lattre de Tassigny

To carry out the reforms in Indochina new men, or rather, a new man, was needed. The High Commissioner, M. Pignon, and the Commanding General, Marcel Carpentier, were, to use the French description, *fatigues*. The military command was worn out, disillusioned, and no longer capable of directing offensive action. The civil administrators of the High Commissioner's office were known to be reluctant to carry out just such reforms as were now demanded And friction between the civil and military authority was recognized generally as being one of the reasons for the failure of both.

The solution to these problems arrived in Saigon on 17 December in the person of General de Lattre. Armed with the seal of political authority as well as the baton of military command, he immediately took complete control of the French administration and of the armed forces. His first job was to restore guts and backbone to the fighting man. This he did by appeals to the soldiers' pride, by

---

18. (S) Msg, Donald Heath, NIACT-1157, to SecState, 1 Jan 51, DA-IN-6870, 4 Jan 51, CCS 092 Asia (6-25-48) sec 9.

insisting on stern discipline, by replacing passive commanders, and especially by setting an example of determination and confidence. Shortly after his arrival he reversed the order, given by M. Pignon, for French civilians to evacuate Hanoi, and declared that the Tonkin delta would be held. He set about organizing a peripheral defense around Hanoi and Haiphong, digging in, constructing mutually supporting positions having adequate fields of fire, organizing mobile reserve units for counterattack at threatened points. And, most important in the minds of American military observers in Indochina, he began planning for offensive operations aimed at defeating the Viet Minh on Communist-held ground.

MAAG Indochina

The dramatic entrance of General de Lattre upon the cluttered stage of Indochina presaged a change in the French attitude toward the American military aid program and toward the MAAG in Saigon. While welcoming American assistance the former French commanders had shown considerable suspicion of American military personnel sent to Saigon to administer the program. Upon their arrival in Indochina General Carpentier had made the observation, tinged with asperity, that the group was larger than he had anticipated and had arrived without his agreement. At the end of August, the first full month of MAAG activity in Saigon, Mr. Gullion reported "some atmosphere of reluctance about French cooperation." He attributed this to the fact that the French High Command had not understood the necessity for, or the advantages of, having the MAAG in Indochina, and had even mistaken its functions. Perhaps more important for explaining the French attitude were the fears of some officials that the MAAG personnel would attempt to interfere excessively in the political and military affairs of Indochina. Despite some improvement in MAAG's relations with the French during the immediately ensuing months the latter continued to regard the group with something less than enthusiastic approval.[19]

---

19. (S) Msg, Gullion to State Dept, "MDAP Monthly Report No. 1 (August 1950)," 20 Sep 50; (S) Msg, Gullion to SecState, "MDAP Monthly Report No. 2 (September 1950)," 6 Nov 50; (S) Msg, Gullion to SecState, "MDAP Monthly Report No. 3 (October 1950)," 1 Dec 50. All in G-3 091 China, sec II A, bk I, Case 31.

From the time the first elements of MAAG arrived in Indochina at the end of July the agency was hampered in accomplishing its mission by several annoying conditions. The chief functions of the group were to screen and pass on to the Department of Defense the French requests for military aid, and then to observe and supervise the distribution and use of the equipment that was provided under the program. For these tasks the thirty-eight officers and enlisted men authorized for the MAAG were too few. And although the authorization was later increased the group continued to suffer from a shortage of personnel.

Screening of French requests was performed on the basis of the Joint Chiefs of Staff screening criteria (to eliminate non-military items, etc.), French and Indochinese needs, and availability of personnel trained to use the materiel requested. To accomplish this screening the cooperation of the French military authorities was necessary, but it was not immediately forthcoming. The MDAP monthly report from Saigon for October 1950 contains a somewhat bitter complaint about the poor liaison between French officials and the MAAG. This, according to the report, "led the French Command to deny the abandonment of Cao Bang even after it had taken place, to withhold information on the extent of French losses in the North, to keep the Legation and MAAG in ignorance of military developments in Tonkin and of French plans for coping with the new situation." Both Legation and MAAG "made every effort to impress upon the French authorities the imperative need for adequate military briefings if the MDAP were to have its maximum effect and by the end of the month definite signs of improvement were to be noted."[20] Nevertheless, sufficient information on the status of French-Indochinese forces continued to be unavailable to MAAG. No troop bases, or even order of battle, were furnished by the French, and screening had to be done by "educated guess." Furthermore, the loose French supply and accounting procedures often made it impossible for the Americans

---

20. (S) Msg, Gullion to SecState, "MDAP Monthly Report No. 3 (October 1950)," 1 Dec 50, same file.

to determine exactly what the forces in the peninsula had on hand. As a result MAAG personnel sometimes hesitated to blue-pencil French requests even when they felt them to be excessive.[21]

In observing and supervising the use of end items provided under MDAP the Army Section of the MAAG was impeded by French restrictions. Because Air Force equipment was employed chiefly at fixed installations, such as airbases, its day-to-day use and maintenance could be checked. Similarly the Naval member of MAAG could inspect ships, which were in more or less constant use and readiness. Army members, however, were not allowed to go into the combat areas to view the employment and care of ground force supplies. Inspections of troop units were scheduled beforehand with the French Command. Units to be inspected had been sent to rearward areas and prepared for the event. The entire inspection was performed with parade-ground spit and polish and with French officers accompanying the American, partly, it would seem, to make sure that the latter did not see too much. Moreover, such inspections were limited to MDAP equipment only, the French jealously guarded from view that which they themselves had furnished. The value of the inspections for calculating French needs and for determining the efficiency with which American materiel was used was undoubtedly impaired by these procedures.

For distributing MDAP equipment on its arrival in Indochina, the MAAG dealt almost exclusively with French authorities, who obviously desired to keep contacts between Americans and Vietnamese at a minimum. Not until the end of 1951 was the MAAG able to require that signatures of Vietnamese officials appear on manifests of supplies

---

21. (C) Interv, Capt W.W. Hoare, Jr., USA, with Lt Col S. Fred Cummings, USA (Logistics Officer, Army Sec, MAAG Indochina from Nov 51 to Nov 52), 1 Nov 54, Memo in JCS HS files.

delivered to native units. There is no evidence, however, that earlier shipments destined for any of the Associated States were withheld by French authorities.[22]

By the end of December 1950 the change wrought by General de Lattre was already noticeable and the MDAP report for January 1951 stated that "relations between the MAAG and the French Command were unquestionably better than at any previous point of the Indochina program."[23] This fact testifies to a different attitude toward MDAP on the part of the new commander than that of General Carpentier who, as late as November, was described as "mildly skeptical about American aid."[24]

Pentalateral Mutual Defense Assistance Pact

On 23 December at Saigon Minister Heath signed an "Agreement for Mutual Defense Assistance in Indochina" with representatives of the Associated States and France. This agreement, which had been in the process of negotiation for several months, provided for military assistance, in accordance with Public Law 329, 81st Congress, as amended, to the four states fighting in the peninsula. Generally similar to MDAP agreements between the United States and other recipient nations, the agreement stated: "With respect to aid received from the United States of America, each State shall designate a member or representative of the High Military Committee and authorize such person to receive . . . the title to the materials received." With respect to MAAG Indochina, the Associated States and France were "to extend to such personnel facilities freely

---

22. Ibid.; (C) Interv, Hoare with Maj H.L. St.-Onge, USA, and Maj Edwin J. Nelson, USA, both at various times Adjutants of MAAG Indochina and aides to Brig Gen Francis G. Brink (first CG of MAAG Indochina), 27 Oct 54, Memo on file in JCS HS.
23. (S) Msg, Heath to State Dept, "MDAP Monthly General Report for the Month of January 1951," 23 May 51, G-3 091 Indo China, sec II A, bk I, Case 31.
24. (TS) Memo, Marshal of the Royal Air Force the Lord Tedder to Gen Omar N. Bradley, 9 Nov 50, CCS 092 Asia (6-25-48) sec 8.

and fully to carry out their assigned responsibilities, including observation of the progress and the technical use made of the assistance granted."[25]

Development of U.S. Policy toward Indochina, July-December 1950

At the time of the outbreak of the Korean Conflict American policy toward Indochina was that set forth in NSC 64 and NSC 48/2. There was general agreement among the governmental agencies concerned that the peninsula, and especially Tonkin, provided the keystone of the Southeast Asian arch without which the free nations in that area would crumble. There was also a general agreement that everything possible must be done to maintain Indochina, although with its forces tied down in Korea the United States would have to confine itself to providing military aid in the form of munitions and equipment. Within the government in Washington, however, it was the Department of Defense that showed itself the most anxious about the dangers in Southeast Asia, and this anxiety was stimulated by constant roweling on the part of the Joint Chiefs of Staff. The Chiefs seemed to see more clearly than the State Department the threat to the United States strategic position in the Far East inherent in a Communist Viet Nam, and they were more eager to act with the resources at hand in order to salvage it for the free world.

This advanced position of the Joint Chiefs of Staff became clear in the first week of July, when the Chiefs were required to comment on a National Security Council (NSC) paper dealing with "The Position and Actions of the United States with Respect to Possible Further Soviet Moves in the Light of the Korean Situation." How to counter an offensive by the Viet Minh alone was not the question here. It was rather what to do in the event the Peiping satellite of Moscow should provide overt military

---

25. State Dept, "Mutual Defense Assistance in Indochina-Agreement between the United States of America and Cambodia, France, Laos, and Viet Nam," Treaties and Other International Acts Series 2447 (GPO, Washington 25, D.C.), p. 4.

assistance to Ho Chi Minh, an action which seemed not improbable in view of the Korean example. If, said the Joint Chiefs of Staff, such assistance is given the Viet Minh forces, "the United States should increase its MDAP assistance to the French and urge the French to continue an active defense, with the United States giving consideration to the provision of air and naval assistance." Also, the United States should ask the United Nations to call upon its members to make forces available to resist the Chinese Communist aggression.[26] On 14 August, in commenting on a revision of the same NSC paper, the Joint Chiefs of Staff recommended that in the event of overt attack by organized Chinese Communist forces against Indochina the United States should support France and the Associated States, in concert with the United Kingdom, accelerate and expand the present military assistance program, and mobilize to the extent necessary to meet the situation. Other government agencies represented in the NSC, however, drew back from such a strong position. The National Security Council's decision was to accept the recommendation of the Joint Chiefs of Staff on supporting French and Indochinese forces and on stepping up MDAP assistance. Mobilization, however, was not accepted and was replaced with a stipulation that, should the Chinese Communists attack in Indochina, the United States should not permit itself to become engaged in a general war with Communist China.[27]

A similar difference in attitude appeared during the preparations for talks between the Foreign Ministers of France and Great Britain and the Secretary of State in September. A State Department position paper on Indochina was submitted to the Joint Chiefs of Staff for comment and recommendation. This paper recommended that Secretary of State Dean Acheson emphasize, in speaking to the French, the importance of liberal implementation of the Elysee agreements and that despite the urgency of the military

---

26. (TS) JCS 1924/14, 5 Jul 50, CCS 092 USSR (3-27-45) sec 45.
27. (TS) JCS 1924/26, 14 Aug 50, same file, sec 48; (TS) NSC 73/4, 25 Aug 50, same file, sec 49.

situation the political program must not be delayed. The French should be urged to speed the formation of new national armies and to intensify their information activities in Asia. The Secretary was also to recommend staff talks between the United States, United Kingdom, and France regarding "pooling and coordination of resources in Southeast Asia in the event of invasion."[28]

In their comments on this paper the Joint Chiefs of Staff noted that

> the recommendations as a whole do not reflect the urgency which, from the military point of view, should be attached to planning, preparing for, and providing adequate means to insure the security of Indochina. . . . Intelligence reports indicate that the Viet Minh military preparations may be sufficiently complete in the very near future to launch a large-scale effort to seize control of all of Indochina. Prior to 1 January 1951, the currently planned level of United States military aid to the French and native allied forces of Indochina should increase their military capabilities but not to the extent of counterbalancing Viet Minh capabilities. In view of these considerations, the Joint Chiefs of Staff suggest that the proposed United States position take cognizance that the situation in Indochina is to be viewed with alarm and that urgent and drastic action is required by the French if they are to avoid military defeat in Indochina. . . .

The Joint Chiefs of Staff recommended the French be urged to conclude the Pau conference immediately and successfully, to give widespread publicity to its accomplishments, and to initiate bolder political measures. In regard to the proposed military staff talks, the Joint Chiefs of Staff asked that the "coordination of resources" be changed to "coordination of operations." They also wished Secretary Acheson to indicate to the French that

---

28. (S) State Dept SFM D-7/1c, "September Foreign Ministers Meeting - Indochina," 28 Aug 50, CCS 092 Asia (6-25-48) sec 6.

increases in military aid would be provided in accordance with operational plans acceptable to the United States and compatible with United States capabilities. But, because of the situation in Korea, the Joint Chiefs of Staff asked that the Secretary "Inform the French that, regardless of current U.S. commitments for provision of certain assistance to French Indochina, the United States will not commit any of its armed forces under present circumstances."29

The records of the September Tripartite Foreign Ministers Meetings do not indicate that Secretary Acheson exerted much pressure on the French in accordance with the desires of the Joint Chiefs of Staff. He seems instead to have wished to let the Joint Chiefs of Staff work out their problems in the proposed military staff talks. In accordance with the National Security Council's policy and the recommendation of the Joint Chiefs of Staff the Secretary refused a French request for the United States to furnish tactical air support for the French forces.30

In October the concern of the Joint Chiefs of Staff for the preservation from Communism of Southeast Asia prompted them to press for a stronger and more precise American policy than that contained in NSC 64. They were particularly conscious of the fact that there was "no clearly stated United States policy covering the contingency of an attack on Indochina by Viet Minh forces supplied and/or otherwise aided by Communist China."31

---

29. (S) Memo, Bradley to Louis Johnson, "Indochina," 7 Sep 50, same file.
30. (S) FMN Min - 4, "Minutes of the Fourth Meeting held in the Waldorf-Astoria," 14 Sep 50; (TS) Memo of Conv, New York, bet Robert Schuman, Foreign Minister of France, and Secretary of State Dean Acheson, (12 Sep 50). Both in State Dept files.
31. (TS) JCS 1992/29, 7 Oct 50, CCS 092 Asia (6-25-48) sec 6.

The deteriorating situation in Indochina after the Cao Bang incident demanded a revision of American policy. And the apparent collapse of Communist resistance in North Korea seemed to offer the opportunity, for if the Korean Conflict could be quickly wound up the United States global strategic position would be greatly strengthened and some American armed forces would be freed for employment in other areas.

On 18 October General J. Lawton Collins laid before his colleagues on the Joint Chiefs of Staff a written proposal for reappraising the government's stand. "I believe that the loss of Indochina would be such a blow to the U.S. strategic position in the cold war that its loss is unacceptable, if we can possibly avoid it," he wrote. "All practicable measures" to deny Indochina to the Communists should be explored, including "even the use of U.S. armed forces if the situation can be saved in no other way." The Army Chief of Staff forwarded a study prepared by G-3, recommending that the United States "be prepared to commit its own armed force" if all else failed. But any such commitment, it was added, must be subject to important qualifications: it must not endanger the US strategic position in the event of a world war, it must offer a reasonable chance of success, and it should be done in concert with other UN members.[32]

The Joint Chiefs of Staff considered General Collins' views in preparing comments on a proposal by the Southeast Asia Aid Policy Committee for a new National Security Council decision of United States policy toward Indochina. This proposal roughly conformed to the ideas of the Joint Chiefs of Staff, although it did not provide for the use of American armed forces and in their opinion did not reflect the urgency of the current situation in Indochina.[33] The Chiefs, however, delayed their comments while awaiting a report from Brigadier General Francis G. Brink, commander

---

32. (TS) Memo by CSA, "Possible Future Action in Indochina," 18 Oct 50, same file, sec 7.
33. (TS) SEAAPC, SEAC D-21, Rev 1, "Proposed Statement of U.S. Policy on Indo-China for NSC Consideration," 11 Oct 50, same file, sec 6.

of the MAAG in Saigon. They had instructed General Brink
to confer with General Juin during the latter's visit to
Indochina and to furnish them an estimate of the chances
of French success against the Viet Minh. By the time
the Joint Chiefs of Staff were ready to present their
recommendations on the paper by the Southeast Asia Aid
Policy Committee the Chinese Communists had struck in
North Korea and a longer war, tying down United States
forces for some time to come, was in prospect. The
Chiefs would not, therefore, advise using American combat forces in Indochina in the foreseeable future.

The Joint Chiefs of Staff sent their recommendations
on the Southeast Asia Aid Policy Committee's proposal to
the Secretary of Defense on 28 November. But instead of
merely commenting on the paper they proposed their own
broad policy, which was, in effect, a revision of NSC 64.
As NSC 64/1 it was presented on 21 December to the National
Security Council for consideration.

The proposal by the Joint Chiefs of Staff listed both
short-term and long-term objectives for the United States
in Indochina, of which the short-term aims were the most
significant for this history. These objectives were the
following:

SHORT-TERM OBJECTIVES

a. The United States should take action, as a
matter of urgency, by all means practicable short of
the actual employment of United States military forces,
to deny Indochina to communism.
b. As long as the present situation exists, the
United States should continue to insure that the primary responsibility for the restoration of peace and
security in Indochina rests with the French.
c. The United States should seek to develop its
military assistance program for Indochina based on
an over-all military plan prepared by the French,
concurred in by the Associated States of Indochina,
and acceptable to the United States.
(1) Both the plan and the program should
be developed and implemented as a matter of
urgency. It should be clearly understood,
however, that United States acceptance of the

plan is limited to the logistical support which the United States may agree to furnish. The aid provided under the program should be furnished to the French in Indochina and to the Associated States. The allocation of United States military assistance as between the French and the national armies of Indochina should be approved by the French and United States authorities in Indochina.

(2) Popular support of the Government by the Indochinese people is essential to a favorable settlement of the security problem of Indochina. Therefore, as a condition to the provision of those further increases in military assistance to Indochina necessary for the implementation of an agreed over-all military plan, the United States Government should obtain assurances from the French Government that:

    (a) A program providing for the eventual self-government of Indochina either within or outside of the French Union will be developed, made public, and implementation initiated at once in order to strengthen the national spirit of the Indochinese in opposition to communism.

    (b) National armies of the Associated States of Indochina will be organized as a matter of urgency. While it is doubtful that the build-up of these armies can be accomplished in time to contribute significantly to the present military situation, the direct political and psychological benefits to be derived from this course would be great and would thus result in immediate, although indirect, military benefits.

    (c) Pending the formation and training of Indochinese national armies as effective units, and as an interim emergency measure, France will dispatch sufficient additional armed forces to Indochina to insure that the restoration of peace and internal security in that country will be accomplished in accordance with the timetable of the over-all military plan for Indochina.

(d) France will change its political and military concepts in Indochina to:

i. Eliminate its policy of "colonialism."

ii. Provide proper tutelage to the Associated States.

iii. Insure that a suitable military command structure, unhampered by political interference, is established to conduct effective and appropriate military operations. The effective implementation of these changes will require competent and efficient political and military leaders who will be able to cope with the conditions in that country.

(3) At an appropriate time the United States should institute checks to satisfy itself that the conditions set forth in subparagraph c-(2) above are being fulfilled.

d. The United States should exert all practicable political and diplomatic measures required to obtain the recognition of the Associated States by the other non-communist states of Southeast and South Asia.

e. In the event of overt attack by organized Chinese Communist forces against Indochina, the United States should not permit itself to become engaged in a general war with Communist China but should, in concert with the United Kingdom, support France and the Associated States by all means short of the actual employment of United States military forces. This support should include appropriate expansion of the present military assistance program and endeavors to induce States in the neighborhood of Indochina to commit armed forces to resist the aggression.

f. The United States should immediately reconsider its policy toward Indochina whenever it appears that the French Government may abandon its military position in that country or plans to refer the problem of Indochina to the United Nations. Unless the situation throughout the world generally, and Indochina specifically, changes materially, the United

States should seek to dissuade the French from referring the Indochina question to the United Nations.

    g. Inasmuch as the United States-sponsored resolution, "Uniting for Peace," has been adopted by the General Assembly of the United Nations, and should a situation develop in Indochina in a manner similar to that in Korea in which United Nations forces were required, the United States would then probably be morally obligated to contribute its armed forces designated for service on behalf of the United Nations. It is, therefore, in the interests of the United States to take such action in Indochina as would forestall the need for the General Assembly to invoke the provisions of the resolution, "Uniting for Peace."

    5. The Joint Chiefs of Staff recommended the following long-term objectives for Indochina:

LONG-TERM OBJECTIVES

    a. United States security interests demand that this government, by all means short of the actual employment of United States military forces, seek to prevent the further spread of communism in Southeast Asia generally and, in particular, in French Indochina.

    b. The United States should seek to insure the establishment of such conditions in Indochina that no foreign armed forces will be required for the maintenance of internal security.

    c. The United States should continue to press the French to carry out in letter and in spirit the program referred to in paragraph 4-c-(2)-(a) above, providing for the eventual self-government of Indochina either within or outside of the French Union.

    d. The United States should continue to favor the entry of the three Associated States of Indochina into the United Nations.

    e. The United States should encourage the establishment of an appropriate form of regional security arrangement embracing Indochina and the other countries of Southeast Asia under Articles 51 and 52 of the United Nations Charter.[34]

---

[34]. (TS) NSC 64/1, 21 Dec 50, same file, sec 9.

An "Analysis," written by the Joint Strategic Survey Committee, accompanied the draft policy of the Joint Chiefs of Staff and contained an explanation of the strategic concept that kept the Joint Chiefs of Staff from recommending armed intervention. Involvement of United States forces against Viet Minh forces, according to the Joint Strategic Survey Committee, would be likely to lead to a war with Communist China, which would probably have to be taken as a prelude to global war. The chief enemy in a global war, "in all probability," would be the USSR, and the principal theater would be Western Europe. And the strength of the Western Powers was insufficient to fight a war on the Asian mainland and at the same time accomplish the predetermined Allied objectives in Europe.[35] This line of reasoning was the one generally accepted by the American Government at the time.

Despite the sense of urgency communicated by the strong words of the Joint Chiefs of Staff, NSC 64/1 was not adopted by the National Security Council. Although the Chiefs complained intermittently about the lack of a more definite statement of policy, NSC 64 remained the basic United States position on Indochina for months. Nevertheless, the Joint Chiefs of Staff strove to realize the objectives that they advocated and other agencies of the government gradually moved toward their point of view. The policy enunciated in NSC 64, therefore, although not superseded, was at least modified by the prevailing climate of opinion in Washington, and this progression toward a stronger stand on the Indochina question was apparent at the end of 1950.

---

35. Ibid.

CHAPTER IX

FROM 1 JANUARY 1951 TO THE DEATH OF GENERAL DE LATTRE ON 11 JANUARY 1952

Military Situation in Indochina Improves

During 1951 the French military position in Indochina showed a definite, but not constant, improvement. In the early part of the year General de Lattre, by consolidating his defenses, was able to repulse a series of attacks and inflict heavy losses on the Viet Minh while keeping his own relatively low. In November the French Commander undertook a limited, though not particularly well-considered, offensive in the Hoa Binh area southwest of Hanoi.

The successes achieved by the French forces under de Lattre were made possible by American military assistance. The effect of United States support in the civil war became apparent in mid-January, when the Franco-Vietnamese forces defeated the largest offensive, in terms of manpower and military organization, that the Viet Minh had yet mounted. It was estimated that about 40,000 rebel troops fought in the battle of Vinh Yen, and that their losses may have been as high as 6,000 effectives. Minister Heath reported from Saigon that the French victory could "in very large part be attributed to the action of French air, artillery, especially 105 mm. howitzers, and napalm, all of which were provided to the French Forces under the MDAP." The aid program, he continued, "has thus in its first full-scale test been fully vindicated."[1]

A certain amount, perhaps the decisive part, of the equipment used in repulsing the Viet Minh offensive, arrived at Hanoi only in the nick of time and as the result of personal intervention by General Brink, who asked General MacArthur's headquarters to have materiel shipped from FECOM stocks outside the established MDAP

---

1. (S) Rpt, Heath to State Dept, "MDAP Monthly General Report for the Month of January 1951," 23 May 51, G-3 091 Indo China, sec II-A, bk I, DRB AGO.

channels. The value of this assistance was acknowledged by General de Lattre to the American Minister, the Chief of the MAAG, and to the press. His public expressions of gratitude went far toward promoting better relations between the French and the Americans in Indochina. The attitude of the French toward the MAAG changed from one of suspicion and annoyance to one of qualified approval and eased the work of that agency during the months that followed.2

After the battle of Vinh Yen the French and Vietnamese forces undertook a series of minor advances, recapturing several outposts around the Tonkin delta perimeter. At the same time they repulsed a number of Viet Minh attacks, reportedly inflicting severe losses on the enemy, and forged ahead with a campaign to clean the rebels out of the delta area itself. During the first week of April the French reported intercepting a radio broadcast by Ho Chi Minh, ordering his troops, who had been maneuvering in daylight in organized units since January, to revert to guerrilla warfare. But while this report indicated some discouragement in Viet Minh ranks, the rebels did not immediately give up the initiative in Indochina. Their attacks continued, though in general with little or no success, until the rainy season slowed all military operations in the country.3

With the return of good weather in the autumn the French returned to the offensive for the first time since their defeat at Cao Bang in the preceding year. In a well-executed, surprise move they advanced out of the delta to capture and fortify positions in the Cho Ben-Hoa Binh area southwest of Hanoi. The purposes of this operation were political as well as military. De Lattre hoped thus to disrupt Viet Minh communications and collection of rice, while impressing public opinion with his initiative and skill and demonstrating to the United States the fact that he was using American equipment to good advantage.

---

2. Ibid.; (S) Rpt, Heath to State Dept, "MDAP Monthly General Report for the Month of February 1951," 23 May 51, same file; NY Times, 23 Jan 51.
3. Ibid.; NY Times, 15 Feb, 7 Apr, 24 Apr, 5 Jun, 7 Jun, 8 Jun, 10 Jun 51.

The so-called Hoa Binh offensive, however, proved to be something less than a strategic success. It overextended French lines and weakened the defense of the Hanoi perimeter, opening the door to heavy Viet Minh infiltration into the delta area. By the end of the year it was apparent to American observers in Indochina that the French would be hard pressed to maintain the position at Hoa Binh (which was being subjected to counterattack by regular Viet Minh troops), since at the same time they had to protect the delta from rebel infiltration.[4] Nevertheless, the French and Vietnamese forces were in a far better condition with respect to training, spirit, equipment, organization, and strategical situation at the time of de Lattre's death than when he had taken over the High Command.

Political Situation in Viet Nam during 1951

The general improvement in the military situation in Indochina during 1951 brought no corresponding development in Vietnamese internal political affairs. The basic problem continued to be lack of public support for the Bao Dai government and for the struggle against Ho Chi Minh. Behind the antipathy and indifference of the natives lay their unabated dislike of the French colonial officials, who seldom relaxed their resistance to the reforms dictated from Paris, or ceased to interfere in the internal affairs of Viet Nam. Bao Dai could not shake off the label that identified his regime with French policies and his new army with the French High Command. It is not inexplicable, therefore, that the Vietnamese National Army failed to capture the imagination and loyalty of the people, or that Premier Tran Van Huu was unable to form a government truly representative of the country.

Despite the concessions to Indochinese nationalism embodied in the Pau Conventions, the reduction of French control over the economic and political life of the

---

4. (S) Msg, Gullion to State Dept, "MDAP Monthly Report No. 14 (November 1951)," 8 Jan 52; (S) Msg, Gullion to State Dept, "MDAP Monthly Report No. 15 (December 1951)," 21 Mar 52. Both in G-3 091 Indo China, sec I-A, bk I, DRB AGO.

Associated States was scarcely visible to the average man in Viet Nam. The turnover of authority was painfully slow and only grudgingly conceded by French officials. For some of the delays the French were not willfully responsible. It was difficult, for instance, to find in Viet Nam men sufficiently experienced in governmental administration to handle the agencies to be transferred. But the easing of the military situation, which ought to have provided breathing space for establishing the new system, seems instead to have reduced in the French the sense of urgency for carrying out the political reforms initiated in more trying times. Mr. Gullion reported from Saigon that as early as March the now more confident French officials, including General de Lattre, had begun to utter doubts about the wisdom of maintaining the then current tempo and limits of Vietnamese independence.[5] Even the United States Government, which had been pushing the French toward more rapid reforms, relaxed its pressure. The official attitude of the State Department was that the Pau Conventions, formally instituted in December 1950, had satisfied Indochinese nationalst aims. American officials, however, continued urging the French not to lag in implementing the conventions or in establishing the national armies.[6]

The equivocal character of French policies was reflected in the actions and attitudes of General de Lattre who, until his death on 11 January 1952, was probably the most important single factor in Vietnamese politics. On the one hand the High Commissioner considered himself a "kingmaker," who would go down in history as the father of Indochinese independence. In April, at a ceremony commemorating the victory of Vinh Yen, he pledged himself to "fulfill the independence of Vietnam." "I have come," he announced, "to accomplish your independence, not to limit it."[7] On the

---

5. (S) Rpt, Gullion to State Dept, "MDAP Monthly Report for Indo-China for the Month of March 1951," 19 May 51, same file, sec II-A, bk I.
6. (TS) State Dept, Pleven D-1/1, "Negotiating Papers for Truman-Pleven Talks - Jan 29-30 - U.S. Aid to Indochina," CCS 092 Asia (6-25-48) sec 10.
7. (TS) SM-143-51, 16 Jan 51, same file; (S) Geneva Conf Background Paper, Indochina Chronology, pp. 64-65.

other hand, General de Lattre was a representative of France and in his mouth the word "independence" meant independence within the French Union. A few weeks before uttering his April pledge the general had remarked to Minister Heath, "'these states (the Associated States of Indochina) could hardly hope to enjoy the same status as members of the British Commonwealth since France had spent too much to protect them.'"[8] That the Indochinese would never be satisfied with the restricted independence the French had in mind was to become increasingly apparent as the months passed.

Nor were the native nationalists content with the rate at which authority was being transferred to the Bao Dai government. General de Lattre seems to have wished to clear up the Viet Minh rebellion before devoting much of his time and energy to political reorganization. Certainly the demands of the military situation were more immediate, and for this reason the one reform that the High Commissioner was most active in accomplishing was the establishment of the Vietnamese National Army, which he expected to use in achieving a satisfactory end to the war. But his attitude in this respect was not conducive to harmonious relations with the Vietnamese government and people, who wanted to see immediate evidence of independence.

Furthermore, the general was impatient of administrative details and with the failures and mistakes of the inexperienced native officials. This trait caused him to intervene personally in the internal affairs of Viet Nam, much to the annoyance of Bao Dai and his premier, Tran Van Huu. During the year the Emperor frequently complained to Minister Heath about de Lattre's interference in such matters, and referred with disgust to the "colonial-minded advisors" retained by the High Commissioner.[9]

---

8. (S) Rpt, Gullion to State Dept, "MDAP Monthly Report for Indochina for the Month of March 1951," 19 May 51, G-3 091 Indo China, sec II-A, bk I, DRB AGO.
9. Ibid.; (S) Rpt, Gullion to State Dept, "MDAP Monthly Report for May 1951," 22 Jun 51, same file.

Cabinet Crisis in Viet Nam

On 20 January the Viet Nam cabinet was dissolved with the object of forming a new government, still under Tran Van Huu, but with a broader base representative of the major non-Communist political groups. This attempt to draw into the government the dissident nationalist parties ended in a fiasco, presaging the failure of the Premier ever to win any great measure of popular support. After a month of negotiations, intrigues, and squabbles Tran Van Huu emerged with a cabinet very much like the last. The Premier also held the portfolios of the Defense Ministry, the Ministry of Foreign Affairs, and the Ministry of the Interior.[10] Just how much General de Lattre and other French officials were involved in the governmental shake-up cannot be determined, but Mr. Gullion reported that in April "Some of the animosity at French intervention in the cabinet crisis in February had begun to subside."[11]

National Army of Viet Nam - A Political Failure

The reshuffling of Huu's government was only one of the factors that delayed the organization of the Vietnamese National Army during the first half of 1951. A similar crisis in France, which began at the end of February and lasted until 9 March, resulted in the replacement of the Pleven cabinet by one under Henri Queuille. The uncertain conditions accompanying the change seemed to paralyze activity in Saigon as well as in Paris. In addition, the development of the army was impeded by disagreements between the French and the Vietnamese governments over the amount of money each should contribute to its support, by the failure of the Saigon government to complete its budget, by the lack of trained cadres, and by the inability of Premier Huu to find a suitable Defense Minister and a Chief of Staff. Also, while MDAP materiel for the French Union Forces was

---

10. (S) Rpt, Heath to State Dept, "MDAP Monthly General Report for the Month of February 1951," 23 May 51, same file.
11. (S) Rpt, Gullion to State Dept, "MDAP Monthly Report for April 1951," 21 May 51, same file, bk II.

arriving at a generally good rate (seven ships unloaded over 10,000 long tons at Saigon during April), equipment for the projected Vietnamese battalions was coming in slowly. And while recruiting for twenty-four battalions was proceeding satisfactorily, the new army was meeting competition from the French Union Forces, who recruited locally more than 7,000 Vietnamese during March and April. Not unnaturally, such activity on the part of the French gave rise to changes of bad faith in their agreement to establish national armed forces in Viet Nam.[12]

Despite confusion and delay some increase in the national armies of the Associated States was achieved during the year, mainly owing to the efforts of General de Lattre. As of 1 May the regular Army of Viet Nam consisted of about 38,500 men. Cambodia and Laos, whose needs were comparatively small, had under arms 7,500 and 4,000 men, respectively. The program for the Vietnamese army called for the formation of four divisions during 1951. A subsequent expansion to eight divisions was decided upon later in the year. By the time of General de Lattre's death the Vietnamese Regular Army comprised thirty-seven battalions, with a strength of approximately 65,000 men. These were augmented by various auxiliary units (59,000 men) and semimilitary forces. In the Associated States as a whole, men in the regular and auxiliary forces numbered over 132,000; those in semi-military forces about 76,500.[13] Had they not been seriously deficient in training, leadership, and the will to fight, these forces combined with the 189,000 troops of the French Union in Indochina, should have given the French High Command an overwhelming superiority against the Viet Minh.

The primary purpose in establishing the National armies had been to stimulate public enthusiasm for the "independent" governments of the Associated States and for the struggle against the Viet Minh Communists. In

---
12. Ibid.
13. (S) JIC 529/10, 10 Jan 52, CCS 092 Asia (6-25-48) sec 22 BP pt 3; (TS) JIC 529/9, 2 Jan 52, same file, sec 22; (TS) JIC 529/4, 20 Jun 51, same file, sec 15; (TS) Navarre Briefing Doc, Jun 53, in OMA files.

this respect, the project cannot be described as a great success. The measure of its achievement in 1951 can be seen in the results of the various mobilization measures authorized by the Vietnamese cabinet on 15 July. By a series of decrees the Huu government asserted the principle of obligatory military service and authorized the conscription of 60,000 men in four increments for a period of two months training after which they were to form a partially trained, readily available reserve. It also announced its plans to draft 800 specialists and technicians for the National Army and to select 1,000 candidates for training as reserve officers. That this program did not meet the demands of the situation was the firm conviction of observers in the American Legation, who reported:

> Actually, the severely limited scope of the planned mobilization falls far short of supplying Viet Nam's basic military needs. The calling up of 60,000 men for only two months of training is an expensive gesture which is ill afforded by the shaky military budget; further, two months of training will provide no semblance of a trained manpower pool. Similarly, the callup of only 1000 candidates for reserve officer training is woefully inadequate of estimated requirement; at least four times that number of both categories of personnel are needed to round out the present four division national army. This estimate, of course, makes no allowance for normal attrition or for the necessity of a rapidly expanded force.[14]

But even this modest program fell short of realization. Little more than half of the specially selected candidates ever reported for training. The second increment of conscripts was released after only five weeks training and the fourth increment was never summoned at all. Of the first increment of 15,000 men, only 7 per cent could be persuaded to enlist in the

---

14. (S) Rpt, Gullion to State Dept, "MDAP Monthly Report for August 1951," 13 Nov 51, G-3 092 Indo China, sec II-A, bk III, DRB AGO.

National Army after completing their training. And the quota of 800 specialists that were to be drafted was reduced to 500.[15]

The response to the mobilization program was scarcely an indication of popular support for the Viet Nam government or the National Army. Some French officials blamed the non-arrival of MDAP materiel as well as financial difficulties for the indifferent success of the project. But American observers noted that the Vietnamese government had done a poor job of selling mobilization to a people for whom the Confucian contempt of military service was traditional. Public apathy, which the National Army and mobilization were intended to decrease, actually was the chief stumbling block of the mobilization scheme.[16]

Another mark of the National Army's failure as a means of exploiting patriotic sentiment was the defection of some of the Cao Daist forces. In June the Cao Dai Chief of Staff led 2,500 of his troops out of Viet Nam into Cambodia to "await developments." The immediate causes of this action probably were attempts to subordinate the suppletory forces, such as those of the Cao Dai, to the National Army, and the curtailment of the subsidy paid by the French to the Cao Dai troops. A more basic reason, however, was the feeling that Viet Nam had not been given full independence and was not likely to achieve it under Tran Van Huu.[17]

---

15. Ibid.; (S) Rpt, Gullion to State Dept, "MDAP Monthly Report No. 16 (January 1952)," 24 Mar 52, same file, sec I-A, bk I; (S) Rpt, Gullion to State Dept, "MDAP Monthly Report No. 19 (April 1952)," 23 May 52, same file.
16. Ibid.; (S) Rpt, Gullion to State Dept, "MDAP Monthly Report for October, 1951," 11 Dec 51, same file, sec I.
17. (S) Geneva Conf Background Paper, Indochina Chronology, p. 65.

De Lattre-Huu Conflict

Toward the end of the year the political situation in Viet Nam was further complicated by growing enmity between the High Commissioner and the Premier, presaging the fall of Tran Van Huu in 1952. General de Lattre had long been disturbed by the inability of Huu to develop the vigorous and popular government necessary to military as well as political success. Also, with some reason, he had misgivings concerning Huu's use of state funds and the Premier's monopoly of the most important posts in the government. Huu, on the other hand, seemed convinced that the High Commissioner was bent on having the determining voice in all Vietnamese affairs, whether purely internal or foreign. The tensions between the two men, which persisted until de Lattre's death, exacerbated the old French-Vietnamese quarrels and undoubtedly weakened the efforts of both in the war against the Viet Minh.[18]

The conflict, which was actually a struggle for control of Vietnamese policy, became apparent in October when both men returned from visits to the United States. By November General de Lattre was hinting that before too long he might use his "influence" to replace Huu. The Premier, feeling more and more insecure, waved the banner of nationalism, sought the support of dissident groups, including the Cao Dai and the Dai Viet, and revived certain democratic projects, such as the establishment of popular assemblies. At the end of November, when de Lattre and Huu went to Paris to attend the first meeting of the High Council of the French Union, their rivalry became even more bitter. It ended, of course, with de Lattre's death, but by that time Huu's position vis-a-vis the French had grown so weak that his government fell only a few months later.[19]

---

18. (S) Rpt, Gullion to State Dept, "MDAP Monthly Report No. 14 (November 1951)," 8 Jan 52; (S) Rpt, Gullion to State Dept, "MDAP Monthly Report No. 15 (December 1951)," 21 Mar 52. Both in G-3 091 Indo China, sec I-A, bk I, DRB AGO.
19. Ibid.

First Meeting of the High Council of the French Union, 29-30 November

The de Lattre-Huu dispute affected the meeting of the High Council of the French Union in a manner disappointing to those Vietnamese who supported the Premier's nationalist aspirations. Before the meeting the Vietnamese delegation had been expected to press for an alteration of the quadripartite committee structure laid down in the Pau Conventions, a system permitting the French to dominate committees that supervised the governmental departments and activities of the Associated States. It was also expected to ask for admission to the United Nations (desired by the United States but considered premature by the French) and for changing the system of representation between Viet Nam and France by an exchange of ambassadors. Premier Huu, however, probably because he felt de Lattre was anxious to pull his portfolios from his grasp, refrained from risking his position by advocating ambitious reforms. The meeting never seriously tackled basic questions but contented itself with settling a few minor matters and deciding certain procedural questions, although the French did agree to UN membership for the Associated States. Once again a major inter-state conference ended without satisfying the demands of Indochinese nationalism.[20]

Everything considered, the political position of the anti-communist elements in Viet Nam improved very little during 1951. Americans in the Legation at Saigon observed a few hopeful developments such as the growth of the National Army, a revival of export trade and commerce, and the beginnings of a conscious Vietnamese administration. But the essential objective of attracting wide popular support for the government was not achieved. The French, who were given a breathing spell by de Lattre's military prowess, sank back into some of the old colonial ruts instead of building new roads to a strong Vietnamese government whose independence could be recognized and respected by loyal citizens.

---

20. Ibid.

Viet Minh

While Viet Nam was plodding toward freedom at snail's pace the Viet Minh in 1951 took the final steps in achieving an orthodox Communist organization. At two congresses in February and March the Lao Dong (Workers) Party was formed and the Viet Minh League consolidated into the Lien Viet (National United) Front. By these actions the Communists tightened their control of the Viet Minh movement, and their hard core, the Lao Dong, was officially recognized as the dominant directing force. The Lao Dong now exercised direct authority over the civilian population in the Viet Minh occupied areas, which hitherto the Communists had controlled only through their positions in the government and in the armed forces. As in almost all Communist "reforms" there was a purge of government officials at all levels. Those who remained in power were solidly Communist and supporters of the Soviet bloc of nations.[21]

Toward the end of the year the Viet Minh began to suffer severely from the defeats that General de Lattre had inflicted upon its troops. A food shortage arose when French successes interfered with Communist rice collection by tightening defenses around the rice producing areas and stiffening peasant resistance against Viet Minh demands. This resistance was also one of the factors that led to a serious financial deficit, owing to the difficulty of collecting taxes. In addition, the Viet Minh had to combat corruption and inefficiency in its own ranks. The combination of these factors, combined with the losses suffered in combat, partially offset the advantages obtained from the tighter Communist control of the rebel movement.[22]

Development of American Policy toward Indochina

Although in 1951 the French thought that they discerned an important change in the United States Government's attitude toward the Indochina War, there

---

21. (S) Geneva Conf Background Paper, Indochina Chronology, pp. 67-68.
22. Foreign Report, 6 Sep 51, pp. 7-8, Economist Newspaper Ltd., London.

was actually little modification of the basic policies laid down in the preceding year. NSC 64 was not to be superseded till June 1952, and while NSC 48/2 was replaced in May by NSC 48/5, the section of the latter paper that directly concerned Indochina provided merely for a continuation of current policies, including the decision not to commit United States armed forces.[23] Whatever evolution of policy took place was the result of American participation in various military and diplomatic conferences, of the setting up of certain machinery for liaison and consultation between the French, British, and American commands in the Far East, and of ad hoc decisions on several specific questions. None of these actions, however, either represented or occasioned any considerable alteration in American aims during the year.

Singapore Conference

The first important international military conference that concerned Indochina in this period was held at Singapore. With the concurrence of the Joint Chiefs of Staff, Secretary Acheson, during the Tripartite Foreign Ministers Meetings in September 1950, had made an agreement with the British and French that military commanders of the three nations in the Far East should meet to discuss the defense of Southeast Asia. The meeting finally took place in May, but only after the Joint Chiefs of Staff objections to holding it at all had been overridden. At the time the Chiefs had agreed to United States participation in discussions, the Korean Conflict had been going well for the United Nations forces. The Chinese intervention in October and November, however, placed such heavy demands on American fighting strength that the Joint Chiefs of Staff could visualize no practical means of assisting Indochina other than increasing the flow of supplies in the event of emergency. Therefore there was little that could be accomplished by a conference. Considering existing limitations on American action, any matters that might

---

23. (TS) NSC 48/5, 17 May 51, CCS 092 Asia (6-25-48) sec 14.

require consultation with the French in Indochina could be handled through General Brink, who had already conferred with Generals Juin and Carpentier. Furthermore, the Joint Chiefs of Staff regarded the Chinese intervention as having so changed the general strategical situation in the Far East that new basic decisions on the political level were required. Until such decisions were made there would be little value in holding the tripartite military discussions.

All of these arguments were advanced by the Joint Chiefs of Staff when they recommended to Secretary of Defense Marshall early in January that no military conference on Indochina be held in the near future.[24] But an agreement had been made, the French were insistent that the meeting be held, and the State Department was exerting polite pressure on the Department of Defense to carry out the obligation. Political considerations were therefore thought to be overriding and on 9 February Secretary Marshall directed the Joint Chiefs of Staff to proceed with the arrangements. The Joint Chiefs of Staff complied. They were resolved, however, to limit the scope of the discussions and not permit them to deal with "matters of strategy affecting United States global policies and plans." Instead of sending the Commander in Chief, Far East, who was preoccupied with the Korean operations, the Joint Chiefs directed the Commander in Chief, Pacific (CINCPAC) to designate an officer from his command to take part in the conference as the United States representative. This officer was to be assisted by General Brink.[25]

After some delay in working out arrangements and agenda for the meeting General de Lattre, General John Harding, Commander of British Forces in the Far East, and Vice Admiral A. D. Struble, USN, met in Singapore on 15 May. Before the conference, the Joint Chiefs of

---

24. (S) Memo, RAdm A. C. Davis, Dir JS, to SecDef, "Proposed Military Talks Regarding Defense of Indochina," 10 Jan 51, same file, sec 10; (S) Memo, Bradley to SecDef, same subj, 8 Dec 50, same file, sec 9.

25. Ibid.; (S) Memo, Marshall to JCS, 9 Feb 51, same file, sec 11.

Staff had made plain to the British and French their view that the discussions should be confined to studying the situation in Southeast Asia and that the conclusions reached by the participants would in no way commit their respective governments.26 And it was on this basis that the delegations at Singapore put forth their recommendations.

Although the talks were concerned with the defense of all Southeast Asia, there was general agreement that Indochina presented the most critical problem and that the defense of Tonkin was the key to the security of the entire area. The delegates in their report recommended a continuation of the accelerated delivery of material aid already programmed and the initiation of periodic meetings between military representatives of the three powers to discuss the Indochinese logistical situation. They also proposed increasing the exchange of intelligence information between the Commanders in the Far East using existing channels, and, in addition, conferences at regular intervals between the chiefs of the British and French military intelligence staffs in Singapore and Saigon, with participation by American intelligence officers. Such meetings, the conferees wrote, would help to alleviate the difficulties that all, and especially the French, were experiencing in securing adequate information about Chinese Communists armed forces and lines of communication, and about arms smuggling to communist guerrilla forces.

The delegates considered the possibility of an invasion of Indochina by the Chinese Communists, and included in their report a French estimate of the reinforcements that would be required to defend Tonkin against them. In respect to this matter, however, they made no recommendation other than that the situation and estimate of reinforcements be noted. They finished their work by making recommendations on certain specific logistical questions in Indochina, on control of contraband, and on control of shipping in Southeast Asian waters in the event the Communists began operations on the high seas.27

---

26. (TS) JCS 1992/77, 10 May 51, same file, sec 13.
27. (TS) Rpt of Singapore Conf, 19 May 51, same file, BP pt 2.

The important recommendations contained in the report of the Singapore Conference was not immediately put into effect. Instead, they provided subjects for military and political negotiations between the three governments for the rest of the year. For the most part the British and French were anxious to have them carried out. The Joint Chiefs of Staff, however, were somewhat averse to American participation in further tripartite military conversations on the defense of Indochina, including those periodic conferences on intelligence and logistics problems recommended in the report. They feared that the British and French might try to erect out of such collaborative sessions a new Combined Chiefs of Staff organization or an over-all three-power command for Southeast Asia. They wished to keep their hands free so that a new global war might not find them encumbered by pre-established combined commands (other than NATO, in which the contribution expected of the European allies justified its establishment). But disagreements between the three governments over the recommendations of the Singapore Report, as well as changing circumstances, obliged the Joint Chiefs of Staff at the end of the year to accede to participation in a new three-power military conference in January 1952.

The Pleven Visit

Even before the Singapore Conference met, and while the Joint Chiefs of Staff were still arguing against it, two bilateral meetings were held in Washington between American officials and important figures in the French Government. The first, and the more important, took place on 29-30 January when the Prime Minister of France, M. Rene Pleven, visited the United States for talks with President Truman. In a series of conversations the President and M. Pleven agreed that while it was necessary to resist aggression in the Far East, nevertheless "The U.S. and France should not over-commit themselves militarily in the Far East and thereby endanger the situation in Europe." They also agreed that the "interested nations" should maintain continuous contact on the problems of the area, but when M. Pleven proposed the establishment of a British, French, United Sates consultative body to coordinate Far Eastern policies the President declined, expressing United States preference for existing mechanisms.

With specific reference to Indochina, the Prime Minister assured President Truman that France would continue to resist the Communist aggression. Mr. Truman thereupon promised to expedite deliveries of increased quantities of material under the aid program. But the French wanted more than this. For the National Armies, they said, 58 billion francs (approximately 166 million dollars) would be required, of which the combined budgets of France and Viet Nam could supply only 33 billion (approximately 97 million dollars). They therefore made a formal request for the United States to furnish additional aid of 70 million dollars to make up the deficit. President Truman "held out no hope" for the provision of such assistance. As Secretary Acheson informed the National Security Council later, "We cannot become directly involved in local budgetary deficits of other countries." The Secretary of State, however, initiated detailed studies concerning the matter, in the hope of devising "some other method to assure that necessary funds for the development of the National armies be forthcoming."[28]

During the conversations the French also asked for an aircraft carrier for service in Indochina. The CVL Langley had recently been transferred to France for use in Mediterranean waters and the Joint Chiefs of Staff were unwilling to provide another at this time. Secretary of Defense Marshall, however, informed M. Pleven that the conditions imposed on the employment of the Langley would be lifted to permit its operation in Indochinese waters if the French chose.[29] The carrier, which was being refitted in the United States, joined French naval forces in July, enabling the French to keep at least one carrier constantly in service in Indochina.

---

28. (S) NSC 105, 23 Feb 51, CCS 337 (1-19-51); (TS) Doc C-24, Msg, Acheson to AmLegation Saigon, 30 Jan 51, in (TS) Doc Hist of US Pol toward Indochina.
29. Ibid.

The threat of a Chinese Communist invasion of Tonkin, which by this time colored every assessment of the Indochinese situation, was also discussed by the President and the Prime Minister. In accordance with Joint Chiefs of Staff advice, the French were informed that in the event an invasion forced the French to retire from Tonkin the United States would not commit any ground troops but would, if possible, assist in the evacuation of French forces.[30] The Joint Chiefs of Staff had been working on this problem for some weeks. On 26 December 1950 General Juin had written to Secretary Marshall saying that if the Chinese Communists came in, the French would have to pull out of Indochina. A National Intelligence Estimate published a few days later contained the opinion that even a relatively small force of Chinese, combined with the Viet Minh, would be able to drive the French from the delta in a short time.[31] The Chiefs therefore in mid-January directed CINCPAC to prepare plans to give United States naval and air support in case the French requested aid in evacuating their forces from Tonkin under Communist pressure. These preparations were not to be disclosed to the French but, after the Truman-Plevan discussion of the subject, General Bradley recommended to Secretary Marshall that CINCPAC be permitted to coordinate his plan with General de Lattre. On 28 March the Joint Chiefs of Staff authorized CINCPAC to consult with the French Commander.[32]

Other subjects, such as the European situation, were also talked over by the President and the Prime Minister, but probably the most important result of the conversations was a better understanding by each party of the other's attitude toward Indochina.

---
30. Ibid.
31. (S) Ltr, Juin to Marshall, 26 Dec 50, CCS 092 Asia (6-25-48) sec 10; (S) CIA NIE-5, "Indochina: Current Situation and Probable Developments," 29 Dec 50.
32. (TS) JCS 1992/49, 15 Jan 51, CCS 092 Asia (6-25-48) sec 10; (TS) Msg, JCS 86957 to CINCPAC, 28 Mar 51, same file, sec 12.

President Truman throughout hewed to the line of established American policy. M. Pleven succeeded in planting one new seed of thought in the minds of American officials, the idea that France would require direct budgetary support in order to carry out the plans for the National Army of Viet Nam. The germination of this seed, however, was put off until the following year.

Auriol Visit

Two months after the Prime Minister's visit the President of France, M. Vincent Auriol, arrived in Washington, bringing with him the Foreign Minister, Robert Schuman. Once again conversations were held at which Indochina was a subject for discussion. Because, in the eyes of the United States Government, no important change had taken place in the Indochinese situation since the Truman-Pleven talks, there was no alteration of the American position. The conferences with Auriol and Schuman, therefore, added nothing to the results of the Pleven visit.

The Visit of General de Lattre

Of more significance for the development of United States policy toward Indochina was the visit of General de Lattre in September. And, oddly enough, it was in the preparations made by the Joint Chiefs of Staff for his visit, rather than in the conversations themselves, that its greatest importance lay. For in considering the position they would take in discussion with the French Commander, the Chiefs came to the conclusion that the current policy had been outmoded by events and needed revision. On 14 September they recommended to the Secretary of Defense that such a review be made by the National Security Council.[33]

The considerations that prompted this recommendation were not explicitly stated by the Joint Chiefs of Staff, but an advance in their thinking was implicit in the position-paper adopted for the coming talks. One of the

---

33. (TS) Memo, Bradley to SecDef, "United States Policy Toward Indochina," 14 Sep 51, same file, sec 17.

items in their paper read: "It would be in the United States security interests to take military action short of the actual employment of ground forces in Indochina to prevent the fall of that country to Communism." This statement was a modification of the established policy that no United States armed forces would be committed in Indochina other than air and naval forces required to aid in an evacuation of Tonkin by the French. It was followed by another important paragraph:

> If the Chinese Communist Government intervened in Indochina overtly, appropriate action by U.S./U.N. forces might include the following:
> (1) A blockade of the China coast by air and naval forces with concurrent military action against selected targets held by Communist China, all without commitment of United States ground forces in China or Indochina; and
> (2) Eventually, the possible participation of Chinese Nationalist forces in the action.[34]

The ideas contained in this paragraph were not new. For months the Joint Chiefs of Staff had been considering them in connection with the Chinese Communist intervention in Korea. Since July, however, the opening of armistice negotiation in Korea had given them increasing importance, for the conclusion of an armistice would release strong Communist forces that might be directed against Indochina. Taken altogether, the paper provided a basis for a review of United States Indochina policy, and the ideas behind it were eventually included in the National Security Council's study that superseded NSC 64 nine months later.

The actual conversations between General de Lattre and Defense Department officials were for the most part about the aid program for Indochina. A good deal of time was spent in explaining to the general and his aides the limitations, such as those imposed by Congressional appropriations, under which the MDAP

---

34. (TS) JCS 1992/93, 11 Sep 51, same file.

operated. Various procedures for administering the
program were also agreed upon. General de Lattre had
brought with him a list of critical items badly needed
in Indochina: trucks, combat vehicles, signal equipment,
and automatic weapons, among others. General Collins
promised delivery by 1 January, provided shipping was
available, of all of the ground force items on the list
except 2,700 radios, only one-fourth of which could be
provided. The United States Government, General Collins
assured de Lattre, would do all it could for Indochina,
and would attempt to make deliveries as early as
possible.[35]

In this, as well as in other conversations with
Secretary Acheson and State Department representatives,
General de Lattre put forth the thesis that the conflicts
in Korea and Indochina were actually one war and should
be fought as such. The implications of his theory were
that there should be a single command for both and a
single logistical organization under which requirements
of the Indochina War would have equal priority with
those of Korea. He was unable, however, to sell this
idea to American officials or to the Joint Chiefs of
Staff, who told the Secretary of Defense (since 17
September, Robert A. Lovett) that while they recognized
the two wars as "but two manifestations of the same
ideological conflict between the USSR and the Western
World. . . . It would be wholly unacceptable . . . to
attempt, under existing circumstances, to integrate
the forces of the Western World engaged in the two
wars . . . ."[36]

General de Lattre's visit had other effects than
those of his formal conferences with political and
military representatives. In a number of public
statements, which were given wide coverage in the press,

---

35. (S) Memo of Conv bet French delegation headed
by Gen de Lattre and Defense officials headed by SecDef
Robert A. Lovett and Gen Collins, 20 Sep 51, in CMA files.
36. Ibid.; (S) Doc C-33, "Extracts from memorandum
of conversation among Acheson, Schuman, and DeLattre,
Sept 14, 1951," in (TS) Doc Hist of US Pol toward Indochina; (TS) Memo, JCS to SecDef, "Combat Operations
in Indochina," 19 Nov 51, CCS 092 Asia (6-25-48) sec 19.

he succeeded in dramatizing for the American people
the issues of the Indochinese war. He painted a somewhat too rosy picture, however, proclaiming that the
Associated States were indeed independent, that France
had abandoned all rights and privileges but was retaining the risks and burdens of the war, that the governments of the Associated States were gaining in popular
support, and that popular elections would be held as
soon as the military situation permitted. Nevertheless, his statements were not unwelcome to the United
States Government, since they helped to justify, in
the public mind, the material sacrifices the government
was making in support of the French and Indochinese.

Somewhat to the annoyance of American personnel
in Saigon, the controlled Indochinese press extolled
the general's trip to Washington as a tremendous victory
for French policy. The Legation reported:

> De Lattre was also credited with being
> successful in his presentation in the United States
> of the "one war (Korea and Indochina) in the Far
> East" theme; press accounts made it appear that
> his visit had resulted in a vast increase and
> acceleration of shipments of arms and materiel
> for Indochina . . . .
> De Lattre also issued a rather flamboyant
> open letter to Bao Dai in which he claimed to
> have radically changed American thinking about
> Indochina, with the implication that all aid
> programs would now be very greatly stepped up.[37]

The French statements were greatly exaggerated because no
basic change in American policy, or even in the aid program,
had occurred. Some necessary adjustments in the administration of the MDAP relative to Indochina had been made,
however, and delivery of certain critical items were
speeded. Also, General de Lattre departed from Washington
in an atmosphere of mutual respect and understanding,
and there was considerable disappointment in the American
capital at the news of his death in January.

---

37. (S) Rpt, Gullion to State Dept, "MDAP Monthly
Report for October 1951," 11 Dec 51, G-3 091 Indo
China, sec I, DRB AGO.

First Tripartite Intelligence Conference

One of the few recommendations of the Singapore Conference that were realized in 1951 was the institution of tripartite intelligence conferences in Southeast Asia. The first of these conferences, however, met with United States officers participating only as "observers." At the end of August the Joint Chiefs of Staff had informed the British and French Chiefs of Staff by memorandum that they were willing "to direct U.S. intelligence officer participation in joint meetings with the French and British Armed Forces Intelligence Staffs in Saigon and Singapore on a regular basis . . . ." The British, misunderstanding a reservation in the Joint Chiefs of Staff memorandum, proceeded to make arrangements for an initial conference in October, to which the French agreed. At first the Joint Chiefs of Staff declined to take part in this meeting, considering it premature but when informed by the British Chiefs of Staff that the British felt themselves committed to meet with the French in any case, they consented. Because they regarded certain items in the proposed agenda as being beyond the competence of such a conference, the Joint Chiefs of Staff directed CINCPAC to designate a representative to attend only as an observer. They did not want this representative to subscribe to, or aid in preparing, "agreed estimates" that might bind them in the future.[38]

The conference met in Saigon on 9-10 November, having been twice postponed. American armed services attaches stationed in the various Southeast Asian capitals and an officer of the Far East Air Force

---

38. (TS) Memo, Bradley to SecDef, "Tripartite Military Staff Talks on Southeast Asia Held at Singapore 15-18 May 1951 (Action on Conference Report)," 30 Aug 51, CCS 092 Asia (6-25-48) sec 17. (S) Ltr, Brit Jt Services Mission to Secy JCS, "Military Staff Talks on South East Asia," 24 Sep 51; (TS) JCS 1992/102, 9 Oct 51; (S) Ltr, Brit Jt Services Mission to Secy JCS, "Tripartite Military Staff Talks on South East Asia," 15 Oct 51; (TS) JCS 1992/105, 24 Oct 51; (TS) Msg, JCS to CINCPAC, JCS 85523, 30 Oct 51. All in same file, sec 18.

attended, along with the official representative of the Joint Chiefs of Staff, Captain E. T. Layton, USN, designated by CINCPAC. Some disappointment was expressed by both British and French that the Americans were not there as full participants. But Admiral Radford, in forwarding the report of the conference to the Joint Chiefs of Staff, remarked that "as observers the U.S. delegation met the objectives of the conference, i.e., 'the further exchange of information,'" and recommended that the observer status be continued for future meetings.

With respect to Indochina the information revealed at the Saigon Conference was not of such a nature as to be startling to the Joint Chiefs of Staff. A member of the French delegation presented an estimate of the situation but gave no data on French plans or operations. His conclusions nevertheless were interesting because of the moderate optimism they expressed, in contrast to recent estimates of General de Lattre who had been publicly predicting an end to the war in as few as fifteen months if China did not interfere. The French delegation, while they saw no important threat in the near future from either the Viet Minh or Red China, expected no "spectacular change in the situation, but only slow suffocation of the moral and armed strengths of the Viet Minh."

The conference was on the whole successful, and "some sound and valuable information" was exchanged. Perhaps more important, it made the delegates aware of each others problems, as well as of procedural shortcomings that could be remedied in future meetings.[39]

---

39. (TS) Ltr, CINCPAC to JCS, "Tripartite Intelligence Conference held at Saigon, 9 and 10 November 1951," 15 Jan 52, same file, sec 23; (S) Rpt, Gullion to State Dept, "MDAP Monthly Report for October, 1951," 11 Dec 51, G-3 091 Indo China, sec I, DRB AGO.

Origins of The Tripartite Chiefs of Staff Meeting in January 1952

In late autumn it was becoming more and more apparent that the British and French Governments were not wholly satisfied with United States interpretations of the results of the Singapore Conference. The disagreement between the allies rested on a basic conflict. The British and French wanted an over-all strategy for the defense of Southeast Asia closely coordinated between the three powers by some sort of tripartite organization. They also desired to have the United States more deeply committed to the defense of the area than American policies would allow. On the other hand, the United States held that cooperation should be achieved generally through existing mechanisms and strove to avoid any definite commitment in Southeast Asia that might limit its military flexibility in the event of a global war.

Early in November the British Government brought this issue to the surface by an Aide-Memoire addressed specifically to the problem of the Chinese threat in Southeast Asia. The British position was that

> 2. That part of the Singapore Report dealing with operational aspects made it clear that in the event of Chinese invasion of South East Asia considerable reinforcements would be required for successful resistance and that these could only come from outside the area. The provision of such reinforcements involves priorities which could only be settled in the light of an agreed tripartite policy for the defence of South East Asia and the relation of that defence to global strategy.
> 3. His Majesty's Government believe that a meeting of the United Kingdom, United States and French Chiefs of Staff to formulate such a policy and to make recommendations to the three Governments would be desirable. They consider that the forthcoming Meeting of the N.A.T.O. Military Committee in Rome affords a convenient opportunity for such a meeting . . . .[40]

---

[40]. (TS) Memo, Kreps to JCS, "Proposed Tripartite Discussions on the Defense of Southeast Asia," 8 Nov 51, CCS 092 Asia (6-25-48) sec 19.

The Joint Chiefs of Staff wanted nothing to do with the suggested meeting. "In effect," they wrote the Secretary of Defense, "this proposal by the British reopens the entire question of the establishment of a single military organization for the strategic direction of the armed forces of the Western World in a global war." They would not agree to the formation of such an authority "even by implication" at this time. Not only would it superimpose another structure over the NATO command organization but it would be premature, it would be labeled warmongering, and, since the USSR did not seem intent on global war at this time, it was unnecessary. Furthermore, the alignment of the Western nations and their contributions in a future conflict was not rigidly fixed and could not be forecast with sufficient accuracy to justify an immediate decision on a future command organization. The Joint Chiefs of Staff therefore declined the invitation, adding, however, that they would not object to conversations restricted to economic and political matters affecting Southeast Asia.[41]

But at the end of November, when General Bradley attended the NATO meeting in Rome, the British and French strongly urged him to agree to tripartite discussion between the Chiefs of Staff on the Singapore Report. They proposed to hold a conference in Washington early in January. Despite his protest that the Joint Chiefs of Staff thought a meeting unnecessary they prevailed upon him to have the matter reconsidered when he returned to the United States.[42] This he did and on 28 December the Joint Chiefs of Staff, having changed their minds, assented to a conference but with the provision that the discussions would involve no commitment on their part. They issued invitations for a meeting in Washington, and this meeting was actually in session when the news of General de Lattre's death arrived on 11 January.[43]

---

41. (TS) Memo, Bradley to SecDef, "Proposed Tripartite Discussions on the Defense of Southeast Asia," 12 Nov 51, same file.
42. (TS) Memo, Bradley to Maj Gen C. P. Cabell, USAF, Dir JS, 6 Dec 51, same file.
43. (TS) Memo, Bradley to SecDef, "Conference with French and British on Southeast Asia," 28 Dec 51, same file, sec 21. See Ch. X, below, for the account of the Washington Conference.

By the end of 1951 other agencies of the American Government had joined the Joint Chiefs of Staff in calling for a review of United States policy toward Indochina.[44] Almost half a year was to pass, however, before a new statement of policy was formally approved by the President and the National Security Council. Nevertheless, the ideas that prompted the Joint Chiefs of Staff to urge a revision as far back as September appeared in their actions and planning even before the new National Security Council decision was made, and colored their conversations at the Washington Conference. Although the official policy had not changed perceptibly during 1951 a stronger attitude toward the Indochina problem was in the Washington air as the new year opened.

Progress of Aid to Indochina

During the first four months of 1951 MDAP aid flowed to Indochina at a constant and fairly good rate, averaging over 10,000 long tons per month exclusive of aircraft and vessels delivered under their own power. In May, however, shipments fell off sharply and the average monthly tonnage unloaded at Saigon from July through September was only 4,147 long tons. The lowest point was reached in October, when only 1,772 long tons of MDAP cargo were received in Indochina.[45]

---

44. Ibid.
45. (S) Rpt, Gullion to State Dept, "MDAP Monthly Report for June 1951," 24 Jul 51, G-3 091 Indo China, sec II-A, bk II, DRB AGO; (S) Rpt, Gullion to State Dept, "MDAP Monthly Report for October, 1951," 11 Dec 51, same file, sec I. The figures given in this study relative to the amounts and value of MDAP material delivered to Indochina are only approximate and not always trustworthy. They are obtained from summaries and the periodic reports of various agencies concerned with the administration of the program, and the data given by one office sometimes differ from those of another. Furthermore, discrepancies are to be found within single reports, so that at the present a true, detailed account of the aid program is unavailable.

The French and Vietnamese began in May to express considerable anxiety over the delay of expected shipments for the National Army. A seven months delay in its activation schedule was attributed to this cause by the Vietnamese government. From Saigon the United States Legation reported:

> . . . In assessing the matter at the end of the month /May/ it was determined that out of 34 planned battalions--of which 27 already exist--only eight battalions had been fully equipped and three partially equipped, whereas 16 battalions have been activated with only equipment supplied from French reserve. The final 7 battalions, which are to be activated by February, apparently have little prospect of obtaining army equipment from the FY 1951 program. In the Legation's opinion this is a serious situation since ultimate solution of the entire Indochinese problem is strongly dependent on accelerating the development of an adequate Vietnamese national army.[46]

Expressions of French concern about the slow rate of arrival of MDAP equipment culminated in General de Lattre's complaints to American officials during his visit in September.

This dissatisfaction was not without a reasonable basis. MDAP shipments had been lagging generally behind schedule, and not only those slated for Indochina, but those programmed for other recipient nations as well. In October Secretary Lovett listed for President Truman the reasons why deliveries had been sluggish during the preceding eight months. "One important factor," he wrote, "has been the indefinite extent and nature of the total program which the Defense Department was to undertake when related to the amount of funds that would be available for its implementation." In addition,

---

46. (S) Rpt, Gullion to State Dept, "MDAP Monthly Report for May 1951," 22 Jun 51, same file, sec II-A, bk I; (S) Rpt, Gullion to State Dept, "MDAP Monthly Report for June 1951," 24 Jul 51, same file, bk II.

there was a shortage of machine tools, "spot shortages" of some critical materials, strikes in important industries, some shortage of production capacity and of skilled personnel, and a lack of experience in producing newly developed items of equipment.[47] Constant efforts were being made in the United States to correct this situation with the result that equipment shortages in Indochina were considerably lessened in 1952. The French admitted, among themselves, that in 1952 owing to United States aid, "the supply situation became virtually sound and the services could . . . claim to function normally."[48] Nevertheless, the French never wholly stopped complaining about deficiencies in the aid program. "The squeaking wheel gets the most grease" can be translated into almost any language.

The extraordinary measures taken by the Defense Department to speed deliveries after the de Lattre visit caused the volume of shipments to Indochina to increase greatly. In November 25,200 measurement tons of cargo were shipped and during December 30,050 measurement tons. This tempo of supply was maintained generally throughout the following year.[49]

The magnitude of the United States contribution is indicated by the MDAP Status Report for December, which contained a resume of the shipments of items listed as critical by General de Lattre in September. As of 31 December, of 4,500 general purpose vehicles requested, 2,977 trucks and 854 trailers had been shipped or were in port awaiting shipment; of 300 combat vehicles, 40 had left port and 205 were at port awaiting shipment; 600 radio sets had been shipped; and of 8,900 machine guns, 4,172 had been shipped and 4,743 were in port awaiting shipment. Thirty LCM's, 36 LCVP's, 26 Coast Guard Patrol Craft, and 1 LST had left the United States for Indochina. In January 1952 FECOM stocks

---

47. (TS) JCS 2099/138, 30 Oct 51, CCS 092 (8-22-46) sec 61.
48. (TS) Navarre Briefing Doc, Jun 53, p. 48, in OMA files.
49. Ibid.; (S) MDAP Status Reports for Months of November and December 1951.

were levied upon for 622 additional trucks. By the end of the month the bulk of the items on General de Lattre's list had been shipped.50

A summary of the MDAP aid to Indochina as of the end of 1951 shows that since the beginning of the program for that country 260,045 measurement tons of supplies, valued at 163,600,000 dollars, had been shipped. A total of 320,100,000 dollars had already been programmed, and this figure was to rise in January 1952 to 460,000,000 dollars.51

ECA Program in Indochina

By mid-1951 the economic aid program administered by the United States STEM in Saigon was making itself felt in support of the military effort. Through it, funds were provided for road construction and improvement (over 3 million dollars), for the purchase of earth-moving equipment and asphalt for the improvement of airstrips, for procuring medical supplies, marine engines and ferries, tin plate used in canning army rations, and for many other items directly or indirectly aiding the armed services. In addition, it was taking care of civilian needs, such as housing and medical facilities, all important to civilian, and therefore, to army morale. In fighting disease and social unrest the ECA program was contributing much to the battle against Communism in the Associated States.52

---

50. Ibid.; (S) MDAP Status Report for Month of January 1952.
51. Ibid.; (S) MDAP Status Report for Month of February 1952.
52. (S) Rpt, Gullion to State Dept, "MDAP Monthly Report for April 1951," 21 May 51, G-3 091 Indo China, sec I, DRB AGO; (S) Rpt, Gullion to State Dept, "MDAP Monthly Report for June 1951," 24 Jul 51, same file, sec II-A, bk II.

French Attitude toward the United States Aid Programs

As indicated earlier in this chapter, the year had begun auspiciously for Franco-American relations in Indochina. MDAP materiel had furnished the substance of General de Lattre's defensive victories and the High Commissioner had proven suitably grateful. But as the ECA program developed there was a recrudescence of the former French attitudes of suspicion and jealousy of Americans in Indochina. In noting the reappearance of French distrust, the Legation in Saigon attributed it to an upsurge of old colonial phobias, to the professional jealousy of military men, to fear of losing prestige, and to exaggerated fears that American participation in the military effort might stimulate Chinese Communist retaliation.[53] And while these feelings were directed much less toward MDAP and MAAG than toward STEM, they could not help but limit to some extent the freedom of action afforded General Brink's group. There was no question however, of a return to the antagonistic attitude toward MAAG of the pre-de Lattre days.

The chief target of French suspicions was STEM, probably owing to the fact that this agency dealt directly with the governments of the Associated States and not through the French. Also, the publicity given STEM's work had resulted in a growth of American prestige in Indochina. An event symptomatic of the French state of mind occurred in June, when a United States-Vietnamese Economic Assistance Agreement was scheduled for signing. The French interposed some rather factitious objections at the last minute, thereby delaying completion of the agreement until September. And when an American news story ascribed the delay to the French, General de Lattre responded with a "rather irritated" press release.[54]

During his visit to Washington the High Commissioner, whose jealousy of French Union prerogatives was well-known, indicated he had not been happy, early in 1951, about "a number of young men with a 'missionary zeal'

---

53. Ibid.
54. Ibid.

[who] were dispensing economic aid with the result that there was a feeling on the part of some that they were using this aid to extend American influence." He added, however, that his relations with the economic mission had since become much better.[55] But in this he perhaps was being only diplomatic, for the French attitude of suspicion persisted.

As the year ended another disquieting note was introduced into Franco-American relations as they concerned MDAP in Indochina. In its report for December the Legation in Saigon informed the State Department:

> As the difficulties of the military situation here increased [as a result of the Hoa Binh offensive] the Legation has noted the disturbing tendency of both the French high officials and medium-level bureaucrats to misrepresent the volume and timing of American military aid deliveries. The theme has been "too little and too late." Mr. MASSOT and M. DUPONT, who are members of Parliament and shortly to visit Viet Nam, have made statements in the French Assembly to this effect. The Minister for the AS, M. LETOURNEAU, is himself responsible for the statement that by the end of the year only 43 shiploads of war material had been delivered to IC amounting to some 70,000 tons and valued at somewhere about 60 million francs. Actually, some 93 ships had offloaded in the ports of IC with a total tonnage approximately 90,000 tons with a value many times that cited by the French.
>
> Appropriate steps were taken at MAAG conferences with the French General Staff to induce these officers, who very well know the actual amount of deliveries, to correct misstatements and prevent further publication of tendentious and erroneous articles.[56]

---

55. (TS) Doc C-34, Mns, 2nd Mtg, Dep State with de Lattre, 17 Sep 51, in (TS) <u>Doc Hist of US Pol toward Indochina</u>.

56. (S) Rpt, Gullion to State Dept, "MDAP Monthly Report No. 15 (December 1951)," 21 Mar 52, G-3 091 Indo China, sec I-A, bk I.

The implications of this report were made explicit in the report for the following month:

> there was an intensification of the trend noticed last month for the French to exculpate themselves in advance of a deteriorating military situation by criticizing the amount and timeliness of American aid.[57]

While earlier French complaints about the rate of MDAP deliveries may have had some justification, there was none for the misrepresentations described in the Legation reports. Such actions might well have given American authorities cause to fear that the French would blame a general defeat in Indochina on an alleged failure of United States military aid. In any case these pronouncements could not fail to have a bad effect on the atmosphere in which the assistance program was conducted.

Despite the vastly increased rate of MDAP deliveries in the last two months of 1951 it cannot be said that the aid program for the year was entirely successful. During a considerable part of the period the flow of materiel was behind schedule. Although the subsequent history of the Indochina war indicates that the resultant delay in activation of some National Army battalions probably did not affect the final outcome, it does leave room for speculation about what greater contribution those battalions might have made in 1952 and 1953 had they received the benefit of the lost months of training. On the whole, however, the United States had done fairly well under the circumstances and it must be remembered that in 1951 the men fighting in Korea had first call on American equipment. The "limited war" was also a limiting war.

---

57. (S) Rpt, Gullion to State Dept, "MDAP Monthly Report No. 16 (January 1952)," 24 Mar 52, same file.

CHAPTER X

FROM JANUARY 1952 TO THE END OF THE TRUMAN ADMINISTRATION

The year 1952 saw little progress in the struggle in Indochina. On neither the political front, nor on the military, did the French and Vietnamese achieve an important victory. On neither did they suffer an important defeat. At the end of the year the situation in Viet Nam was about what it had been at the time of General de Lattre's death, a little better in some respects, a little worse in others. Yet, although the anti-Communist forces had been able to "hold their own," the free world's prospects of victory in that area actually declined. The French and the loyal Vietnamese were in a position where, if they did not go forward, they had to slide backward.

Time was on the side of the Communists. This is not to say that the Viet Minh forces were growing so fast that they would soon be able to crush the French. They were not. The French and Vietnamese regular troops constantly outnumbered the Viet Minh regulars. They had superior equipment. They were supported by air and naval forces to which the rebels could offer little active opposition. In addition, they held well-fortified positions that could not be easily overrun. But in France itself the people and the government were becoming more and more weary of a war that seemed to drag on without end. There were increasingly numerous indications that if the war could not be won quickly in Indochina it might be lost in France. And the war was not being won.

The Military Situation in Indochina

The death of General de Lattre deprived the French in Indochina of a commander who had great prestige, energy, and experience, combined with the will to fight. His successor, General Raoul Salan, could not adequately fill his shoes. Conservative, overcautious, and defensive-minded, Salan conducted the war with a "barbed-wire strategy" reminiscent of the first World War. His concept of operations seems to have been to fortify strong points and wait for the enemy to attack them in the hope of inflicting many more casualties on the attackers than his own forces suffered. In this he had just enough success during 1952 to keep his strategy from being discredited. The result was that the Viet Minh forces usually held the initiative.

Unlike General de Lattre, General Salan did not wear, over his soldier's cap, the hat of High Commissioner. The duties of that office were given to M. Jean Letourneau, who as Minister Resident, nevertheless retained his position in the French Cabinet as Minister for the Associated States. Thus the French Government returned to the system that had worked so poorly in the years prior to 1951, that of dividing responsibility for French affairs in Indochina between a civil administrator and a military commander.[1] And since the Minister Resident was a more powerful figure than the High Commander, the stultifying hand of politics was once more in a position directly to restrain and blunt the sword of strategy. The extent to which political considerations affected the conduct of operations in Indochina cannot be determined, but it may be surmised that General Salan did not have a free hand.

Unfortunately for the new French Commander, he had to enter upon his duties under rather distressing circumstances. He had to contend with a general letdown in morale following the death of de Lattre, whom many in Indochina had regarded as the one man who could bring the war to a successful end. Also, he had to give up Hoa Binh, thereby acknowledging failure of the one strategically offensive operation undertaken by the French since the autumn of 1950. And in addition, he had to fight in the shadow of what the French were convinced was a constantly growing threat of Chinese Communist intervention. According to a United States intelligence estimate of

---

1. (S) Rpt, Gullion to State, "MDAP Monthly Report No. 19 (April 1952)," 23 May 52, G-3 091 Indo China sec I-A, bk I, DRB AGO.

August 1952 "The French /were/ apprehensive that substantial French victories would bring about such intervention, with which the French, because of their limited capabilities, would be unable to cope."[2]

Progress of the Fighting in Spring and Summer, 1952

The Viet Minh attacks against the French position at Hoa Binh had been accompanied by extensive infiltration of the Tonkin Delta area. In February, when the French evacuated Hoa Binh, this infiltration grew to serious proportions and occasioned the heaviest fighting since 1950. With considerable success the French employed mobile units against the Viet Minh forces within the delta perimeter and by July had restored the area to a relatively calm condition. In the process they reportedly crippled one Viet Minh division and inflicted severe losses on some other units, thus reducing the capabilities of the rebels, and also their morale, for several months.[3]

During the late summer the French undertook two limited operations south of the Delta against an isolated enemy regiment. These actions were successful in producing a considerable number of Viet Minh casualties but fell short of their aim, which was complete annihilation of the regiment. In the meantime Ho Chi Minh's main forces reportedly were being reorganized and put through a course of training, including combined maneuvers, in preparation for the fall campaign.[4]

The Autumn Campaign in 1952

When dry weather appeared, at the end of September, General Salan was in a position to attack, and probably

---

2. (S) CIA NIE-35/2, "Probable Developments in Indochina Through Mid-1953," 29 Aug 52, p. 3; (S) Rpt, Gullion to State, "MDAP Monthly Report No. 16 (January 1952)," 24 Mar 52, G-3 091 Indo China, sec I-A, bk I, DRB AGO.
3. (TS) Navarre Briefing Doc, Jun 53, in OMA files; (TS) Ann B to CINCPAC Staff Study, "Evaluation of Military Operations in Indochina," 18 Apr 53, CCS 092 Asia (6-25-48) BP pt 9.
4. Ibid.

to defeat, the Viet Minh regular forces. He had a substantial numerical superiority (about 26,000) in numbers of troops. He could dispose of superior equipment, fire power, mobility, and air support. He could operate on interior lines, backed by the fortifications of the Delta perimeter. He knew in general the strength and disposition of his enemy. He could have seized the initiative--but he did not. The French, by default, permitted the Viet Minh to take the offensive.

Early in October the Communist forces began attacking French outposts in the Thai country west and north of the Delta. The area was one of secondary economic and political importance and the French felt that these attacks were merely diversions calculated to draw friendly forces outside the perimeter. Between 10 and 15 October, however, concerted attacks drove in the outposts of the fortified position at Nghia Lo, which fell to the Viet Minh on 18 October. The French Command then decided to fortify a strong position in the path of the enemy advance and there await the attack. It therefore concentrated at Na San its forces that were in the area and flew in reinforcements from the Delta. After fighting a delaying action along the Black River the French completed their concentration on 20 November.

Meanwhile opportunity was knocking for the second time on the French door. On 29 October General Salan, with the aim of diverting some Viet Minh forces from the Black River, had launched a column from the Delta northwest along the east side of the Red River. This force successfully cut across the Viet Minh lines of communication, destroying about 500 tons of supplies in dumps. But, once astride the enemy lines of communication, the French column withdrew, casting aside what American observers believed to be the chance to inflict a decisive defeat on the Communist forces. The French Command preferred to fight a defensive battle at Na San.

The attack on Na San began on 24 November and ended nine days later when the Viet Minh withdrew, having suffered severe casualties (over 1,500 counted dead). From the French point of view this was a successful battle. But members of the CINCPAC staff who analyzed the campaign concluded that the battle had contributed little toward ending the war and that in order to achieve an unimportant victory the defensive-minded French Command had thrown away a chance to fight a decisive battle under favorable circumstances.[5] Furthermore, except for the region around Na San, the Viet Minh remained in possession of the territory they had invaded. Although it was an area of secondary importance its capture was a psychological and political victory for the Communists and enhanced their prestige among the native population.

The autumn campaign in Tonkin convinced many American officials that unless some fairly drastic change was made in the French conduct of the war there would be a prolonged period of stalemate in Indochina during which the French-Vietnamese situation might well deteriorate. Two solutions to this problem were put forward. The first was to persuade the French to adopt and carry out an aggressive plan of campaign aimed at a decisive defeat of Viet Minh forces. The second was to persuade them to give their commanders sufficient forces, preferably by raising the number of Vietnamese regular units, so that even a Salan might be enticed from behind his barbed wire to strike a massive blow at the enemy. During the following year both solutions were tried at once.

The Political Situation in Indochina--No Progress

If, by the end of 1952, the military outlook in Indochina was dreary, nothing in the political scene was any brighter. The government of Bao Dai had little more popular support in December than it had enjoyed in January and seemed to have few prospects for gaining such support in the foreseeable future. Its appeal for the average Vietnamese was not strengthened by the appointment, in April, of Letourneau as Minister Resident. M. Letourneau was known to regard the independence of Viet Nam as having already been completed and to

---

5. Ibid.

oppose any major revision of the 8 March Accords.[6] The French seemed determined to cling to their position in Indochina like a drowning man refusing to let go a sack of gold that is dragging him down.

On 2 June, in an effort to obtain a government with a broader base of popular and regional representation, the cabinet of Tran Van Huu was replaced by one under Nguyen Van Tam. Unfortunately, Tam was not only a French citizen but was well-known as an ardent French supporter, even more closely identified with French policies than Huu had been. The new Premier made many fine promises to the people, which were received with skepticism. He installed a Provisional National Council, ostensibly a sort of representative assembly, but the members were hand-picked by him. The Council never played any important role in Vietnamese affairs and, of course, never captured the imagination of the people. In 1952, at least, Tam was unable to do either the Bao Dai government or the French any good.[7]

The state of affairs in Viet Nam during this period is illustrated by a passage in the April MDAP report from the American Legation in Saigon.

> Vietnamese Deputy Minister of Defense declared that Government has decided not to call up the fourth increment of conscripts in order that funds and present cadres could be used in accelerating the formation of two additional regular VN divisions to make a total of six by the end of 1952. He added that the draft is in any case not a primary source of manpower for the Army in view of the fact that there are

---

6. (S) CIA NIE 35/2, "Probably Developments in Indochina Through Mid-1953," 29 Aug 52. (S) Rpt, Gullion to State, "MDAP Monthly Report No. 19 (April 1952)," 23 May 52, G-3 091 Indo China, sec I-A, bk I, DRB AGO.

7. (S) Rpt, Gullion to State, "MDAP Monthly Report No. 21 (June 1952)," 31 Jul 52, same file; (S) Geneva Conf Background Paper, Indochina Chronology, pp. 70-71; Hammer, Struggle for Indochina, pp. 281-291.

sufficient volunteers and enlistees to create
a regular army of any size required, provided
sufficient funds and material are provided.
He referred significantly to the uselessness
of training conscripts only to have them
defect to, or be kidnapped by, the Viet
Minh . . . .[8]

Clearly, in the opinion of the Vietnamese government the national mobilization, from which much had been expected, had not succeeded.

In spite of this history of failures the situation in Indochina itself did not seem hopeless to the American Government. But more and more, as the end of the year approached, the word "stalemate" appeared in reports from Saigon, in intelligence estimates dealing with Indochina, and in conversations among United States officials concerning that country. In modern war, however, unlike a game of chess, stalemate is not the end of the game. American planners during 1952 sought to prevent the introduction of a new red queen, Communist China, and at the same time to strengthen friendly forces to the point where the stalemate could be broken.

Development of American Policy toward Indochina

This period witnessed the development of four important trends in the Indochinese war as it affected United States policy. Firstly, Washington was taking its place with Paris and Saigon as a center of political and military strategic planning for the war. For not only was the vital military aid program determined in the United States capital; increasingly numerous tripartite and bilateral conferences between American, British, and French officials concerning the situation in Southeast Asia were held there. Secondly, the United States Government was being drawn into closer and closer cooperation, on a high military level, with the British and French on the problems of the area. The Joint Chiefs of Staff, fearing that this tendency might lead to a combined command of some sort, or to increased American responsibility in the Indochinese conflict, sometimes

---

8. (S) Rpt, Gullion to State, "MDAP Monthly Report No. 19 (April 1952)," 23 May 52, G-3 091 Indo China, sec I-A, bk I, DRB AGO.

protested against it, though with little success. Thirdly, the threat of Chinese Communist intervention was beginning to dwarf other factors in the Southeast Asian picture, especially for the French, who seemed obsessed with this danger. Finally, France itself was beginning to crack under the triple burden of the Indochinese war, European rearmament, and the chronic instability of its own government. Although this trend was by no means ignored in United States planning, its rapid progress leading to the Geneva settlement was not generally foreseen.

The Washington Chiefs of Staff Conference

All of these trends were operating, directly or indirectly, on United States policy at the time of the tripartite Chiefs of Staff conference in Washington on 11 January. The preparations for this conference had already been made at the end of the previous year and the Joint Chiefs of Staff went into it ready to discuss measures for implementing the recommendations of the Singapore Report and to exchange informal views with the British and French on ways to fight the extension of Communism in Southeast Asia. As it turned out the problem that received the most attention during the discussions was how to deter Chinese Communist aggression in the area, and particularly in Indochina.

General Juin, the spokesman for the French delegation, assured the conferees that the French could at least hold their present positions in Viet Nam against the Viet Minh. He was, however, especially alarmed about the possibility of a Chinese Communist invasion of Tonkin. In this he was joined by the British, who feared for Burma and Malaya should Tonkin fall. Despite intelligence reports about extensive construction and repair work on Chinese lines of communication leading into Indochina, the Joint Intelligence Committee had advised the Joint Chiefs of Staff that although capabilities for it existed such an invasion did not seem imminent.9 The Joint Chiefs of Staff, however, felt that the possibility was great enough to justify serious consideration of deterrent measures.

---

9. (S) JIC 529/10, 9 Jan 52, CCS 092 Asia (6-25-48) BP pt 3.

More than that, the Joint Chiefs of Staff inclined to the view that Chinese Communist aggression was all of a piece, and in this respect the problem of Indochina was linked to that of Korea. The United States Government had already been discussing with other participants in the Korean Conflict a statement, to be issued on the signing of a Korean armistice, warning Peiping that a renewal of aggression in Korea would bring a United Nations reaction not necessarily confined to that area. When, therefore, the possibility of issuing a similar warning against aggression in Southeast Asia was broached at the conference the Joint Chiefs of Staff agreed with the British and French Chiefs of Staff that they should recommend that this measure be considered by their respective governments.[10]

This agreement logically brought the conference to the question of what to do if such a warning were issued and then ignored by the Chinese Communists. Retaliation in the form of atomic bombs was mentioned, and the Joint Chiefs of Staff brought up the possibilities of naval blockade of the China coast and employment of Chinese Nationalist forces. The delegates, however, decided to turn the problem of determining the form of retaliation over to an Ad Hoc Committee composed of military representatives of the three powers, plus Australia and New Zealand, who, since September 1951, had been allied with the United States in the Tripartite Security Pact (ANZUS). According to the terms of reference provided by the conference delegates, the Ad Hoc Committee was to:

    a. Determine the collective capabilities of the nations represented on the committee which could be made available for retaliation;
    b. Make recommendations for eventual transmission to Governments through the respective Chiefs of Staff as to what specific military measures might be taken as a collective effort

---

10. (TS) Notes recorded by Secy and DepSecy JCS at the U.S.-U.K.-Fr. CsofS Tri Talks on Southeast Asia (hereinafter: Notes on the Washington Conf), 11 Jan 52, same file, sec 22.

against the Chinese Communists not only in threatened areas but also directly against China.[11]

Although he concurred in the appointment of the Ad Hoc Committee and in the terms of reference, General Juin was not quite satisfied with this solution. He wanted a commitment for air and naval support in the event the Chinese Communists should invade Tonkin before the warning was issued and before the committee had completed its work. General Bradley, speaking for the United States, replied that this was a matter for the governments to decide, that the United States Government was currently giving urgent consideration to the situation in Southeast Asia but had not yet made a decision. The Chiefs of Staff thereupon turned to the problems of implementing the report of the Singapore Conference.

The agreements reached during the remainder of the discussions may be summarized briefly. It was decided that the United States delegates to the Tripartite Intelligence Conferences on Southeast Asia would henceforth attend as participating members rather than as observers. Further, the United States would exchange information with the British concerning control of shipping and contraband bound for the Communists in Southeast Asia and China. The United States refused, however, to participate in establishing a supply base for the French at Singapore or to alter the machinery of the MAAG through which military aid for Indochina was supplied.[12] With agreement on these points the conference closed.

The Cooper Statement--An Implied Warning

The Joint Chiefs of Staff and officials of the State Department realized that it would be some time before the warning contemplated at the Washington Conference could be issued. Not only would they have to wait for the Ad Hoc Committee to complete its deliberations but the required political decision would require lengthy consideration by the governments concerned. They nevertheless

---

11. (TS) "Terms of Reference to the Ad Hoc Committee," 11 Jan 52, same file.
12. (TS) Notes on the Washington Conf.

agreed that the earlier a warning was issued, the better it would be.[13]

But if, pending a political agreement, the United States Government was not free unilaterally to threaten retaliation, a less drastic warning could be given as an interim measure. Thus, on 28 January, Mr. John Sherman Cooper, United States delegate to the UN General Assembly, solemnly announced to the Assembly's Committee I (Political and Security):

> At this time I must, on instructions of my Government, state clearly that any . . . Communist aggression in Southeast Asia would, in the view of my Government, be a matter of direct and grave concern which would require the most urgent and earnest consideration by the United Nations.[14]

This statement did not commit the United States to any armed reaction against a Chinese Communist attack in Indochina. It did imply, however, that such an attack might meet a United Nations effort similar to the defense of Korea.

The Five-Power Ad Hoc Committee

On 5 February the United States representative on the Ad Hoc Committee, Vice Admiral A. C. Davis, submitted the report of the committee to the Joint Chiefs of Staff. He sent along with it his own analysis of the report and of the discussions that had taken place in the committee meetings, a document more revealing of the individual national positions than the report itself.

The British and French, Admiral Davis stated, had been unwilling to "meet the terms of reference," which

---

13. (TS) Summary of notes recorded by DepSecy JCS at State-Defense Meeting held on 16 and 23 Jan 52, in DepSecy, JCS files.
14. State Dept Bulletin, No. 659, 11 Feb 52, p. 224.

required recommendations on what might be done if retaliatory action against a Chinese Communist aggression was instituted by the governments of the five powers. Instead, they had undertaken to decide, within the committee, that real retaliatory action should not be taken and that military measures should be aimed merely at defending the area attacked. Both British and French members had opposed the measures, advocated by the United States delegate, of blockading the Chinese coast. Both had also opposed bombing China except in direct support of operations close to that part of the border over which the Chinese Communist armies were attacking. Their opposition was rationalized by their assumptions that blockade and bombing would be at once impractical and ineffectual.

According to Admiral Davis, the French position was based on a desire to prevent forces from being diverted outside the scene of operations in Indochina; the French wanted all the aid and commitments they could get in connection with their immediate problem in Tonkin. The British position, more definitely expressed than the French, indicated an intention to avoid any measures that might unduly irritate Peiping or Moscow. The British wished to defend Hong Kong and Indochina, but not to take any drastic action against Communist China itself.[15] In the report of the Ad Hoc Committee the British member averred that blockade would at least ruin Hong Kong economically if it did not lead to its fall, while there was little doubt that bombing China would cause retaliatory action against the colony.

One possible course of action all delegates agreed to reject. "We consider," they reported, "/that/ the use of Chinese Nationalist Forces in their present state of training and equipment is inadvisable and unlikely to cause the Chinese Communists to desist from their aggressive action." As to atomic weapons, their use was not mentioned. Admiral Davis had been instructed by the Joint Chiefs of Staff not to consider them.

---

15. (TS) Memo, Davis to JCS, "Report of the Five Power Ad Hoc Committee on Southeast Asia," 5 Feb 52, CCS 092 Asia (6-25-48) sec 24.

Despite their knowledge of the U.S. Joint Chiefs of Staff's aversion to anything resembling a combined command for Southeast Asia, the British and French members inserted in the report a plea for setting up machinery for the joint implementation of any agreed military measures. The United States member, of course, registered his opposition. In his analysis of the report Admiral Davis remarked,

> . . . the British and French are determined to persist in their desire to set up a form of combined command in the Southeast Asia area. In the Ad Hoc Committee report this intention is toned down . . . but the original draft on this point as proposed by the British, together with attendant discussion, indicates that they think any direct support operations by us should come under the French in Indochina and under the British in Hong Kong. . . . it seems to me that . . . they would like not only to determine what we shall do with our own forces in the event of our taking military action with respect to the Southeast Asia problem, but also to command our forces while these limited actions are being taken.[16]

In Admiral Davis' opinion the committee, except for clarifying basic differences, had accomplished little. He was convinced that the British and French had expressed themselves on the basis of firm, national politico-military positions, and that the United States views would not be supported by their governments even if the British and French committee members had approved them. The time had come, he thought, to "firm up some sort of Defense-State position before engaging in further argument on the strictly military level."[17]

It was apparent that the deliberations of the Ad Hoc Committee had put the British, French, and United States

---

16. Ibid.; (TS) Rpt by Ad Hoc Cmte on South East Asia, 5 Feb 52, same file.
17. Ibid.

Chiefs of Staff no nearer to agreement on the form of retaliation against Chinese Communist aggression. It was also obvious that their basic differences would have to be resolved before the contemplated warning could be issued. The Joint Chiefs of Staff did not need to be reminded of the fact that the United States Government required a new, firm policy toward the problem of Southeast Asia as a basis from which negotiations could be carried on. Such a policy had been the subject of study by the NSC staff since late in 1951. This study was about to emerge from the mill and the Chiefs wished to wait for a final decision on it before undertaking any further military talks with the British and French concerning the area.

The Development of NSC 124/2

The initial draft of the new policy toward Southeast Asia, NSC 124, was submitted by the NSC staff on 13 February. Insofar as it applied to Indochina, it was directed more toward countering a possible invasion by the Chinese Communists than toward helping the French and Vietnamese to win their struggle in Tonkin. Furthermore, the measures recommended for use in the event of overt Communist aggression were tied either to the framework of the United Nations or to joint action with the British and French.[18]

In their official comments on the NSC draft the Joint Chiefs of Staff pointed out that in recent conferences the British and French had shown themselves opposed to even the concept of military action against China other than in an area of aggression. But without military measures directed against China itself the local defense of Indochina would have, in the Chiefs' opinion, no reasonable chance of success. Therefore, unless the National Security Council could give assurance that at least the British and French would agree to such measures, the new policy should provide for unilateral action by the United States to save Southeast Asia. Only on this basis could the Joint Chiefs of Staff make reasonable plans and determine their costs and requirements.

---

18. (TS) NSC 124, 13 Feb 52, same file.

What the Joint Chiefs of Staff wanted was a political decision by the National Security Council on whether or not the United States Government, in order to save Southeast Asia from Communism, was willing to take military actions that would, in effect, constitute war against Communist China. If the answer was affirmative the Chiefs could then estimate the costs of specific courses of action and the National Security Council could make further decisions concerning them. The Joint Chiefs of Staff alerted the National Security Council to the fact that preparations for the contemplated measures in Southeast Asia could be made only at the expense of other programs, such as that for NATO, unless United States military production was stepped up and "forces in being" were increased.[19]

There ensued several months of discussion and negotiations between the Departments of State and Defense and the NSC staff. During this time the National Security Council decided to give more consideration, in the new statement of policy, to what the United States should do for Indochina in the current situation, that is, in the absence of overt Chinese Communist aggression. Finally, on 25 June, President Truman approved a revision of NSC 124--which, as NSC 124/2, included the first comprehensive United States policy toward Indochina.

In NSC 124/2 the United States Government recognized that the primary threat to Southeast Asia lay in the possible deterioration of the situation in Indochina as a result of the French and Associated States Governments weakening in their resolve to continue, or becoming unable to continue opposing the Viet Minh rebellion. It also recognized that the successful defense of Tonkin was "critical" to the retention in non-Communist hands of mainland Southeast Asia. For the purpose of holding the entire area, NSC 124/2 provided that:

---

19. (TS) Memo, Vandenberg to SecDef, "United States Objectives and Courses of Action with Respect to Communist Aggression in Southeast Asia," 3 Mar 52, same file, sec 25.

7. With respect to Southeast Asia, the United States should:

   a. Strengthen propaganda and cultural activities, as appropriate, in relation to the area to foster increased alignment of the people with the free world.

   b. Continue, as appropriate, programs of economic and technical assistance designed to strengthen the indigenous non-communist governments of the area.

   c. Encourage the countries of Southeast Asia to restore and expand their commerce with each other and with the rest of the free world, and stimulate the flow of the raw material resources of the area to the free world.

   d. Seek agreement with other nations, including at least France, the UK, Australia and New Zealand, for a joint warning to Communist China regarding the grave consequences of Chinese aggression against Southeast Asia, the issuance of such a warning to be contingent upon the prior agreement of France and the UK to participate in the courses of action set forth in paragraphs 10 c, 12, . . . and such others as are determined as a result of prior trilateral consultation, in the event such a warning is ignored.

   e. Seek UK and French agreement in principle that a naval blockade of Communist China should be included in the minimum courses of action set forth in paragraph 10 c below.

   f. Continue to encourage and support closer cooperation among the countries of Southeast Asia, and between those countries and the United States, Great Britain, France, the Philippines, Australia, New Zealand, South Asia and Japan.

   g. Strengthen, as appropriate, covert operations designed to assist in the achievement of U.S. objectives in Southeast Asia.

h. Continue activities and operations designed to encourage the overseas Chinese communities in Southeast Asia to organize and activate anti-communist groups and activities within their own communities . . . .

i. Take measures to promote the coordinated defense of the area, and encourage and support the spirit of resistance among the peoples of Southeast Asia to Chinese Communist aggression and to the encroachments of local communists.

j. Make clear to the American people the importance of Southeast Asia to the security of the United States so that they may be prepared for any of the courses of action proposed herein.

8. With respect to Indochina the United States should:

a. Continue to promote international support for the three Associated States.

b. Continue to assure the French that the U.S. regards the French effort in Indochina as one of great strategic importance in the general international interest rather than in the purely French interest, and as essential to the security of the free world, not only in the Far East but in the Middle East and Europe as well.

c. Continue to assure the French that we are cognizant of the sacrifices entailed for France in carrying out her effort in Indochina and that, without overlooking the principle that France has the primary responsibility in Indochina, we will recommend to the Congress appropriate military, economic and financial aid to France and the Associated States.

d. Continue to cultivate friendly and increasingly cooperative relations with the Governments of France and the Associated States at all levels with a view to maintaining and, if possible, increasing the degree of influence the U.S. can bring to bear on the policies and actions of the

French and Indochinese authorities to the end of directing the course of events toward the objectives we seek. Our influence with the French and Associated States should be designed to further those constructive political, economic and social measures which will tend to increase the stability of the Associated States and thus make it possible for the French to reduce the degree of their participation in the military, economic and political affairs of the Associated States.

 e. Specifically we should use our influence with France and the Associated States to promote positive political, military, economic and social policies, among which the following are considered essential elements:

  (1) Continued recognition and carrying out by France of its primary responsibility for the defense of Indochina.

  (2) Further steps by France and the Associated States toward the evolutionary development of the Associated States.

  (3) Such reorganization of French administration and representation in Indochina as will be conducive to an increased feeling of responsibility on the part of the Associated States.

  (4) Intensive efforts to develop the armies of the Associated States, including independent logistical and administrative services.

  (5) The development of more effective and stable Governments in the Associated States.

  (6) Land reform, agrarian and industrial credit, sound rice marketing systems, labor development, foreign trade and capital formation.

(7) An aggressive military, political, and psychological program to defeat or seriously reduce the Viet Minh forces.

(8) US-French cooperation in publicizing progressive developments in the foregoing policies in Indochina.

9. In the absence of large scale Chinese Communist intervention in Indochina, the United States should:

    a. Provide increased aid on a high priority basis for the French Union forces without relieving French authorities of their basic military responsibility for the defense of the Associated States in order to:

        (1) Assist in developing indigenous armed forces which will eventually be capable of maintaining internal security without assistance from French units.

        (2) Assist the French Union forces to maintain progress in the restoration of internal security against the Viet Minh.

        (3) Assist the forces of France and the Associated States to defend Indochina against Chinese Communist aggression.

    b. In view of the immediate urgency of the situation, involving possible large-scale Chinese Communist intervention, and in order that the United States may be prepared to take whatever action may be appropriate in such circumstances, make the plans necessary to carry out the courses of action indicated in paragraph 10 below.

    c. In the event that information and circumstances point to the conclusion that France is no longer prepared to carry the burden in Indochina, or if France presses for an increased sharing of the responsibility for Indochina, whether in the UN or directly with the U.S. Government, oppose a French withdrawal and consult with the French and British concerning further measures to be taken to safeguard the area from communist domination.

10. In the event that it is determined, in consultation with France, that Chinese Communist forces (including volunteers) have overtly intervened in the conflict in Indochina, or are covertly participating to such an extent as to jeopardize retention of the Tonkin Delta area by French Union forces, the United States should take the following measures to assist these forces in preventing the loss of Indochina, to repel the aggression and to restore peace and security in Indochina:

    a. Support a request by France or the Associated States for immediate action by the United Nations which would include a UN resolution declaring that Communist China has committed an aggression, recommending that member states take whatever action may be necessary, without geographic limitation, to assist France and the Associated States in meeting the aggression.

    b. Whether or not UN action is immediately forthcoming, seek the maximum possible international support for, and participation in, the minimum courses of military action agreed upon by the parties to the joint warning. These minimum courses of action are set forth in subparagraph c immediately below.

    c. Carry out the following minimum courses of military action, either under the auspices of the UN or in conjunction with France and the United Kingdom and any other friendly governments:

    (1) A resolute defense of Indochina itself to which the United States would provide such air and naval assistance as might be practicable.

    (2) Interdiction of Chinese Communist communication lines including those in China.

    (3) The United States would expect to provide the major forces for task (2) above; but would expect the UK and France to provide at least token forces therefor and to render such other assistance

as is normal between allies, and France to carry the burden of providing, in conjunction with the Associated States, the ground forces for the defense of Indochina.

11. In addition to the courses of action set forth in paragraph 10 above, the United States should take the following military actions as appropriate to the situation:

    a. If agreement is reached pursuant to paragraph 7-e, establishment in conjunction with the UK and France of a naval blockade of Communist China.

    b. Intensification of covert operations to aid anti-communist guerrilla forces operating against Communist China and to interfere with and disrupt Chinese Communist lines of communication and military supply areas.

    c. Utilization, as desirable and feasible, of anti-communist Chinese forces, including Chinese Nationalist forces in military operations in Southeast Asia, Korea, or China proper.

    d. Assistance to the British to cover an evacuation from Hong Kong, if required.

    e. Evacuation of French Union civil and military personnel from the Tonkin Delta, if required.

12. If, subsequent to aggression against Indochina and execution of the minimum necessary courses of action listed in paragraph 10-c above, the United States determines jointly with the UK and France that expanded military action against Communist China is rendered necessary by the situation, the United States should take air and naval action in conjunction with at least France and the UK against all suitable military targets in China, avoiding insofar as practicable those targets in areas near the boundaries of the USSR in order not to increase the risk of direct Soviet involvement.

13. In the event the concurrence of the United Kingdom and France to expanded military action against Communist China is not obtained, the United States should consider taking unilateral action.[20]

The Joint Chiefs of Staff Act on NSC 124/2

With Presidential approval of NSC 124/2 the Joint Chiefs of Staff had a firm governmental policy on which to base their planning. Moreover, they had successfully inserted into the new policy the consideration of unilateral action against a Chinese Communist aggression in Southeast Asia. They therefore, on 29 August, directed CINCPAC to make unilateral plans, which, in addition to preparing for unilateral action, would develop a United States position in the event that an agreement for allied combined planning was reached. CINCPAC had previously been instructed to establish plans for a naval blockade of Communist China, for supporting participation of Chinese Nationalist forces in hostilities, for assisting in evacuation of the Tonkin Delta, and for military action against selected targets held by Communist China. He was now instructed:

> In order to be prepared to assist our Allies in war in defense of Indochina and approaches thereto, prepare plan for Air and Naval action against Communist Forces and for action against Chi Communist communications lines and facilities operating in support of Communist Forces.

He was to develop his plans under three assumptions: firstly, that the Korean Conflict was continuing and no FECOM naval forces would be available to him; secondly, that conditions in Korea would permit him to have limited naval forces from FECOM; and thirdly, that there was an armistice in Korea and FECOM naval forces above minimum FECOM requirements could be used in Southeast Asia. Implementation of his plans was to be undertaken only upon authorization by the Joint Chiefs of Staff.[21]

---

20. (TS) NSC 124/2, 25 Jun 52, same file, sec 31.
21. (TS) Msg, JCS 917321 to CINCPAC, 29 Aug 52, same file, sec 34.

The plans called for in the JCS instructions were capabilities plans, based on the forces available in the Pacific and Far Eastern areas. CINCPAC, however, requested authority to make plans based on the requirements for the task contemplated. On 22 December the Joint Chiefs of Staff partially acceded to his request, instructing him to make both capabilities and requirements plans.[22]

The Five-Power Military Conference on Southeast Asia

A few days after the promulgation of NSC 124/2 United States representatives at a Tripartite Foreign Ministers Conference in London tentatively assented to holding another five-power military meeting on the problem of Chinese Communist aggression in Southeast Asia. Mindful that the Five-Power Ad Hoc Committee had failed owing to the lack of agreed political assumptions the Working Committee of the conference drew up a set of "provisional conclusions," which, if approved by the governments concerned, would permit the military representatives to produce a useful report. The Joint Chiefs of Staff found, however, that the "provisional conclusions" expressed chiefly the usual British and French opposition to action against China outside the area of aggression and their desire for a combined command organization. Furthermore, the conclusions did not fit with the provisions of NSC 124/2. The Chiefs therefore refused their assent to such a meeting, recommending instead a joint tripartite conference of heads of state, or their representatives, and Chiefs of Staff, which could settle political and military disagreements at the same time. As a prelude to the conference, the Joint Chiefs of Staff recommended, a meeting of purely military representatives should be held, but only after preliminary agreement had been reached on terms of reference substantially conforming to the pattern of NSC 124/2.[23]

But once again JCS resistance to a military meeting without agreed political guidance was overcome. At a

---

22. (TS) JCS 1992/188, 31 Oct 52, same file, sec 35; (TS) Msg, JCS 927061 to CINCPAC, 22 Dec 52, same file, sec 37.
23. (TS) JCS 1992/171, 10 Jul 52, same file, sec 32.

Defense-State conference on 16 July State Department representatives argued that a five-power military representatives conference would serve as "a step toward bringing the other powers to an acceptance of the United States concept of the solution to the problems incident to Southeast Asia" and that the terms of reference proposed by the Joint Chiefs of Staff could not be made acceptable to the other four powers. Faced with these arguments the Joint Chiefs of Staff consented to soften their position and agreed to more general terms of reference. According to these terms the conferees were to assume that the five powers had jointly decided to take action against Communist China in the event of further Chinese Communist aggression and that a joint warning had been issued to Peiping. From a purely military point they were to determine the collective military capabilities that might be made available and to make recommendations on the feasible military courses of action for causing the Chinese Communists to cease their aggression.[24]

On 6 October, their governments having agreed to these terms of reference, the military representatives of the United Kingdom, France, Australia, and New Zealand met with the United States delegation, headed by Major General J. S. Bradley, USA, in Washington. After eleven days of deliberation the conferees submitted a report containing over-all conclusions that conformed generally with JCS positions of long standing. The representatives agreed that:

> Air, ground and naval action limited only to the areas of aggression and contiguous areas of China offers little prospect of causing Communist China to cease its aggression.
> The imposition of a total sea blockade, in conjunction with /such action/ . . ., might have a significant cumulative effect. This course of action offers little assurance of forcing the Chinese Communists to cease aggression.
> A combination of all coercive measures including the defense of the areas of aggression,

---

24. (TS) JCS 1992/174, 26 Jul 52, same file, sec 33.

interdiction of the lines of communication, a full sea blockade and air attacks on all suitable targets of military significance in China, insofar as they are within the Allied capabilities, plus such reinforcements in time and scale as may be practicable in the immediate area, offers the best prospect of causing Communist China to cease an aggression.[25]

It was the opinion of Major General Bradley, expressed in a separate report to the Joint Chiefs of Staff, that these conclusions represented a step forward from positions established in the February Ad Hoc Committee meetings. But it was apparent from the discussions, he said, that the agreement was forced by the terms of reference. When the representatives had attempted to settle on the strategy against Communist China that could be undertaken with the forces available the British and French had displayed the same interests, attitudes, and fears described by Admiral Davis in February. Australia and New Zealand, not unnaturally, adhered in general to the United Kingdom position. Without agreements reached at a high political level, Major General Bradley concluded, or unless there were a decided change in United States policy, further five-power military talks on Southeast Asia would serve no useful purpose.[26]

The Joint Chiefs of Staff Act on the Five-Power Conference Report

The Joint Chiefs of Staff concurred with Major General Bradley's opinion that further five-power military meetings were useless without prior jointly agreed political guidance. They were encouraged, however, by the conference report. They recommended to the Secretary of Defense that NSC 124/2 be amended to provide for securing assent "under the auspices of the United Nations

---

25. (TS) Rpt of the Five Power Mil Conf on South East Asia, 17 Oct 52, same file, sec 34.
26. (TS) Memo, Maj Gen J.S. Bradley to JCS, "Report of the Five Power Military Representatives Conference on Southeast Asia," 23 Oct 52, same file.

or in conjunction with France and the United Kingdom and any other friendly government" for undertaking the "combination of all coercive actions" set forth in the report as offering the best prospect of stopping Chinese Communist aggression. They also recommended that the report be used as a basis for securing international agreement on those actions.

Turning to another item in the conference report, the Joint Chiefs of Staff advised Secretary Lovett that the French should be encouraged at every opportunity to increase and speed the development of the native armies and supporting facilities in Indochina. The five-power military representatives had concluded that the forces in Tonkin were insufficient to halt a massive Chinese attack. Under existing circumstances the only large scale reinforcements that could arrive in time to stop an invading army would have to come from United States forces in the Pacific and Far East. And not only were facilities for basing United States air and ground forces lacking in Indochina, but commitment of such forces in that limited area would reduce capabilities for direct action against Communist China. The solution, according to the Joint Chiefs of Staff, lay in building up indigenous combat forces to the extent necessary to meet the threat, and the French should be assisted and encouraged in carrying out this responsibility.[27]

Like its predecessor, the Ad Hoc Committee Report, the Five-Power Conference Report expressed the desire of the British and French for some sort of staff agency to coordinate the planning of the five powers in Southeast Asia. It also registered the opinion of the United States delegation that, insofar as American participation was concerned, CINCPAC already had sufficient machinery for fulfilling the United States obligation to cooperate in the area. Since this was, of course, the position of the Joint Chiefs of Staff, they let the issue rest until French and State Department pressure revived it.[28]

---
27. (TS) JCS 1992/191, 13 Nov 52, same file, sec 35.
28. Ibid.

Early in December the French Government, through diplomatic channels, urged the United States Government to participate in a liaison group drawn from the staffs of the British, French, and United States commanders in Southeast Asia. The French had accommodated themselves to the JCS views so far as to project purely liaison, rather than planning or operating, functions for the group. In passing the French proposal on to the Joint Chiefs of Staff, the State Department expressed the view that "it would be advantageous to increase the effectiveness of military liaison arrangements among the countries which have military interests or commitments in Southeast Asia."[29]

The Joint Chiefs of Staff thereupon agreed to the establishment of liaison machinery in Southeast Asia subject to three conditions. Firstly, it should permit participation "on an on-call and need to know basis," not only by each of the five powers, but by additional Southeast Asian countries if this later appeared desirable. Secondly, it should allow representatives of any participating nation to communicate with representatives of one or more other nations either in person or through liaison officers. Necessary coordination should be accomplished on a bilateral basis whenever possible. Finally, it should not result in the establishment of any formal body or committee; there would be no need for regular meetings or for a permanent chair.[30]

On 27 February 1953 the Joint Chiefs of Staff acted on their decision. They instructed CINCPAC to invite the principal local military commanders of the other four powers to send representatives to an exploratory meeting for the purpose of discussing liaison arrangements, including machinery for coordinating national plans.[31] This directive led to the Five Power Military Representatives Conference at Pearl Harbor in April.

---

29. (TS) Ltr, Matthews to Cabell, 9 Dec 52, same file, sec 36.
30. (TS) Memo, Cabell to SecDef, "Machinery for Implementing Five-Power Coordinations of Plans," 11 Dec 52, same file.
31. (TS) Msg, JCS 932447 to CINCPAC, 27 Feb 53, same file, sec 38.

Undoubtedly the promulgation of NSC 124/2 was the most important development in United States policy toward Indochina in 1952. In pursuing the objectives of that policy the United States Government, by the end of the year, was becoming more and more involved in the Southeast Asian struggle against Communism. It contrived, of course, to keep responsibility for the war in the hands of the French, it refused to be drawn into a combined military command in Southeast Asia, and it sidestepped any commitment to participate in a purely local defense of Indochina. Nevertheless, the United States had agreed to at least liaison arrangements for coordinating five-power planning in Southeast Asia. United States representatives were backing the French position on Indochina in the United Nations and in international conferences. They were assuring the French Government of continued American support of, and appreciation for, France's efforts in the war. Furthermore, the Truman Administration was expanding the military aid program for Indochina and was publicizing its contribution to the war. By the time President Eisenhower entered the White House at least a part of American prestige rested upon French and Vietnamese success in Tonkin.

American Public Opinion on Indochina

At least one provision of NSC 124/2 was slighted during 1952. This was the obligation to educate the American people concerning the importance of Southeast Asia to United States security to prepare them for the courses of action contemplated by the National Security Council. True, government officials seized upon various occasions, such as international conferences, to make statements on the subject. But these occasions were relatively few in number. It is apparent, after study of the New York Times and other news media, that no concerted effort was made to arouse public opinion. It may be that in an election year, with the unpopular Korean Conflict very much at issue, the Administration feared to present the public with the prospect of another armed action. Nevertheless, this failure was important for the future. In a progress report on NSC 124/2 prepared in August 1953, officials of the State and Defense

Departments estimated that there was as yet no indication that public opinion would support a contribution to the Indochina war other than the current type of aid program. United States military participation, they said, would not be acceptable to the public.[32]

Development of the Aid Program during 1952

Throughout 1952 United States equipment supplied under MDAP passed in a steady stream over the docks of Saigon and Haiphong. A monthly average of approximately 21,300 measurement tons of end items were shipped, exclusive of aircraft and vessels delivered under their own power. The monetary value of this materiel was approximately $171,100,000. These deliveries brought the total of end items shipped to Indochina between June 1950 and 31 December 1952 to 539,847 measurement tons with a value of $334,700,000. As of the end of 1952 the total value of MDAP material programmed under the budgets for Fiscal Years 1950-1953 had risen to $775,700,000.[33]

No breakdown of statistics on major items of equipment shipped during 1952 is available. By the end of June 1953, however, the United States had shipped to Indochina under the MDAP 1,224 tanks and combat vehicles, 20,274 transport vehicles, 120,792 small arms and machine guns, 2,847 artillery pieces, over 220 million rounds of small arms ammunition, and more than 5 million rounds of artillery ammunition. Also, 302 naval vessels and 304 naval and Air Force aircraft had been delivered.[34] Obviously, the United States contribution to the Indochina struggle was not a small one.

---

32. (TS) Memo, Actg SecState and Actg SecDef to Exec Secy NSC, "Progress Report on NSC 124/2 -- United States Objectives and Courses of Action with Respect to Southeast Asia," 5 Aug 53, same file, sec 44.

33. (S) MDAP Status Report for the Month of January 1953.

34. (S) MDAP Status Report for the Month of July 1953.

The Lisbon Program

In addition to the regular MDAP end item shipments, a program for giving direct support to the French military budget was undertaken by the United States Government early in 1952. In the autumn of 1951 the French announced that their financial difficulties would entail a cut in dollar imports, with resultant injury to their defense program, and to their heavy industry.[35] The United States Government therefore decided to support the French budget to the extent of 200 million dollars by letting contracts in France, chiefly for end items to be used in Indochina. On 25 February 1952 a "memorandum of understanding" on this matter was drawn up by French and United States officials at the Lisbon meeting of the NATO Council. Under this program Indochina was to receive materiel worth 126 million dollars, the remaining 74 million dollars to be used for requirements in France itself. The French Government, however, considered that this permitted the release for Indochina of an equivalent from the French military budget, so that, in the French view, the entire 200 million dollars went for the support of the war.[36]

By 31 December 1952, $127,100,000 worth of Lisbon-type aid had been programmed, and $47,100,000 worth had been delivered. In July the United States Government agreed to support the French Fiscal Year 1953 budget to the extent of $525,000,000, over half of which was to come from MDAP funds. It is not clear, however, what part of this sum was used for Indochina and what part for French requirements in Europe.[37]

---

35. (TS) JCS 2099/171, 13 Feb 52, CCS 092 (8-22-46) sec 68.

36. (S) MDAP Status Report for the Month of March 1952; (C) Msg, USEmb Paris to SecState, 3697, 29 Dec 52, in OMA files, Indochina 2a (1952). Twenty-three million dollars of the 126 million dollars for Indochina was spent in the United States for items that France could not supply.

37. (S) MDAP Monthly Status Reports for the Months of November 1952 and January 1953.

The Pleven Proposal

In early March the French Government intimated that it was not satisfied with the 200 million dollars promised at Lisbon. Unless additional aid was given, the Minister of National Defense wrote, France would have to cancel some of her intended military production then in progress. In May, M. Pleven, then Defense Minister, submitted a list of heavy items, the production of which he proposed the United States finance. The cost of this program was estimated at 623 million dollars. The United States Government, and especially its military services, were reluctant to expend so large a sum, but did promise 196 million dollars for the procurement of jet aircraft and ammunition. According to the MDAP Status Report for July 1952:

> The official reaction of the French to the U.S. position /was/ extremely unfavorable. President Auriol . . . expressed on two occasions to the U.S. Special Representative in Europe (Ambassador William H. Draper, Jr.) his personal disappointment and said that the U.S. decision promised to create grave difficulties for France. . . . Mr. Pleven has stated that, as a result of the U.S. decision, he may have no alternative but to resign.[38]

Despite Gallic disappointment, in June 1953 French officers in Indochina admitted, inter se, that because of United States aid the French taxpayer was carrying less of the burden of the war in 1953 than he had in 1952.[39]

Equipment Shortages in Indochina

French complaints about lagging MDAP deliveries generally subsided after the first few months of 1952. M. Letourneau, during a visit to Washington in June

---

38. (S) MDAP Status Report for the Month of July 1952.
39. (TS) Navarre Briefing Doc, Jun 53, in OMA files.

expressed to officials of the Department of Defense his satisfaction with the program except in the troublesome categories of aircraft and spare parts.40 Throughout the year these items were in short supply in Indochina, and Air Force deliveries were behind schedule. Ammunition, too, was sometimes a problem.

When French complaints about these shortages became less strident, General Brink, and later his successor, Brigadier General T.J.H. Trapnell, took up the chorus. As the autumn fighting season approached, MAAG Indochina began to bombard the Pentagon with requests to speed overdue deliveries. On 9 August General Trapnell sent a message to the Chief of Staff, Air Force, saying:

> Successful accomplishment of French Air Force mission of air superiority, interdiction, log opr of grd forces in Indochina is being threatened and jecpardized by lack of implementation of existing Air Force MDA programs. Generally, some C 47 maint Equip and sprares /sic/ have not been dlvr under FY 50 program, 35% of line items of FY 51 consisting primarily of comm equip; acft spares and acft maint equip, 30 of 70 acft programmed under FY 52 program remain undlvr as well as the initial RG of acft spares . . . . The Army spt program curr contains no shortage items of critical nature however the Air Force program contains all above listed item.41

As the year wore on such messages became more frequent. CINCPAC, too, added his voice in support of General Trapnell. On 27 September Secretary Lovett approved a recommendation of the Joint Chiefs of Staff placing combat requirements for Indochina alongside requirements for Korea in first priority for allocation of equipment. Finally,

---

40. (S) Memo for Rec by Ch, Liaison Div, OMA, "Conferences with Minister Letourneau and Members of His Staff, 16-17 June 1952," nd, in OMA files, Indochina 2a (1952).
41. (S) Msg, Trapnell MG 3824 A, to CSUSAF, DA-IN-170843, 9 Aug 52, same file.

in late December, the Deputy Secretary of Defense, William C. Foster, saw fit to admonish the Service Secretaries:

> It has been brought to my attention, both as a result of my recent inspection trip to the Far East and by numerous communications from Department of Defense representatives and others, that the MDA Program for Indochina may not be receiving proper emphasis. Specific instances of lack of support for this Program have generally been in the area of items to support maintenance activities, spare parts and depot equipment, and in the delivery of some types of ammunition. . . .
>
> Because of the high priority assigned to the supply of materiel to Indochina, I consider that all requirements for this Program should be met on an urgent basis and that no delay in the delivery of major items of equipment, spare parts to support this equipment, and ammunition should be permitted by any of the Military Departments. . . .[42]

Despite efforts to remedy the situation General Trapnell reported that, as of 1 January 1953, while Army and Navy deliveries were generally in good order, the Air Force MDAP stood as follows:[43]

Program	% Complete
FY 50	97%
FY 51	67%
FY 52	22%
FY 53	None

The lag in deliveries was attributed in part to improper planning by the French and the MAAG in Indochina, but a good share of the responsibility was placed on the Military

---

42. (S) Memo, Foster to SecA, SecNav, and SecAF, "Indochina Mutual Defense Assistance Program," nd, same file.
43. (S) Memo, Trapnell to Dir OMA, "Field Estimate of current and future effectiveness of the French Union Forces in Indochina," 22 Jan 53; same file, sec 2 (1953).

Departments for not placing proper emphasis on the program.[44] French inefficiency also contributed much to the constant shortage of spare parts. Poor organization, poor training, lack of personnel, lack of an inspection system, no stock control system for spare parts, and lack of an aggressive attitude in correcting malpractices hampered French maintenance activities. All of these factors raised the French rate of utilization of spare parts to a level much too high according to American standards.[45]

French Requests for Additional Aircraft

When M. Letourneau talked with Department of Defense representatives during his June visit he asked not only for immediate shipment of aircraft already programmed but for additional aircraft, including transport, fighter, and light bomber types. U.S. Air Force officers, however, considered that instead of more aircraft the greatest French need was to improve the utilization rate of those they already had. The French were using their C-47's only 35 hours per month whereas the United States standard was 100 hours monthly. French rates for fighters and bombers were similarly low. The Air Force therefore declined to furnish more than ten out of sixty-nine B-26's requested by the French for Fiscal Year 1953. It refused to supply ten additional C-47's until the French had developed a basis of justification for them. It turned down a request for a squadron of C-119's because Air Force officers thought the French were not prepared to maintain them. Finally, a request for jet fighters was refused on the

---

44. (S) Memo, DepAsst to SecDef for ISA to DepSecDef, "Indochina MDA Program," 16 Dec 52, same file, sec 2a (1952).
45. (S) Memo, Trapnell to Dir OMA, "Field Estimate of current and future effectiveness of the French Union Forces in Indochina," 22 Jan 53, same file, sec 2 (1953); (S) Memo for Rec by Ch, Liaison Div, OMA, "Conferences with Minister Letourneau and Members of His Staff, 16-17 June 1952," nd, same file, sec 2a (1952); (C) Interv, Hoare with Cummings, 1 Nov 54, in JCS HS files.

grounds that the French Air Forces were unopposed in Indochinese skies. The United States representatives agreed, however, to maintain the four French fighter squadrons by replacing worn-out F-6F's with F-8F's and by providing attrition aircraft.[46]

But these decisions were not final, even for 1952. On 14 August General Trapnell cabled that the French High Command was planning offensive operations, for the fall campaign, that required the dropping of three paratroop battalions in each operation. In order to carry out their plan, he said, the French would require additional transport planes. The Department of Defense, after careful study, decided that the French could use fifty additional C-47's. These aircraft were in short supply in the United States, but a solution to the problem was worked out in a conference among Army, Air Force, Department of State, and Department of Defense officials. Nine C-47's were provided from France, 20 were diverted from the MDAP allotment to Belgium, and 21 were lent by the U.S. Air Force for about four months on Memorandum Receipt.[47] When these transfers were accomplished, however, the French were so pinched for C-47's for crew training in France that the Department of Defense was obliged to lend them four additional planes intended for U.S. Air Forces in Europe.[48]

American Mechanics Go to Indochina

As we have seen, the offensive planned by the French High Command in Indochina was not undertaken. The fifty C-47's were nevertheless used extensively in providing airlift in support of the Na San defense. They were, in fact, used so frequently that the limited French ground

---

46. (S) Memo for Rec by Ch, Liaison Div, OMA, "Conferences with Minister Letourneau and Members of His Staff, 16-17 June 1952," nd, in OMA files, Indochina 2a (1952).
47. (TS) Memo, Foster to JCS, "Requirement for Additional Transport Aircraft in Indo-China," 12 Sep 52, CCS 092 Asia (6-25-48) sec 34.
48. (TS) Msg, AFOMS-OP to Ch MAAG, France, AF-OUT-9100, 25 Nov 52, in OMA files, Indochina 2a (1952).

crews were unable to maintain them. The French therefore asked that 150 U.S. Air Force mechanics be sent to Indochina for one month to perform 50 and 100 hour checks on C-47's. This request was backed by both General Trapnell and Ambassador Heath. The United States Government responded by sending a mobile maintenance team of about 28 men from the FEAF to perform direct maintenance on C-47's being used by the French forces. It sought to avoid bad publicity, however, by informing "all concerned" that the action was only a temporary augmentation of the MAAG for the purpose of training French ground crews and insuring the early return of the C-47's on loan. These men were to be withdrawn at the earliest possible date.[49]

United States Offer to Train Vietnamese Forces

The question of United States participation in training of the Associated States Armies was not much discussed in the halls of government during 1952. But, for the first time, it was considered seriously. On 8 April the Service Secretaries recommended to Secretary Lovett the consideration of a program "whereby an expanded MAAG would undertake the training and equipping of a national army capable at least of preserving internal security."[50] Not long thereafter an offer of assistance in training was made. But, as Secretary of State Acheson later remarked:

> the French, always skittish over what they might regard as undue American interference, /did not take/ up this offer. Certainly it is not up to the Americans to press on the French assistance along these lines.[51]

---

49. (TS) Doc C-54, Msg, Heath, 1149 to SecState, 5 Dec 52, in (TS) <u>Doc Hist of US Pol toward Indochina</u>; (TS) Memo, SecAF to SecDef, 7 Jan 53, in OMA file "Indochina Maintenance Support Exercise"; (TS) Msg, OSD to Ch MAAG Indochina, DEF 927097, 22 Dec 52, in OMA files, Indochina 2a(1952).
50. (TS) Memo, SecA, SecNav, and Actg SecAF to SecDef, "Draft State Department Paper on Indochina dated 27 March 1952," 8 Apr 52, CCS 092 Asia (6-25-48) sec 28.
51. (TS) Doc C-52, Summary Mns, "Ministerial Talks in London, June 1952," 14 Jul 52, in (TS) <u>Doc Hist of US Pol toward Indochina</u>.

Assessment of MDAP in 1952

Although the handling of the MDA Program still left something to be desired, the United States, by the end of 1952, had given the French in Indochina equipment for ground, naval, and air forces far superior to that in the hands of the Viet Minh. Despite the hampering of air operations by shortages of planes and spare parts it would be difficult to support a contention that French forces would have done much better had those shortages not existed. Wedded to his barbed-wire entanglements, General Salan used his air force too often as a defensive arm. More French aircraft would have meant more Viet Minh casualties at Na San and the Black River. But it is doubtful, even had they all the planes they could man, that the French could have broken the Communist forces in a defensive operation. What seemed to be needed most in Indochina, and what the United States did not offer under MDAP, was guts. This is not to say that the French were cowards on the battlefield. On the contrary, their officers and men conducted themselves bravely in action. But they were not so brave at the planning board, partly, perhaps, because they felt they were not being well-supported at home.

The French Home Front Begins to Crack

Throughout 1952 France's allies were disturbed by symptoms of weakening in her determination to carry on the war. These symptoms were appearing not only in expressions of public opinion, but in parliamentary debates and even in statements by government officials.

The number of Frenchmen, including politicians, who opposed the war seemed to be growing constantly. They based their position chiefly on four arguments. Firstly, they pointed to the drain on the French treasury and the resultant effect on France's economic condition in general. Secondly, they held that France could not afford any longer the losses of manpower represented by the casualties in her armed forces (the French claimed 90,000, excluding Vietnamese, between 1945 and 1 October 1952).[52] Thirdly, maintaining the bulk of the French

---

52. (NATO S) Summary Record of NATO Council Mtg, Paris, 16 Dec 52, in JCS records.

Army in Indochina was holding up the development of French forces for NATO and delaying the establishment of an adequate defense organization in Europe. Finally, after the conclusion of the EDC Treaty in May, they argued that the prospect of German rearmament demanded the recall to France of the forces in Indochina. Otherwise, they said, Germany would become militarily strong while France remained weak in Europe. Such arguments appealed to segments of political opinion on the Right as well as on the Left, to conservatives who had supported the war as well as to Socialists who had opposed it. Most of all, they appealed to the almost universal French fear of Germany.[53]

French Socialists and Communists had long urged negotiations with the Viet Minh for ending hostilities. On the whole public opinion had given them little support. By 1952, however, an important part of the Radical Socialist Party favored a political agreement with Ho Chi Minh. This faction was led by a former cabinet minister, Pierre Mendes-France, who as early as 1950 had expressed his opposition to continuing the war.[54] At a Radical Socialist Congress in Bordeaux in October 1952, former Premier Edouard Daladier proclaimed that instead of wasting men and arms in Indochina France should be defending the French Union in North Africa, an area far more important for her future.[55]

The defection of a large group of Radical Socialists from the ranks of those who favored continuing the war was especially significant. The Radical Socialists had participated in the several Center-Right coalition governments that, of late years, had been carrying the burden of the struggle in Indochina. They drew their support, traditionally, from the middle class and particularly from the intellectual professions, always an important factor

---

53. *The Economist* (London), 5 Jan 52, p. 30; 5 Apr 52, pp. 4-6; 21 Jun 52, pp. 821-822. NY Times, 2 Jul 52, p. 4; 31 Jul 52, p. 1; 19 Oct 52, p. 2.

54. *Journal Officiel, Assem Nat*, 18 Oct 50, pp. 7003-7004.

55. *L'Information Radicale-Socialiste*, Oct 52, quoted in Hammer, *Struggle for Indochina*, p. 309.

in French public opinion. The growth of Mendes-France's following weakened the coalition governments and was a definite indication that France's will to fight was at least beginning to deteriorate.

Early in 1952 the British began to regard the French internal situation as serious in its possible effects on Southeast Asia. In March the British Embassy in Washington sent an unofficial aide-memoire to the State-Department calling attention to recent statements of M. Letourneau. The Minister for the Associated States had said publicly, in reply to a question whether or not the French were prepared to enter into discussions with the Viet Minh, that France could not on principle reject any opportunity to end hostilities. He had also indicated that France would not reinforce its troops in Indochina. This had followed a statement by Foreign Minister Schuman that France "would not refuse an accord which would put an end to the conflict under conditions which would be honorable for France."[56] The British also felt there was reason to believe that French representatives had recently been in contact with the Viet Minh and, indeed, might be seeking Russian mediation.

The United States Government, however, was not alarmed. The Joint Intelligence Committee advised the Joint Chiefs of Staff that while there was a possibility of an eventual French withdrawal, the British estimate that it might be imminent was exaggerated. Reported French approaches to the Communists, they wrote, could not be confirmed. Furthermore, the factors disturbing the British had been considered in the preparation of a National Intelligence Estimate on 3 March in which United States intelligence experts had concluded that the French effort in Indochina would continue through mid-1952. This estimate was

---

56. (TS) Copy of Unofficial Aide Memoire on "Indochina" handed by member of Brit Emb to Asst SecState for Far Eastern Affairs, 15 Mar 52, CCS 092 Asia (6-25-48) sec 26; NY Times, 7 Jan 52, p. 4.

projected through mid-1953 in another National Intelligence Estimate of 29 August.[57]

Despite the fact that these predictions were borne out it is difficult to escape the conclusion, on the basis of hindsight, that the United States Government was overestimating the strength of French determination. American officials, while not ignoring the warning signals that were flashing, seem to have comforted themselves with repeated assurances by the French Government that France would not give up the struggle. They realized of course, that if the situation in Indochina failed to improve, the French will and ability to continue resisting the Viet Minh would eventually weaken. They thus recognized that there was a limit to the time the French government would have to win the war before being faced with a collapse of the home front. But as late as June 1953 the belief was expressed, in a National Intelligence Estimate, that the French would maintain their current troop strength (and, by implication, their position) in Indochina through mid-1954, albeit "without enthusiasm."[58] And too seldom, during 1952, did United States officials, in planning for and supporting the Indochinese war, display the sense of urgency that would have been called for had the debacle of early 1954 been foreseen.

---

57. (TS) Encl B to SM-762-52, Memo, Lalor to JCS, "Indochina," 22 Mar 52, CCS 092 Asia (6-25-48) sec 26; (S) NIE 35/1, "Probable Developments in Indochina through mid-1952," 3 Mar 52; (S) NIE 35/2, "Probable Developments in Indochina through mid-1953," 29 Aug 52.

58. (S) NIE 91, "Probable Developments in Indochina through Mid-1954," 4 Jun 53.

CHAPTER XI

THE EISENHOWER ADMINISTRATION AND THE NAVARRE PLAN

During 1953, while America's material support for the Indochinese war reached ever higher levels, the United States took on a large new commitment for financial aid to the French cause. It did so to give every advantage and encouragement to a program of French military operations that seemed to offer real hope of bringing the Indochina affair to a decisive conclusion. American officials acted also in awareness that the present opportunity was probably their last chance to sustain a positive French effort. The resolute support given by the incumbent French Government to its new commander in the field contrasted disturbingly with the steadily declining willingness of the French public to make further sacrifices and the talk of negotiated settlement that even the government leaders had taken up.

The Main Course of United States Policy

At the moment of the turn of the year, to be sure, policy development was in virtual suspension. France was once more without a government, until Rene Mayer won the endorsement of the National Assembly on 7 January 1953. The United States awaited the inauguration of President Dwight D. Eisenhower and his new administration later in the month.

Dedicated to making a fresh and comprehensive approach to America's problems abroad, the Eisenhower Administration nevertheless faced the fact that the aims of the United States Government in Southeast Asia were hardly susceptible to fundamental revision. Reassessment would only highlight anew the national interests and purposes already set forth in the dossier of NSC papers that awaited the incoming officials. Indochina must be defended against Viet Minh domination. Unless the United States wished to assume the whole task its leaders must continue to work with and through the French.

For his part, Premier Mayer came to office in January 1953 pledged to lessen the burdens of France in Indochina by seeking greater help from the Atlantic allies. French spokesmen were intent on wringing every possible advantage from the resolution recently adopted by the North Atlantic Council. On 17 December 1952 that body had formally recognized that French resistance to aggression in Indochina made an essential contribution to the security of the free world and hence deserved "continuing support from the NATO governments." The United States had been a party to the North Atlantic Council action. When Secretary of State John Foster Dulles arrived in Paris early in February he encountered a request for larger assistance "in order that France may carry out the mission devolving upon her in the common interests of the free world."[1]

For meeting French importunities the Secretary of State had at hand one telling and quite legitimate argument. The American people had just installed an administration pledged to government economy; that administration in turn had to deal with a Congress that was even more disposed to reduce expenditures abroad and jettison unproductive programs. Therefore, to win authorization for additional American aid the French requests must in every case be backed by cogent justification and convincing performance in the field.

At the moment the French could claim little military progress in Indochina. Acquiescence in the Viet Minh initiative in October 1952 had set the pattern for the remainder of the fighting season. Thereafter the French did little more than react to each new attack. The C-47

---

1. (U) Doc C-55, "Resolution on Indo-China Adopted by the North Atlantic Council on 17th December, 1952," and (TS) Doc D-4, Account of SecState Conversations in Paris, 2 Feb 53, sent Saigon as A-117, 5 Mar 53. Both in (TS) Doc Hist of US Pol toward Indochina, 1940-1953. For quotation from French Govt Communique, 2 Feb 53, see Keesing's Contemporary Archives (London), vol. IX (1952-1954), p. 12740A (hereinafter: Keesing). For Mayer statement on assuming office, see ibid., p. 12674A.

aircraft, originally gathered to permit aggressive operations involving a 3-battalion drop, were soon fully employed in supplying isolated strong points, particularly the briskly defended bastion at Na San.

While the French made much of the heavy losses their entrenched defenders had inflicted on the enemy, April 1953 brought dramatic evidence that the Viet Minh still held the initiative. In an entirely new aggression whose international repercussions nearly carried the matter to the United Nations, enemy forces invaded Laos. Overrunning the two northeast provinces and surging to within ten miles of the royal Laotian capital, they posed a threat to Thailand's border. By a major exertion the French command established strong points at the Plaine des Jarres and elsewhere in the path of the invaders. Logistical difficulties and the approach of the rainy season induced the Viet Minh to withdraw during May.

Thus the military situation during the first part of 1953 underscored the need for new measures and further effort. At the year's beginning officials in both Washington and Saigon were considering means of enlarging the forces in Indochina. Since the political conditions that denied any increase in the French manpower contribution seemed inalterable, the troops would have to be Vietnamese. A project for placing 40,000 additional natives under arms received approval from the Franco-Vietnamese Military High Committee on 24 February 1953. After training and organization into light battalions the new forces would free veteran French and Vietnamese army units for an offensive role by replacing them in static defense posts. American officials saw the further advantage that every increase in the Vietnamese forces deepened the identification of the native population with resistance to the Viet Minh and hastened the time when the National Army might take over the exclusive defense of its country.

Surveys conducted in Washington and by General Trapnell's MAAG organization in Saigon indicated that the

United States could readily find MDAP resources to provide arms, ammunition, and other unit equipment for the additional battalions.[2] The Joint Chiefs of Staff endorsed the augmentation of the Vietnamese National Army as an indispensible first step that merited American support, but they listed other necessary measures as well. Pentagon officials generally were on guard against any French disposition to view the marshalling of more forces as the sole requirement for conclusion of the war. They emphasized that plans for aggressive use of the new battalions must form part of an integrated program encompassing all military, political, economic, and psychological warfare means. From Saigon General Trapnell warned that the augmentation project would be of little worth unless coupled with a revitalization of the French training system and a genuine shift from defensive to offensive attitudes among French military planners and commanders.[3]

United States material support for the Vietnamese Army augmentation project began during March.[4] If the

---

2. (TS) "Report by the Ad Hoc Committee /Farrell Cmte/ to the Assistant to the Secretary for International Security Affairs on Forty Additional Vietnam Battalions," nd, Encl to (TS) Memo, Kyes, Actg SecDef, to SecArmy, Navy, and Air Force, "Forty Additional Vietnam Battalions," 19 Feb 53, CCS 092 Asia (6-25-48) sec 37. App A to the Farrell Cmte Rpt was (TS) Ltr, Trapnell to Collins, 20 Dec 52, which had precipitated the study.

3. (TS) Memo, Collins to SecDef, "Broadening the Participation of the United States in the Indochina Operation," 13 Mar 53, CCS 092 Asia (6-25-48) sec 38. (TS) "French Strategic Concept of Operations in Indochina with General Discussion of Current and Long-Range Plans," Tab A to (TS) OSD ISA staff study, "Conversations with M. Letourneau, 1000, 27 March 1953, nd, "Washington Talks - March '53, Indochina - Letourneau," Alden files, OMA. (TS) Msg, Ch MAAG IC to DEPTAR for DJS, MG 4492A, 17 Dec 52, DA-IN-218456, CCS 092 Asia (6-25-48) sec 36.

4. (TS) Memo, Maj Gen G. C. Stewart, Dir OMA, to Asst SecDef ISA, "Augmentation of Vietnam Army," 23 Mar 53, "Indochina 1953," Alden files, OMA.

French took the further steps that appeared necessary in American eyes, requests for additional aid were to be anticipated. American leaders were prepared to consider such requests sympathetically, but insistence had grown since the first of the year that the French must undergird the situation by presenting a comprehensive plan for termination of the Indochinese hostilities within an acceptable time period.

French spokesmen would have their opportunity later in March when Premier Mayer and his colleagues arrived in response to President Eisenhower's invitation to hold consultations in Washington. In preparation for this visit Secretary Dulles had pointedly informed the French officials of the American attitude. Continued stalemate in Indochina he termed unacceptable. The situation required increased effort under a plan envisioning liquidation of the regular enemy forces within something like 24 months. Stressing the legislative limitations on United States executive action, the Secretary declared that Administration spokesmen could forcefully present the need for appropriations to Congress only if they were convinced that a sound strategic plan for Indochina existed and would be energetically carried out.[5]

President Eisenhower was no less explicit during his first interview with Premier Mayer aboard the *Williamsburg* on 26 March. While he paid tribute to the valiant French defenders and reiterated the American Government's recognition that Indochina was a fighting front of prime significance in the free world's resistance to aggressive Communism, the President demanded a plan.[6] In following sessions M. Jean Letourneau, Minister in charge of Relations with the Associated States, undertook to sketch at least the military portion of the French program. A rough cost estimate was submitted in writing; the Minister offered only his oral presentation of the strategic outline.

---

5. (S) Doc D-5, Msg, Dulles to AmEmb Paris, 4907, 19 Mar 53, in (TS) Doc Hist of US Pol toward Indochina, 1940-1953.

6. (S) "Notes made by Assistant Secretary Frank C. Nash of Initial Meeting with the French (Mayer) Delegation," nd, "Indochina 1953," Alden files, OMA. (TS) Doc D-7, Msg, Dulles to AmEmb Paris, 4992, 26 Mar 53, in (TS) Doc Hist US Pol toward Indochina, 1940-1953.

The Letourneau Plan relied primarily on an expansion of the Vietnamese National Army during 1954 and 1955 that would add some 80,000 to the 40,000 personnel augmentation already scheduled for the current year. Completion of this program would raise the Vietnamese ground forces to at least 250,000 in 1955, exclusive of Suppletifs. Concurrently, operations would unfold in three successive steps. While the recruits were being trained, regular French and native forces would pacify the regions outside the Tonkin Delta, working generally from south to north. Later the newly formed light battalions would begin occupying the cleared areas, releasing regular units for assembly as a striking force in the Delta. The last stage of the plan would see a powerful French Union army engaging and destroying the Viet Minh battle corps, compressed by the previous operations into northern Tonkin. This final drive might culminate in the spring of 1955.

The accompanying cost data displayed important gaps, but M. Letourneau's figures at least indicated that American aid was expected in providing equipment for the expanding Vietnamese armies. In addition, for 1954 and 1955 the fiscal account contained expenditures totalling more than 500 million dollars that were not covered by the French or Associated States budgets. The French voiced no formal request that the United States plan to assume these deficits, but their intentions were clear.[7]

At his final session with Premier Mayer on 28 March the President did not mask the disappointment with which American authorities viewed the Letourneau Plan, owing

---

7. (TS) JCS 1992/214, 10 Apr 53, CCS 092 Asia (6-25-48) sec 39. (TS) "Rough Cost Estimates submitted by Letourneau Group in Washington on 30 March 1953 for Indo-China Effort 1953-55," nd, "Indochina 1953," Alden files, OMA. (TS) Doc D-12 Msg, Dulles to AmEmb Saigon, 1967, 7 Apr 53, in (TS) Doc Hist of US Pol toward Indochina, 1940-1953.

particularly to the slowness of its timetable. But Mr. Eisenhower emphasized that the United States remained eager to help; its officials would give the plan thorough study. Premier Mayer suggested that consultations between military technicians would be helpful, particularly in establishing more precisely the catalogue of material requirements. He invited the dispatch of a United States military mission to Saigon for this purpose.[8]

In their appraisal for Secretary of Defense Charles E. Wilson, the Joint Chiefs of Staff displayed marked reluctance to accept the Letourneau Plan as the best that could be hoped for. While they termed it "workable," the Joint Chiefs considered the plan deficient in aggressive spirit. The devotion of effort to clearing rear areas before concentrating for decisive blows against the main Viet Minh forces and supply lines in the north seemed to them rather like trying to mop up the water without turning off the faucet. Early pressure against the enemy communications with Red China would be more useful than chasing guerrillas into the hills in central Annam. Further, the extensive French reliance on operations by units of battalion-size precluded the type of coordination and concentration of power that American military authorities wished to see. Finally, the Letourneau Plan did not appear to match the expansion of the Vietnamese Army with an equal emphasis on the training of native military leaders and the prompt transfer of responsibility to their hands.

The Joint Chiefs of Staff concluded, however, that the enlistment of larger Vietnamese forces was vital to this or any other plan for termination of the Indochinese hostilities. Hence they certified the troop augmentation phase of the program as deserving of United States material support. But the Joint Chiefs did not relax their demand for substantial improvement in the French strategic plan. They recommended that as much political pressure as appeared feasible be placed on the French to obtain a clear-cut commitment to modernize training methods, to expedite the transfer of responsibility to qualified native military leaders, and to seize the initiative and act out the

---

8. (S) Doc D-10, Msg, Dulles to AmEmb Paris, 5040, 30 Mar 53, in same file.

plan with determined vigor, organizing where possible on a regimental and divisional basis and giving special attention to cutting the enemy supply lines.9

Negotiations carried on with the French by Secretary Dulles and other United States authorities a few days later disregarded the particulars but followed the spirit of the JCS recommendations. During these late April conversations in Paris the Secretary of State reemphasized the difficulties faced by Administration leaders and clearly implied that they despaired of making an effective appeal to the American Congress on the basis of the Letourneau program. But if the French offered an overall plan for an additional effort in Indochina that the military advisors of the United States Government could endorse as having every reasonable chance of success, the prospect of gaining a sizeable appropriation would brighten. It was up to the French. "You help us to help you" was the Secretary's charge. Meanwhile the American negotiators gave notice that in view of critical French requirements arising from the enemy invasion of Laos the United States would immediately advance 60 million dollars in aid from the anticipated appropriations for Fiscal Year 1954.10

Soon thereafter came the appointment of a new Commander-in-Chief for Indochina, Lieutenant General Henri Navarre. Although the French pictured the relief of General

---

9. (TS) Memo, JCS to SecDef, "Proposed French Strategic Plan for the Successful Conclusion of the War in Indochina," 21 Apr 53, CCS 092 Asia (6-25-48) sec 40.
10. (S) Doc D-13, "Bipartite U.S.-French Conversations, First Session--April 22, 1953," in (TS) Doc Hist of US Pol toward Indochina, 1940-1953. Meanwhile the Joint Chiefs restated their reservations about the Letourneau Plan with new emphasis at a meeting with USecState W.B. Smith, who relayed their expressions to Paris; (TS) Doc D-14, Msg, Smith to AmEmb Paris, TOPSEC 9, 24 Apr 53, same file. For account of the second bipartite session in Paris, 26 Apr 53, see (S) Msgs, Amb Dillon, Paris 5672 to SecState, 26 Apr 53, "Indochinese Problems (Fall Offensive 1953-54)," Alden files, OMA.

Salan as a routine rotation of assignments, the event had a decidedly favorable import for the United States desire to see the Letourneau Plan recast as a more aggressive concept. General Navarre arrived in Saigon during the latter half of May breathing a spirit of vigor and determination reminiscent of Marshal de Lattre.

Under this encouraging sign Defense officials in Washington readied the United States military mission to Indochina suggested by Premier Mayer in March. Assignment as head of the mission went to Lieutenant General John W. "Iron Mike" O'Daniel, Commander in Chief, United States Army, Pacific, whom the Joint Chiefs of Staff named on recommendation of his CINCPAC superior, Admiral Arthur W. Radford. The terms of reference given General O'Daniel in June set the task of his small joint group at something more than the mere gathering of information. By "thorough discussion" the mission members were expected to influence General Navarre and his subordinates to revise the Letourneau Plan along the more aggressive lines and with the accompanying measures that would meet the criticisms listed by the Joint Chiefs of Staff. Thus the result of its own efforts would largely control the mission's final estimate of the adequacy of French plans for winning the war and the justification for further American aid.[11]

The outcome of the O'Daniel Mission marked it with every appearance of success. Following intensive inspections, surveys, and discussions in Indochina from 20 June through 10 July 1953 the United States group repaired to Hawaii to write its report. Already cabled to Washington was the prime result of the visit--the Navarre Plan, which General O'Daniel described as "a new aggressive concept

---

11. (TS) Memo for Rec, Col E.H.J. Carnes, DSecy JCS, "Joint Political-Military Mission to Indochina," 29 May 53. (TS) Memo, JCS to SecDef, "Terms of Reference for Military Mission to Indo-China," 10 Jun 53. Both in CCS 092 Asia (6-25-48) sec 42. (TS) Memo, SecDef to JCS, "Terms of Reference for Military Mission to Indochina," 12 Jun 53, same file, sec 43.

for the conduct of operations in Indochina."[12] The Navarre Plan, which seemed almost a conscious, point-by-point disposal of the previous objections of United States military authorities, called for an immediate shift to the offensive. For the remainder of the rainy season it listed a series of local operations and increasing guerrilla warfare. Next, General Navarre schemed to anticipate and disrupt the Viet Minh fall campaign by loosing an offensive of his own in Tonkin as early as 15 September 1953. During the remainder of the fighting season he intended to operate aggressively, emphasizing attacks on the flanks and rear of the enemy and drawing support from the recovery of a maximum number of units from areas not directly involved in the battle. The High Command would also apply itself to the progressive incorporation of battalions into regiments and regiments into divisions, creating new supporting units as needed. Further, General Navarre pledged to continue the development of the native armies and the transfer to their leaders of responsibility for the conduct of operations.

General O'Daniel hailed the new plan as a design that would accomplish the decisive defeat of the Viet Minh by 1955. A still more favorable outlook would result if General Navarre succeeded in the quest for additional French forces that now found him in Paris. General Navarre's personal qualities and the air of confidence and energy that appeared to surround the new high command had impressed General O'Daniel greatly. Subsidiary agreements providing for additional United States intelligence activity in Indochina, timely sharing of French operational plans with General Trapnell's MAAG organization, and a modest beginning at American participation in improvement of the French training system only deepened the impression of willing cooperation and receptiveness to advice. As a final evidence of French sincerity the mission chief noted that General Navarre and other high officers had repeatedly invited him to return in a few months "to witness the progress we will have made." General O'Daniel

---

12. (TS) Msg, Ch MAAG IC sgd O'Daniel to CINCPAC, 301148Z Jun 53, readdressed by CINCPAC to CNO as 030401Z Jul 53, same file. (TS) "Report of the U.S. Joint Military Mission to Indochina, 15 July 1953," same file, BP pt 9.

recommended that a follow-up mission under his leadership be scheduled.[13]

General Navarre and his plan inspired confidence and conviction in Paris as well. Presentations made during his July visit induced the home authorities to adopt the Navarre concept as official policy. Thus the recently invested government of Premier Joseph Laniel stood committed to enlarged effort and active pursuit of victory in Indochina. What was the more extraordinary, it backed this commitment with indications of willingness to send out additional forces from Metropolitan France, to the number of nine infantry battalions plus certain supporting units.

But all depended on increased assistance from the United States. Commanding no more secure base in the National Assembly than its numerous predecessors, the Laniel government could not face the political hazards of such a course without very substantial American support of the French budget, far exceeding the current arrangements. When Premier Laniel first broached the matter to Washington late in July he mentioned a figure in the neighborhood of 400 million dollars. The sum reflected not merely the heightened cost of the war owing to activation of the Navarre Plan but the further fact that at this very time the French military budget, of political necessity, must be reduced. France would commit more men, but less money. Before objection could be voiced the Premier turned quickly to sketching the unpalatable alternative. Unless the additional funds were forthcoming, he said, the only prospect was for eventual French withdrawal from Indochina, with the only unsettled questions being the method and date.[14]

The United States Government faced a crucial decision. Yet the very statement of the problem's conditions virtually dictated the answer. American officials recognized

---

13. (TS) "Report of U.S. Joint Military Mission to Indochina, 15 July 1953," same file.
14. (TS) Doc D-36, Msg, Amb Dillon, Paris 370 to Sec State, 29 Jul 53, in (TS) Doc Hist of US Pol toward Indochina, 1940-1953.

the Laniel government as the first in seven years that seemed prepared to make the exertion necessary to bring victory in Indochina. And if that happy outcome could be achieved, a most favorable train of consequences would follow. Leaving Southeast Asia secure against any but a major Communist aggression, the French might turn their full attention to European and domestic problems. Relief from the long drain of the Indochinese war should permit restoration of French financial stability, end the protracted vacillation over joining the European Defense Community, and allow France to assume a confident and active role in the councils of the free world coalition.

Against this bright picture American officials placed the somber conclusion that the Laniel regime was almost certainly the last French government from which a positive approach to the Indochinese conflict could be expected. If Premier Laniel's effort failed, the mounting popular and parliamentary sentiment in France in favor of some kind of negotiated peace would surely find expression in the policy of the next cabinet. Any settlement negotiated under such conditions could hardly fail to spell the eventual loss of all Indochina to Communism and confront United States policymakers with the still more momentous decision of whether to intervene with force in Southeast Asia.[15]

Costly though it would be and undeniably surrounded by risk, full support of the Laniel-Navarre program seemed the only course compatible with the interests of the United States. The National Security Council on 6 August 1953 agreed to recommend such a policy, providing the Department of State, the Foreign Operations Administration, and the Joint Chiefs of Staff were willing to affirm that the French program held promise of success and could be implemented effectively.[16]

---

15. (TS) Rpt by State Dept, "Further United States Support for France and the Associated States of Indochina," Encl to (TS) Memo, Exec Secy NSC to NSC, same subj, 5 Aug 53, CCS 092 Asia (6-25-48) sec 44.
16. NSC Action No. 874, set forth in (TS) "Record of Actions by the National Security Council at its One Hundred and Fifty Eighth Meeting, August 6, 1953," CCS 334 NSC (9-25-47) sec 11.

The Joint Chiefs of Staff five days later advised the Secretary of Defense that "if vigorously pursued militarily in Indochina and supported politically in France" the Navarre Plan did offer sufficient promise of success to warrant American aid. But the record of French performance suggested caution in accepting declarations of intention at full value. The Joint Chiefs urged that American material and financial support be conditioned on demonstrated French adherence to the plan and continued willingness to receive and act upon U.S. military advice.[17]

During the week following their submission of the 11 August recommendations every member of the Joint Chiefs of Staff except Air Force General Nathan F. Twining yielded place to a successor. Admiral Radford assumed the duties of Chairman while General Matthew B. Ridgway became Chief of Staff, U.S. Army, and Admiral Robert B. Carney appeared as the Chief of Naval Operations.

Before the month's end the new Joint Chiefs acted to head off Secretary Wilson's transmittal to the State Department of the views of their predecessors. It was not merely that they wished to add an observation on the vital need for creating a political situation in Indochina that would provide the natives with incentive to give wholehearted support to the French. Reports received from General Trapnell and the service attaches in Saigon regarding the languid pace of Navarre Plan implementation had convinced the new military leaders that even the qualified endorsement given by the previous JCS group had been too favorable. Given the fading hope that the French command was really going to act with energy and dispatch, their assessment of the plan's promise of success would no longer allow them to say "_Accordingly_, the Joint Chiefs of Staff believe . . . that the necessary support should be provided . . . ." The word would have to be "Nevertheless."[18]

---

17. (TS) Memo, Bradley to SecDef, "The Navarre Concept for Operations in Indochina," 11 Aug 53, CCS 092 Asia (6-25-48) sec 44.
18. (TS) Memo, Radford to SecDef, "The Navarre Concept for Operations in Indochina," 28 Aug 53, same file, sec 45.

Among other things General Trapnell had reported profound doubt that the French had either the intention or the capability of mounting the major offensive listed for 15 September. Most successful of the well-publicized operations General Navarre had carried out so far had been the 2-battalion paratroop raid on the enemy supply center at Lang Son in July. The MAAG Chief felt that while this strike and operations in the Quan Tri and Phan Thiet areas had improved morale and helped instill an aggressive spirit, the results in terms of destroying enemy potential and wresting initiative from the Viet Minh had been negligible. All three attaches concurred in his statement that the French appeared to have no plans for a general fall offensive.[19]

These views were confirmed on 1 September when General Navarre submitted a new timetable that hardly bore out his previous vows to seize the initiative and operate aggressively. If the enemy attacked in late September or early October the French and Associated States forces would counterattack. In the event no Viet Minh drive developed, the French command would launch a diversionary operation. The general offensive against the enemy battle corps was now scheduled for October 1954. It appeared that General Navarre intended to piece out the 1953-1954 fighting season with limited-objective local offensives designed to keep the enemy off balance while waiting for French reinforcements and the activation of newly-trained Vietnamese units.[20]

Into the various U.S. Government consultations during the first days of September 1953 the Joint Chiefs of Staff carried their concern over the modest progress and apparently waning enthusiasm of the French command. But the fact remained that the Laniel-Navarre program offered a chance--and a last chance at that--of putting the Indochinese war on the right track. It could be hoped that

---
19. (TS) Msg, Ch MAAG IC, MG 1442A to CINCPAC, 24 Aug 53, DA-IN-299535, "Navarre Letter - Actions Taken," vol I, Alden files, OMA.
20. (TS) Msg, Ch MAAG IC, MG 1488A to CINCPAC, 1 Sep 53, DA-IN-1796 (2 Sep 53), "Indochinese Problems (Fall Offensive 1953-54)," Alden files, OMA.

the assurance of wholehearted support from the United States would banish General Navarre's hesitation in carrying forward his plan.[21]

On 1 September the French Government submitted its formal statement of the Indochina program and the request for U.S. assistance on which it depended. The total figure now stood at 385 million dollars. Building on its previous consideration of the matter the National Security Council on 9 September recommended to the President that the United States grant additional assistance to France in an amount not exceeding 385 million dollars, on certain conditions. The French Government must give assurances that it was determined to put the Navarre Plan promptly into effect and pursue it vigorously, without at the same time retreating substantially from its NATO commitments in Europe. The government must further undertake to provide a full record of aid expenditures and agree to take into account the comments and advice of American military authorities on campaign plans in Indochina. In the realm of political action assurance was demanded that the French would press forward with their program for granting entire independence to the three Associated States. The French must regard the 385 million as the final dollar contribution during 1954 and must recognize the right of the United States to terminate its aid upon invalidation of any of the above understandings.[22]

---

21. (TS) Notes, State-JCS Mtg, 4 Sep 53, files D Secy JCS. (TS) State Dept Memo, R.B. Knight to MacArthur, "Comments on Supplementary French Material on the Navarre Plan," 3 Sep 53, Encl to (TS) Memo, Secy JCS to Twining, Ridgway, and Carney, 3 Sep 53, CCS 092 Asia (6-25-48) sec 45.
22. (TS) Rpt by State Dept, "Assistance for Indochina," Encl to (TS) Memo, Exec Secy NSC to NSC, "Further United States Support for France and the Associated States of Indochina," 8 Sep 53, same file. NSC Action No. 897, set forth in (TS) "Record of Actions by the National Security Council at its One Hundred and Sixty First Meeting, September 9, 1953," CCS 334 NSC (9-25-47) sec 12.

Presidential approval followed, and by 29 September a formal agreement incorporating these points had been worked out between French officials and the American Ambassador in Paris.23 In giving particular attention to accounting safeguards surrounding the actual transfer of funds from one government to the other the agreement's terms reflected American determination not to become involved again in anything resembling the Lisbon aid grant of 1952. Unsatisfactory experience and considerable Congressional criticism had followed that earlier venture, because by making an unconditional lump sum contribution to the support of the French budget U.S. officials had left themselves no means of checking the money's final disposition. This time the U.S. representatives took pains to make clear they were agreeing to finance a specific action program--the Navarre Plan--up to an agreed dollar figure. Payment would proceed in installments, taking the form of reimbursement of the French Treasury for certified expenditures as they occurred. Subsequently it took experts of the two governments until early March 1954 to work out the detailed accounting procedures the United States required.24

---

23. (S) Doc D-46, "US-French Supplementary Aid Agreement on Indochina," and (U) Doc D-47, State Dept Press Release No. 529, "Joint Communique Issued by the Governments of the United States and France," 30 Sep 53, both in (TS) Doc Hist of US Pol toward Indochina, 1940-1953.

24. (TS) Doc D-42, Msg, Dulles to AmEmb Paris, 868, 9 Sep 53, in same file. Some of the sharpest criticism of Lisbon type aid appeared in the report of a survey team, sponsored by Senator Styles Bridges, that the Senate Appropriations Cmte had sent to Paris. News accounts of the report carried the heading "Senate Study Asserts France is Substituting Aid for Taxes"; NY Times, 13 Jul 53, pp. 1, 18. After a strong attempt during 1953, OMA/OSD officials gave up the attempt to identify and account for end-items purchased with Lisbon funds and shipped to Indochina by the French; (C) MR by R.N. Lind, nd /Jan 54?/, "Indochinese Problems (Fall Offensive 1953-54)," Alden files, OMA.

Even before the Paris agreement was completed Washington officials had plunged into the exacting series of resurveys, adjustments, and negotiations necessary to produce the pledged 385 million dollars. The Congress had already adjourned; in any event seeking a supplemental aid appropriation on the Hill would have introduced worrisome uncertainties and delays. The job must be done by applying executive decision to the reassignment of funds already in hand. Fortunately a previous decision had already set aside 100 million dollars from the current MDAP appropriation for just such a contingency. Other large sums could be recovered by stringent rescreening throughout the foreign assistance program, relying finally on a liberal interpretation of the President's authority to shift funds under the Mutual Security Act.[25]

Discretion no less than legal requirement imposed the necessity of informing and consulting Congressional leaders regarding the new commitments to France. The President's acceptance of the NSC recommendations involved an important change in the orientation of the foreign assistance program from what had been explained and defended before legislative committees during the recent session, and the program would undoubtedly generate large further requests for appropriations during the coming year. Consultation now might assure future support, and careful explanation might lessen discontent over the apparent discrepancies between Congressional intent and the actual purposes to which some of the funds were now assigned. Whereas a very large portion of the present grant was earmarked for the payment and rationing of Vietnamese troops, legislative leaders had hitherto insisted that U.S. aid dollars be expended primarily for "shot and shell." Administration spokesmen would also wish to explain that

---

25. (TS) MR by Col J.G. Anding, "Indochinese Special Program," 4 Sep 53, "Indochinese Problems (Fall Offensive 1953-54)," Alden files, OMA. Means of financing the grant and the need for clearing with Congressional leaders were discussed in Ann B to (TS) Rpt by State Dept, "Assistance for Indochina," Encl to (TS) Memo, Exec Secy NSC to NSC, "Further United States Support for France and the Associated States of Indochina," 8 Sep 53, CCS 092 Asia (6-25-48) sec 45.

concern for proper accounting of the funds had led them to channel all the additional assistance for the Indochinese forces through the French Government. Congressional opinion in the past had strongly favored bypassing Paris to award more aid directly to the three Associated States.[26]

While these preparations and readjustments continued in Washington, the October reports of American military observers in Indochina took on a somewhat more encouraging tone. True, the intention of speeding the transfer of military responsibility to Vietnamese authorities had received a serious setback. Having taken over the occupation of the supposedly quiet Bui Chu sector in the Tonkin Delta, light native battalions experienced a severe defeat in September when regular Viet Minh units re-entered the area. Control was returned to the French command, the morale of the new national army suffered, and charges and recriminations over the affair left considerable bitterness between the French and Vietnamese. It was disturbing, too, to find General Navarre disclaiming any agreement with General O'Daniel to welcome the establishment of a small U.S. intelligence team in Hanoi.[27]

In most other respects, however, the observers reported modest progress. The activation of Vietnamese units was actually ahead of schedule, and elements of the promised French reinforcement had begun to arrive, including one battalion transferred with American assent from Korea. Unhampered by any extensive enemy activity at the opening of the fighting season, General Navarre had been able to launch Operation MOUETTE, an excursion in force southward from the Delta in the direction of Thanh Hoa. While General Trapnell discounted the French claim that MOUETTE had

---

26. Ibid. (C) Memo, N.E. Halaby, DepAsst SecDef (ISA) to Stassen, Dir FOA, "Consultations with Senator Homer Ferguson in Detroit," 14 Sep 53, "Indochina Problems (Fall Offensive, 1953-54)," Alden files, OMA.

27. (TS) Msg, CH MAAG IC, MG 1766A, to CINCPAC, DA-IN-17890, 31 Oct 53. (C) Msg, USARMA Saigon, OAEMA MC 299-53, to CSUSA for G-2, DA-IN-16870, 23 Oct 53. Both in "Indochina 1953," Alden files, OMA. (S) Geneva Conf Background Paper, Indochina Chronology, pp. 80-81.

inflicted serious loss and disruption of plans on the enemy, he at least saw signs that an offensive attitude was gaining impetus at all levels of the French command.[28]

Although halting and deficient in spots, the Navarre Plan was recognizably in operation in October 1953. As the great new contributions of American aid came to bear in the approaching months, it might yet be pressed to fulfillment.

The Joint Chiefs of Staff had been closely involved in the months-long U.S. endeavor to commit the French to an Indochina plan holding reasonable promise of success. But the comments and evaluations they had supplied represented only part of the Joint Chiefs' attention to the Indochina problem. Besides making numerous detailed decisions regarding the aid program, yet to be recounted, their responsibility included planning for contingencies other than the successful conclusion of the war toward which the main American effort was directed.

Late in January 1953, the Joint Chiefs of Staff set in motion a study of possible U.S. military action to prevent the overrunning of Indochina by Communist forces, should the French find it necessary to withdraw.[29] Before the final paper reached them at mid-year, the Joint Chiefs had undertaken several other broadly related considerations.

During early April 1953, the Five-Power Conference of military commanders with responsibilities in Southeast Asia, occurred at Pearl Harbor. The conference report recommended the establishment of a formal and continuous relationship among designated military representatives of the five nations, who would be charged with coordinating the plans produced by each of the parties for the defense of Southeast Asia. With the approval of the Secretaries of State and Defense, the Joint Chiefs of Staff, late in May, authorized American participation in the proposed machinery

---

28. (TS) Msg, CH MAAG IC, MG 1609A, to CINCPAC, DA-IN-9615, 1 Oct 53, CCS 092 Asia (6-25-48) sec 46. (TS) Msg, CH MAAG IC, MG 1766A, to CINCPAC, DA-IN-17890, 31 Oct 53, "Indochina 1953," Alden files, OMA.

29. (TS) Memo, Secy JCS to JSPC, "Possible Military Courses of Action in Indochina," 23 Jan 53, CCS 092 Asia (6-25-48) sec 37.

and named Admiral Radford, Commander in Chief, Pacific, as the U.S. Military Representative.[30]

The new arrangement added a further dimension to the important planning responsibilities already assigned to CINCPAC. Admiral Radford was even then completing the series of CINCPAC Operation Plans called for by the JCS directive of the previous December, and he continued to give close attention to developments in Indochina.[31] Indeed, the Joint Chiefs had completed their action on the Five-Power Conference report under strong urging from Admiral Radford that the critical situation introduced by the Viet Minh invasion of Laos made imperative an immediate start on coordinated Southeast Asia planning.[32]

Admiral Radford's grim estimates undoubtedly influenced the Chief of Naval Operations, Admiral W.M. Fechteler, toward the expression of concern he made on 5 May over the danger to the security of all Southeast Asia inherent in the Laotian crisis. On that day, Admiral Fechteler asked for study of what action the United States could take to prevent spread of Communist control over the area.[33]

---

30. (S) JCS 1992/218, 29 Apr 53; (S) Rpt, "Conference of Representatives from the Principal Military Authorities Representing Australia, France, New Zealand, United Kingdom and the United States in the Southeast Asia Area, Pearl Harbor, 6-10 April 1953," nd. Both in same file, sec 40. (TS) Memo, Fechteler to SecDef, "Implementation of Measures for Coordination of Five-Power Southeast Asia Plans," 6 May 53; (TS) Msg, JCS to CINCPAC, JCS 939436, 21 May 53. Both in same file, sec 41.

31. (TS) Msg, JCS 927061 to CINCPAC, 22 Dec 52, same file, sec 37. For CINCPAC Operation Plan Nos. 40-53, 40-53A, and 44-53, all issued during Jun 53, see CCS 381 (4-16-49) BP pt 2.

32. (TS) Msg, CINCPAC to CNO and JCS, 032130Z May 53, CCS 092 Asia (6-25-48) sec 41.

33. (TS) Memo, Fechteler to JCS, "Current Situation Southeast Asia," 5 May 53, same file. (TS) Msg, CINCPAC to CNO, 271130Z Apr 53, same file, sec 40. Adm Radford had just completed a visit to Indochina.

The resulting paper presented a catalogue of measures for discussion rather than a single recommended course and hence ranged freely over all the possibilities, including U.S. armed intervention. It omitted previous qualifications about using "as much pressure as is feasible" and listed bluntly all the measures the United States might demand of the French to improve their capabilities in Indochina. These included transferring at least two French divisions to Indochina, expediting the revision and aggressive implementation of present campaign plans, following U.S. suggestions for expanding and modernizing training, and improving the low rate of aircraft utilization by assigning more French Air Force personnel to Indochina and hiring civilian flight and maintenance crews. As a further step short of intervention, the United States might insist on direct participation in both training and operational planning. Anticipating by more than four months the actual developments of the coming autumn, the JCS paper suggested speeding and increasing the American aid program and issuing a minority political announcement that would stress the U.S. interest in Southeast Asia and indicate concern over continued Communist moves in the area.[34]

Complementary to these brusque considerations were the plans for U.S. military action should the French withdraw, taken up by the Joint Chiefs of Staff a few weeks later.[35] Feeling assured that the Viet Minh alone did not have the military capability of driving the French out, the Joint Chiefs recognized two conditions under which withdrawal might take place. Intervention by the Chinese Communists might force an evacuation, or political deterioration in France could bring a government decision to abandon the Indochina struggle.

In the latter situation several alternatives would lie open to American decision. The United States might deploy its own and available Allied forces to Indochina in sufficient strength to take over entirely the former French objective of "reducing Communist activity to the status of scattered guerrilla bands." Or the United States might employ only enough ground forces to hold critical strong points vacated by the French, while providing air and naval support for such operations as the Vietnamese National Army might undertake. In either case, intensified

---

34. (TS) JCS 1992/220, 8 May 53, same file, sec 41.
35. (TS) JCS 1992/227, 22 Jun 53, amended by Dec On, 2 Jul 53, same file, sec 43.

development of the native forces would continue under strong American tutelage, and the second alternative placed reliance in the ultimate capability of the Vietnamese Army to destroy the Viet Minh.

Hopefully, the Joint Chiefs of Staff considered that French withdrawal might not occur until the expansion of native forces had reached an advanced stage. In that event, the United States might be able to forego the commitment of ground troops and achieve results by providing air and naval support, or logistic support, for the Vietnamese operations, always assuming U.S. participation in an intensified training effort.

The still graver possibility of intervention in force by the Chinese Communists necessarily led the Joint Chiefs of Staff into broader considerations. They could not escape the conclusion that if Red Chinese aggression drove the French to withdraw there was no feasible course of military action that the United States could take <u>in Indochina</u> to prevent Communist forces from overrunning the country. Military opinion held that even the extension of full U.S. and Allied counteraction to the portion of China contiguous to the Tonkin border would not suffice to halt the aggression. If it wished to succeed, the United States must contemplate applying all available coercive measures against the Chinese mainland, including naval blockade and air attack on all targets of military significance.[36]

Preventing the Far Eastern situation from reaching so serious a state as this was a prime objective of American policy. The U.S. Government had encountered continued French and British reluctance to subscribe to a joint declaration advising Red China that any further acts of aggression would call forth a united retaliation that might not observe geographic limitations such as those imposed on the Korean action. Secretary Dulles found that more general warnings were easier to arrange. Both the Franco-American communique at the close of Premier Mayer's visit in March 1953 and the public declarations of the July conference of British, French, and U.S. Foreign Ministers

---

36. Ibid. (TS) JCS 1992/187, 28 Oct 52, same file, sec 34.

had cautioned the Chinese Communists not to use a Korean armistice as an opportunity to gather forces for some other adventure in Asia.37 On 2 September the American Legion Convention in St. Louis heard Secretary Dulles deliver a more pointed admonition to the rulers of Communist China. After repeating President Eisenhower's statement that "any armistice in Korea that merely released aggressive armies to attack elsewhere would be a fraud," the Secretary turned to the risk that "as in Korea, Red China might send its own army into Indochina."

> The Chinese Communist regime should realize that such a second aggression could not occur without grave consequences which might not be confined to Indochina. I say this soberly in the interest of peace and in hope of preventing another aggressor miscalculation.38

In issuing a unilateral U.S. warning against further incursions in Southeast Asia, Mr. Dulles discretely gave the Red rulers only an oblique view of American military strategy. Whereas the Secretary suggested that retaliatory action might not be limited to Indochina, the Joint Chiefs of Staff had concluded that such action <u>could</u> not be so confined.

The French and Indochinese Political Scenes

A turbulent year in the politics of both France and the Associated States opened in January 1953. During that month the election of village councils throughout the pacified areas of Viet Nam marked a first step toward the establishment of democratic institutions. Participation by 80 percent of the eligible voters indicated a high

---

37. (U) Doc D-9, State Dept Press Release No. 160, "Communique on United States-France Talks," 28 Mar 53, and (TS) Doc D-32, Msg, Dulles to AmEmb Paris, 158, 14 Jul 53. Both in (TS) <u>Doc Hist of US Pol toward Indochina, 1940-1953</u>. (S) Geneva Conf Background Paper, Indochina Chronology, p.79.

38. (U) Doc D-39, State Dept Press Release No. 469, "Address by the Honorable John Foster Dulles, Secretary of State, Before the American Legion . . . , September 2, 1953," 1 Sep 53, in (TS) <u>Doc Hist of US Pol toward Indochina, 1940-1953</u>.

level of political interest and a clear rejection of the
Communist call for an election boycott. The results, however, showed no striking gain in popular support for the
Vietnamese government currently sponsored by the French.[39]

In Cambodia, January found King Norodom Sihanouk dissolving the National Assembly, arresting "obstructionist"
delegates, and assuming personal direction of the government. The monarch then plunged into a year-long course
of unpredictable behavior that included explosive press conference statements in New York, a week of self-imposed exile
in Thailand, and the filing of numerous demands and protests
in Paris--all designed to win Cambodia an independence within the French Union equal to that of India within the
British Commonwealth.[40]

In these circumstances the French continued their
halting progress toward satisfaction of native demands for
freedom and sovereignty. In February, the French command
and Minister Letourneau entered agreements with Bao Dai
that provided for a freer development of the Vietnamese
National Army in a status distinct from the French forces.[41]
In May, the Mayer government gave pledges to the Cambodians
looking toward transfer of control over the native army,
relaxation of economic restrictions, and French acknowledgement of the judicial integrity of the local courts.
A few weeks earlier the Paris authorities had revised the
form of French political representation in Indochina in a
way that betokened somewhat more regard for the dignity
and separate autonomy of the three Associated States.[42]

Any favor these moves may have gained was sacrificed
when the French decreed a devaluation of the Indochinese
currency on 10 May 1953. As a measure to end both the
government scandals and the financial drain resulting from

---

39. Hammer, Struggle for Indochina, pp. 289-291. (S)
Geneva Conf Background Paper, Indochina Chronology, p. 74.
    40. (S) Geneva Conf Background Paper, Indochina Chronology, p. 74. NY Times, 19 Apr 53, p. 1; 15 Jun 53, p. 1;
21 Jun 53, p. 1.
    41. (S) Geneva Conf Background Paper, Indochina Chronology, p. 75. NY Times, 26 Feb 53, p. 3.
    42. NY Times, 10 May 53, p. 1; 23 Apr 53, p. 4.
(S) Geneva Conf Background Paper, Indochina Chronology,
pp. 77-78.

the extensive traffic in piastres, devaluation was long overdue, but when French officials set the new rate of exchange with only a few hours notice to the local governments they acted without regard for the pledges of prior consultation given in 1949. The event demonstrated once again how little true sovereignty the French had so far accorded the Associated States. Native protests were still resounding when the Mayer government fell on 21 May and France entered a protracted cabinet crisis.[43]

Emerging at last late in June under the leadership of Joseph Laniel, the French Government turned a new face toward Indochina. In assuming the premiership, Laniel had declared that it was essential to end the present malaise in the relations between France and the Associated States in a spirit of accommodation and understanding. In genuine dedication to this aim the new Premier began a wholesale replacement of the clique of colonial administrators, whose long tenure in Indochina had made them symbols of French arrogance and repression. His ouster of M. Letourneau also ended the curious arrangement whereby the French Commissioner-General in Saigon had held membership in the Paris cabinet as Minister for relations with the Associated States.[44]

Then, on 3 July 1953, the Laniel government invited the three Indochinese states to enter new consultations, during which France intended to "perfect" their independence and complete their sovereignty.[45] Since this new start differed little in appearance from numerous others announced by French officials over the years, native leaders approached the proposal with skepticism. But Foreign Minister Bidault soon informed Secretary Dulles that the statements of 3 July had been made in earnest. To clear up the matter of independence, France was prepared to accept virtually any terms the native states demanded, so long as Laos, Cambodia, and Viet Nam agreed to continued membership in the French Union.[46]

---

43. Hammer, *Struggle for Indochina*, pp. 300-301. (S) Geneva Conf Background Paper, Indochina Chronology, p. 78.
44. Keesing, p. 12995B. NY Times, 2 Jul 53, p. 3.
45. NY Times, 4 Jul 53, p. 3. (S) Geneva Conf Background Paper, Indochina Chronology, p. 79.
46. (TS) Doc D-33, Msg, Dulles to AmEmb Paris, 180, 15 Jul 53, in (TS) *Doc Hist of US Pol toward Indochina, 1940-1953*.

Thereafter, in public addresses the Secretary of State frequently referred to the 3 July declaration as having removed all basis for criticism of French policy. Since that date, he told the United Nations, "the Communist-dominated armies in Indochina have no shadow of a claim to be regarded as the champions of an independence movement."[47] This turn in French policy, coupled with the support of General Navarre evidenced by the decision to send nine battalions to Indochina, did much to convince Washington officials in September that the Laniel government deserved additional American aid.

The sincerity of the French declaration was in fact borne out during long, forebearing, and ultimately successful negotiations with the refractory Cambodians concerning the transfer of control over fiscal matters and the police, army, and judiciary. A less difficult series of exchanges with Laotian representatives brought a more clear-cut result. The negotiations culminated in October in a treaty of friendship and association that recognized Laos as "a fully independent and sovereign state" while reaffirming its membership in the French Union.[48]

In the third state of Viet Nam, however, political ructions set aside any immediate hope of orderly progress. The announcement that Chief of State Bao Dai and Premier Nguyen Van Tam were departing for Paris to open preliminary negotiations with the French touched off an outburst of nationalist agitation. Early in September an unofficial "Congress of National Unity and Peace" gathered to demand unconditional independence, domestic reforms, and the immediate election of a National Assembly. Bao Dai countered

---

47. (U) Doc D-44, State Dept Press Release No. 505, "Address by the Honorable John Foster Dulles, Secretary of State, Made in General Debate of the United Nations Assembly, . . . September 17, 1953," 17 Sep 53; (U) Doc D-35, State Dept Press Release No. 387, "Report to the Nation by the Honorable John Foster Dulles, . . . July 17, 1953," 17 Jul 53. Immediately following the declaration the US Government sent an expression of its "great pleasure and satisfaction at realistic and forward-looking steps by new French Government in approach to Indochina problem"; (S) Doc D-30, Msg, Smith to AmEmb Paris, 64, 4 Jul 53. All in (TS) Doc Hist of US Pol toward Indochina, 1940-1953.

48. NY Times, 18 Oct 53, p. 1, 23 Oct 53, p. 1. For text of the Franco-Laotian treaty see Keesing, pp. 13230B-13231A.

by summoning his own National Congress, which he expected would define and endorse a more moderate set of terms for the Vietnamese negotiators.

When it met on 12 October, however, the second convention displayed the same fractious and uncompromising character as the first. Its members demanded that France annul the 1949 agreements and grant complete independence forthwith; then negotiations might begin toward a treaty of alliance between equals. Swept on by their nationalist ardor, the delegates next passed a declaration that Viet Nam would not participate in the French Union. By nightfall Bao Dai's lieutenants had succeeded in restoring only enough control to induce the congress to add "in its present form." Unmodified was the further resolve that the ultimate treaty with France must be ratified by a Vietnamese National Assembly elected by universal suffrage.[49]

The Vietnamese resolutions aroused outraged resentment in Paris. Even spokesmen of the political factions that most actively supported the war now demanded to know what France was fighting for if not the preservation, in some form, of her empire overseas. When seeking larger contributions from Britain and America, the government might find it useful to dwell on the front-line role of France in the defense of Southeast Asia against Communist domination, but for home consumption this honor was not enough. If France was to be repaid in ingratitude and disdain by the very people she sought to defend, her sacrifices in Indochina must end.[50]

No disavowal issued by Bao Dai or Premier Tam could entirely stitch up the damage that had been done to the fabric of French popular and parliamentary support for the war. Large areas of that support had already frayed and given way under the seven-year accumulation of weariness with the apparently endless struggle. While no other party in the National Assembly wished to be identified with the demands for French withdrawal chanted by the

---
49. Hammer, Struggle for Indochina, pp. 304-305. Keesing, p. 13229AB.
50. Hammer, Struggle for Indochina, pp. 305-306. NY Times, 21 Oct 53, p. 2; 22 Oct 53, p. 3.

Communist deputies, sentiment for a negotiated settlement in Indochina had steadily grown. By October 1953 an influential portion of the Radical Socialist Party had reached the view that a military solution was impossible without an unthinkably large commitment of francs and Frenchmen. Hence political negotiations, during which the cost of past mistakes would have to be paid, seemed the only way out.[51]

M. Pierre Mendes-France emerged as the leading spokesman for this faction among the Radicals. Aspiring to the premiership during the five-week cabinet crisis in mid-1953, he fell 13 votes short of the necessary 314. Of the six candidates who presented themselves to the National Assembly, only Mendes-France received the 105 ballots of the Socialists, who responded eagerly when he hinted of having a perfected plan for ending the war by negotiation. But the Assembly as a whole was not yet ready to entrust the future of the French Empire to his care. Besides the automatic opposition of the 100 Communists and the negative votes of various factions on the right, Mendes-France encountered massive abstentions, totaling more than 200 delegates, among the right and center parties.[52]

The following week M. Georges Bidault missed the premiership by only one vote. Undoubtedly he spoke for a large body of opinion in the Assembly when he said that the security of the Associated States must be assured "by victory if necessary, by negotiation if possible." "The only thing we cannot envisage is a retreat which would be inconsistent with the respect due to our dead, with the support we owe to our allies, and with the spirit of the achievements we have accomplished in Indochina in the past."[53] Later in June Premier Laniel came to office pledged to examine every possibility of ending the Indo-chinese war, including negotiation on any basis acceptable to France's allies and the Associated States.[54] No French

---

51. Hammer, *Struggle for Indochina*, pp. 307-309.
52. *NY Times*, 5 Jun 53, p. 1. *Keesing*, pp. 12933AB, 12994AB.
53. *Keesing*, p. 12994B.
54. *Ibid.*, pp. 12995B-12996A.

government could any longer hope to stand that did not give the Assembly such assurances.

To most Frenchmen the case for settlement by negotiation seemed greatly strengthened when on 27 July the United Nations command completed the armistice agreement in Korea. With pardonable exaggeration *Time* reported that a great cry swelled across France: "Finish *la sale guerre* by negotiation--like the clever Americans in Korea."[55] Surely, it was argued, this event provided instruction in what to do when a military solution appeared impossible. Deputies frequently cited the Korean example during the October debates in which they also vented their bitterness over the Vietnamese Congress resolutions. Edouard Daladier favored a simple declaration to the Viet Minh: "We offer you peace; will you accept it?" He could see no dishonor in this course after seven years of war, considering that the Americans had done the same thing in Korea after only two years of fighting.[56]

At the end of a debate in which repeated calls for peace by negotiation had aroused few replies favoring continuation of the war, Premier Laniel delivered his statement. First he emphasized that there was no basis for pessimism over the military prospect in Indochina and hence no reason to seek peace merely out of despair. Yet his government stood constantly ready to undertake negotiations, whether with the Soviet Union, with Red China, or locally with the Viet Minh, on any basis that did not involve abandonment of Viet Nam's freedom. "It is true that the war in Indochina is unpopular," said the Premier. "There is, however, something which is still more unpopular in France--namely, to betray one's friends and to fail in one's duty."[57]

In the early hours of 28 October the Assembly endorsed a set of resolutions that instructed the government to continue seeking every opportunity of negotiation. It should also encourage the Associated States to take over a progressively greater share of the military responsibility

---
55. *Time*, 15 Mar 54, p. 25.
56. *Keesing*, p. 13231B. *NY Times*, 24 Oct 53, p. 3.
57. *Keesing*, pp. 13231B-13232A.

while completing their independence within the framework of the French Union. Finally, the resolutions called for a more equitable division of the burdens of the Indochinese war among the free nations.[58]

This last point may have been included more out of habit than conviction. A new attitude toward foreign assistance was arising. Whereas in the past American contributions had been welcomed as lifting some of the burdens of the French taxpayer, now there were expressions of fear that the acceptance of more aid only committed France to continuing the war indefinitely. When the 385 million dollar grant was announced late in September Le Monde reviewed the prospect in an article titled "Should We Take the Money?"[59]

At the same time the French continued their flat rejection of any recourse to the United Nations. During April 1953 Secretary Dulles had urged France to bring the matter of the Laotian invasion before the UN Security Council, thus giving the Indochinese conflict an international standing that would make it more readily subject to negotiation and settlement between the Western Powers and the Soviet Union. Refusing to take the action themselves, French authorities were "emphatic almost to the point of hysteria" in opposing a similar move by the Government of Thailand. They appeared to fear that United Nations debate could not be confined to Indochina and might quickly extend to other aspects of French colonial administration, particularly in North Africa. Pride in the French military tradition made equally abhorrent any internationalization of the war on the Korean pattern that would transfer control of the operations to a United Nations command.[60]

---

58. NY Times, 28 Oct 53, p. 2.
59. Ibid., 1 Oct 53, p. 9.
60. (S) Doc D-21, Dulles, Memo of Conv /with Mayer and Bidault/, 27 Apr 53; (S) Doc D-24, Msg, Amb Dillon, Paris 5766, to SecState, 3 May 53; (S) Doc D-27, Memo of Conv /between State Dept officials and Amb Bonnet/, "Thailand's Appeal to SC regarding Threat to Thailand from Vietminh Invasion," 22 May 53; (S) Doc D-28, Msg, Dulles 2297, to AmEmb Bangkok, 1 Jun 53. All in (TS) Doc Hist of US Pol toward Indochina, 1940-1953.

In another respect, however, the French Government saw an intimate connection between the Indochinese war and the UN action in Korea. As agreement on a Korean armistice drew near, American authorities heard increasing insistence from Foreign Minister Bidault that the political conference scheduled to follow the truce must extend its attention to Indochina. The French people, said Bidault, would be profoundly disturbed by any appearance that their Western allies regarded a diplomatic solution as proper for Korea but inadmissable for Indochina. The Korean conference must be seized as an opportunity for broader discussions aimed at achieving a general Far Eastern settlement. If for procedural reasons this conference under UN auspices could not properly add to its agenda a matter that France had always refused to submit to the United Nations, then the French would still demand that settlement of the Indochinese war be discussed with the Chinese Communist representatives outside the formal sessions.[61]

Adhering at first to a strict interpretation of the purposes of the coming conference, Secretary Dulles relented in response to the ceaseless agitation of the French. If the negotiations over Korea developed a favorable atmosphere, the conference, with a somewhat different slate of participants, might move on to consideration of Indochina. In his American Legion address early in September the Secretary declared that the United States wanted peace in Indochina as well as in Korea.

> . . . The political conference about to be held relates in the first instance to Korea. But growing out of that conference could come, if Red China wants it, an end of aggression and restoration of peace in Indochina. The United States would welcome such a development.[62]

---

61. (TS) Doc D-33, Msg, Dulles to AmEmb Paris, 180, 15 Jul 53; (C) Doc D-34, "Text of the French Memorandum," nd; /14 Jul 53/; (C) Doc D-37, French Emb, "Aide-Memoire," 31 Jul 53. All in (TS) <u>Doc Hist of US Pol toward Indochina, 1940-1953</u>.

62. (U) Doc D-39, State Dept Press Release No. 469, "Address by the Honorable John Foster Dulles, Secretary of State, Before the American Legion . . . , September 2,

Returning to the question of negotiation two weeks after the October debates, Premier Laniel announced "in the clearest and most categorical fashion" that the French Government did not consider that the Indochinese problem necessarily required a military solution.

> No more than the United States does France make war for the sake of war, and if an honorable solution were in view, either on the local level or on the international level, France, I repeat, like the United States in Korea, would be happy to welcome a diplomatic solution of the conflict.63

American authorities could only hope that the constant emphasis they placed on the perils of negotiating from weakness was registering with proper effect in French minds. If so, the United States might still hope to see a vigorous implementation of the Navarre Plan that would materially strengthen the French bargaining position.

Main Features of the U.S. Aid Program

During 1953 the United States continued and enlarged its deliveries of arms, ammunition, and equipment to the French and native forces in Indochina, on a first priority basis. Scheduled deliveries of ground force and naval materials were met with increasing regularity, and as the Air Force supply pipeline filled, even the persistent shortages of aircraft spare parts and maintenance equipment began to yield before the massive American effort. In January 1953 the French themselves were willing to state

---

1953," 1 Sep 53. SecState amplified his remarks at a press conference the next day; (U) Doc D-41, State Dept Press Release No. 475, "Restoration of Peace in Indochina," 3 Sep 53. Both in (TS) Doc Hist of US Pol toward Indochina, 1940-1953.

63. Laniel address before the Council of the Republic, 12 Nov 53, translation quoted in Hammer, Struggle for Indochina, p. 312. A less polished translation of the same remarks appeared in NY Times, 13 Nov 53, p. 1.

that no ground unit had failed to meet its activation date because of lack of MDAP equipment. By that date, too, the U.S. material aid program had worked a transformation of the French Air Force in Indochina from a conglomerate assortment of German, French and American aircraft, generally of World War II models, into a reasonably standardized organization with modern equipment of propeller-driven types.[64]

No lessening of the momentum of the American aid program was in sight. The appropriations made by Congress in 1953 exceeded the previous year and allowed the assignment of 312.3 million dollars for end-item assistance to Indochina during Fiscal Year 1954, plus 30 million dollars to be expended under the Military Support Program. In addition, Congress appropriated an unprecedented 400 million dollars for direct financial assistance to France.[65]

The general schedule of MDAP equipment deliveries, carefully screened and programmed in advance on a fiscal year basis, moved forward with relative tranquility. It was the special requests and accelerated procurements generated by the vicissitudes of war and the recurring inspirations of French military planners in Indochina that demanded unusual exertion and adjustment by American officials. One of the least trying of these exercises during 1953 resulted from the French request for an additional aircraft carrier.

During the March conversations in Washington Minister Letourneau had asked whether a loan of U.S. naval vessels could be arranged, similar to the World War II loan of fifty destroyers to Great Britain. Navy Department officials could not refrain from noting that the example cited had involved a material *quid pro quo*, but they agreed to explore the possibility.[66] In May the French Embassy

---

64. (S) Hq MAAG IC, "Field Estimate of Effectiveness of French Union Forces," 23 Jan 53, "Indochina 1953," Alden files, OMA.
65. (S) "Implementation of the Mutual Defense Assistance Program for Indochina (Jan-June 1954)," Ann B to (TS) OCB "Progress Report on NSC 5405," 14 Jul 54, CCS 092 Asia (6-25-48) sec 75.
66. (C) MR by Cdr W.C. Wells, "Temporary Loan of an Aircraft Carrier to France," 7 Jun 53, "Indochina 1953," Alden files, OMA.

placed a specific request with the State Department for loan of an aircraft carrier of the same CVL type as the Lafayette (formerly the USS Langley) and the Arromanches (formerly HMS Colossus) the French already possessed.

The supporting argument was persuasive. Normally the French committed one vessel to the Indochinese operations and maintained the other in home waters, where it provided continuous training in carrier operations for replacement air units. During the current year the necessity of sending the Arromanches and the Lafayette successively to Toulon for extensive overhaul would disrupt this arrangement. Training, refitting, and combat operations could proceed without interruption only if France received a third CVL by the last quarter of the year.67

A hint that President Eisenhower had interested himself in the request smoothed its passage through the Washington machinery. The Joint Chiefs of Staff on 11 June endorsed the military soundness of the loan, and Secretary Wilson soon instructed the Navy Department to seek the necessary enabling legislation from Congress. On 5 September the USS Belleau Wood was formally transferred to French authorities at San Francisco.68

Against the remaining experience of 1953 this affair appears unusual in two respects. First, the loan was justified by recognizable need and guaranteed in effectiveness by a demonstrated French capability to man and maintain the carrier; second, the request did not involve aircraft. Far more typical was the January interview of General Salan with the U.S. Ambassador at Saigon, Donald R. Heath. The Indochina commander said it would be ideal to have another squadron each of F-84's, B-26's, and C-47's, as well as more carrier-based aircraft.

---

67. (C) Fr Emb Note No. 307 to State Dept, 23 May 53, Ann to (C) JCS 1992/225, Memo by SecDef, "Temporary Loan of an Aircraft Carrier to France," 10 Jun 53, CCS 092 Asia (6-25-48) sec 42.
68. (C) Memo, JCS to SecDef, "Temporary Loan of an Aircraft Carrier to France," 11 Jun 53, same file. (C) Memo, SecDef to SecNav, same subj, 19 Jun 53. In a telephone call

At the moment, however, his only specific request was for extension of the loan of the twenty-one C-47's the United States had provided in the fall of 1952. Delaying the return of these planes to the U.S. Far East Air Force by two months or so would allow them to serve out the period of good weather in Indochina.[69]

American authorities complied by extending the loan at least until 1 April 1953. Their action likewise continued the temporary duty in Indochina of the U.S. Air Force personnel who had been assigned in December 1952 as a mobile maintenance team to service the American-owned C-47's.[70]

As the 1 April date approached, General Mark W. Clark, the U.S. Far East Commander, reported observations made during his March visit to Indochina. Convinced that an urgent French requirement for C-47 aircraft would continue until mid-May, he recommended that only eight of the twenty-one planes be returned to the Far East Air Force as scheduled, leaving thirteen C-47's on loan to the French for another two months.[71]

---

to SecNav on 29 May 53, Actg SecState W.B. Smith "indicated to him that the President desired favorable action on the French request"; (C) MR by Cdr W.C. Wells, same subj, 7 Jun 53. Both in "Indochina 1953," Alden files, OMA. NY Times, 6 Sep 53, p. 18.

69. (S) Msg, Amb Heath, Saigon 1511, to SecState, 29 Jan 53, DA-IN-232451 (30 Jan 53), CCS 092 Asia (6-25-48) sec 37.

70. (UNK) OMA staff study, "Supply Action-French Forces Indochina," 28 Apr 54, "Navarre Letter - Actions Taken," vol II, Alden files, OMA. (TS) Memo, SecAF to SecDef, 7 Jan 53, "Indochina Maintenance Support Exercise," Alden files, OMA.

71. (TS) Msg, CINCFE C61640, to DEPTAR for Collins, DA-IN-251110, 26 Mar 53, and (TS) Msg, CINCFE C61719, to DEPTAR for G-3, DA-IN-253811, 3 Apr 53, Ann C and D to (TS) Memo, JCS to SecDef, "Proposed French Strategic Plan for the Successful Conclusion of the War in Indochina," 21 Apr 53, CCS 092 Asia (6-25-48) sec 40. The disposition of C-47's suggested by Gen Clark coincided with a plan already submitted by the French; (S) Dept of French Air Force paper, "Reinforcement of Transport Aircraft In Indo-China," 27 Mar 53, encl to (TS) Memo, Maj Gen Thomas E. De Shazo, Ch MAAG France to Nash, 23 Apr 53, "Indochina 1953," Alden files, OMA.

Quick approval followed in Washington, but the Joint Chiefs of Staff could not accept General Clark's further suggestion. While a survey team reported that the condition of forward air-strips in Indochina would not permit C-119 aircraft to be employed in their prime role as movers of tanks and other heavy equipment, the Far East Commander saw important alternative uses for their huge lift capacity. General Clark believed at least two C-119's should be sent to Indochina, but since the French Air Force had neither aircrews nor maintenance men qualified for the task, he had to recommend that a full complement of U.S. personnel accompany the planes. The Joint Chiefs of Staff replied on 21 April that the standing policy of non-involvement of American personnel in combat operations in Indochina barred the venture.[72]

General Clark had made his recommendation in rising concern over the Viet Minh invasion of Laos. Within a few days the Joint Chiefs received a call to action from another first-hand observer, Admiral Radford. Picturing the seriousness of the military situation in the strongest terms, he noted that the French had got themselves into a dispersed defensive position that laid them open to defeat in detail and left them almost entirely dependent on air transportation for supplies. Admiral Radford reported that General Salan was now saying he could arrange for pay on a contract basis if civilian pilots, crews, and mechanics could be recruited to operate the C-119 aircraft he desired. Feeling that the United States could not afford to omit any action that would improve the French capabilities, Admiral Radford urged that a minimum of six of the big transports be delivered immediately.[73]

---

72. (TS) Msg, CINCFE C 61640, to DEPTAR for Collins, DA-IN-251110, 26 Mar 53, and (TS) Msg, CINCFE C 61982, to DEPTAR for G-3, DA-IN-258870, 18 Apr 53, Ann C and E to (TS) Memo, JCS to SecDef, "Proposed French Strategic Plan for the Successful Conclusion of the War in Indochina," 21 Apr 53. (TS) Dft Msg, CSUSA to CINCFE, encl to (TS) Memo for Rec, Secy JCS, 21 Apr 53. Both in CCS 092 Asia (6-25-48) sec 40. (TS) MR by Lt Col V.W. Alden, 6 Apr 53, "Indochina 1953," Alden files, OMA.
73. (TS) Msg, CINCPAC to CNO, 271130Z Apr 53, CCS 092 Asia (6-25-48) sec 40.

Meanwhile authorities higher than the Joint Chiefs of Staff had taken the matter in hand. Secretaries Dulles and Wilson were already meeting with the French in Paris when the Laos crisis arose to dominate their discussions. Premier Mayer himself voiced the plea for several C-119 aircraft and suggested that U.S. military personnel might operate them under the cover of civilian dress and credentials. The Americans countered by offering to qualify three French crews by giving them fifteen days of training at U.S. air bases in Germany. Upon arrival in Indochina the French flight personnel would man three C-119's loaned from General Clark's command with American ground crews.[74]

Secretary Wilson sent authorization for implementing this arrangement to his Defense subordinates in Washington on 28 April. That same day the Joint Chiefs of Staff raised the number of C-119's to six, and State, Defense, and CIA officials concerted their efforts to find civilian pilots and flight personnel in the Far East who could operate the planes under contract with the French Government.[75]

With NSC approval the orders went out on 1 May. The U.S. Air Force in Europe would train six French aircrews in C-119 procedures. The Far East Air Force would immediately deliver six of the aircraft to Indochina with spare parts and maintenance crews on a loan basis, to be flown initially by the civilian contract pilots then being gathered. French airmen arriving from Europe would

---

74. (TS) Doc D-19, Memo of Conv, "Secretary's Meeting with M. Mayer, French Prime Minister . . . ," 26 Apr 53, in (TS) Doc Hist of US Pol toward Indochina, 1940-1953. (TS) Msg, Amb Dillon, Paris 5708, to SecState, 28 Apr 53, "Additional Transport A/C for French Indochina (C-119)," Alden files, OMA.

75. (TS) Msg, SecDef to ADMINO SECDEF (Wilson to Kyes), 282012Z Apr 53, CCS 092 Asia (6-25-48) sec 40. (S) Doc D-23, Memo, Walter S. Robertson to SecState, "Flying Boxcars (C-119's) for Indochina," 28 Apr 53, in (TS) Doc Hist of US Pol toward Indochina, 1940-1953.

subsequently replace the civilian aircrews. Further, the orders directed postponement of the return of any of the thirteen C-47 aircraft still on loan to the French.76

Between 6 May and 1 June 1953 the C-119's logged 517 combat flying hours, made 176 sorties, and carried 883 tons, comprising an estimated one-third of the supply support given by the French Air Force to the northern operations during the period. But every American observer who offered his views emphasized that the big planes had delivered nothing that could not have been lifted more economically by C-47's, which required one-quarter as much maintenance effort. Further, the experience strongly confirmed the opinion that the heavy C-119's could be efficiently operated only from modern, all-weather airstrips. Their operations had brought on the collapse of the runway at Gia Lam, putting Hanoi's main airport out of commission.77

Still the French professed a strong desire to retain the six aircraft indefinitely. Not until early July were members of the O'Daniel Mission able to convince the French command that the nature of operations in Indochina did not justify the use of C-119's except in an emergency requiring the air drop of heavy equipment. By agreement the six planes and their U.S. maintenance crews were withdrawn to the Philippines, there to be kept in readiness for return on short notice whenever a heavy drop operation became necessary.78

---

76. (TS) Memo, DepAsst SecDef (ISA) to Dir OMA, "Situation in Indo-China," 1 May 53. (TS) Msg, CSAF TS 2938, to CINCUSAFE, 1 May 53. (TS) Msg, CSAF TS 2937, to CGFEAF, 1 May 53. All in "Additional Transport A/C for French Indochina (C-119)," Alden files, OMA. (TS) Msg, OSD to CH MAAG IC, DEF 937911, 1 May 53, CCS 092 Asia (6-25-48) sec 41.
77. (S) Msg, Sturm, Hanoi 802, to SecState, 3 Jun 53; (S) Msg, CH MAAG IC, MG 1014A, to DEPTAR for G-3, 11 Jun 53, DA-IN-276684 (12 Jun 53). Both in "Additional Transport A/C for French Indochina (C-119)," Alden files, OMA. (TS) "Report of U.S. Joint Military Mission to Indochina, 15 July 1953," CCS 092 Asia (6-25-48) BP pt 9.
78. (TS) Msg, COMFEAF TS 4054, to HQ USAF for AFOOP, VC 0433 D/O, 30 Jun 53; (TS) Msg, COMFEAF TS 4178, to HQ

Concurrently the arrival of replacement aircraft from rehabilitation centers in Europe allowed a phasing out of the thirteen C-47's and their American ground crews. The last of these departed in mid-August 1953, after almost a year of service in Indochina.[79]

The Laos emergency had provided exasperating new evidence of the inability of French Air Force leaders to take a realistic view of their capabilities. When French sources released publicity to the effect that all would turn right if only the United States would deliver an armada of transport planes to the eagerly waiting French pilots in Indochina, General Trapnell's indignation exploded in a long dispatch to his Washington superiors. Time and again the MAAG Chief had counseled French authorities that the supply and maintenance facilities on which their operations depended were inadequate to support even the aircraft already on hand.

The French Air Ministry had set a limit of 10,000 on the personnel assigned to Indochina, a figure that necessarily covered some 2,500 guards and ordinary laborers. The technicians in that complement had been able to maintain the existing planes at an average monthly utilization rate of approximately 40 hours--less than half the USAF standard. A desperation effort during the Laos emergency was yielding a higher figure, but only at the cost of virtual abandonment of maintenance and overhaul at echelons above the tactical level. To talk of accommodating more aircraft with these same personnel and facilities was pure moonshine. Yet General Trapnell seemed unable to shake the incomprehension of the local French officials. In the same interview they would acknowledge the critical shortage of skilled mechanics, deplore the arbitrary ceiling imposed by the home authorities, and enter an urgent request for more aircraft.[80]

USAF for AFOOP, VC 0453 D/O, 9 Jul 53. Both in "Additional Transport A/C for French Indochina (C-119)," Alden files, OMA.
    79. (S) Msg, CH MAAG IC, MG 1452D, to CSAF and COMFEAF, CAF-IN-97794, 26 Aug 53, "Indochina 1953," Alden files, OMA.
    80. (S) Msg, CH MAAG IC, MG 728A, to OSD for Stewart, 1 May 53, DA-IN-263746 (2 May 53). See also (S) Msg, USAIRA Saigon AFC-31-53, to CSAF, CAF-IN-98999, 29 Apr 53. Both

Other U.S. observers fully supported General Trapnell's view. Accordingly the Joint Chiefs of Staff informed the Secretary of Defense on 20 May that the shortage of airlift capacity in Indochina was due not to lack of planes but to the inadequate manning of the French supply, maintenance, and operating organizations that prevented maximum utilization of the aircraft already on hand. Although agreeing with the repeated statements of American officers that more personnel were needed, the French had failed to correct the deficiency. The Joint Chiefs recommended that Mr. Wilson urge the Secretary of State to make representations to the French Government stressing the need for remedying the situation. The State Department complied, but the very day its instructions reached the Paris Embassy the cabinet of Premier Mayer resigned and France entered a five-week interregnum.[81]

American officials recognized that behind the flight line there were other French Air Force deficiencies that even a major increase in personnel would not cure. Supply was an unwieldy and uncertain operation. The French system suffered from faulty organization, poor location of facilities, lack of periodic inspections, and absence of the modern stock control records and procedures that would allow effective planning.

The small Air Force Section of the U.S. Military Assistance Advisory Group in Indochina had done what it could to remedy these shortcomings and instill an aggressive attitude toward the correction of malpractices. In July the effort was reinforced by the arrival on six-month temporary duty of fifty-five U.S. Air Force specialists

---

in "Additional Transport A/C for French Indochina (C-119)," Alden files, OMA. Gen Trapnell used the same arguments when opposing a French plan for creating a separate Vietnamese Air Force; (S) Msg, CHMAAG IC, MG 910D, to OSD for Stewart, DA-IN-271079, 25 May 53, "Indochina 1953," Alden files, OMA.
 81. (TS) Memo, Bradley to SecDef, "Aid to French Airlift Capability in Indochina," 20 May 53, CCS 092 Asia (6-25-48) sec 41. (S) Doc D-26, Msg, Smith to AmEmb Paris, 5693, 21 May 53, in (TS) <u>Doc Hist of US Pol toward Indochina, 1940-1953</u>.

in supply, maintenance, armament, communications, and other logistic functions. Assigned to French units down to the squadron level, they began providing instruction in current American procedures in matters ranging from corrosion control to depot organization.[82]

By August General Trapnell had new developments to report. French Air Force officials appeared to presume that they could make virtually unlimited calls on the bounty of the United States now that the Korean armistice had removed their only high-priority competitor in the bidding. Hence they saw a ready solution to the French logistic support and maintenance difficulties. In effect the French proposed that the United States ship spare parts and other materials in such massive quantities that maldistribution in Indochina would pass unnoticed. As a further measure perhaps used equipment might simply be returned in exchange for new models. The MAAG Chief rejected these proposals, both as being too costly and on the ground that they contravened one of the basic purposes of U.S. aid, which was to assist the recipient countries in developing the ability to sustain their own military establishments.[83]

Further, General Trapnell reported a French request that twenty-five C-47 aircraft and auxiliary equipment be provided within the next 30 days to permit the activation of a fourth transport squadron in Indochina. For the logistical support of this venture the local command planned to transfer 1,000 unskilled native troops to the French Air Force, and it had the promise that 650 technicians would be sent from Metropolitan France.

---

82. (TS) "Report of U.S. Joint Military Mission to Indochina, 15 July 1953," CCS 092 Asia (6-25-48) BP pt 9. NY Times, 18 Jul 53, p. 2. (S) "Air Force Section, Military Assistance Advisory Group, Indo-China, Briefing (classified) for 14 November 1953," in "Indochina Background Book," Alden files, OMA.
83. (S) Msg, CH MAAG IC, MG 1463A, to OSD/OMA, CSUSAF, and CNO, 27 Aug 53, DA-IN-593 C (28 Aug 53), CCS 092 Asia (6-25-48) sec 45.

The MAAG Chief did not concur in the request, feeling strongly that no new air unit should be activated until qualified personnel to utilize and maintain the planes were actually assembled. But he also recognized that the French desire to have sufficient aircraft to mount operations involving a simultaneous drop of three paratroop battalions was justified and deserved U.S. support. Any offensive potential must be encouraged and exploited. General Trapnell therefore offered three alternative plans and mentioned a fourth only to reject it. The poor billeting facilities, health hazards, and other difficulties encountered over the past year by the U.S. Air Force personnel assigned to service C-47's in Indochina led him to advise against any further recourse to long-term loans of planes and maintenance crews.[84]

The suggestion accepted by Washington authorities involved an expansion of the C-119 arrangement the O'Daniel Mission had worked out with the French Air Force in July. Whenever the French planned an operation such as a three-battalion drop that required greater airlift than their own forces provided they could call on the MAAG organization for assistance. On 72-hour notice from General Trapnell the Far East Air Force would then loan up to twenty-two C-119 aircraft for a period not to exceed five days for each operation. The planes would be operated by French crews in the combat zone but maintained by American ground personnel.[85]

By 1 October General Trapnell was able to say that detailed arrangements for applying this scheme had been accepted by the French authorities. Twelve French aircrews stationed in Indochina were undergoing C-119 refresher training. But before October had passed the MAAG Chief was receiving new pleas for aircraft. The French still longed for the C-47's and wanted more B-26 bombers as well.

---

84. Ibid. Concurrently the French advanced the same request in Washington; (TS) MR by Lt Col V.W. Alden, "French Request for Twenty-Five C-47 Aircraft for Indochina," 28 Aug 53, "Indochina 1953," Alden files, OMA.

85. (S) Msg, HQ USAF AFOOP-OC-T 55078, to Ch MAAG IC and COMFEAF, 17 Sep 53, CCS 092 Asia (6-25-48) sec 46.

General Trapnell wearily reissued his previous nonconcurrence. He noted that the shortage of technical personnel was already resulting in substandard maintenance and low utilization rates for the very types of aircraft now requested. Adding more planes would only compound the French logistical difficulties.86

When occasion arose in November to invoke the plan for short-term loan of C-119 transports a U.S. officer on the scene urged unusual care and promptness in carrying out the American responsibility, since General Navarre would undoubtedly "use any foul up as excuse to eliminate C-119 solution in lieu of additional squadron of C-47's.87

While dealing with the French requests for aircraft seemed an endless labor, American officials found time for other aid considerations as well. Improvement and acceleration of the training given by the French to the Vietnamese forces was an objective constantly held in mind by U.S. authorities during 1953. Experience highly qualified the Americans to give advice in this field, but no real opportunity to influence the French training system presented itself.

Early in the year a high-level committee in the Defense Department recommended against seeking any direct American participation in the Vietnamese training program in the foreseeable future. Besides repeating General Trapnell's prediction that the French would vehemently oppose any such suggestion, the committee stressed the language problem that American instructors would encounter. The Joint Chiefs of Staff expressed the same view to the Secretary of Defense in March, noting further that an exchange of missions between Indochina and Korea was scheduled that should make French officers familiar with the methods used by the United States in training the ROK forces.88

---

86. (TS) Msg, Ch MAAG IC, MG 1609A to CINCPAC, DA-IN-9615, 1 Oct 53, same file. (S) Msg, Ch MAAG IC, MG 1713D, to CSUSAF, DA-IN-15700, 23 Oct 53, "Indochina 1953," Alden files, OMA.
87. (TS) Msg Ch MAAG IC MG 1823A, sgd McCarty to COMFEAF, DA-IN-21074, 13 Nov 53, same file.
88. (TS) "Report by the Ad Hoc Committee to the Assistant to the Secretary for International Security

The results, however, were disappointing. In April General Trapnell reported that French observers had returned from Korea with little but a list of reasons why U.S. training procedures could not be effectively applied in Indochina. The MAAG Chief labeled these findings "completely fallacious" and asserted that French authorities had simply fabricated an argument "to justify resistance to any change or modernization of 'traditional' French methods."89

The unfavorable first report from Indochina led Secretaries Dulles and Wilson to reopen the subject during their visit to Paris later in April. Getting the French to observe and adopt the instructional methods so successfully applied in Korea had been a leading objective of Mr. Dulles from the moment he assumed office. Now, maintaining a friendly tone, he said it did not come as a surprise that the initial French reaction had been negative, for the Americans themselves had been slow to realize the capabilities of the South Koreans. But the Secretary counseled the French government leaders not to undervalue the results that could be achieved with proper effort. Secretary Wilson supported his colleague by pointing to the new faith, confidence, and unity that had flowered in the ROK Army when natives were given training and responsibility.90

Affairs on Forty Additional Vietnam Battalions," nd, Encl to (TS) Memo, Kyes, Actg SecDef to SecA, SecNav, and SecAF, "Forty Additional Vietnam Battalions," 19 Feb 53, CCS 092 Asia (6-25-48) sec 37. (TS) Memo, Collins to SecDef, "Broadening the Participation of the United States in the Indochina Operation," 13 March 53, same file, sec 38.

    89. (S) Msg, Ch MAAG IC MG 619A, to ACofS G-3 and CINCFE, DA-IN-257701, 15 Apr 53, Ann A to (TS) Memo, JCS to SecDef, "Proposed French Strategic Plan for the Successful Conclusion of the War in Indochina," 21 Apr 53, same file, sec 40.

    90. (S) Doc D-13, "Bipartite U.S.-French Conversations, First Session--April 22, 1953." For previous indications of SecState interest in getting French to study and adopt Korean training methods see (TS) Doc D-2, Msg, Dulles to AmEmb Saigon, 1644, 10 Feb 53, and (TS) Doc D-4, Account of SecState conversations in London, 4 Feb 53, sent Saigon as

The French response held little encouragement. M. Letourneau spoke of the Korean visits as "very useful," but he dwelled on the standing French assertion that Indochina and Korea presented entirely different problems and conditions.

During their July surveys in Indochina the members of the O'Daniel Mission gave particular attention to the French training system and facilities. Lack of centralized control and uniform standards stood out among the deficiencies they noted. The mission members also observed that many training centers were operating at far under capacity, at a time when greatly expanded instruction of Vietnamese recruits, officer candidates, and higher commanders was clearly needed. To achieve that end the Americans recommended thorough reorganization along lines that would impose real command supervision on the French training effort.

General O'Daniel felt that corrective action was assured, since General Navarre had agreed to follow the American MAAG concept and create a similar French organization to oversee all training of the native forces. Moreover the French Commander had welcomed the idea of having three U.S. officers assigned to the agency. This arrangement General O'Daniel declared would provide an excellent opportunity for continued American influence, short of direct U.S. participation in the training program.

General O'Daniel also saw encouraging evidence that lessons drawn from observation of the U.S. training procedures in Korea were already having a beneficial effect in Indochina. While French officials continued to minimize the usefulness and applicability of American methods, he found a growing interest among senior commanders in making visits to the Korean training centers.[91]

A-117, 5 Mar 53. All in (TS) <u>Doc Hist of US Pol toward Indochina, 1940-1953</u>.
    91. (TS) "Report of U.S. Joint Military Mission to Indochina, 15 July 1953," CCS 092 Asia (6-25-48) BP pt. 9.

Like other features of the Indochinese military situation, training seemed headed for improvement and expansion under the new direction of General Navarre. With American encouragement and assistance he might press on to important results.

Conclusion

Committed to supporting the Navarre Plan as an ultimate attempt to dispose of the Viet Minh threat to Indochina's freedom, American officials and agencies faced a period of exacting decision and increased activity as the fall campaign opened in 1953. The Mutual Defense Assistance Program under which most of the U.S. effort fell had been designed for aiding peacetime expansion of the military establishments of friendly governments. More than one observer had suggested that when applied to Indochina the aid program needed greater flexibility than the legal and institutional structure of MDAP allowed, in order to meet the urgent and rapidly changing requirements of an active theater of war.[92] If, through fulfillment of General Navarre's promise to take the offensive, that theater now became more active still, the coming months would undoubtedly see the development of new, more direct, and more expeditious aid procedures to meet the special Indochinese situation.

At the moment the American aid program appeared in good order. By 31 October 1953 obligation of the funds provided for Fiscal Year 1954 had begun and just short of 75 per cent of the material programmed under the MDAP budgets for Fiscal Years 1950-1953 had been shipped. The monetary value of all items delivered to Indochina stood at 674 million dollars; deliveries during the first ten months of 1953 had accounted for nearly 44 per cent of the cumulative total.[93]

There were still occasional failures, such as the deficiencies in Air Force procurement that brought

---

92. (S) HQ MAAG IC, "Field Estimate of Effectiveness of French Union Forces," 23 Jan 53, "Indochina 1953," Alden files, OMA.

93. (S) MDAP Status Report for the Month of November 1953.

protests from General Trapnell as late as October, but in many lines the French received not only more material than they could effectively use but more than they could properly store as well.[94] The contribution of military equipment as a means of encouraging and supporting the French was already being fully exploited. In September 1953 the foremost French request was not for more direct material aid but for 385 million dollars in cash.

As the fall campaign season opened American officials anticipated that General Navarre's operations would generate further urgent demands for costly equipment. But they did not foresee the Dien Bien Phu emergency, which was to drive American agencies to an extreme exertion and almost double again the cost of U.S. support to the French forces in Indochina.

---

94. (S) Msg, Ch MAAG IC MG 1755A, to OSD for Stewart, 30 Oct 53, DA-IN-17762 (31 Oct 53), "Indochina Operating Files," Alden files, OMA. (TS) "Summary of the French Situation Report Prepared by the Staff of French Expeditionary Forces, Far East, for General Navarre (30 Jun 53)," in "Navarre Letter - Actions Taken," vol I, Alden files, OMA.

CHAPTER XII

SUPPORT FOR THE NAVARRE PLAN
19 NOVEMBER 1953 - 14 JANUARY 1954

With the opening of the 1953-1954 fighting season French Union Forces in Indochina under the command of Lieutenant General Henri Navarre undertook to seize the initiative from the Viet Minh Army. Concurrently, the French were employing all available military and diplomatic channels to seek increased American material support. Washington, entirely aware that time was running out, was much occupied with satisfying the French needs, but also devoted attention to the problem of redrafting American policy toward Southeast Asia.

The provision of material aid in 1953-1954 was conditioned by three requirements which the United States had placed on the French in the early fall. These were (1) perfection of the political and economic independence of the Associated States, (2) adoption of a plan for dynamic military action, and (3) expansion and training of indigenous armies. While the first of these stipulations was primarily a matter for State Department concern, the other two were of direct interest to the Department of Defense and the Joint Chiefs of Staff.

In order to determine how well the French were living up to the military conditions, the Joint Chiefs of Staff had directed Lieutenant General John W. O'Daniel to return to Indochina with a small joint mission and report on his findings. The General forwarded the report on the two-week stay of his mission to the Joint Chiefs on 19 November 1953.

Basically optimistic in tone, General O'Daniel's report announced that "clear indications of real military progress by French Union Forces since our previous visit to Indochina /in July/ are evident." If General Navarre had not completely succeeded in wresting the initiative from the Viet Minh, he had at least definitely kept the enemy off balance and had established a far better military situation than existed during the 1952-1953 campaign. The French command had recovered sufficient forces from static positions to establish a mobile combat reserve in the Tonkin Delta and had proceeded to activate native light infantry battalions as scheduled. But there were some black spots. By American standards the French continued to be over-cautious in the conduct of the war and less effective in using available means. Furthermore, progress in training native units remained unsatisfactory. Insufficient naval materiel and inadequate maintenance and logistic support for air units in Indochina were other deficiencies.

By way of conclusion General O'Daniel reiterated American policy: "we should fully support General Navarre, in whose success we have such a large stake." Yet General O'Daniel's recommendations for American action to remedy the deficiencies were limited to measures that the French would be willing to accept. As such, they fell short of introducing large-scale American influence in the planning of operations and in the training of Vietnamese forces. Specifically, the general suggested the assignment of a small number of additional officers to MAAG Indochina for liaison with French headquarters and for duty with the French command training native armies. He also recommended the continuation of existing arrangements by which the United States loaned C-119's upon call to the French. Later, when the French command developed sufficient maintenance capability, the United States might furnish C-47's on a permanent basis. Finally, more naval craft could be put to good use.[1]

Not all views of the Indochina situation were as sanguine as General O'Daniel's. Commenting on the joint

---

1. (TS) O'Daniel, "Progress Report on Military Situation in Indochina as of 19 November 1953," CCS 092 Asia (6-25-48) sec 50 BP pt 10. For a resume of the report see (TS) Msg, CGUSARPAC O'Daniel to JCS, RJ 68496, 190707Z Nov 53, DA-IN-22712, same file, sec 50, and (TS) App to Encl A to (TS) JCS 1992/260, Rpt by JSPC, "Report of U.S. Joint Military Mission to Indochina," 17 Dec 53, same file, sec 52.

mission's report, Vice Admiral Felix Stump, Commander in Chief, Pacific, concurred that considerable military progress had been made; however, he pointed out additional flaws. Political and psychological factors remained intertwined with the purely military aspects of the problem. Not enough had been done to turn these vital factors to the advantage of the West. Therefore CINCPAC thought it very important that the highest levels of the French and United States Governments reaffirm their intention of prosecuting the war to a satisfactory conclusion. Admiral Stump also stated his opinion that complete victory was unlikely until there was sufficient native troops to garrison captured areas and until the Indochinese had been won over by anti-Communist psychological warfare.[2]

Immediately following General O'Daniel's visit, the French command itself took action underscoring Admiral Stump's more reserved optimism. In a move reminiscent of the defensive concepts of previous years, French Union Forces on 20 November 1953 launched operation CASTOR to seize control of the Dien Bien Phu basin in mountainous western Tonkin, near the Laotian border. Although the objective was to consolidate a strong position from which to interdict supply routes when the Viet Minh made its annual incursion into Laos, selection of the site was dictated by the need for an airstrip. Happily, the Japanese had established a pierced-steel-planked runway at Dien Bien Phu during World War II. But since the requirements for air support received first consideration, the needs of other arms for good defensive positions were sacrificed.[3]

Dropping by parachute, the first waves of French troops easily overcame the surprised Viet Minh garrison. Repairing the runway was delayed, however, when a heavy bulldozer broke away from its canopy and crashed to the

---

2. (TS) Msg, CINCPAC to CNO, 020135Z Dec 53, DA-IN-25651, same file, sec 51.
3. Capt M. Harrison, "Dien Bien Phu," *An Cosantoir* (Irish Defense Journal), vol XIV, no. 6 (Jun 54), pp. 270-286.

ground. As a result, succeeding waves of troops had to drop rather than land. A substitute bulldozer was subsequently located, and the French began the work of organizing a strong defensive fortress to be manned by twelve battalions.[4]

As an immediate outcome of more active operations the French High Command increased its pressure for American material support. High on General Navarre's list were the oft-sought twenty-five additional C-47's. In October Major General Thomas J.H. Trapnell, Chief of the U.S. Military Assistance Advisory Group, Indochina, had advised against providing these planes until the French had demonstrated the capability to support and use them efficiently. However, the November visits of General O'Daniel and Vice President Nixon provided General Navarre a chance to renew his importunities. Although General O'Daniel supported the MAAG position, General Trapnell withdrew his objections to providing the aircraft when the American Ambassador pointed out that the planes might provide just the psychological lift needed to encourage French initiative.[5] The Vice President also saw the question as a political matter and carried it to President Eisenhower, who decided that political advantages outweighted military objections. Secretary of State Dulles informed Paris of the decision to provide twenty-five C-47's while Admiral Radford passed the word to Lieutenant General Jean E. Valluy, French Representative on the NATO Standing Group.[6]

---

4. Ibid. See also (S dg C) Msg, USARMA Saigon to CSA for G-2, OARMA MC 319-53, 231330Z Nov 53, DA-IN-23791 (24 Nov 53), CCS 092 Asia (2-25-48) sec 50, and (S) Mns, QUINTEL Mtg, 1 Dec 53, App to Encl to (S) JCS 1992/276, Memo by CNO, "Report on the Sixth QUINPART Intelligence Meeting," 11 Feb 54, same file, sec 57.
5. (S) Msg, Heath to SecState, OSD, 846, 132250Z Nov 53, DA-IN-21426 (14 Nov 53), same file, sec 49.
6. (S) Doc D-50, Msg, SecState to AmEmb Paris, 1930, Saigon, 920, 6:17 p.m., 23 Nov 53, in (TS) Doc Hist of US Pol toward Indochina. (S) CM-40-53, Memo by CJCS to JCS, "Additional C-47 Aircraft for French Forces Indo-China," 25 Nov 53.

The President and Mr. Dulles soon had an opportunity to discuss Indochina face-to-face with the French Premier and Foreign Minister when the tripartite French-U.K.-U.S. conference finally convened in Tuckers Town, Bermuda, 4-8 December 1953. Although the principal topics on the agenda were European security and the Soviet proposal for a four-power conference in Berlin, the Big Three did find time for one session on the Far East.

In preparation for the conference, the Joint Chiefs of Staff directed the Joint Intelligence Committee to evaluate repetitive French reports indicating that the Chinese Communists might support the Viet Minh with jet aircraft. The committee could not find corroboration for French fears. It reported to the Chiefs that although the Chinese were capable of furnishing jet or conventional aircraft support for the Viet Minh, U.S. intelligence did not indicate either an increase in this capability or an intent by the Chinese to intervene with jets in Indochina. The Joint Chiefs agreed, and so informed the Secretary of Defense.[7] They took no other part in preparing material for use in the Indochinese phase of Bermuda discussions.

When the conference turned to Far Eastern matters, Premier Joseph Laniel was indisposed, so the French position was sketched by Foreign Minister Georges Bidault. He briefed the President and Prime Minister on the military situation, acknowledging American aid and emphasizing French Union sacrifices. Although they were making every effort to establish the Associated States as truly independent nations, the French were handicapped by the lack of native leaders capable of governing the people. For example, when the French had asked Bao Dai whether the transfer of all authority with real independence was enough, this question "had brought him to the Riviera like Galatea to the willow."

---

7. (TS) JCS 1992/254, 25 Nov 53, CCS 092 Asia (6-25-48) sec 50. (TS) Memo, CJCS for JCS to SecDef, "Support of Viet Minh Forces in Indochina by Chinese Communist Jet Aircraft," 1 Dec 53, same file, sec 51.

The most significant of M. Bidault's remarks dealt with the prospects for negotiations. France, he asserted, would not make peace except under conditions that would respect the individual liberty of the Indochinese people. However, he did think that a five-power conference, including China, France, the United Kingdom, the United States, and the Soviet Union, called in a specific framework for a discussion of Southeast Asian problems, might be acceptable to France, provided the Associated States could be present. In reply Mr. Churchill praised the French efforts. President Eisenhower seconded his war praise but added that the United States viewed a Five-Power Conference "with a jaundiced eye."[8]

A major accomplishment of the Bermuda talks was the drafting of a reply to the Soviet Union agreeing to the convocation of a four-power foreign ministers meeting at Berlin in early January 1954. Taking note of a Soviet proposal that the foreign ministers should discuss the possibility of holding a five-power conference including Red China, the West agreed only that the participating governments could state their views on this topic at Berlin.[9] M. Bidault had made it clear that France could not turn its back on an opportunity to negotiate a settlement of the Indochinese war; thus, the agreement to go to Berlin and to talk about China was not without danger to the West.

The Bermuda conversations did not resolve questions about the provision of additional American aid to Indochina. The twenty-five planes approved for transfer in late November represented only a portion of total French needs. General Navarre was in a difficult position; he had to produce military success in very little time. And he saw success threatened by material shortages. He had gleaned the impression in recent months from highly-placed American military and civilian visitors to Indochina that the United States was determined to undertake an extensive effort in providing material aid. Yet MAAG and stateside agencies did not seem to be quite the cornucopia General Navarre visualized.

---

8. (S) Mns, 5th Plen Tri Mtg of Heads of Government, Bermuda, 5:30 p.m., 7 Dec 53, CCS 337 (4-19-50) BP pt 2.
9. (U) Tri US-UK-Fr Note to USSR, 8 Dec 53, State Dept, Bulletin, 21 Dec 53, pp. 852-853.

Rather than sitting down with General Trapnell for a frank discussion of the problem, in mid-December General Navarre dispatched a strong letter to MAAG contrasting promise and performance. Not only had MAAG screened French requests but Washington agencies had further reduced agreed programs. The French Commander stated that the discrepancy between means in personnel and means in material threatened to necessitate a complete re-examination of his 1954 operational plan. He wanted Washington to speed deliveries of material programmed in earlier years and to inform him when he could expect 1954 items. In addition, he asked for reconsideration of the reductions applied to the 1954 program.[10]

Since the Office of Military Assistance suspected that this complaint was an attempt to establish an alibi in advance for failure to achieve military success, it provided General Trapnell with the information for a polite but firm protest against delaying operations. End-items programmed in earlier years were on the way, and within budgetary limitations the 1954 program was being met.[11]

General Trapnell's courteous answer opened the door for American consideration of French battle needs on an ad hoc, emergency basis. On 18 December the Chief of MAAG wrote General Navarre:

> I have been advised that the military requirements for Indochina have the highest MDAP priority, and that although the military departments did not expect to make deliveries of FY 54 programmed items in time for use during the current dry season, urgent action had been taken to provide items critically in need during this season.

---

10. (S) Msg, Ch MAAG IC to OSD for OMA for Stewart, MG 1988-B, 091500Z Dec 53, DA-IN-27610 (10 Dec 53), "Navarre Letter, Actions Taken," vol I, Alden files, OMA.

11. (S) Memo, Col J.G. Anding, Actg Dir OMA, to Asst SecDef (ISA), "Indochina FY 1954 MDAP," c. 11 Dec 54; (S) Msg, OSD sgd Ruffner to Ch MAAG IC, DEF 954347, 142329Z Dec 53; (S) Msg, OSD sgd Nash to Ch MAAG IC, DEF 954441, 162145Z Dec 53. All in "Navarre Letter, Actions Taken," vol I, Alden files, OMA.

In addition, he invited the French Staff to work with MAAG in readying lists of critical items. These lists would be submitted to Washington and delivery expedited to meet operational requirements.[12] Requests went forward on this basis and General Trapnell was able to assure Admiral Radford during their Christmas conference at Manila that no deficiencies in the American aid program or deliveries would cause any embarrassment or change in French plans in the immediate future.[13]

Perhaps one of the concerns contributing to General Navarre's petulance had been a new political crisis in Viet Nam. The world learned on 27 November 1953 that Ho Chi Minh had informed the Stockholm newspaper *Expressen* of Viet Minh willingness to negotiate with France for an armistice. His terms were cessation of hostilities and real respect for the independence of Viet Nam.[14] Coincidentally, President Auriol of France announced on 27 November a liberal formula by which the Associated States could be independent, yet remain members of the French Union. By this announcement France moved to carry out the 3 July declaration and to satisfy American pressure for granting Indochina its independence.[15] The effect of the Ho interview and President Auriol's statement was to stir up anew nationalistic feelings in Viet Nam. In early December Premier Nguyen Van Tam tried to capitalize on nationalistic sentiments by demanding that Chief of State Bao Dai establish an anti-Communist coalition government to negotiate peace with the Viet Minh and work out the terms of association with France. Then, having failed to win popular support, on 17 December Van Tam handed his government's resignation to the Chief of State. While the resignation may have been little more than the normal

---

12. (S) Msg, Ch MAAG IC to SecDef for OMA for Nash, MG 2057 B, 180907Z Dec 53, DA-IN-29482 (18 Dec 53), same file.
13. (S) Msg, CJCS to OSD for Nash, 250935Z Dec 53, DA-IN-31007 (29 Dec 53), same file.
14. (S) Geneva Conf Background Paper, Indochina Chronology, p. 83.
15. (U) "Summary of statement of President Auriol on Free Association of States within the French Union," Tab D to State Dept (S) Bermuda Conf preparation paper, BM D-10d, "Indochina," 2 Dec 53, CCS 337 (4-19-50) sec 10.

Indochinese political machination, it did nothing to improve the situation.[16]

Against the background of somewhat more vigorous French military and political action and a Vietnamese domestic crisis, the Joint Chiefs of Staff gave considerable attention to Indochinese affairs in December 1953. They had to decide what disposition to make of General O'Daniel's recommendations. In addition, the National Security Council Planning Board was rewriting the statement of American policy toward Southeast Asia and the Chiefs had to provide military guidance on this subject.[17]

First on the agenda was a report by the Joint Strategic and Logistics Plans Committees on General O'Daniel's mission. The committees had arrived at six conclusions which paralleled those of the joint mission. On the asset side of the ledger they found that there was no indication of French or Vietnamese disposition to envisage negotiations with the enemy and that there was evidence of real military progress in the implementation of the Navarre Plan. As liabilities, the committees incorporated in their conclusions four deficiencies found by General O'Daniel: lack of sufficient naval small craft, and inadequacies in the training of native forces, in the operation of the joint amphibious command, and in the maintenance and supply capability of the French air arm.

The committees recommended that the report submitted by the O'Daniel Mission be accepted by the Joint Chiefs as the basis for further planning and seconded the

---

16. NY Times, 17 Dec 53, pp. 1 and 3; Hammer, Struggle for Indochina, p. 306. The crisis was not resolved until 11 Jan 54 when Bao Dai appointed his cousin, Prince Buu Loc, Prime Minister.

17. (TS) JCS 1992/256, 3 Dec 53; (TS) Memo, Maj Gen J.K. Gerhart to DJS, Lt Gen F.F. Everest, "Review of U.S. Policy Toward Southeast Asia," 9 Dec 53; (TS) DM-72-53, to JCS, 14 Dec 53. All in CCS 092 Asia (6-25-48) sec 51.

general's principal suggestions. These recommendations included the assignment of two Army officers to MAAG for duty with the French training command and the assignment of four officers, one from each Service and one from the Marine Corps, for liaison duties between MAAG and the French headquarters. The committees' report also incorporated General O'Daniel's recommendation that the Chief of Staff, USAF, continue the arrangements for French use of up to twenty-two C-119's from the Far East Air Command. Finally, they suggested that the Chief of Naval Operations expedite delivery of naval craft programmed for 1954 and in the meantime lend the French four LSM's or their equivalent.[18]

Before approving the committees' conclusions and recommendations, the Joint Chiefs of Staff amended them at the Army's suggestion to reflect more completely Admiral Stump's comments. Qualifying remarks were added to the two more roseate conclusions. As amended, the report indicated that the French had made limited progress in carrying out the Navarre concept, but that the military situation had not yet altered significantly in their favor. To the opinion that the French or Vietnamese did not contemplate negotiations with the enemy the Chiefs added the thought that a seemingly plausible offer from the Viet Minh might lead to a parley, expecially in the absence of any real French Union military progress. In addition, the Joint Chiefs of Staff wrote in a new conclusion, as follows: "Primary military requirements for a French Union victory in Indochina include the development of large and effective indigenous forces and the effective utilization of psychological warfare among the natives."

The Chiefs, however, did not develop this new conclusion into recommendations for implementing action. Instead they accepted the recommendations from the committees' report and added only General O'Daniel's suggestion that French Union officers be invited to inspect U.S. training methods in the Republic of Korea.

---

18. (TS) JCS 1992/260, 17 Dec 53, same file, sec 52.

As amended, the report became a basis for further planning, and the recommendations became directives to appropriate Service Chiefs on 31 December 1953.[19]

Even before the Chiefs had approved the recommendations, General O'Daniel in Honolulu was urging early implementation. The French Government had now authorized General Navarre to accept a few additional American officers for intelligence work, for duty with the training command, and for liaison with French services. This authorization, commented General O'Daniel, offered a splendid opportunity for the United States to influence French planning and training. Two days later, however, General O'Daniel suggested that the invitation for French Union officers to inspect Korean training installations be held up until the end of the fighting season. Implementation of the recommendations approved by the Chiefs went forward on the basis of these amplifying comments.[20]

While the Joint Chiefs of Staff were dealing with the O'Daniel report the Planning Board of the National Security Council had been redrafting the 18-month old statement of American objectives and courses of action in Southeast Asia.[21] The Board took up this task because in the interim the French situation in Indochina had further deteriorated.

---

19. (TS) Memo by CSA, "Report of U.S. Joint Military Mission to Indochina," /Army ditto/, c. 30 Dec 53, same file. (TS) JCS 1992/264, 30 Dec 53, same file, sec 53. (TS) JCS 1992/260, Dec On, 31 Dec 53, same file, sec 52.
20. (S) Msg, CGUSARPAC O'Daniel to CSA, RJ 68589, 262125Z Dec 53, DA-IN-30757 (26 Dec 53); (S) Msg, CGUSARPAC to SecDef for Nash, RJ 68591, 282242Z Dec 53, DA-IN-30971 (29 Dec 53). Both in same file, sec 53.
21. (TS) NSC 124/2, 25 Jun 52 (circ to JCS as Encl B to (TS) JCS 1992/168, 2 Jul 52), same file, sec 32.

A major problem was the assessment of the probable consequences of a French defeat in Indochina. In June 1952 the Security Council had agreed that the loss of any Southeast Asian country would have critical consequences for the United States and would probably lead to the relatively swift realization of Communist domination over the whole area. But in November 1953 the Central Intelligence Agency would go no farther than to say: "A Viet Minh victory in Indochina would remove a significant military barrier to a Communist sweep through Southeast Asia, expose the remainder of that region to greatly increased external Communist pressures, and probably increase the capabilities of local Communists . . . ." However, the Deputy Director for Intelligence of the Joint Staff registered a dissenting view: "The establishment of Communist control over Indochina by military or other means would almost certainly result in the Communization of all of Southeast Asia . . . ."[22]

In Planning Board sessions Major General J. K. Gerhart, Special Assistant to the Joint Chiefs of Staff for National Security Council Affairs, argued convincingly in support of the Joint Staff estimates.[23] Accordingly, when the Planning Board submitted its redraft to the appropriate agencies at the end of December 1953, the principal change in the new policy statement was increased emphasis on the dangers present in the Indochinese situation. The starting point was the same statement that had appeared in NSC 124/2: "Communist domination, by whatever means, of all Southeast Asia would seriously endanger in the short term, and critically endanger in the longer term, United States security interests." The redraft, thanks to General Gerhart's pleading, pointed out that the loss of Indochina would

---

22. (TS) SE-52, CIA Sp Est, "Probable Consequences in Non-Communist Asia of Certain Possible Developments in Indochina Before Mid-1954," 10 Nov 53, p. 1, JIG files.

23. (TS) Interv, Samuel A. Tucker with Lt Col J.W. Vogt, Office of the Spec Asst to JCS for NSC Affairs, 4 Jan 55, memo in JCS HS files. (TS) "An Account of the Events and Decisions Leading to the Loss of North Indochina," prepared for the record by the Office of the SpecAsst to JCS for NSC Affairs, 1st Draft, 25 Oct 54, pp. 26-27. (Hereinafter cited as Gerhart "Account.")

have "the most serious repercussions on U.S. and Free World interests in Europe and elsewhere." The loss of a single country might lead to loss of the entire area, with grave economic consequences; it might seriously jeopardize U.S. security interest in the Far East, and subject Japan to severe economic and political pressures making it difficult for the United States to prevent Japan's eventual accommodation to Communism.

Two agents could transform these threats into reality. First, there was the new, stronger, hostile, aggressive China. Overt Chinese attack on Southeast Asia would require the extensive diversion of American strength from other areas. However, the Chinese Communists were more likely to continue their efforts to dominate the region covertly through subversion and armed rebellion. The second potential source of disaster was France itself. Although the Laniel Government was committed to seeking the destruction of the Viet Minh forces, the Planning Board warned that a successor government might well accept an improvement in the military situation short of Viet Minh defeat as the basis for serious negotiation within the next year. If the Laniel-Navarre Plan should fail, or appear doomed to failure, the French might seek to negotiate for the best possible terms, irrespective of whether these offered any assurance of preserving Indochina for the free world.

In coping with Communist expansion in Asia to date the United States had issued its warning to China, participated with other interested nations in military talks on measures which might be taken in the event of open aggression, and increased the flow of military and economic aid to France and the Associated States. The Board cautioned that, in planning for the future, the United States Government should bear two considerations in mind. It was necessary to coordinate actions affecting one country with actions for the region as a whole, and to accommodate those actions to the individual sensibilities of the governments, social classes, and minorities of Southeast Asia.

Having sketched the problem, the Planning Board rephrased the general objective of the United States thus: "To prevent the countries of Southeast Asia from passing into the communist orbit; to persuade them that their best interests lie in greater cooperation and stronger affiliations with the rest of the free world; and to assist them to develop toward stable, free governments with the will and ability to resist communism from within and without and to contribute to the strengthening of the free world."

Following the format of the June 1952 statement, the Planning Board recommended generalized courses of action for the area as a whole. Both words and acts--in the form of technical assistance, economic aid, and the encouragement of economic cooperation--should be employed to persuade indigenous governments that their best interests lay in close cooperation with the free world. Further, it was essential that the United States encourage and support the spirit of resistance among southeast Asians to Chinese Communist aggression in all its forms. But this was only one side of the street, and working both sides was obviously required. To this end the United States should continue its actions to make China aware of the grave consequences of aggression. Words were not enough; it was necessary to promote the coordinated defense of Southeast Asia, "recognizing that the initiative in regional defense measures must come from the governments of the area." Finally, the American people at home should be made aware of the importance of the region so that they would be prepared to support the proposed courses of action.

The Planning Board continued by taking up the individual countries of Southeast Asia. And of course Indochina led all the rest. Actions toward that bloc of nations were grouped under two assumptions: one, that Communist China would not overtly intervene in the war; the other, that it would. Should China remain a silent partner of the Viet Minh, the main targets for U.S. action would continue to be the French and the Indochinese. And in dealing with them America was forced to carry water on both shoulders. The United States had to build up the independence of Indochina, which could only occur at the short-range expense of France, while inducing the French to fight vigorously for the longer-range interests of the free world.

This dilemma was implicit in the statements of specific actions. Suggesting first action primarily in the military field, the Planning Board proposed that, while recognizing France's basic responsibility for the defense of the Associated States, the United States should expedite or even increase its aid to French Union Forces. The objective would be to foster an aggressive military, political, and psychological offensive, including covert operations designed to eliminate organized Viet Minh forces by mid-1955. At the same time, American aid would help in the development of native forces that could eventually be capable of maintaining internal security. On the diplomatic and political front the United States would assure the French that America appreciated the sacrifices being made in the common interest of the free world. But it was also necessary to encourage and support steps by both France and the Associated States in the development of a working relationship between them based on equal sovereignty within the French Union.

A further series of proposed actions dealt with the possibility that France might sue for peace. To offset this contingency, the United States should employ every feasible means for influencing the French Government and people against a conclusion of the war on terms inconsistent with American objectives. France should be allowed no illusions about being able to obtain acceptable terms in advance of achieving a marked improvement in the military situation. It would be equally illusory for the French to consider establishing a coalition Viet Nam government with Ho Chi Minh. Drawing upon Korean experience, the Planning Board also recommended that the United States flatly oppose any idea of accepting a cease-fire prior to opening negotiations because of the probable result--irretrievable deterioration in the French Union military position. One means by which the United States could block undesirable negotiations was to insist that the French obtain Vietnamese approval of all actions taken in response to any Viet Minh offers. Finally, if the French persisted in opening talks with Ho Chi Minh, the American Government should seek to influence the outcome of the negotiations by demanding that France consult with U.S. officials.

The Planning Board recommended as a final course, assuming that the Chinese did not intervene, that the United States prepare for taking the actions set forth under the contrary assumption. Turning to this assumption of Chinese intervention, the board rephrased those paragraphs of NSC 124/2 which also dealt with the possibility of China's entering the war. It did not significantly alter the substance of those earlier proposals. First, an appeal should be addressed to the United Nations for action against aggression; at the same time the United States would seek maximum international support and cooperation in whatever military action might be necessary. America itself should furnish naval and air assistance, as practicable, to French Union ground troops, provide major forces for interdicting Chinese Communist communication lines, and supply logistic support needed by other participating states. Other military action, as appropriate, might include a blockade of China, providing the French and British concurred; covert operations to aid guerrillas in China; utilization of Chinese Nationalist forces where desirable and feasible; assistance to the British in Hong Kong; and evacuation of French Union military and civilian personnel from the Tonkin Delta if required. Finally, if the United States, the United Kingdom, and France determined that expanded action against China was needed, the three powers should take naval and air action against military targets in China which directly contributed to the Chinese effort in Indochina; however, targets near the Soviet border would not be attacked unless absolutely necessary. The United States might even consider taking action against China unilaterally if the other two powers would not come along.[24]

The courses of action recommended by the Planning Board in NSC 177 reflected an assumption that France would continue to fight. However, the Board had recognized the possibility that a successor government might sue for peace. Therefore, General Gerhart proposed that the Board

---

24. (TS) NSC 177, 30 Dec 53, Encl to (TS) JCS 1992/265, 4 Jan 54, CCS 092 Asia (6-25-48) sec 53.

also draft recommended courses of action to be adopted in the event that France gave up the struggle. The Board concurred, subject to the restriction that the study receive even more limited distribution than normal, because if the French were to get wind of the existence of American planning for such a contingency they might slacken their efforts.[25]

Since the Board needed military advice, the Joint Chiefs of Staff directed the Joint Strategic and Logistic Plans Committees to review the validity of another study of this same contingency that the Chiefs had noted in July 1953.[26] As in the earlier study, the committees accepted certain basic assumptions. These were as follows: (1) the United States could take over French responsibilities in an orderly manner at the invitation of the Associated States; (2) Korea would remain quiescent so that two American divisions could be withdrawn from there; (3) elsewhere U.S. commitments would remain undisturbed unless the return home of French forces from the Orient permitted American withdrawals from Europe; and (4) Communist China would not overtly intervene in the war.

The committees reaffirmed the conclusion that the successful defense of Indochina was essential since loss of the area would have critical psychological, political, and economic consequences for the United States. Should the American Government determine to participate with military forces in this defense, it should commit sufficient strength to insure military success. The course of action offering the United States the greatest assurance of such success was to support and step up the development of native troops and to deploy American and Allied forces to Indochina for operations that would have the objective of reducing Communist strength to scattered

---

25. (TS) Interv, Tucker with Vogt, 4 Jan 55, memo in JCS HS files. (TS) Gerhart "Account," p. 31.
26. (TS) Memo, Gerhart to DJC, "Review of U.S. Policy Toward Southeast Asia," 9 Dec 53; (TS) DM-72-53, to JCS, same subj, 14 Dec 53. Both in CCS 092 Asia (6-25-48) sec 51. (TS) JCS 1992/227, 22 Jun 53, amended by Dec On, 2 Jul 53, same file, sec 43.

guerrilla bands. A second course, which would be acceptable as a temporary measure provided the United States were prepared to follow through with more vigorous action if necessary, was supporting and developing native forces and deploying sufficient strength to hold critical strong points evacuated by the French. Such holding operations would require air and naval support until the native armies could themselves take effective operations against the Communists. The committees rejected two additional courses, requiring less extensive American intervention, as insufficient and likely to result in military defeat.[27]

Although the Joint Chiefs did not consider this report immediately, the Services were in general agreement with its conclusions. Therefore, General Gerhart and the Planning Board drew upon it in drafting their study of additional courses of action that could be adopted in the event of French withdrawal from Indochina.

The board foresaw that the threat of French withdrawal might take two forms. There was, first, the possibility that France might seek peace unless America offered to participate in the war with military forces. Should this contingency arise, two choices would be open to the United States. Either the American Government might do nothing to prevent the loss of Indochina or it might provide the forces needed to keep France in the war. The logistic implications of this latter action were spelled out by the Planning Board in some detail.

The second threat foreseen by the Board was even more ominous. The French Government might refuse to continue the struggle even if the United States did agree to commit troops. Under these circumstances again America might write off Indochina. On the other hand, it could

---

27. (TS) JCS 1992/262, 24 Dec 53, same file, sec 53.

consider taking one of the four alternative courses that had just been evaluated by the Joint Staff. The Board submitted this study for NSC consideration in December 1953 as the Special Annex to NSC 177.[28]

Meanwhile, the military situation in Indochina had not been improving. On Christmas Day, 1953, the Viet Minh launched its annual invasion of Laos, which compelled the French to divert troops for its defense. In early January General Trapnell gloomily reported that the situation bore a striking similarity to the pattern of last year's campaign in which sizeable French Union Forces were widely dispersed and in defensive attitudes. The French had been surprised, moreover, to find that the Viet Minh units surrounding Dien Bien Phu were supplied, for the first time, with antiaircraft artillery that could successfully knock down fighter bombers. Only light bombers (B-26's) could now be used, and General Trapnell warned Washington to expect requests for additional aircraft of this type and for U.S. personnel both to maintain the C-47's, B-26's, and C-119's and to fly C-119's on missions to non-combat areas.

Although Admiral Stump had thought General O'Daniel too optimistic, he now believed General Trapnell was unduly pessimistic. He recommended to Washington that all possible assistance be given to General Navarre. It was CINCPAC's belief that "timely assistance by the U.S. in this critical period through which Gen. Navarre and the French Union Forces are now passing will be instrumental in bringing about ultimate victory."[29]

---

28. Since the Special Annex was subsequently withdrawn and destroyed, no copy exists in JCS files. The above material was drawn from the author's interview with Lt Col Vogt, 4 Jan 55, JCS HS files, and from (TS) JCS 1992/267, 4 Jan 54, CCS 092 Asia (6-25-48) sec 53. See also (TS) Gerhart "Account," p. 33.

29. (S) Geneva Conf Background Paper, Indochina Chronology, p. 84. (TS) Msg, Ch MAAG IC to CINCPAC, MG 8 A, 020730Z Jan 54, DA-IN-31633 (2 Jan 54); (TS) Msg, Ch MAAG IC to DA, MG 9 A, 020926Z Jan 54, DA-IN-31639 (2 Jan 54); (TS) Msg, CINCPAC to CNO, 040139Z Jan 54. All in CCS 092 Asia (6-25-48) sec 53.

These reports from the field arrived in Washington at about the same time the Joint Chiefs were asked to review the two Planning Board studies, NSC 177 and the Special Annex. CINCPAC's comments pointed up the need for early action along lines outlined in NSC 177, which assumed the French would fight if America continued its aid programs. Accordingly, on 6 January 1954 the Joint Chiefs of Staff informed the Secretary of Defense that they were in general agreement with the Planning Board draft.[30]

General Trapnell's message emphasized the importance of having plans ready for the possibility of French failure and withdrawal. Such plans, incorporated in the Special Annex to NSC 177, came before the Joint Chiefs of Staff for approval on 6 January 1954. However, the Joint Strategic Survey Committee had reported that this Planning Board study was not sufficiently explicit. Admittedly, the United States would suffer critical consequences if Indochina fell; therefore, reasoned the Joint Strategic Survey Committee, the United States should not accept the alternative of writing off the area if the French proposed to quit in the absence of American military participation. Instead, the committee recommended that the Chiefs press for a decision on whether the United States should intervene, if necessary, to preserve Indochina. Such a decision would provide definitive policy for the development of further national diplomatic and military plans.

The Joint Strategic Survey Committee recognized that if the French withdrew in spite of American intervention the world-wide situation might oblige the United States to accept the loss of Indochina. Nevertheless, the American Government should be prepared to do what it could to offset such a development. Therefore, the committee recommended that the Special Annex be revised to reflect the following views:

---

30. (TS) Memo, CJCS for JCS to SecDef, "NSC 177 - United States Courses of Action with Respect to Southeast Asia," 6 Jan 54, same file, sec 54.

Should the French make an arbitrary decision to withdraw from the conflict in Indochina despite all offers of United States assistance, the United States should in any event, and as a minimum urge the French to phase their withdrawal over a protracted period and to take all practicable measures to prepare the indigenous forces better to assume the responsibilities of their own defense. Additionally, the United States, preferably in conjunction with its Allies, should provide such military assistance to the indigenous forces of Indochina as is determined to be advisable and feasible in the light of conditions then prevailing, and as is consistent with United States objectives both with respect to Southeast Asia and world-wide. The level of military assistance which might be advisable and feasible cannot be predetermined, but might encompass anything from a continuation of materiel aid as a minimum to Alternative A (vigorous intervention) as a maximum.[31]

The Chief of Naval Operations suggested further amendments. He wished to write in the thought that if U.S. forces were to participate in the war, they should do so in sufficient strength to insure an early and lasting military victory. Admiral Carney also wished to strengthen the arguments in favor of the most vigorous alternative course, supporting native troops while deploying American and Allied forces for operations which would reduce the Communists to scattered guerrilla bands. However, he recommended adding one qualification to the acceptable courses: "precautionary reservations are necessary by reason of the fact that circumstances under which the French forces withdraw, and other related strategic circumstances cannot be accurately predicted."[32]

---

31. (TS) JCS 1992/267, 4 Jan 54, same file, sec 53.
32. (TS) JCS 1992/268, 5 Jan 54, same file, sec 54.

At their meeting on 6 January 1954 the Joint Chiefs of Staff considered the JSSC report and Admiral Carney's recommended amendments without reaching final decision.33 On the following day at a meeting of the Armed Forces Policy Council Admiral Radford indicated that the Joint Chiefs of Staff had hastily prepared some comments on the Special Annex to NSC 177, but needed more time for proper study of the paper. The Deputy Secretary of Defense, Mr. Roger M. Kyes, then attacked the accuracy of the logistical requirements set forth under the alternative courses of American intervention. He did not address himself to the principal problem at hand--that of being prepared for a French request for U.S. intervention. This was the very problem which the Joint Chiefs of Staff believed should receive timely examination. Nevertheless, Secretary of Defense C. E. Wilson supported Mr. Kyes and decided to request that the Special Annex be withdrawn from further consideration. In addition, the Department of Defense suggested to the Security Council that, in the future, requests for military advice, such as that contained in the Special Annex, should be addressed to the Secretary of Defense, not to the Joint Chiefs of Staff.34

When the National Security Council met on 8 January President Eisenhower sustained the objections of Secretary Wilson and ordered the withdrawal and destruction of the Special Annex to NSC 177. However, the council did touch upon the question of how far the United States would go

---

33. The (TS) Gerhart "Account," p. 34, indicates that the Joint Chiefs of Staff on 6 January 1954 approved a memorandum to the Secretary of Defense calling for immediate decision on whether or not the United States would intervene in Indochina if necessary to prevent the French from seeking to conclude the struggle on terms likely to result in the loss of the area to the Communists. Furthermore, this memorandum rejected as an unacceptable course of action the alternative of refusing to commit U.S. forces to the French military effort. However, official records of the Joint Chiefs of Staff available to the Historical Section do not indicate that this memorandum was formally adopted.

34. (TS) AFPC Advice of Action, "U.S. Objectives and Courses of Action with Respect to Southeast Asia (NSC 177)," 11 Jan 54. (TS) Interv, Tucker with Vogt, 4 Jan 55, memo in JCS HS files. (TS) Gerhart "Account," p. 35.

to stave off French defeat at Dien Bien Phu. Admiral
Radford pointed out that the United States had a large
share at stake and suggested that U.S. pilots, trained
to suppress anti-aircraft guns, could do much even in
one afternoon's operations to save the situation at
Dien Bien Phu. Although President Eisenhower did not
rule out U.S. air and naval intervention, he did oppose
committing U.S. ground troops. He favored maximum aid
short of intervention, including even volunteer air
operations such as the Flying Tigers had provided in
China prior to World War II.

At Admiral Radford's suggestion, the council decided
that General O'Daniel should be stationed continuously in
Indochina under appropriate liaison arrangements and with
sufficient authority "to expedite the flexible provision
of U.S. assistance to the French Union forces." It was
not intended that General O'Daniel should concern himself
with the Military Assistance Advisory Group but rather
that he would provide the means through which the United
States might exercise more influence on military strategy
and the training of native troops. The council, additionally, requested the Department of Defense, in collaboration with the Central Intelligence Agency, to study
and report on all feasible further steps, short of the
overt use of American forces in combat, which the United
States might take in achieving the success of the Laniel-
Navarre Plan.[35]

Six days later the National Security Council moved
to adopt the Planning Board statement of policy toward
Southeast Asia, NSC 177. After the President approved
the study, it was circulated as NSC 5405 and referred to
the Operations Coordinating Board for coordinated implementation.[36] It was the charter for American action in
the months to come, assuming the French fought on. However, the Secretary of Defense and the council had sidestepped the question, raised by the Joint Chiefs of Staff,
of what the United States would do if France gave up the
struggle.

---

35. (TS) NSC Action 1005, 8 Jan 54, CCS 334 NSC
(9-25-47) sec 13. (TS) Msg, JCS to CINCPAC, JCS 955317,
082226Z Jan 54, CCS 092 Asia (6-25-48) sec 54. (TS)
Gerhart "Account," pp. 36-38.
36. (TS) NSC Action 1011-a, 14 Jan 54.

CHAPTER XIII

THE BERLIN CONFERENCE AND ITS AFTERMATH
15 JANUARY-15 MARCH 1954

The forthcoming Berlin Conference presented the United States with a dual-edged problem: how to counter the expected Soviet demand for a five-power conference including Communist China "to consider measures for the relaxation of international tension," and how to persuade France that it should attain a position of strength before negotiating a settlement of the Indochinese war. Admission of Communist China to a conference would automatically be a long step toward general recognition, which the United States was particularly anxious to avoid. The stated purpose of the Berlin Conference was to bring about a settlement of the German and Austrian questions and there was no reason why the Far East should be touched upon. Korea and Indochina were the major sources of tension in the Orient and so far Communist China had shown no disposition to accept a settlement in either area that would preserve the interest of the free world.[1]

---

1. (U) Unofficial Trans of Soviet Note, 26 Dec 53; (U) Tri U.S.-U.K.-Fr. Note to USSR, 1 Jan 54; (U) Unofficial Trans of Soviet Note, 4 Jan 54. All atchd to State Dept Background Paper, BER D-8/50, 12 Jan 54, CCS 337 (4-19-50) BP pt 2A. (S) State Dept Paper, PREP D-1/2, "Revision of Tactics Section (pages 1 and 2) of Report of Tri-partite Working Group, Paris, October 21 - November 2," 12 Dec 53; (S) State Dept Psn Paper, BER D-1/2, "Tripartite Draft Re Anticipated Soviet Request for Five-Power Conference Including Communist China," 15 Jan 54. Both in CCS 337 (4-19-50) BP pt 2. (S) State Dept Rebuttal Paper, D-8/17a, "Indochina," 11 Jan 54, same file, BP pt 2A. (S) State Dept Talking Paper, PTB D-3/2, "Bilateral Discussion in Berlin with the French, Indochina," 19 Jan 54, same file, BP pt 3.

The United States Government had to persuade France that it would be disastrous to open negotiations with the Communists before improving her military position in Indochina. Moreover, America had to provide the wherewithal for France to make such improvements. The new statement of policy toward Southeast Asia, NSC 5405, had reaffirmed that the United States would furnish the French all aid short of actual military participation and would even consider direct military support if the Chinese Communists intervened. On the basis of that policy the American task was to strengthen France's hand to the point where she would hold out for a settlement that protected United States security interests in the Far East.

Although the Joint Chiefs of Staff did not participate extensively in direct preparations for the Berlin Conference, they had been asked by the National Security Council what the United States should do to improve the French position in Indochina. Forwarding their reply to the Secretary of Defense on 15 January, the Chiefs repeated many of the suggestions that had come to them recently from General O'Daniel and Admiral Stump.

Several of the JCS recommendations reaffirmed courses of action to which the United States was already committed. For example, the Chiefs recommended that the United States Government should place renewed emphasis on vigorous French prosecution of the Navarre Plan and that equal emphasis should be placed on American measures in support of French efforts. Specifically, the Joint Chiefs suggested that the three Services expedite items programmed for Indochina during the 1950-1954 period but still undelivered, and revise programs in accordance with combat needs. Such revision might call for additional funds for the 1954 MDA program. The Chiefs also recommended that the American Government re-examine national strategy toward Indochina, with a view to developing a unified effort in Southeast Asia to counter Communism on a regional basis--the basis on which the Communists fought. Further, the United States might consider scaling down French commitments to the North Atlantic Treaty Organization in order to permit deployment of additional forces to the Orient. The Chiefs also recommended that both France and the United States increase their political warfare activities.

The Joint Chiefs of Staff responded to recent French requests for additional airpower by proposing that the United States provide material and financial support while France augmented her air force in Indochina with maintenance and air crew personnel already available. America should restrict its contribution of manpower to certain specialists, but should also examine the idea for establishing unofficial, volunteer air units composed of United States personnel.[2]

Before the Secretary of Defense took any action on the JCS recommendations, the question of assisting France had again moved up to the highest governmental levels. At a White House meeting on 16 January the President, Secretary Dulles and Under Secretary W. B. Smith of the State Department, Deputy Secretary Kyes and the Director of the Office of Foreign Military Affairs, Vice Admiral A. C. Davis, of the Department of Defense, and Mr. C. D. Jackson, White House adviser on cold war strategy, discussed what the United States should do about Indochina.

General Smith opened the discussion by setting the problem in somewhat the same framework as the Joint Chiefs. He felt that a comprehensive plan for dealing with Southeast Asia as a whole was necessary. Mr. Kyes, however, protested that planning for comprehensive assistance to the entire area could lead to a relaxation of the belief that Indochina should be saved at almost any cost. Siding with Mr. Kyes, President Eisenhower on the one hand indicated that the United States would have to continue the gamble that present efforts would be effective, but emphasized, on the other hand, that everything possible should be done to improve the situation.

The group recognized that a major problem arose from French reluctance to accept American assistance in training native soldiers and in improving the conduct of operations. Searching for a way to combat this reluctance, the President suggested the appointment of an experienced

---

2. (TS) Memo, DJS for JCS to SecDef, "Steps which the United States Might Take to Assist in Achieving Success of the Navarre Plan," 15 Jan 54, CCS 092 Asia (6-25-48) sec 54.

American officer, such as General J. A. Van Fleet, either as Ambassador to the Associated States or as a member of the Ambassador's staff. As the upshot of the discussion, President Eisenhower appointed a Special Committee to develop a detailed program for securing military and political victory without United States overt participation in the war. This committee was composed of the Director of Central Intelligence, Allen Dulles; General Smith; Mr. Kyes; Admiral Radford; and Mr. Jackson.[3]

While the Special Committee undertook its study, events did not stand still. During the middle of January Premier Laniel formally requested additional material aid and United States maintenance personnel for the French air force in Indochina. This request was substantially the same as General Trapnell had forewarned Washington to expect; the Joint Chiefs of Staff had already recommended to the Secretary of Defense that the United States provide aircraft but not personnel.[4] Specifically, the Premier asked for eighteen B-26's so that the two light-bomber squadrons in Indochina could be equipped with twenty-five planes each. Other advice from Saigon and Paris, however, indicated the French would need only ten additional B-26's to bring the two squadrons up to a total strength of fifty planes. In addition, the Premier requested twenty-five more B-26's for a third squadron. The French also wanted an assurance that General Navarre could continue to use the twelve U.S. C-119's for long-distance transportation. This grant would mean that the four C-47 squadrons could concentrate on operational support. France likewise asked that the United States supply spare parts in ample quantities and on regular consignments for the C-47's, B-26's and C-119's.

---

3. (TS) Memo, C.D. Jackson to A. Dulles, Kyes, Radford, & Smith, "Indo-China and Southeast Asia," 18 Jan 54; (TS) Uniden Memo (Gen G.B. Erskine to Radford), "Proposed Procedure for Implementation of the President's Decision Regarding Indo-China," 18 Jan 54. (TS) Uniden Memo for Rec, "Meeting at White House - 16 January 1954," nd, "Navarre Letter, Actions Taken," vol I, Alden file, OMA.
4. See Ch XII, pp. 20-21, and above pp. 2-3.

Not limiting its requests to material requirements, the French Government requested that the United States ship 400 technical maintenance specialists to Indochina, to service U.S.-provided aircraft. Premier Laniel emphasized the temporary nature of this assignment and promised to replace Americans with Frenchmen as soon as possible.[5]

The French request gave added emphasis to the need for further information in Washington. Accordingly, Admiral Radford urged CINCPAC to speed General O'Daniel on his way to Indochina. The general's mission was two-fold. First, he was to try to win consent from the French High Command for the idea that he remain in Saigon indefinitely, and, second, he was to evaluate the adequacy of the American assistance program and tabulate additional requirements. However, because of French sensitivity, CINCPAC was asked to provide General O'Daniel with cover by ordering him to make an inspection tour of all MAAG's in Southeast Asia.[6]

When the National Security Council met on 21 January, it considered the new French request for aid and the JCS recommendations for improving the French position. In presenting these suggestions, Admiral Radford observed that some of the recommendations might be referred to the Special Committee for further study. Others, however, should be put into effect immediately. Specifically, the United States should at once render maximum material support, and train French Union Forces in the use of American equipment. To this end the United States should expedite the shipment, in conformance with JCS priorities,

---

5. (TS) Msg, Achilles (AmEmb Paris) to SecState, 2668, 2 p.m., 19 Jan 54, CCS 092 Asia (6-25-48) sec 55. (TS) Msg, Achilles to SecState, 2663, 11 a.m., 19 Jan 54. See also: (S) Msg, Heath (Saigon) to SecState, 1151, 9 a.m., 3 Jan 54, DA-IN-31713 (3 Jan 54); (TS) Msg, Achilles to SecState, 2629, 2 p.m., 15 Jan 54; (TS) Msg, Achilles to SecState, 2642, 1 p.m., 16 Jan 54.
6. (TS) Msg, CJCS to CINCPAC, JCS 955862, 202345Z Jan 54.

of undelivered items programmed during 1950-1954, make changes in the current program as requested by MAAG Indochina, make deliveries in accordance with the changes, and, if necessary, do all this without prior approval of the Office of the Secretary of Defense. In addition, funds should be found so that current Indochina MDA programs could be adjusted to satisfy the additional training and material requirements submitted by MAAG. Since the Department of Defense was already acting on these recommendations, the National Security Council took no formal action.

Admiral Radford also discussed with the Security Council the French request for B-26's and American maintenance personnel. While favoring the provision of aircraft, he felt that the French could themselves, from resources available in France, find the necessary flight and maintenance personnel for an expanded air force. If necessary, United States Air Force personnel in NATO units could be utilized temporarily to replace and release French ground, maintenance, and supply personnel for service in the Far East. The United States could also train these French personnel in Europe.7

The National Security Council agreed that Admiral Radford should explore directly with Lieutenant General Jean E. Valluy, French representative to the NATO Standing Group in Washington, the problems of providing immediate aid to the French air forces. After discussing the matter with Air Force and OSD officials, Admiral Radford was able to inform General Valluy that ten B-26's would soon be on their way to Indochina and that the United States would also consider providing aircraft for the third B-26 squadron when the French could furnish flight and maintenance personnel. The admiral also assured General Valluy that spare parts would arrive as needed. However, it did

---

7. (TS) Dft Statement by Radford to NSC, "Report on 'steps which the U.S. might take to assist in achieving the success of the Navarre Plan' in Indochina," 20 Jan 54. (TS) Interv, Tucker with Vogt, 14 Jan 55, memo in JCS HS files.

not seem feasible for the United States to provide maintenance crews. Problems of language and accommodations, unfamiliarity with French methods, and the time factor all militated against using Americans.[8]

Even while these matters were under discussion, the French command in Saigon was pleading for immediate help. Viet Minh forces surrounding Dien Bien Phu were expected to attack soon, or to move against Luang Prabang in Laos. To counter either course the High Command needed aircraft and personnel.[9] Therefore Paris instructed its military representative in Washington to seek American help again.

General Valluy thanked Admiral Radford for the two B-26's already programmed for Indochina and the ten additional aircraft that had been promised. But he announced that France had been able to locate and ship only ninety maintenance specialists. Drawing French personnel from NATO wings would not solve the immediate problem, for these technicians would still need training on American-type craft. Therefore, he renewed the request that the United States provide 400 ground crewmen. Fortunately, providing additional flight crews did not present as great a problem; the French Government was working out arrangements with General A. M. Gruenther, Commander in Chief, U.S. European Command, for USAF units on the Continent to train French aviators in the use of B-26's.[10]

The French soon reported, however, that twelve B-26's were only enough to take care of the past year's attrition. They still needed ten more to bring squadron strength up to twenty-five each. Admiral Radford then ascertained that ten more used B-26's might be transferred from the Far East

---

8. (TS) Memo for Rec, Capt G.W. Anderson, 21 Jan 54.
9. (TS) Msg, Ch MAAG IC to OSD/OMA, MG 146 A, 210350Z Jan 54, DA-IN-34719-C, CCS 092 Asia (6-25-48) sec 55. (TS) Msg, USAmb Saigon to SecState, NIACT 1307, 4 p.m., 23 Jan 54, same file, sec 56.
10. (TS) Memo, Valluy to Radford, "U.S. Military Aid to Indochina," DFM(54) 16, 26 Jan 54. (TS) Msg, USNMR Paris sgd Gruenther to CSA, ALO 189, 011610Z Feb 54, DA-IN-36621, CCS 092 Asia (6-25-48) sec 56.

Air Force to Indochina. When the Admiral asked General Valluy to give assurances that Americans, if sent to Indochina, would not be exposed to capture, the general gave a categorical statement to this effect. He further assured the admiral that United States personnel could be brought home at the end of the fighting season, about 15 June.[11]

Admiral Radford took up the French request for B-26's and United States personnel with other members of the Special Committee. Since France apparently had no more trained mechanics for the Orient, General Smith favored sending 200 USAF crewmen to Indochina. Mr. Kyes objected that this action would commit the United States to such an extent that it would have to prepare for complete intervention. In reply General Smith distinguished between mechanics and combat troops; he did not think the United States was taking on any commitment to provide the latter. However, he felt, and Admiral Radford concurred with him, that Indochina was so important to the United States that America should intervene with naval and air forces if worst came to worst.

Confronted with Mr. Kyes' reservations, the Special Committee agreed that final decision should be left to the President. However, the members of the committee did recommend that the United States should provide the ten additional B-26's (making a total of twenty-two) and could send 200 USAF maintenance personnel to Indochina. They felt the government should defer a decision on the third light bomber squadron and on the second contingent of 200 ground crewmen, pending the results of General O'Daniel's talks with General Navarre and the outcome of further French efforts to provide the additional mechanics themselves. President Eisenhower accepted all three

---

11. (TS) Memo for Rec, Anderson, 26 Jan 54; (TS) Memo for Rec, Anderson, 27 Jan 54.

recommendations. Accordingly, General Twining ordered the Far East Air Force to carry out the President's decisions.[12]

Meanwhile, on 25 January, Secretary of State Dulles met with his French, British, and Soviet counterparts at Berlin. As anticipated, Soviet Foreign Minister Vyacheslav M. Molotov utilized his first chance to speak by proposing that "a conference of the Ministers of foreign affairs of France, the United Kingdom, the United States of America, the U.S.S.R., and the Chinese People's Republic should be called in May-June 1954 for the purpose of considering urgent measures for easing the tension in international relations."[13] Mr. Dulles agreed that the conference might consider the Soviet suggestion.[14] And the conference did, for five days, before Mr. Dulles succeeded in sidetracking the matter for later discussion.[15]

While the conference was still considering the Soviet proposal, the fact that the United States had agreed to send maintenance personnel to Indochina was divulged by Joseph and Stewart Alsop. The leak occasioned considerable furor in France and the United States.[16] Finally President Eisenhower found it necessary to intervene personally to calm the uproar. At his press conference on 3 February,

---

12. (TS) Memo for Rec, Brig Gen C. H. Bonesteel, III, OSD, "Meeting of the President's Special Committee on Indochina, 29 January 1954," 30 Jan 54. (S) Memo, DepSecDef to SecAF, 29 Jan 54, circ as Encl B to (TS) JCS 1992/340, 21 Jun 54, CCS 092 Asia (6-25-48) sec 72. (TS) Msg, Hq USAF to COMFEAF & Ch MAAG IC, AFOOP-OC-C TS 7323, 302339Z Jan 54, "Navarre Letter, Actions Taken," vol I, Alden files, OMA.
13. State Dept, Foreign Ministers Meeting (Washington, GPO, 1954), pp. 13-24, 220.
14. Ibid., pp. 24-29.
15. Ibid., pp. 29-54.
16. Joseph and Stewart Alsop, "Where is Dien Bien Phu?" Washington Post and Times Herald, 27 Jan 54. (S) Msg, Achilles (Paris) to SecState, 2758, 1 p.m., 27 Jan 54. (TS) Memo for Rec, Anderson, 27 Jan 54; (U) Ltr, Sen John Stennis to Radford, 1 Feb 54.

he acknowledged that USAF technicians were on their way to Indochina, but implied that they would be part of the MAAG group training the French in the use of American equipment.[17]

A week later, permitting direct quotation, he informed newspaper correspondents that "no one could be more bitterly opposed to ever getting the United States involved in a hot war in that region than I am. Consequently, . . . every move that I authorize is calculated, so far as humans can do it, to make certain that that does not happen." Nor could he conceive of a greater tragedy for America than to become heavily involved in an all-out war in any of those regions, particularly with large units. He told the correspondents of French guarantees that Americans would not be subject to capture, and the French Government publicly repeated the guarantees for the benefit of American audiences. When both Republican and Democratic Senators endorsed the President's remarks, officials in the Executive Branch breathed a sign of relief.[18]

In Indochina, meanwhile, the Viet Minh divisions surrounding Dien Bien Phu had not yet attacked. Instead, General Giap withdrew some of his forces and at the end of January moved again in the direction of Luang Prabang, royal city of Laos. Further depleting their combat reserves in the Tonkin Delta, the French moved to counter the Viet Minh thrust. But they bemoaned their lack of the troops and aircraft that could have decisively defeated the Viet Minh invasion.[19]

This new indication that the initiative lay with the Viet Minh and not with the French brought another somber report from Saigon. Severely indicting General Navarre's defensive concepts, the United States Military Attache to Viet Nam likened Dien Bien Phu to another Na San. He reported that the Viet Minh command had concentrated its battle

---

17. Unofficial Transcript of Eisenhower News Conference, 3 Feb 54, NY Times, 4 Feb 54. Congressional Record, vol 100, no. 3, p. 1470. (UNK) Memo for File, Radford, 27 May 54.
18. NY Times, 10 Feb 54, p. 2; 11 Feb 54, pp. 1, 6, 16; 4 May 54, p. 4.
19. (S) Msg, Heath (Saigon) to SecState, 1360, 31 Jan 54 DA-IN-36566, CCS 383.21 Korea (3-19-54) sec 145. (S) Geneva Conf Background Paper, Indochina Chronology. (S) D/A, G-2, Background Paper GI-D-33, "History of Indochina War," 7 Apr 54, CCS 092 Asia (6-25-48) sec 62.

corps in western Tonkin, but the French, with their forces dispersed throughout Indochina, were not in position to take advantage of the opportunity for offensive operations to destroy the enemy. Although the French Union Forces outnumbered the Viet Minh two to one and had overwhelming fire power and air transport capability, their tactics remained defensive. Patrolling was the exception, not the rule, for French units. Likewise, French Union Forces were not maintaining contact with the Viet Minh army, but were waiting to be attacked.

In Laos, also the French had failed to demonstrate tactical initiative. Instead they had been content to let six Viet Minh battalions tie down twenty French Union battalions rather than capitalize on the chance to defeat the Viet Minh forces decisively. The attache gave as his opinion that General Navarre had been directed by his government to conduct a minimum-casualty holding operation, improving his position where feasible, with a view to eventual negotiations. The Viet Minh, on the other hand, seemed to be fighting a clever war of attrition with time running in its favor. In conclusion, the attache reported that "informed United States military opinion here" considered the greatest deterrents to successful French action to be lack of energetic support from Paris, inadequate training of combat units and staffs, and a defensive philosophy. These defects could not be remedied by the unlimited provision of modern United States military equipment.[20]

Secretary Dulles and Mr. Nash in Berlin were so concerned about this report that they asked General Trapnell for his comments. According to the Chief of MAAG, General Navarre was revealing an increasing tendency to seek "miracle" solutions instead of forthright and energetic action according to "universally accepted principles of war." General Trapnell considered that the French had adequate supplies and equipment for large scale sustained operations,

---

20. (S) Msg, USARMA VN to CSUSA for G-2, MC 39-54, 032355Z Feb 54, DA-IN-37222 (4 Feb 54), same file, sec 57.

but in the absence of any genuine offensive plan, it appeared that they had little intention of moving decisively toward the defeat of the Viet Minh battle corps.[21]

General Trapnell's comments contrasted strikingly with those of General O'Daniel, who had returned to Washington following his visit to Indochina. General O'Daniel pointed out that since the French were bound by treaty to protect Laos, they had no choice but to counter the Viet Minh invasion by committing their reserves. However, he was confident that General Navarre would carry out his planned offensive and achieve military success during the 1954-1955 season. Agreeing that more than American supplies was needed, General O'Daniel had arranged for the assignment of five United States liaison officers to General Navarre's headquarters where they would have the opportunity to help correct French weaknesses.[22]

These comments reflected General O'Daniel's satisfaction with the results of his third visit to Indochina. Although General Navarre had not agreed that it would be desirable for the American general to remain at his elbow, he had consented to short visits from General O'Daniel every four to six weeks. The agreement to station the five liaison officers in Saigon also was an encouraging step toward increasing American influence in French councils. Although General Navarre in his conversations with General O'Daniel had stressed his needs for further supplies and equipment, he did agree to consider suggestions that the United States also provide help in psychological warfare activities and in training native troops.

General O'Daniel's inspection of Dien Bien Phu and the Tonkin Delta caused him to be optimistic about the immediate military situation. Although he recognized that the Viet Minh forces could make Dien Bien Phu untenable if they had medium artillery, he estimated that the French Union Forces could withstand any attack the Viet Minh was capable of launching there. The French were receiving reinforcements, and native troops were being raised and trained. General O'Daniel was confident that these additional units, supplied with American equipment, would permit the French Union to dominate all areas and bring the Viet Minh army to battle by

---
21. (S) Msg, Ch MAAG IC to DA, MG 318A, 090950Z Feb 54, DA-IN-38234 (10 Feb 54), same file.
22. (S) Gen O'Daniel's comments on cable MC 39-54.

the fall of 1954. One additional step the United States might take, provided the French and Vietnamese agreed, was to assign American reserve officers to train the natives. On the whole, the future looked bright.[23]

Admiral Stump, however, again sounded a note of caution. He did not believe the five liaison officers and occasional short visits by General O'Daniel were an adequate substitute for the continuous assignment of a high-ranking American to Indochina. While he agreed with General O'Daniel that there was no immediate danger of the French Union's suffering a major military reverse, he viewed with grave concern French failure to launch an offensive.[24]

Admiral Radford shared CINCPAC's concern and was anxious to have General O'Daniel permanently assigned to Indochina. The French agreed to accept General O'Daniel to replace General Trapnell as head of MAAG if he would surrender one star so that he would not be senior to General Navarre, and provided that he would have no greater authority or responsibility than had General Trapnell.[25]

General Navarre's terms meant that General O'Daniel would still not be able to exercise any substantial influence upon French strategy and training. General Ridgway protested that a distinguished senior officer was being demoted and the United States was losing prestige in the Far East without gaining compensating advantages.

---

23. (TS) Msg, ALUSNA Saigon [O'Daniel] to CINCPAC, readdressed CINCPAC to CNO, 280815Z Jan 54; (TS) Msg, Ch MAAG IC [O'Daniel] to CINCPAC readdressed CINCPAC to CNO/JCS, MG 250A, 020130Z Feb 54. Both in CCS C92 Asia (6-25-48) sec 56. (TS) Rpt of U.S. Sp Mission to Indochina, 5 Feb 54, same file, BP pt 10. (TS) Encl C to (TS) JCS 1992/300, 27 Apr 54, same file, sec 64.
24. (TS) Msg, CINCPAC to CNO/JCS, 042114Z Feb 54; (TS) Msg, CINCPAC to CNO/JCS, 072308Z Feb 54. Both in same file, sec 57.
25. (TS) Mns Mtg of Sp Cmte (Indochina), 9 Feb 54. (C) Memo, Ely to Radford, 13 Feb 54. (S) Msg, Heath (Saigon) to SecState, 1501, 5 p.m., 21 Feb 54. CCS 092 Asia.

At JCS instigation, France was again asked to consider increasing the scope of MAAG's authority. When France again refused, the Department of Defense on 12 March announced General O'Daniel's new assignment and his change in rank and let it be known that no amendments had been made in the terms of reference for MAAG Indochina.[26]

At the same time Washington was examining General O'Daniel's status, it was also considering another piece of the Indochinese puzzle. In December, when the Viet Minh forces invaded Laos, the Laotian Government had issued a call for help. This appeal brought a response from an unexpected quarter and created a new question for consideration by the National Security Council. On 2 February President Syngman Rhee of the Republic of Korea informed General John E. Hull, Commander in Chief, Far East, that, if the United States desired, his country would send one division to fight the Viet Minh invaders in Laos. President Rhee felt that this act would encourage many anti-Communist elements in Southeast Asia and also make manifest Korean appreciation for the aid that the United Nations had been providing since 1950. General Hull thanked the Korean President for his offer and promised to take it up with Washington. In addition, he advised that the suggestion be kept secret until the United States Government had replied. In spite of this advice, Korea announced its offer before Washington acted.[27]

General Ridgway forwarded the Korean offer to the Joint Chiefs of Staff on 16 February. He suggested that the Joint Chiefs obtain governmental approval for

---

26. (TS) JCS 1992/284, Memo, CSA to JCS, 4 Mar 54; (TS) Memo, CJCS for JCS to SecDef, "Reappraisal of General O'Daniel's Status with Respect to Indochina," 5 Mar 54; (C) Msg, OSD sgd Davis to CINCPAC DEF 958261, 122158Z Mar 54. All in same file, sec 59. NY Times, 13 Mar 54.
27. (TS) Msg, CINCFE to JCS & CSA, C66980, 021000Z Feb 54, DA-IN-6799 (2 Feb 54); (S) Msg, CINCFE to JCS & CSA, KCG 2-4, 051000Z Feb 54, DA-IN-37583 (6 Feb 54); (S) Msg, Amb Briggs (Seoul) to SecState, 759, 101045Z Feb 54, DA-IN-38292 (10 Feb 54). All in CCS 383.21 Korea (3-19-45) sec 145. NY Times, 12 Feb 54, p. 1.

advising President Rhee that the United States interposed no objection to sending the division to Laos if the French approved, and that United States commitments to support ROK troops would remain unchanged.[28]

    The National Security Council did not reject the offer and the Joint Strategic Survey Committee tended to favor it. However, General Ridgway now had second thoughts. He was alarmed lest the presence of ROK troops in Laos provide the Chinese Communists with an excuse for active intervention. A similar consideration led Admiral Carney to point out that no matter how the ROK intervention was disguised or described, it would appear to world opinion as a manifestation of American policy.[29] Accordingly, the Joint Chiefs of Staff informed the Secretary of Defense they thought the United States should commend President Rhee for his determination to fight Communists even outside of Korea, but tell him that the offer did not appear to be in the best interest of the free world. They reasoned that President Rhee might have the ulterior purpose of hoping renewed hostilities in Korea would ensue. They also recognized that it would be difficult to justify keeping American and Allied contingents in Korea while ROK troops were fighting Communists in Indochina. Furthermore, it was extremely unlikely that the French would be willing to run the risk of courting Chinese intervention by accepting the offer. Taking up the matter again at its 4 March meeting, the National Security Council agreed with the Joint Chiefs of Staff that the offer should be declined. The President felt that the transcending objection to the offer was the fact that American public opinion would not stand for having United States troops tied up in Korea

---

    28. (TS) JCS 1776/432, 16 Feb 54, CCS 383.21 Korea (3-19-45) sec 145.
    29. (TS) NSC Rec of Action 1043 a, 17 Feb 54. (TS) JCS 1776/433, 17 Feb 54; (TS) JCS 1776/434, 19 Feb 54; (TS) JCS 1776/435, 19 Feb 54. All in CCS 383.21 Korea (3-19-45) sec 145.

while the ROK forces were fighting elsewhere. This consideration was stressed in the American reply rejecting the offer.30

While Washington had been attending to General O'Daniel's assignment and President Rhee's offer, the Berlin Conference had resumed consideration of the Soviet proposal for a five-power meeting. The United States had to recognize the very real pressures on the French Government to give at least the appearance of willingness to negotiate peace for Indochina. And the French had an unassailable argument: the United States itself had agreed to an armistice in Korea and had consented to meet with the Chinese to negotiate a political settlement. Moreover, Mr. Dulles had publicly stated that if the Korean political talks went well and "the Chinese Communists show a disposition to settle in a reasonable way such a question as Indochina, we would not just on technical grounds say no we won't talk about that."31 Since the French seemed determined to open negotiations, the

---

30. (TS) JCS 1776/437, 24 Feb 54; (TS) Memo, CJCS for JCS to SecDef, "Consideration of the ROK Offer to Send a Division to Indochina," 1 Mar 54. Both in same file, sec 146. (TS) JCS 1776/444, 5 Mar 54, same file, sec 147. (TS) NSC Rec of Action 1054 b, 4 Mar 54.
31. (U) DOC D-41, State Dept Press Release No. 475, 3 Sep 53, in (TS) Doc Hist of US Pol toward Indochina, 1940-1953. (UNK) Msg, SecState Berlin to State Dept, 177, 18 Feb 54, as summarized in App to (TS) JCS 1992/286, 11 Mar 54, CCS 092 Asia (6-25-48) sec 59. Article IV of the Korean Armistice Agreement, signed 27 Jul 53, read as follows: "In order to insure the peaceful settlement of the Korean question the military commanders of both sides hereby recommend to the governments of the countries concerned on both sides that, within three (3) months after the armistice agreement is signed and becomes effective, a political conference of a higher level of both sides be held by representatives appointed respectively to settle through negotiation the questions of the withdrawal of all foreign forces from Korea, the peaceful settlement of the Korean question, etc." State Dept, Bulletin, 3 Aug 53, p. 139.

question facing the United States was whether to let the French go their own way and thereby destroy Western unity, or to attend the conference and seek to influence the terms of settlement. The latter course seemed preferable. Nevertheless, the United States wanted to avoid any implication that, by agreeing to negotiate, it recognized the People's Republic as the de jure government of China.

With these considerations in mind Mr. Dulles opposed any portmanteau-type conference with Communist China, such as the Soviets had proposed. Instead, he and the other Western Foreign Ministers worked for an agreement that the five-power conference would limit itself to settlement of the Korean and Indochinese wars, and that other powers participating in the two conflicts might also be invited to attend. French Foreign Minister Georges Bidault proposed that two conferences be held, one for each war, but the Soviet Union held out for a single meeting. The Foreign Ministers compromised by agreeing that a conference would be called to consider the Korean problem and that Indochina would also be discussed.

Foreign Minister Molotov labored long and hard to strike down Mr. Dulles' proposed statement for inclusion in the final joint communique to the effect that no power would be recognizing Communist China by meeting with Chinese representatives. But the West rallied to support the United States. The United Kingdom's Anthony Eden, for example, stated that his government recognized the People's Republic, but did not "seem to recognize them much." The American language was allowed to stand.[32]

The final communique, released on 18 February 1954, announced that the five powers and other countries that had participated in Korean hostilities would meet in Geneva on 26 April for the purpose of reaching a peaceful settlement of the Korean question. The four Foreign Ministers further agreed "that the problem of restoring peace in Indochina will also be discussed at the conference, to which representatives of the United States,

---

32. (TS) Mns 1st-6th Restricted Sessions of Foreign Ministers Mtg, 8-18 Feb 54, in State Dept HD files.

France, the United Kingdom, the Union of Soviet Socialist Republics, the Chinese People's Republic, and other interested states will be invited."33

In public, American officials expressed satisfaction with the results of the conference. Under Secretary Smith congratulated the French for resisting pressure to settle the Indochinese war on Communist terms. Secretary Dulles emphasized particularly the fact that the United States would not be recognizing China by sitting down with its representatives at Geneva. Acknowledging the primary responsibility of France for Indochina, he told the American people of the agreement to discuss peace for this area at Geneva. He added that the United States had a vital interest in Indochina and would continue helping the French Union Forces to defeat Communist aggression there.34

Even in private discussions with the Joint Chiefs of Staff, State Department officials emphasized the positive achievements of the United States at Berlin. They praised the vigor and skill of M. Bidault in helping to preserve western unity in the face of Molotov's blandishments. They ignored the possible consequences of the Indochinese phase of Geneva and stressed only that the Korean phase would be conducted along the lines desired by the United States. The agreement to discuss Indochina, they stated, represented the minimum needed by the French Government to satisfy public clamor at home for peace.35

Within the privacy of the National Security Council, however, Secretary Dulles admitted that the United States had little to gain at Geneva although it probably would lose nothing. It was unlikely that the Geneva Conference would reach an agreement for a free and united Korea.

---

33. "Quadripartite Communique, Issued at Berlin, February 18 /1954/," State Dept, Foreign Ministers Meeting, p. 217.
34. Smith, "Progress Toward Solving Current International Problems," (Address before Chicago World Trade Conference, 23 Feb 54), State Dept, Bulletin, 8 Mar 54, pp. 358-360. Dulles, "Report on Berlin," (Radio-TV Address, 24 Feb 54), ibid:, pp. 343-347.
35. (TS) Summary of Notes Recorded by DepSecy, JCS at JCS-State Mtg, 26 Feb 54.

Further, there was some danger that the French might accept a settlement in Indochina contrary to United States interests. Yet French domestic political difficulties were so great that the United States had been unable to dissuade the Laniel Government from agreeing to the Geneva meeting.[36]

The prospects of going to Geneva to negotiate a settlement were indeed welcomed by the French National Assembly when it debated Indochina on 5 March 1954. Some members of the opposition called on the government to accept Prime Minister of India Nehru's proposal for an immediate cease-fire and negotiations, but both the opposition and the government seemed to be pleased that the Berlin Conference had opened the door for peace. Premier Laniel, however, ruled out an early cease-fire by proposing conditions that were designed to be unacceptable to the Viet Minh. Before concluding a cease-fire, he announced, France would require: (1) total Viet Minh evacuation of Laos and Cambodia; (2) creation of a no-man's land around the Tonkin Delta and withdrawal of Viet Minh units from the delta under a controlled evacuation; (3) withdrawal of Viet Minh forces in central Viet Nam to delimited zones; and (4) withdrawal or disarmament of Viet Minh troops in southern Viet Nam. The Premier also stated that the French Union Forces could not relax their military efforts prior to Geneva, since successful French military operations had obliged the Viet Minh to negotiate in the first place.[37]

On 2 March the President's Special Committee submitted its recommendations for further United States action to preserve Indochina for the free world. The committee had originally only considered steps short of military intervention. However, the group recognized that the

---

36. (TS) Interv, Tucker with Vogt, 14 Jan 55, memo in JCS HS files. (TS) "An Account of the Events and Decisions Leading to the Loss of North Indochina," prepared for the record by the Office of the SpecAsst to JCS for NSC Affairs, 1st dft, 25 Oct 54, p. 44.

37. (S) Msg, Amb Dillon (Paris) to SecState, 3238, 6 p.m., 6 Mar 54. (U) Msg, Dillon to SecState, 3240, 6 Mar 54, DA-IN-868537, CCS 092 Asia (6-25-48) sec 59.

United States might wish to consider taking direct military action if the situation drastically deteriorated or if the French rejected a broad program of American advice and aid. But military action had to be considered in its full context, that is, in relation to American Southeast Asian policy as a whole.

The Special Committee reiterated the conclusions of NSC 5405 that Indochina was the keystone of the Southeast Asian arch and that, consequently, the Associated States must not be allowed to fall under Communist domination. To prevent such a debacle, the French had to defeat Communist military and quasi-military forces and to develop native resistance to Communism. The United States should help the French, but help had to be consistent with the United States, own and allied programs for all of the Far East. The committee felt that the United States had already taken all feasible actions to furnish the assistance that would aid the French to win the coming battle at Dien Bien Phu. The twenty-two B-26's were, of course, a major example. By March 1954 the Defense Department had expended $123,600,000 beyond the funds allocated in 1950-1954 appropriations for aid to Indochina to the detriment of programs for other areas. In addition, it appeared that at least another 100 million dollars would be needed to meet French Union requirements.[38]

Little else could be done to affect the tactical situation. Even the French staff itself had acknowledged to General Navarre that there was more American equipment in Indochina than could be put to immediate use. Therefore, the Special Committee concluded, delivered and programmed American aid to Indochina, plus the potential manpower of the French Union, was sufficient to defeat

---

38. (S) Memo, Asst SecDef (ISA) to DepSecDef, "Developments in U.S. Military Assistance for the French and Associated State /sic/ Forces in Indochina," 8 Jan 54, I-10134. (C) Memo, Dir OFMA Davis for AsstSecDef (ISA) to DepSecDef, "Implementation of Indochina MDA Programs to Assist in Achieving Success of the Navarre Plan," 2 Mar 54.

the Communists eventually. However, the French would have to use their resources properly and hold the military situation relatively stable so that they would have time to develop native resistance to Communism, and to organize and train effective fighting units. To date the French had not been able to utilize Indochinese manpower effectively. It was up to the United States to take the initiative in persuading France and Viet Nam to overcome this deficiency. Yet America had to be wary lest the French exploit United States aid for unilateral advantage. Likewise, the United States had to be careful not to be drawn into combat involuntarily.

The Special Committee incorporated in its report three JCS recommendations that had not yet been fully implemented:

1. France should augment its air force in Indochina with flight and ground-crew personnel drawn from military and/or civilian resources already available. The United States should help the French accomplish this task, explore the possibilities for establishing a volunteer air group, and make arrangements for relieving USAF technicians temporarily assigned to Indochina.

2. The United States should arrange with France for the assignment of additional Central Intelligence agents to Indochina.

3. The Department of Defense should find funds to replace the 124 million dollars taken from other programs to meet Indochinese MDA needs.

The committee further recommended that the United States obtain formal or informal French acceptance of an increase in the strength of MAAG Indochina to provide additional aid to the French in operational planning and in the training of native troops. They should also be urged to use more American help in unconventional warfare, and encouraged and assisted to increase the Foreign Legion in Indochina. Furthermore, the United States purpose of helping the Indochinese people to achieve independence should be duly stressed. Bao Dai and possibly the King of Cambodia should be encouraged to take a more active role in leading their countries.

The Special Committee recommended that the Chief of the Advisory Group, once the French agreed to an increase in his authority, should attempt to get the French High Command to develop and carry out a sound concept and operational plan for intensified operations in order to win a significant, tactical victory soon so that success could be exploited politically. The High Command should adopt the use of native defense groups and local civilian administrators to pacify French-Vietnamese occupied areas. It should also train and properly equip Vietnamese units, with particular emphasis on training officers, non-commissioned officers, and technical personnel. The French Command badly needed to improve its intelligence and security agencies and to expand unconventional warfare activities.

The Special Committee concluded that if these political and military reforms were carried out with full French support at an early date, the unfavorable situation in Indochina would be reversed. Significantly, however, the committee added the suggestion that the Department of Defense be asked to develop a "concept of operations and considerations involved in the use of U.S. armed forces in Indochina should such involvement be determined upon."

A week later the Operations Coordinating Board (OCB) directed the appropriate agencies to begin implementation. The Special Committee, thereafter, turned its attention to studying military intervention and to examining the position the United States should take at the forthcoming Geneva Conference. The conference was only seven weeks away; much had to be accomplished in little time if Indochina was to be saved.39

---

39. (TS) JCS 1992/290, 24 Mar 54, CCS 092 Asia (6-25-48) sec 60. (TS) Memo for Rec, Gen G.B. Erskine, Dir of Sp Opns, OSD, "Terms of Reference for Subcommittee on Indo-China, Related Southeast Asian Matters, and the Geneva Conference," 4 Mar 54.

CHAPTER XIV

PRELUDE TO GENEVA
15 MARCH-7 MAY 1954

Against its best interests the United States had acceded at Berlin to French demands that the Geneva Conference discuss the Indochinese question. The problem then became one of preparing France for the diplomatic struggle awaiting her. The only method likely to bolster the French at the bargaining table was to concentrate on actions to strengthen the French Union's military position in Indochina.

American estimates of the military situation were optimistic in their long-range forecasts. There was no theoretical reason why the French should not be able to crush the Viet Minh, provided they had the will to do so and the material assistance with which to accomplish it. Provision of material aid was a relatively simple matter for the United States. The equipment was available and the pipelines were already established and functioning.

It was in the more nebulous sphere of psychology that the United States encountered real difficulties. Because the United States wished to stop short of actual intervention with its own armed forces, the fighting and the winning had to be done by the French. The Joint Chiefs of Staff were convinced that, with an aggressive plan for a military offensive, good staff planning, and well-trained native troops, the French would have the situation in hand within a year or two. But French leadership had shown slight inclination and little ability to tackle its basic military problems with energy and foresight. Moreover, the French High Command, jealous of its traditions and prerogatives, displayed scant desire to accept American assistance in other than a solid and tangible form.

Well knowing the thankless task they were undertaking, the Americans made a concerted effort after Berlin to convince the French that the highroad to victory would open before them if they would only allow the United States to increase its aid in training, planning, and unconventional warfare. Even while America was attempting to persuade the French to accept help, the political climate in France and the military situation in Indochina were deteriorating rapidly. The will to fight is a thing of the heart, and the French had no heart for the fight. The United States, therefore, had to decide whether it should commit its own military forces and under what conditions intervention should take place.

The Berlin agreement to discuss peace for Indochina at Geneva was a signal to the Viet Minh to improve its military position. General Giap directed his forces to strike vital communications lines between Hanoi and Haiphong, to attack the main French airfields in the Tonkin Delta, and to cut the Savannakhet-Quang Tri highway in Laos. At the same time, Viet Minh irregulars in southern Viet Nam stepped up guerrilla operations.[1]

During the night of 13-14 March the Viet Minh launched the long-expected assault on Dien Bien Phu. Concentrating on one sector at a time, General Giap sent two regiments against the northern and northeastern French positions, each held by one French Union battalion. Employing horde tactics, the Viet Minh forces overran the first French battalion outpost shortly after midnight. Two days later the Viet Minh battle corps captured the second position. Although the French managed to drop two battalions of paratroops to replace personnel losses, they were not able to recover the two lost redoubts. With the capture of these positions the Viet Minh forces threatened directly the airfield upon which the entire isolated fortress depended.[2]

---

1. (S) Geneva Conf Background Paper, Indochina Chronology.
2. (S) Geneva Conf Background Paper, Indochina Chronology. Harrison, "Dien Bien Phu," pp. 270-286. (S) Uniden Intel Briefing, "Current Military Situation, 21 March 1954."

The Viet Minh had not yet been able to capitalize on its new position when General Paul Ely, Chairman of the French Chiefs of Staff, arrived in Washington on 20 March 1954. He had come at Admiral Radford's invitation to summarize his impressions drawn from a recent inspection tour of Indochina and to listen to American suggestions for increasing the scope of U.S. assistance.[3]

Admiral Radford attempted to convince General Ely of the vital importance of winning in Indochina by pointing out that France's position as a world power depended upon what France did in the Far East. The admiral also presented arguments for increasing American help along the lines proposed in recent months by the Joint Chiefs of Staff and the President's Special Committee. He suggested forming an international volunteer air group and improving maintenance practices to augment French airpower. He invited the French to accept American participation in unconventional warfare activities. He offered to send additional American officers to assist the French in training the natives. General Ely, however, after admitting the need for improvements, agreed only to consider and investigate the American offers but declared that increasing the numbers of U.S. personnel in Indochina would jeopardize French prestige in Indochinese eyes.[4]

General Ely showed no such reluctance about accepting American material aid. In fact, the general had come to

---

3. (C) Msg, CJCS to Ch MAAG IC for Ely, JCS 956829, 101951Z Feb 54; (S) Memo, Anderson to Radford, 1 Mar 54. (TS) Memo, [Radford?] to Valluy, "Discussions with General Ely," 18 Mar 54.
4. (TS) Aide Memoire, Radford to Ely, 8 Nov 54. (TS) Memo for Rec, Anderson, "Conversation with General Ely, Chairman, French Chiefs of Staff, on 22 March," 22 Mar 54. (TS) Memo for Rec, Anderson, "Discussions with General Ely, Chairman of the French Chiefs of Staff on Indo-China in the Afternoon of 24 March," 24 Mar 54. (TS) Memo of Conv, Dir CI Cabell, Ely, et al., 23 Mar 54. (TS) Notes of JCS-State Mtg, 26 Mar 54.

Washington with a long list of additional emergency requests for airplanes, naval craft, guns, small arms, ammunition, and other supplies. He asked again for the third squadron of twenty-five B-26s and entered a new request for twelve F-8-Fs, fourteen C-47s, and twenty-four L-20s to replace combat losses, and for twenty helicopters to evacuate the wounded at Dien Bien Phu. He also asked for eighty U.S. maintenance personnel to service the helicopters. The United States felt that the real problem was not lack of aircraft, but French failure to make efficient use of what they had. However, President Eisenhower did not want the United States to be in the position of denying any aid critically needed in Indochina. Therefore the Department of Defense loaned a third light-bomber squadron to the French and gave them all the other aircraft General Ely had requested except the C-47s and the helicopters which were simply not available. As a quid pro quo, Admiral Radford obtained General Ely's consent for the U.S. Air Force to send a team to Indochina for the purpose of investigating the reasons for the low French aircraft-utilization rates. The Department of Defense also found twenty LSMs, parachutes and drop containers, arms and ammunition, and the other equipment requested by General Ely. The United States even agreed that the French air force could use U.S. C-119s to drop napalm on Dien Bien Phu, providing no American crews were aboard.5

Dien Bien Phu was foremost in General Ely's thoughts. The general acknowledged that undoubtedly the Viet Minh's objective was to obtain a military victory that could be exploited politically and diplomatically at Geneva. And he gave the French Union only a fifty-fifty chance of staving off defeat. Yet he shrugged off American suggestions that a

---

5. (TS) Memo, Ely to Radford, 22 Mar 54; (TS) Memo, Ely to Radford, 24 Mar 54; (TS) Memo, Anderson to Col Brohon /Gen Ely's aide/, "French requests for equipment for French forces in Indo-China," 24 Mar 54; (S) Memo, SecDef to SecAF, "Transfer of Additional B-26 Aircraft to Indo-China," 25 Mar 54; (TS) CM-74-54, Memo, Radford to President's Special Committee on Indochina, "Discussions with General Paul Ely," 29 Mar 54. (TS) Notes of JCS-State Mtg, 26 Mar 54.

relief column be sent overland to the besieged fortress. Of course, if the French lost, only five per cent of their troops in Indochina would be captured, whereas the Viet Minh would suffer far heavier casualties. Nevertheless, General Ely admitted that a military defeat at Dien Bien Phu would be a serious blow to morale both in the field and at home. If the fortress fell, Foreign Minister Bidault might not be able to hold out at Geneva for terms that would be acceptable to the United States.[6]

The French Government was apprehensive not only about the outcome at Dien Bien Phu, but also about the possibility of Chinese Communist intervention and instructed General Ely to find out what the United States would do if Red planes appeared over Indochina. General Ely raised this question in an interview with Secretary of State Dulles. Refusing to be drawn into a negotiation, Mr. Dulles indicated that American reaction would depend upon the circumstances. But the United States would certainly not be willing to participate in the war except on a partnership basis that would insure the patriotic cooperation of the Indochinese people.[7]

General Ely also took up his question directly with Admiral Radford. He asked not only whether American aircraft would intervene to counter Chinese planes but also how American intervention would occur. He suggested that precise staff agreements be concluded between CINCPAC and the French command in Indochina "with a view to limiting the air risk which characterizes the present situation."[8]

---

6. (TS) Memo for Rec, Anderson, "Conversation with General Valluy, French Military Mission to the U.S., on 19 March," 19 Mar 54; (TS) Memo for Rec, Anderson, "Conversations with General Paul Ely, Chairman of the French Chiefs of Staff, on the subject of Indo-China," 21 Mar 54; (TS) Memo for Rec, Anderson, "Discussions with General Ely, Chairman of the French Chiefs of Staff, on Indo-China in the afternoon of 24 March," 24 Mar 54. (TS) CM-74-54, CJCS to President's Special Committee on Indochina, "Discussions with General Paul Ely," 29 Mar 54.
7. (TS) Memo of Conv, SecState, Radford, Ely, et al., 23 Mar 54.
8. (TS) Memo, Ely to Radford, 23 Mar 54, CCS 092 Asia (6-25-48) sec 60.

Admiral Radford assured General Ely that considerable advanced planning for limited U. S. participation in the war had already been completed and that CINCPAC had worked out procedures for employing carrier aircraft in Indochina. However, before the United States would commit these forces it would have to have firm agreements with the French on such questions as command and organizational arrangements, the duration of American support, and basing facilities in Indochina. Admiral Radford asked whether the French Government was prepared to request American air support, if the Communists intervened or if, for other military reasons, the French needed more airpower than they could muster. The admiral pointed out that if General Ely considered such a request likely, then "prudence dictated that the matter should be explored on a higher level in order to be ready for such emergency." General Ely replied that since he had been instructed by the French Defense Minister to raise the question of American intervention, it was obvious that France contemplated making such a request if necessary to prevent defeat.

General Ely also asked about American constitutional processes governing the commitment of aircraft. He informed Admiral Radford that the French Parliament would have to consent to the request for help. Admiral Radford replied that the President had also committed himself to take such a question up with Congress;[9] there was no North Atlantic Treaty for Southeast Asia that would permit the President to act without consulting the legislature. Thus, it would take time to arrange for American intervention, and it would have to be done at the governmental level.

Next General Ely asked what would America do if the French needed help to avert a disaster at Dien Bien Phu. Admiral Radford stressed that the United States would have to consider the whole Far Eastern situation and the probable Chinese Communist reaction before deciding to commit its planes. However, he did tell the general that if the French

---

9. On 10 March 1954 President Eisenhower had replied to a question about American activities in Indochina as follows: "There is going to be no involvement of America in war unless it is a result of the Constitutional process that is placed upon Congress to declare it." NY Times, 11 Mar 54, p. 14; 4 May 54, p. 4.

requested aid, and the American Government granted it, as many as 350 fighters operating from carriers could be brought into action within two days. It would be more difficult, however, to arrange for bringing U.S. medium bombers into the fight. General Ely concluded the discussion by saying that he was certain his government would ask for American air support if the Chinese intervened. However, Paris was so fearful of provoking the Chinese that the general would not hazard a guess whether his government would ask American help to save Dien Bien Phu.[10]

Before returning home, General Ely obtained Admiral Radford's signature on the following minute of their discussion:

> In respect to General Ely's memorandum of 23 March 1954, it was decided that it was advisable that military authorities push their planning work as far as possible so that there would be no time wasted when and if our governments decided to oppose enemy air intervention over Indo-China if it took place; and to check all planning arrangements already made under previous agreements between CINCPAC and the CINC Indo-China and send instructions to those authorities to this effect.[11]

The Chief of Naval Operations informed Admiral Stump of the terms of this agreement and notified him that General Ely's aide was on the way to Indochina to tell General Navarre of the Ely-Radford conversations. The aide's arrival would provide CINCPAC with a suitable occasion to renew any liaison with General Navarre which seemed necessary.[12]

The bare bones of this minute were apparently less than General Ely had hoped for. He had presented Admiral Radford with a version that included this paragraph: "There was complete agreement on the terms of General Ely's memorandum, dated 23 March, dealing with intervention by US aircraft in Indochina in case of an emergency, it being understood that

---

10. (TS) Memo for Rec, Anderson, "Discussions with General Ely, Chairman of the French Chiefs of Staff. on Indo-China in the afternoon of 24 March," 24 Mar 54.
11. (TS) Mns of Mtg between Radford and Ely, Friday, 25 Mar 54, sgd "Arthur Radford" and "P. Ely."
12. (TS) Msg, CNO to CINCPAC, 312313Z Mar 54.

this intervention could be either by Naval or Air Force units as the need arises, depending on the development of the situation."[13] In spite of the fact that Admiral Radford refused to initial this statement, General Ely went away from Washington feeling that a request from the French for American intervention would receive a prompt and affirmative reply.

The talks with General Ely confirmed Admiral Radford's opinion that the United States faced a critical situation. The admiral informed President Eisenhower of his fear

> that the measures being taken by the French will prove to be inadequate and initiated too late to prevent a progressive deterioration of the situation. The consequences can well lead to the loss of all of S.E. Aisa to Communist domination. If this is to be avoided, I consider that the U.S. must be prepared to act promptly and in force possibly to a frantic and belated request by the French for U.S. intervention.[14]

Admiral Radford's warning came to the President just as another chain of events culminated in bringing this same question before the National Security Council. The starting point of this second sequence of developments was the agreement at Berlin to hold the Geneva Conference.

The Berlin communique had triggered military action by the Viet Minh to strengthen its hand for Geneva; the agreement also moved the United States to weigh the stakes. How much could the French lose to the Viet Minh without losing the game? In early March 1954 the Secretary of State posed such

---

13. (UNK) Dft Mns, Mtg of Radford and Ely, 26 Mar 54.
14. (TS) Memo, Radford to Pres, "Discussions with General Ely Relative to the Situation in Indo-China," 24 Mar 54, CCS 092 Asia (6-25-48) sec 60.

a question to the Secretary of Defense, and the Secretary of Defense asked the Joint Chiefs of Staff for their military advice on this matter and on other issues that would arise at the Geneva Conference.[15]

The Chief of Naval Operations pointed out to the Chiefs that considering minimum positions was not enough. Since the French had already shown a disposition to negotiate, they might accept terms which looked reasonable on the surface but which would let the Viet Minh subvert Indochina at leisure. Therefore, it was essential that the United States get the French Government to stand by Premier Laniel's terms calling for an evacuation of the Viet Minh forces to delimited zones prior to a cease fire.[16] Likewise, the United States should insist that France attain a strong military situation before negotiating seriously with the Viet Minh.[17]

The Joint Chiefs of Staff agreed with Admiral Carney. They reaffirmed the importance of Indochina to the security interests of the United States and rejected the following possible settlements: (1) the status quo, (2) a cease-fire, (3) a coalition government, (4) partition, and (5) self-determination through a plebiscite. None of these would preserve Indochina for the free world. The only acceptable alternative was military victory. Although much treasure and many lives had already been spent, and although it would be expensive to commit the additional resources that victory would cost, it would be far more costly to roll back the Communist tide once it had gained momentum in Southeast Asia. Therefore, the Chiefs recommended that the United States urge France not to abandon "aggressive prosecution of military operations until a satisfactory settlement has been achieved."

The Chiefs recognized, of course, that France might elect to accept a negotiated settlement in spite of American pressure

---

15. (TS) JCS 1992/285, Memo by SecDef, "Preparation of Department of Defense Views Regarding Negotiations on Indochina for the Forthcoming Geneva Conference," 8 Mar 54, CCS 092 Asia (6-25-48) sec 59.
16. See Ch XLII, p. 20, 21.
17. (TS) JCS 1992/286. 11 Mar 54, CCS 092 Asia (6-25-48) sec 60.

They felt that, if this eventuality occurred, the United States should refuse to associate itself with the terms and should seek ways and means of continuing the struggle directly with the Associated States and other allies. They recommended that the National Security Council should immediately consider the extent to which the United States would be willing to commit its military resources in Indochina in concert with the French, or, if the French withdrew, in concert with other allies or unilaterally.[18]

These JCS views were confirmed by the subcommittee of the President's Special Committee on Indochina. If France insisted upon negotiating a peace that jeopardized the political and territorial integrity of Indochina, then the United States should pursue measures for continuing the war with the help of the Associated States and other allies, particularly Britain. The subcommittee further agreed with the Joint Chiefs of Staff that the matter deserved National Security Council consideration. The Council should examine what political pressures the United States could apply to keep the French in line; it should study actual intervention with American "air, naval and ultimately ground forces"; and it should determine whether it was possible to develop another base of operations in Southeast Asia as a substitute for Indochina, even though such a step would require much time and money.[19]

The JCS and subcommittee recommendations were punctuated by the Viet Minh capture of the two French redoubts at Dien Bien Phu on 15 March. The deteriorating military situation emphasized anew how much had to be done before the Geneva Conference began on 26 April. In December 1953, when the Joint Chiefs of Staff had tried to get the question of possible American intervention before the National Security Council, Deputy Secretary Kyes had quashed the JCS recommendations on the grounds of logistical inaccuracies. In March,

---

18. (TS) JCS 1992/287, 11 Mar 54 (as amended by Dec On, 12 Mar 54), same file, sec 59.
19. (TS) Memo, Gen G.B. Erskine to Sp Cmte, "Military Implications of the U.S. Position on Indo-China in Geneva," w/encl, same subj, 17 Mar 54, OSD 092.31, Admin Secy, OSD files.

however, the military and political situation had changed and the Secretary of Defense approved both the JCS and the subcommittee recommendations and forwarded them to the Secretary of State.[20]

Mr. Dulles also recognized that a very serious situation was developing. Not only was the French military position potentially dangerous, but the political climate within France boded ill for preserving Indochina at Geneva. On 9 March Radical-Socialist Deputy Pierre Mendes-France called upon the French Government to stop the Indochinese war immediately by negotiating directly with the Viet Minh; it should not wait for an international conference that would prolong for some months "the massacre and anguish of /the/ entire nation."[21] Although this statement represented the views of the non-Communist leftist opposition, Mr. Dulles also had reason to be concerned about the attitude of the French Government itself. French hopes were growing that the United States would recognize Red China or at least lighten the trade embargo as a quid pro quo for a satisfactory settlement of the Korean and Indochinese wars. Premier Laniel expected his government to fall if it returned empty-handed from Geneva. And a successor regime would be likely to sell out not only Indochina but also the European Defense Community. Ambassador Dillon in Paris put bluntly the question facing the United States: how far was America prepared to go to prevent further Communist expansion in Southeast Asia, either by fighting or by making the concessions sought by China?[22]

Confronted by the Ambassador's question, which had been partially reiterated by General Ely, Mr. Dulles took up with the National Security Council on 25 March the recommendation by the Department of Defense that the United States Government

---

20. (TS) Ltr, SecDef to SecState, 23 Mar 54, CCS 092 Asia (6-25-48) sec 60.
21. (U) Msg, Amb Dillon (Paris) to SecState, 3312, 11 Mar 54.
22. (TS) Msg, Dillon to SecState, 3294, 9 p.m., 10 Mar 54; (S) Msg, Dillon to SecState, 3313, 7 p.m., 11 Mar 54; (S) Msg, Dillon to SecState, 3315, 8 p.m., 11 Mar 54.

study immediately the question of military intervention. Mr. Dulles pointed out that the United States must have answers to some fundamental questions before the Geneva Conference opened in late April. The questions were: what would the United States do if the French attempted to sacrifice the position of the Free World in Indochina by accepting terms unacceptable to the United States, and what would the United States do if the French decided to get out of Indochina? Mr. Dulles stated that the United States had to be prepared either to write off its interests in Indochina or to assume responsibility there if the French relinquished their hold.

In reply President Eisenhower listed four conditions to be met before U.S. military intervention might take place. The Associated States would have to request assistance; the United Nations should sanction the response; other nations would have to join the United States in answering; and Congressional assent be given. Mr. Dulles thought that the United Nations might give sanction to the call for assistance, but believed that more work would have to be done by the Executive Branch before it presented the case for intervention to the Congress.

After discussing the possibility of developing the Australia-New Zealand-United States pact as an instrument for united action, the Council directed the Planning Board to make recommendations on "the extent to which and the circumstances and conditions under which the United States would be willing to commit its resources in support of the Associated States in the effort to prevent the loss of Indochina to the Communists, in concert with the French or in concert with others or, if necessary, unilaterally."[23]

---

23. (TS) NSC Rec of Action 1074-a, 25 Mar 54. (TS) Gerhart "Account," pp. 44-46.

Secretary Dulles also began to prepare the American people and world opinion for possible U.S. intervention in Indochina. After enumerating ways short of open aggression by which the Chinese Communists were aiding the Viet Minh, the Secretary clarified the American position as follows:

> Under the conditions of today, the imposition on Southeast Asia of the political system of Communist Russia and its Chinese Communist ally, by whatever means, would be a grave threat to the whole free community. The United States feels that that possibility should not be passively accepted but should be met by united action. This might involve serious risks. But these risks are far less than those that will face us a few years from now if we dare not be resolute today.[24]

The Secretary, with the support of Admiral Radford and Mr. Kyes, also sounded out Congressional majority and minority leaders on the conditions to be met before Congress would sanction American participation in the war. Above all else the Congressmen stipulated that the United States should not intervene unilaterally, but only as a member of an international coalition. In addition, Congress would want assurances that France was granting full independence to the Associated States, that it had developed an effective training program for native troops, and that it would not withdraw its own forces but would prosecute an aggressive plan for military action.[25] It became obvious from this meeting with the Congressmen that the government had not yet succeeded in carrying out a task set forth in 1952 and reaffirmed in 1954, namely, making clear to the American people the importance of Southeast Asia to the security of the United States.

---

24. (U) J.F. Dulles, "The Threat of a Red Asia," (address to Overseas Press Club, 29 Mar 54), State Dept *Bulletin*, 12 Apr 54, p. 540.

25. (TS) Msg, SecState to USecState (Geneva), TEDUL 37, 9:35 p.m., 6 May 54. (TS) Interv, Tucker with Vogt, 26 Jan 55, memo in JCS HS files. (TS) Gerhart "Account," pp. 51-52.

Secretary Dulles' resolute call for united action did not deter the Viet Minh forces from pressing their advantage at Dien Bien Phu. At the end of March General Giap's troops assaulted the main bastions of the fortress. By 3 April they had reduced the French stronghold to a triangle with sides of about 2,500 yards, and had captured the northern side of the airfield, making it extremely difficult for the French command to reinforce and supply the fortress, even by parachute.[26]

This critical situation brought a new spate of emergency requests for American help. Could the United States airlift two battalions of paratroopers from North Africa to Indochina? Would the United States provide some carrier planes to be flown by French naval aviators? Could the United States furnish eighteen C-47s to transport a reserve paratroop battalion from Hanoi to Dien Bien Phu? And could six more C-119s be loaned to the French Air Force? The Department of Defense found ways to meet these new French requests after President Eisenhower reiterated that he wanted to give the French all possible assistance short of outright intervention that would truly improve the situation.[27]

---

26. (S dg C) Msg, USARMA Saigon to CSUSA for G-2, MC 106-54, 291030Z Mar 54, DA-IN-48138 (30 Mar 54), CCS 092 Asia (6-25-48) sec 61. Harrison, "Dien Bien Phu," pp. 270-286.

27. (TS) Msg, Dillon (Paris) to SecState, NIACT 3692, 030002Z Apr 54, DA-IN-49168, CCS 092 Asia (6-25-48) sec 61. (TS) Msg, Dillon to SecState, 3693, 8 p.m., 2 Apr 54. (UNK) Memo, CJCS to Pres, 2 Apr 54. (S) Msg, CINCFE to JCS CX67593, 020300Z Apr 54, DA-IN-48943 (2 Apr 54), CCS 092 Asia (6-25-48) sec 61. (S) Msg, CINCFE to JCS, CS 67604, 030319Z Apr 54, DA-IN-49215 (3 Apr 54); (S) Msg, CNO to CINCPACFLT, 051951Z Apr 54. Both in same file, sec 62. (TS) Msg, CJCS to CHMAAG IC (Trapnell), JCS 959547, 071700 Apr 54.

The United States acted promptly to cope with the emergency, but the French Government suddenly decided that material aid would not be enough and put forward the "frantic and belated" request for American intervention that Admiral Radford had advised the President to anticipate. At 2300 on Sunday, 4 April 1954, Premier Laniel and Foreign Minister Bidault told Ambassador Dillon that "immediate armed intervention of US carrier aircraft at Dien Bien Phu is now necessary to save the situation." Two considerations moved the French to make this request. First, the Viet Minh was throwing fresh troops into the battle at a faster rate than the French could reinforce the garrison with paratroops. Second, General Ely had told his government that Admiral Radford had promised to do his best to obtain American help if Dien Bien Phu required U.S. naval air support. The French leaders further justified their request on the ground that, in all but name, Chinese Communists had already intervened in the battle. Premier Laniel admitted that American naval support might bring on Red air attacks against the Tonkin Delta, but his government was ready to accept this risk. Emphasizing that speedy American intervention was essential since the Viet Minh forces were expected to renew their attack within a week, M. Bidault observed that the Geneva Conference would be won or lost at Dien Bien Phu.[28]

After conferring with the President, Secretary Dulles reaffirmed to the French Government that it was not possible for the United States to commit belligerent acts in Indochina before reaching a full political understanding on the formation of a coalition with France and other countries, particularly the British Commonwealth. In addition, he pointed out again that the President was committed to consult with Congress before going to war. In the meantime, however, the United States was giving all aid short of active belligerency and was preparing the public and Congress for intervention in accordance with constitutional processes.[29]

---

28. (TS) Msg, Dillon to SecState, NIACT 3710, 1 a.m., 5 Apr 54.
29. (TS) Msg, SecState to Dillon, 3482, 9:29 a.m., 5 Apr 54.

Although M. Bidault remarked to Ambassador Dillon that unfortunately the time for forming coalitions had passed, the French Cabinet received the American reply with good grace. The Ministers continued to feel, however, that a relatively small commitment of airpower would save the day. Therefore, they asked the United States to provide ten to twenty B-29's to be flown by French pilots from U.S. bases in the Philippines. Ambassador Dillon seconded the request, pointing out that if America failed to help and Dien Bien Phu were lost, the disaster would strengthen the already powerful grip of the Ministers in the French Government who wished for peace at any price.[30]

Yet both political and military logic ran counter to using B-29's at Dien Bien Phu. It would take time and finesse to obtain consent for using Philippine territory as a base for French operations against Asians. It would also take more time than was available to train even experienced pilots to operate B-29's. Even if time were available, however, medium bombers were not a suitable weapon to use against troops in foxholes. After informing General Valluy of these reasons for not loaning the B-29's, Admiral Radford offered to provide additional fighter bombers, which the French command gratefully accepted. Later, General Ely himself claimed that the request for B-29's had been generated by the politicians, not by soldiers and airmen.[31]

The French Government put forward its request for B-29's in lieu of a carrier strike on the same day that the National Security Council met to consider a Planning Board report recommending that "the United States should now reach a decision whether or not to intervene with combat forces, if that is necessary to save Indochina from Communist control, and, tentatively, /on/ the form and conditions of any such intervention." The board further recommended that "The timing

---

30. (TS) Msg Dillon to SecState, NIACT 3729, 8 p.m., 5 Apr 54; (TS) Msg, Dillon to SecState, NIACT 3738, 1 p.m., 6 Apr 54; (TS) Msg, Dillon to SecState, NIACT 3740 4 p.m., 6 Apr 54.

31. (TS) Memo for Rec, Anderson, /Conv with Gen Valluy, 7 Apr 54/, 7 Apr 54; (TS) Memo for Rec, Anderson, /Conversation with Col Brohon, 9 Apr 54/, 9 Apr 54. (TS) Msg, CJCS to CH MAAG IC, JCS 959547, 071700 Apr 54.

for communication to the French of such /a/ decision, or for its implementation, should be decided in the light of future developments." Setting forth steps which the government should begin to take if the United States planned to intervene at some later time, the board suggested the following actions: (1) obtain Congressional approval for intervention, (2) initiate military and mobilization planning, (3) make and publicize moves to ready U.S. air and naval forces for action on short notice, (4) make it clear that no acceptable settlement could be reached without far greater Communist concessions, (5) explore with the British Commonwealth and with Asian nations the formation of a regional coalition, and (6) exert maximum diplomatic pressure on France and the Associated States to resolve the question of the future status of Indochina and prepare the French and Indochinese for inviting the United States and other nations to participate in the war.[32]

Although the National Security Council did note and discuss the report, it "postponed decision on the recommendation" that the United States should determine now whether or not to intervene. This action reflected the views of President Eisenhower, who reiterated his opposition to unilateral American intervention: congressional approval would have to be won and, as a minimum, the Associated States would have to request American participation in the struggle.

Secretary Dulles reported on his conversations with Congressional leaders, and also indicated that his discussions with ambassadors of major U.S. allies had not been encouraging. There was little disposition among the allies to take a strong stand on Indochina. Yet the Secretary rejected the recommendation by the Planning Board that the United States decide whether to intervene. Rather, the Council's discussion focused on the tangential issue of the Southeast Asian coalition. There was apparently some feeling,

---

(TS) Msg, CNO to CINCPACFLT, 071709Z Apr 54, CCS 092 Asia (6-25-48) sec 62. (TS) Msg, SecState to AmAmb Paris, 3534, 8:25 p.m., 7 Apr 54.

32. (TS) NSC Plng Bd Rpt, "NSC Action No. 1074-a," 5 Apr 54, CCS 334 NSC (9-25-47) sec 14.

shared by the President, that bringing the coalition into existence would so strengthen the bargaining position of the West at Geneva that intervention would become unnecessary. In addition, the coalition could bolster the political strength of other countries in Southeast Asia to resist Communism and thus prevent the loss of the entire area should Indochina fall. Although both Secretary of Defense Wilson and Admiral Radford opposed the partition of Indochina and pointed out the likely psychological impact on France of the loss of Dien Bien Phu, the Council decided only to direct U.S. efforts prior to the Geneva Conference towards organizing an alliance composed initially of ten nations. These ten were the United States, the United Kingdom, France, Viet Nam, Cambodia, Laos, Australia, New Zealand, Thailand and the Philippine Islands. In addition, the Council agreed that the United States should attempt to win British support for American objectives in the Far East and should press the French to accelerate their program for granting independence to the Associated States. At the same time President Eisenhower directed the Department of Defense to obtain Congressional approval for increasing the number of U.S. maintenance technicians in Indochina and for extending the tour of duty of personnel already there. If Congress approved these steps, then the United States could send the French additional aircraft suitable for employment against the Viet Minh.[33]

The National Security Council's action allowed the Department of Defense to intensify its efforts in assisting the French to save Dien Bien Phu, but only by providing material aid. Yet there was very little more material aid that would help. The Air Force inspection team and General Trapnell both reported that the factors limiting French utilization of American aircraft were the lack of flight crews and inadequate base facilities, and not shortage of aircraft or maintenance deficiencies. Most maintenance

---

33. (TS) NSC Rec of Action 1086, 6 Apr 54. (TS) Interv, Tucker with Vogt, 26 Jan 55, memo in JCS HS files. (TS) Gerhart "Account," pp. 51-54.

problems had largely been solved by the efficient performance of U.S. Air Force technicians. General Trapnell informed Washington that the B-26 situation was the most critical. The French had only thirty-four flight crews to fly forty-three operational aircraft. Loaning additional B-26's to the French air force would hardly alleviate this unbalance. However, the French air force did have flight crews for the naval Corsairs which the United States had just agreed to provide, and it could use American maintenance personnel to keep these planes flying. The U.S. Navy obliged by ordering a few of its ratings to Indochina to service the twenty-five carrier planes.[34]

The critical situation in Indochina had at last produced a change of heart in General Navarre. He finally agreed to use more fully the American officers on his staff and to accept some twenty-five to fifty U.S. personnel for helping with the training of native forces.[35] On the whole, however, French military authorities were doing little to improve Franco-American relations. Although Admiral Radford had stayed up all night to obtain governmental approval for airlifting paratroops from North Africa to Indochina, after the arrangements were completed the French announced that the troops would not be ready to leave for almost two weeks. In addition, the French navy sent the aircraft carrier Belleau Wood, which had been loaned to France by the United States, to the Far East with a cargo of planes for sale to the Indian Government. The carrier would therefore arrive in Indochinese waters at a crucial time without aircraft. Finally, General Ely persisted in his misinterpretation of his March conversations with Admiral Radford. On 7 April he complained to the admiral that

> The diplomatic exchanges of views stemming from the conditional answer made by the U.S. Government to our request for emergency intervention of the U.S. Air Forces /sic/ in support of our forces at Dien Bien Phu cause me to fear that this intervention would be subject to time lag which would be too long.

---

34. (TS) Msg, Ch MAAG IC to CJCS, MG 968A, 091015Z Apr 54, DA IN-50634 (9 Apr 54); (TS) Msg COMFEAF to CSUSAF, V-VC0173, 120721Z Apr 54, TS: 8374 (12 Apr); (TS) CM-84-54, Memo, CJCS to SecDef, 12 Apr 54.
35. (TS) Memo, CJCS to SecState, "Conversations with Col Brohon, Assistant to General Ely, Chairman of the French

> . . . I . . . wish that requested emergency
> intervention should not remain subordinated to political
> exchanges of views which will not fail to take a lot
> of time, in view of the fact that they must be conducted
> with several other governments.[36]

Admiral Radford replied by giving his version of the conversations. He and the Secretary of State had made it absolutely clear

> that the decision to employ U.S. forces in combat was
> one that could only be made at the highest governmental
> level and in the light of constitutional processes
> and congressional action. I did state that no such
> participation by U.S. forces was possible without a
> formal request by the French Government, and that I
> was certain that such a request, if made, would
> receive prompt and thorough consideration by the United
> States Government.
> Events connected with the request have proved my
> prediction to be true. The Secretary of State is
> moving with great urgency to cope with the situation.
> It is receiving the continuing attention at the
> highest levels of the United States Government.
> Meanwhile, every possible effort is being made to
> take all action, short of actual intervention by U.S.
> armed forces, to assist in the defense of Dien Bien
> Phu until international arrangements involving the
> nations who are so directly affected, can be completed.[37]

The Secretary of State was coping with the situation by attempting to bolster sagging French morale. He pointed out to Foreign Minister Bidault that even if the battle of

---

Chiefs of Staff," 10 Apr 54, CCS 092 Asia (6-25-48) sec 62. (TS) Msg, CJCS to CINCPAC for Gen O'Daniel, JCS 959753, 101700Z Apr 54.

36. (S) Msg, SecState to Paris, 3541, to Saigon, 1886, 1:35 p.m., 8 Apr 54. (TS) Msg, Ely to Valluy for Radford, c. 7 Apr 54, incorporated in (TS) Memo for Rec, Anderson, 7 Apr 54.

37. (TS) Ltr, Radford to Ely, 12 Apr 54.

Dien Bien Phu were lost, France would not have lost the war and he explained again that the United States could not become a belligerent until the American people had been prepared for such a step. His efforts were only partially successful. The French Government could recognize the realities of American politics, but it could not overlook French political considerations. M. Bidault felt compelled to reply that if Dien Bien Phu fell "it would be most unlikely that either /the/ Associated States or France would be willing to continue /the/ war even with full American military support."38

Secretary Dulles, as directed by the National Security Council, was also laboring to build the ten-nation Southeast Asian security coalition. The French were in general sympathy with the idea, but they did not agree that building such an alliance would of itself induce the Communists to lighten their terms for settling the war. They only saw that the coalition would not be formed in time to save Dien Bien Phu.39

To speed the process of organizing the regional defense organization, Secretary Dulles resorted to personal diplomacy. He flew to Europe on 10 April, announcing that he was going "to consult with the British and French Governments about some of the very real problems that are involved in creating the obviously desirable united front to resist Communist aggression in Southeast Asia." His purpose, he told the American people, was not to extend the fighting, but to end it. He did not intend to prevent the Geneva Conference from arriving at a peaceful settlement; instead, he wanted to create the unity of free wills that was needed to assure a peaceful settlement.40

---

38. (TS) Msg, SecState to Amb Paris, NIACT 3512, 7 p.m., 6 Apr 54; (TS) Msg, Dillon to SecState, NIACT 3756, 11 a.m., 7 Apr 54.
39. (TS) Msg, Dillon to SecState, 3774, 7 p.m., 7 Apr 54.
40. Dulles, "Consultations with United Kingdom, France. regarding Southeast Asia," WH press release, 10 Apr 54, State Dept Bulletin, 19 Apr 54, p. 590.

The Secretary's trip was reasonably successful. From London Mr. Dulles and Foreign Minister Eden announced that "we are ready to take part, with the other countries principally concerned, in an examination of the possibility of establishing a collective defense, within the framework of the Charter of the United Nations, to assure the peace, security and freedom of Southeast Asia and the Western Pacific." A day later Secretary Dulles and Foreign Minister Bidault issued a similar joint declaration. In addition, during early April the Department of State obtained Thai and Philippine acceptance at least in principle for the idea of a regional defense organization.[41]

Mr. Dulles had no more than returned to Washington, however, when the British reneged on their agreement to form the regional defense organization before Geneva. Foreign Minister Eden later explained that Commonwealth politics had dictated the change in British policy. The Colombo Powers, which included three Commonwealth members, India, Pakistan, and Ceylon, were to convene on 26 April and Mr. Eden felt that it would be "most undesirable" for Britain to give any public indication of membership in a program for united action until the Colombo Conference had ended. Furthermore, the establishment of the working group of ten nations, which did not include the three Asian Commonwealth members, would produce criticism that Mr. Eden felt would be "most unhelpful" at Geneva. Secretary Dulles privately attributed the reversal of position to British fear that intervention would bring on overt Chinese participation in Indochina and lead to World War III.[42]

Although the State Department had been unsuccessful in arranging for united action, the first prerequisite for American intervention, the Department of Defense was pushing

---

41. "U.S.-U.K.-French Discussions on Indochina and Southeast Asia," State Dept press releases 194, 197, and Statement by Secy Dulles at Syracuse, 15 Apr 54, State Dept, Bulletin, 26 Apr 54, pp. 622-623.

42. (TS) Msg, SecState (Paris) to ActgSecState, DULTE 3, 8 p.m., 22 Apr 54; (TS) Msg, SecState (Geneva) to ActgSecState, DULTE 7, 2 p.m., 26 Apr 54; (TS) Msg, SecState to USecState (Geneva), TEDUL 37, 9:35 p.m., 6 May 54.

ahead with military planning and preparations. CINCPAC's representative arrived in Saigon to confer with General Navarre on plans for American air support, should it be authorized. A few days later the Department of Defense publicized the move of a carrier task force, including the Essex and the Boxer, into the South China Sea between Indochina and the Philippines. In Washington the JCS planning machinery was thrown into high gear to recommend policies for the guidance of CINCPAC, CINCFE, and COMSAC in preparing operational plans for meeting possible Chinese Communist aggression in Indochina or Korea. The Joint Chiefs of Staff on 23 April accepted the outline plan for Indochina. This plan was based on the assumption that the French Union would continue to supply ground troops while the United States furnished air and naval support.[43]

Although the Joint Chiefs in 1953 and 1954 had repeatedly approved the concept of limited American intervention in Indochina if circumstances required, in early April 1954 General Ridgway suggested that they consider a broader course of action. Returning to a position the Chiefs had held in 1952, he recommended that the United States concentrate its strength against Communist China, the true source of Viet Minh military power. If the United States determined to use armed force to hold Indochina and Southeast Asia, it should line up allied support and warn the Communists that it would take military action to neutralize the sources of Viet Minh strength. It should also initiate mobilization and other supporting measures after enlisting the fullest possible allied military support.

General Ridgway supported his recommendation by pointing out that there were few if any decisive targets in Indochina itself. Although American intervention might result in local successes, it would "consititute a dangerous diversion of limited U.S. military capabilities, and could commit our armed forces in a non-decisive theater to the attainment of non-decisive local objectives." Nothing would please the Communists more.

---

43. (TS) Msg, CINCPACFLT to CNO, 020202Z Apr 54, CCS 092 Asia (6-25-48) sec 61. NY Times, 16 Apr 54, p.2. (TS) JCS 1776/462, 22 Apr 54, CCS 092 Asia (6-25-48) sec 63.

The other Joint Chiefs of Staff did not immediately accept General Ridgway's analysis. Without approving or disapproving the substance, they noted the views and forwarded them to the Secretary of Defense. Later, however, after the fall of Dien Bien Phu and the deterioration of the French position at Geneva, the Chiefs came back to General Ridgway's proposal.[44]

With the Army Chief of Staff calling for action against China, and with the Southeast Asia coalition foundering on British shoals, the Vice President of the United States took action of his own to test public opinion. Asked what the country should do if the French withdrew from Indochina, Mr. Nixon replied "that:"

> there was no reason why the French could not stay on and win, but on the assumption they did withdraw--an assumption he did not accept--Indochina would become Communist in a month.
> The United States as a leader of the free world cannot afford further retreat in Asia. It was hoped that the United States would not have to send troops there, but if this Government could not avoid it, the Administration must face up to the situation and dispatch forces.

Public reaction was so unfavorable that the Department of State took pains to point out that the Vice President had been addressing himself to a hypothetical question. Mr. Nixon also had to wipe out the impression he had created that the Administration was bent on war. He said, "The aim of the United States is to hold Indochina without war involving the United States, if we can," and, "The purpose of our policy is to avoid sending our boys to Indochina or anywhere else to fight."[45]

---

44. (TS) JCS 1992/296, 26 Apr 54, and Dec On, 26 Apr 54, CCS 092 Asia (6-25-48) sec 62. (TS) Memo, CJCS for JCS to SecDef, "Indochina," 22 Apr 54, same file, sec 63. For a discussion of later development of General Ridgway's ideas, see Ch XV.

45. NY Times, 4 May 54, p. 4. J. Parker (State Dept press officer), "U.S. Policy Toward Indochina," 17 Apr 54, State Dept Bulletin, 26 Apr 54, pp. 623-624.

With public opinion and the Congress obviously still unready for unilateral American action and the British unwilling to internationalize the war, the only course open to the Administration was the use of moral suasion to keep the French from selling out at Geneva. There was still a measure of hope that the situation could be saved since the Viet Minh had adopted "nibbling" tactics at Dien Bien Phu, reducing the perimeter progressively, but not overwhelming the defenders.[46]

Still hoping that he could salvage the Southeast Asian coalition and thereby establish a French bargaining position, Secretary Dulles left for Paris and Geneva on 20 April. Three days later Admiral Radford journeyed to Paris and London to discuss the military aspects of the situation with the French and British.

Mr. Dulles found the French Government believing it would have to throw in the sponge when the enemy knocked out Dien Bien Phu. Foreign Minister Bidault and General Ely reported that the situation at the fortress was virtually hopeless; nothing would help short of "'massive' air intervention which the US would have to supply." Recalling that Mr. Dulles thought U.S. participation impracticable without British cooperation, M. Bidault belittled the amount of help that the United Kingdom would give. He urged that the American Government should give the "most serious consideration to armed intervention promptly as the only way to save the situation."

Turning the conversation to the idea of a coalition, the Secretary of State argued "that this was essential to give some cards to work with at Geneva so as to have a chance of obtaining acceptable peace." If Dien Bien Phu were lost, M. Bidault answered, the French people would regard the coalition as nothing more than a trick to keep them fighting, whereas their desire would probably be to pull out of Southeast Asia entirely.[47]

---

46. Harrison, "Dien Bien Phu," pp. 270-286.
47. (TS) Msg, SecState to ActgSecState, DULTE 2, 2 p.m., 22 Apr 54.

General Navarre, growing ever more panicky, told the American Charge d'Affaires that he needed not only airpower but also U.S. ground forces[48] and informed his government that if American air intervention did not arrive promptly he would have to conclude a cease fire, not just at Dien Bien Phu, but throughout Indochina. M. Bidault placed General Navarre's request before Secretary Dulles. Admitting that U.S. help might come too late to save Dien Bien Phu, the Foreign Minister pleaded for the United States to intervene anyway. With Americans at their side, he argued, the French would feel honor-bound to go on fighting. Intervention would thus save the war, if not the battle. In a formal reply Mr. Dulles reminded the French that Congressional authorization was required and that this authorization would be predicated on an international coalition. Mr. Dulles' military advisers had informed him that air intervention would no longer save Dien Bien Phu, so the real question was what to do next. He advised the French to "react vigorously to temporary setbacks and to surmount them. That can be done in relation to the present situation if our nations and people have the resolution and the will. We believe that you can count upon us, and we hope that we can count on you."[49]

General Ely renewed with Admiral Radford the discussion of America's role. Talking as one military man to another, the general asked for intervention. Admitting that airpower could have no direct bearing on the outcome at Dien Bien Phu, he said its effect would be psychological; it would keep the Laniel government in office and France in the war. The admiral could only reply that the Secretary of State had already made the U.S. position clear to the French Government.

In reporting the Ely-Radford talk, Ambassador Dillon commented that the inevitable result of American failure to intervene would be the prompt overthrow of the French

---

48. (TS) Msg. McClintock to SecState, 2098, 241200Z Apr 54, DA-IN-53782 (24 Apr 54), CCS 092 Asia (6-25-48) sec 63.
49. (TS) Msgs, SecState to ActgSecState, DULTE 9, 6 p.m., 23 Apr 54; DULTE 10. 2400, 23 Apr 54; DULTE 1, 2400, 24 Apr 54.

Government and its replacement by a cabinet pledged to negotiate with Ho Chi Minh and to withdraw from Indochina. Such a government would probably not accept U.S. intervention even if it were freely offered.[50]

Ambassador Dillon did not persuade the Secretary of State that the time had come for intervention. Since the security of the United States was not directly threatened, Mr. Dulles believed that the President should not commit forces by executive action. He also thought that intervention was not in the best long-range interests of the country. Pointing out that a successor French government might come to power and repudiate American help, he advised against taking a step that would gravely strain relations with the British, Australians, and New Zealanders. He preferred to risk dealing with a successor government rather than to intervene unilaterally.[51]

The French were no more successful in obtaining American intervention than the Americans were in winning British agreement to establish the Southeast Asia coalition in time to affect the Geneva negotiations. Mr. Eden repeated that Britain could not sit with a working group to draft terms of reference until the Colombo conference had met. Even if the coalition were formed, he doubted gravely that Britain would agree to take part in fighting to save Indochina. Nor did the British Government want the United States to intervene without consulting it. Mr. Eden

---

50. (TS) "Resume of Conversations with French and British Representatives by Admiral Radford, Chairman, Joint Chiefs of Staff, in Paris and London, 24-26 April 1954 on the Subject of Indochina," 28 Apr 54. (TS) Msg, Dillon to SecState, NIACT 4060, 251600Z Apr 54, DA-IN-53954 (25 Apr 54), CCS 210.482 (3-18-48) sec 4.
51. (TS) Msg, SecState to ActgSecState, DULTE 3, 8 p.m., 25 Apr 54.

did recognize that if the French lost Indochina, the
Communists would threaten Burma and Malaya. He was
therefore prepared to recommend to his government that a
secret military group composed of American, British,
Australian, New Zealand, and Thai representatives should
meet to consider actions for strengthening the buffer state
of Thailand. Mr. Dulles suggested that this idea be held
in abeyance until there emerged a clearer picture of what
the French were going to do. He and the French Government
succeeded in persuading Mr. Eden to consult further with
the British Cabinet.[52]

The British, however, would go no farther than to agree
that they were prepared to hold the secret military talks
with the United States. They remained adamantly opposed
to intervening in Indochina or to entering negotiations
for the establishment of a coalition for intervention.
Her Majesty's Government based its position on an estimate
by the British Chiefs of Staff that airpower alone would
not be sufficient to save Dien Bien Phu. The British
Chiefs thought that the only way to cope with the situation
was to commit a strong force in the Tonkin Delta. These
troops, in Mr. Dulles' words, would "generally work outward
concentrically consolidating their position as they go with
loyal natives." The British Chiefs admitted that such an
operation would be a tremendous project involving lots of
time and considerable forces.[53]

Admiral Radford discussed this estimate with the
British Chiefs of Staff and with Prime Minister Churchill.
The admiral found that the British military leaders agreed
with the American appreciation of the probable serious
consequences that would follow the loss of all or part of
Indochina. Even after hearing the admiral's views, however,
the British Chiefs continued to feel apprehensive about the

---

52. (TS) Msg, SecState to ActgSecState, DULTE 3,
8 p.m., 22 Apr 54; (S) Msg, SecState to ActgSecState,
SECTO 6, 11 a.m., 23 Apr 54; (TS) Msg, SecState to Actg
SecState, DULTE 10, 2400, 23 Apr 54.

53. (TS) Msgs, SecState to ActgSecState, DULTE 18,
11 p.m., 24 Apr 54; DULTE 5, 2400, 25 Apr 54; DULTE 7,
2 p.m., 26 Apr 54.

likelihood of Chinese intervention if the allies lifted a finger to save the Associated States. Moreover, they were thinking in terms of large-scale ground operations. Their principal concern seemed to be holding Malaya. The Prime Minister's thinking was also concentrated on British interests. If Britain had freely given India its independence, how could the English people be asked to participate in an exercise to save Indochina for the French Empire? Sir Winston seemed to think that the way to halt the spread of world Communism was to hold talks "at the summit."[54]

The day following his conversation with Admiral Radford, the Prime Minister made the British position crystal-clear in a public announcement to the House of Commons.

> Her Majesty's Government are not prepared to give any undertakings about United Kingdom military action in Indochina in advance of the results of Geneva. Her Majesty's Government have not entered into any new political or military commitments. My Right Honorable friend /Eden/ has, of course, made it clear to his colleagues at Geneva that if settlements are reached at Geneva, Her Majesty's Government will be ready to play their full part in supporting them in order to promote a stable peace in the Far East.[55]

Confronted with a British statement that gave no hope of strengthening the French bargaining position, Mr. Dulles and the National Security Council turned their thoughts toward establishing a regional coalition without the United Kingdom.[56] The Secretary of State conferred in Geneva

---

54. (TS) "Resume of Conversations with French and British Representatives by Admiral Radford, Chairman of the Joint Chiefs of Staff, in Paris and London, 24-26 April 1954, on the Subject of Indochina," 28 Apr 54; (UNK) Memo for Rec, /Adm Radford/, 27 Apr 54; (TS) COS(54) 47th Mtg, Mns of Mtg of BCOS and CJCS /with additions and amendments by Capt Anderson/, 26 Apr 54.
55. Quoted in (TS) Msg, SecState DULTE 51, to ActgSec State, 7 p.m., 5 May 54.
56. (TS) Msg, SecState DULTE 21, to ActgSecState, 10 a.m., 29 Apr 54. (TS) NSC Rec of Action 1104 **b**, 29 Apr 54.

with the Foreign Ministers of Australia and New Zealand under the terms of the ANZUS pact. He stressed the necessity for a common stand by all countries in Southeast Asia. The Australians indicated willingness to hold military talks immediately, without making any commitments. They preferred, however, that the discussions take place within the framework of the Five-Power Staff Agency, of which Britain was a member. New Zealand was also willing to begin the talks without awaiting the end of the Geneva Conference. Neither country objected to the inclusion of Thailand.[57]

When the Americans began preparing for talks with the Dominions, the British Foreign Minister reversed his field. He told Mr. Dulles that he was ready to recommend that "Her Majesty's Government should take part at once with the United States, France, Australia, and New Zealand in an examination by the Five Power staff agency of the Indochina and Southeast Asia situation, both now and subsequent to the Geneva conference, . . . including the implications of any Geneva settlement." The British, however, would remain opposed to intervention. Mr. Dulles felt that the staff talks opened an avenue of hope and that they would have a good effect at the conference and on public opinion.[58]

Any good effect an announcement of the talks might have had was completely eclipsed two days later when the French Union defenders of Dien Bien Phu capitulated. The surrender came the day before the Indochinese phase of the Geneva Conference began. The French had been saying for weeks that they could not avoid negotiating peace if they lost Dien Bien Phu. The British, also, were prepared to accept a cease-fire. America, unprepared to intervene unilaterally, stood alone.

---

57. (S) Msg, SecState SECTO 73 to Actg SecState, 10 a.m., 3 May 54.
58. (TS) Msg, SecState to DULTE 51 to Actg SecState, 7 p.m., 5 May 54.

CHAPTER XV

THE GENEVA CONFERENCE

When the Indochinese phase of the Geneva Conference opened on 8 May 1954, the main outlines of America's task during the critical days to come were reasonably clear. The French had to be supported, as much as they themselves and harsh reality would permit. There were three areas in which United States support could be effective: at the conference table, in Indochina, and on the international scene. The nature of the problem, and the nature of the ally, were such that support could not be unqualified. What was, in spite of its gravity, largely a matter of internal affairs to France, was to the United States a major move in its global strategy. There was the risk that in holding France's chin above the quicksand, America might become inextricably mired in a series of commitments inimical to her own national interests. The position of the United States at Geneva was, from the start, difficult and delicate.

The difficulty sprang from the magnitude of the material, psychological and moral changes the United States wished France and the Associated States to accomplish in order to meet its minimum conditions for really effective support and participation; the delicacy lay in convincing them without alienating them. On the eve of the conference, Ambassador Dillon cabled from Paris that, since the U.S. Government had been unable to respond to French requests for military assistance to save Dien Bien Phu, the only available course now was to support fully negotiation of the best possible settlement at Geneva. The Ambassador claimed that it would appear utterly illogical to all Frenchmen were the United States to refuse to associate itself unreservedly with the settlement, and that a refusal would seriously affect our already damaged prestige and have adverse repercussions on NATO and EDC.[1] But the National Security Council had

---

1. (TS) Msg, Dillon 4267 to SecState, 8 May 54.

already established a number of conditions under which the United States would not associate itself with an agreement.

French Armistice Proposal and U.S. Reaction

At its meeting of 8 May, the Security Council decided that the United States ought not to associate itself with any proposal, from any source, directed toward a cease-fire in advance of an acceptable armistice agreement under international controls. Although the Council felt that the United States could concur in the initiation of negotiations for such an armistice, it urged that France and the Associated States should continue to oppose the Viet Minh with all resources at their disposal. In the meantime, to strengthen the position of France and the Associated States during the negotiations, the United States should continue its program of aid and its efforts to organize a southeast Asian regional grouping to prevent further Communist expansion into that area.[2]

The Security Council was also informed by the Secretary of State that he intended to indicate to the French Government the willingness of the United States to discuss at any time the conditions under which the Indochinese conflict might be internationalized. The French had already been advised that American intervention depended upon their fulfillment of three prerequisites: real independence for the Associated States, an aggressive military plan, and an effective program for the training of native troops. In explaining the Administration's position on intervention to leading members of Congress on 5 May, Mr. Dulles stated that the prerequisites had not been fulfilled and that, therefore, conditions did not exist for a successful conclusion of the war. Under these circumstances, intervention was not advisable and, in any event, the United States would not intervene unless other interested nations joined in.[3]

---

2. (TS) Rec of Act, NSC, 196th Mtg, 8 May 54, 1110, "Position of the US with Regard to the French Proposal for Negotiating an Armistice in Indochina."
3. (TS) Msg, Dulles TEDUL 37 to Smith, 6 May 54.

American intervention was the only ace the two nervous partners had between them. The nature of the original French armistice proposals at Geneva was conditioned by incertitude of American intentions, while American support depended upon the nature of the proposals. Four days before the conference, M. de Margerie, of the Ministry of Foreign Affairs, admitted to Under Secretary of State Smith that the French had not advised the United States of their ideas about possible armistice proposals because they had not been able to agree among themselves. He said that the near impossibility of preventing the Communists from profiting by a cease-fire or armistice arrangement was fully realized, but that in a thoroughly bad situation it was necessary to seek the course with least evil consequences. To his expression of hope that the French proposals would receive American support, Under Secretary Smith replied that United States policy still was that anything short of prosecution of the Navarre Plan to victory was not good enough. M. de Margerie observed that that was a "large order" but that he believed the United States would not be "too unhappy" over the French proposals when they emerged. He added that if the United States did not like them, it would not be in too good a position to object, unless prepared to intervene militarily.[4]

When finally communicated to the United States, the tentative French proposals, not yet authorized by the Cabinet, were better than had been expected. They took the line that the problem of Viet Nam was purely Vietnamese, with no question of partition, and that it was only a military struggle for control of the government. Laos and Cambodia were placed in a totally different category, as victims of external aggression. According to the Berlin Agreement, the purpose of the Geneva Conference was to establish peace in all three countries. To this end, there should be a cease-fire guaranteed by adequate military and administrative controls under supervision. Cease-fire would take effect only when such guarantees had been embodied in armistice conventions, which might be different for all three states, and when control machinery had been established and was in place. Controls would be based upon Premier Laniel's March 5th conditions. When cease-fire occurred, regular

---

4. (S) Msg, Smith SECTO 89 to SecState, 4 May 54.

troops would be regrouped into delimited areas and all other forces disarmed. The control machinery would be international and would require a considerable body of personnel. After peace had been re-established by the cease-fire, political and economic problems could be examined.[5]

M. Chauvel, the French delegate, said that the French assumed the Soviets would propose an immediate cease-fire, to be followed by a political settlement based on coalition and immediate elections. Such a maneuver would force the West into the position of opposing cease-fire. In spite of the strong emotional desire of the French public for cease-fire, the Government would be able to defend its proposal on the ground that the conditions demanded were essential for the safety of the troops themselves. Compliance with those conditions would, in effect, delay any cease-fire for a long time, if not indefinitely. In response to the inquiry whether by "international" the French meant "United Nations" supervision, M. Chauvel stated there was no firm position on the question. Subsequent discussion, however, indicated that the French were continuing to oppose the use of UN machinery for fear it would establish a precedent that could be used against them in North Africa and elsewhere. It was also gathered that the British definitely shared this view.[6]

One of the most frantic proponents of cease-fire was none other than General Navarre, to whom had been entrusted the dynamic prosecution of an aggressive strategy made possible by millions in American aid. His fixation with the need to save Dien Bien Phu blinded him to the fact that there was still hope in the over-all military situation. More rugged and courageous, High Commissioner De Jean vigorously opposed the idea of a cease-fire and urgently recommended that Foreign Minister Bidault ignore Navarre's importunities. As the American Charge d'Affaires in Saigon observed, it was the irony of war that the general wished to surrender, while the diplomat wished to forge ahead.[7]

---

5. (S) Msg, Smith SECTO 106 to SecState, 5 May 54; SECTO 132, 7 May 54
6. (S) Msg, Smith SECTO 106 to SecState, 5 May 54.
7. (TS) Msg, McClintock NIACT 2242 to SecState, 6 May 54.

Although the tentative French terms were not an outright request for a cease-fire, the United States delegate cabled that "unless or until we have firm support in the United States for some other solution we are not in a position in Geneva to prevent the French from making such a proposal, which is far below a successful prosecution of the Navarre plan." He doubted whether the French would, in fact, remain firm in negotiations for satisfactory controls. It was his belief that they would slide rapidly toward the almost inevitable Communist counter-proposal of immediate cease-fire without controls. An important element in blocking French capitulation, as the French themselves observed, would be the degree to which the United States could strengthen the French hand by increasing Communist uncertainty of the possibility of American intervention. In the opinion of the United States delegate, success in organizing some form of Southeast Asian coalition would also help to bolster the French.[8]

The comments of the Joint Chiefs of Staff were even more somber. They thought the French proposal would be regarded by the people of Asia as a Communist victory, particularly in the light of the then-current military situation. In their opinion, an armistice under the proposed conditions would lead to a political stalemate attended by progressive deterioration of the French-Vietnamese military position, ultimately resulting in the loss of Indochina to the Communists.

The Joint Chiefs reasoned that even if the Communists were to agree to undertake negotiations pursuant to the French proposals, such negotiations could be expected to result either in rapid capitulation of the French to obtain a cease-fire, or in a protracted wrangle characterized by steadfast Communist adherence to an inflexible position on important issues and by substantial concessions by the French. Moreover, experience in Korea had indicated it was certain the Communists would flagrantly evade, circumvent and violate any agreement to suit their ultimate purpose of subjugating all of Indochina, regardless of what military and administrative controls were embodied in the armistice

---

8. (S) Msg, Smith SECTO 110 to Sec State, 5 May 54.

conventions. Even though the Communists should agree to international control machinery, their practices would render it impotent, as in Korea.

Judging from past performance, the Joint Chiefs were skeptical that the Communists would enter into a preliminary agreement to refrain from new military operations during the course of negotiations. It was much more likely that they would intensify their operations to improve their bargaining position, whereas the French would be under a strong compulsion to avoid casualties.

The Joint Chiefs warned that if the United States associated itself with the initial French terms, it would in all likelihood be confronted subsequently with the painful alternatives of continuing to support the French in successively weakened positions, or of extricating itself at some point along the way. The Chiefs agreed that it was no longer realistic to insist that the French continue aggressively to prosecute the Navarre Plan. At the same time, they adhered to the view that no satisfactory settlement was possible without a substantial improvement in the military situation of the French Union. In the absence of a settlement that would reasonably assure the political and territorial integrity of the Associated States, any armistice entered into would inevitably lead to eventual loss of the area to the Communists.

Therefore, in the light of the current situation, the Joint Chiefs of Staff considered that the United States should adopt the following as its minimum position:

> . . . The United States will not associate itself with any French proposal directed toward cease-fire in advance of a satisfactory political settlement. The United States urges the French Government to propose that negotiations for a political settlement be initiated at once. During the course of such negotiations, French Union Forces should continue to oppose the forces of the Viet Minh with all means at their disposal in order to reinforce the French negotiating position. In the meantime, as a means of strengthening the French hand, the United States will intensify its efforts to organize and promptly activate a Southeast Asian coalition for the purpose

of preventing further expansion of Communist power in Southeast Asia. If the French Government persists in its intention of entering armistice negotiations or accedes to immediate cease-fire negotiations, the United States will disassociate itself from such negotiations in order to maintain maximum freedom of action in taking whatever measures may be feasible for opposing extension of Communist control into Southeast Asia.9

To make clear the reason for United States refusal to associate itself with a cease-fire in advance of a political settlement, the President inserted the phrase "Because of the proof given in Korea that the Communists will not be bound militarily by the terms of an armistice." He also added a clause to the effect that the United States would continue its aid program to strengthen the French.10 The influence of the Joint Chiefs' recommendations, in their revised form, upon the National Security Council position of 8 May is apparent at a glance.

The rather uncompromising position of the Joint Chiefs of Staff contained several internal contradictions that carried over, in more attenuated form, into the stand of the Security Council. As General Ridgway pointed out, the United States had to support some French proposal, after having agreed at Berlin to discuss the problem. From the military point of view, no position was acceptable that would lead to the loss of Indochina, and it was almost inevitable that a settlement based on either partition or coalition government could have no other result. An agreement assuring, within reason, the political and territorial integrity of the Associated States would have been highly desirable, but no such settlement had been proposed. The Army Chief of Staff felt that the French would automatically reject any American attempt to force them to propose a political settlement that did not take into account the realities of the military situation. In that event, The Joint Chiefs' position would oblige the United States to disassociate

---

9. (TS) JCS 1992/308, 6 May 54 (as amended by Dec On, 7 May 54), CCS 092 Asia (6-25-48) sec 64.
10. (TS) JCS 1992/323, 24 May 54, same file, sec 68.

itself from France prior to any discussions on Indochina. Such action would jeopardize the Franco-American alliance, accelerate French settlement for a cease-fire, and open the way for new aggressions in southeast Asia.

General Ridgway believed it would be to the advantage of the United States to support a proposal along the lines of Premier Laniel's conditions because they held out the greatest hope of France's continuing the war. These conditions were: (a) total evacuation of Laos and Cambodia by the Viet Minh; (b) evacuation of the Tonkin delta by the Viet Minh, and creation of a no-man's land around the periphery; (c) withdrawal of Viet Minh troops from central Viet Nam to certain specified and restricted areas; (d) disarmament or evacuation of Viet Minh forces in south Viet Nam; and (e) measures of security and control to prevent any build-up of enemy forces during armistice discussions. If, however, the French began to negotiate without these guarantees, the United States should not be a party to the talks. General Ridgway was convinced that the French people would endorse continuation of the struggle only after it had been demonstrated that an honorable settlement was impossible.[11]

The American attitude was hardly helpful to the French Government, which was at that very moment fighting desperately for the right to negotiate at Geneva at all, instead of trying to reach an agreement with the Viet Minh immediately. Wits in Paris had prognosticated that the Assembly would allow the Government "to keep its head above water but not show its neck." In the words of the American Embassy, "its neck emerged" when it won a vote of confidence by a better margin than had been expected. But the Government's victory was clearly subject to an implicit caveat: should it fail to find a solution at Geneva along the lines indicated by Laniel on 5 March, it would be faced with almost insurmountable pressure to reach an immediate

---

11. (TS) Memo, CSUSA to JCS, "Minimum French Negotiating Position for Indochina Which French Will Support," (8 May 54?), same file, sec 65, For Laniel Conditions, also (U) Msg, Dillon 3240 to SecState, 6 Mar 54.

settlement with the Viet Minh on the best terms obtainable. Those terms would presumably be considerably less than Laniel's conditions.[12]

The French tabled their proposal, now couched in looser terms, on the opening day of the Indochinese conference:

I - For Viet Nam:
1. The grouping of regular units in zones of assembly, to be determined by the conference on the basis of proposals from the commanders-in-chief.
2. The disarmament of elements which do not belong either to the Army or to forces in charge of maintaining order.
3. The immediate liberation of war prisoners and civilian internees.
4. The control of the execution of these clauses by international commissions.
5. Cessation of hostilities with the signing of this agreement.

The re-assembly of troops and the disarmament cited above, provided for in the five points, would begin, at the latest, /number of days/ after the signing of the accord.

II - For Cambodia and Laos:
1. Evacuation of all regular and irregular Viet-Minh forces which have invaded the countries.
2. The disarmament of elements which do not belong either to the Army or to forces in charge of maintaining order.
3. The immediate liberation of war prisoners and civilian internees.
4. The control of the execution of these clauses by international commissions.

---

12. (C) Msg, Dillon to SecState, 4248, 6 May 54, DA-IN-58003 (13 May 54); (S) Msg Dillon to SecState, 4258, 7 May 54, DA-IN-56901 (8 May 54).

III

>These agreements shall be guaranteed by the States participating in the Geneva Conference. Any violation would call for immediate consultation among these States with a view to taking appropriate measures individually or collectively.[13]

The American delegate pointed out that the proposal was an armistice, and not a simple cease-fire, because it provided for cessation of hostilities only after the first four conditions of Section I had been complied with. Nevertheless, he drew attention to a major loophole: inasmuch as assembly and disarming of troops would unavoidably follow, rather than precede, cessation of hostilities, it was possible to make a simple cease-fire out of a paper armistice agreement. He noted that the French had retained the good bargaining position offered by the distinction between the case of Viet Nam and that of Laos and Cambodia.

Under Secretary Smith reported, however, that the French had not thought through much of their proposal. Their tentative thinking on regrouping, for instance, was that the framework would be established by the conference, and that commanders in the field would work out the details, which would then be submitted to the conference for approval. "There was no answer to Allen's remark that Eden did not wish to spend the next two years in Geneva," stated the Under Secretary. An even more serious possibility was that on-the-spot technical conversations between the combatants could develop into a substitute for formal agreements and circumvent the conference proceedings.

The French had no definite idea on the composition of control commissions, other than their not necessarily having to be of the same nationalities as the guarantors mentioned in paragraph III. The French appeared to be showing less opposition than previously to United Nations' responsibility for control and selection of commissions.

It was on the question of guarantees that the American delegate showed most reservation. He stressed

---

13. State Dept, *Bulletin*, 24 May 54, "French Proposal of 8 May," (Unofficial translation), p. 784.

the need for clarification on this point and for very careful consideration lest it amount to an obligation by the United States to underwrite a settlement that, at best, would be highly unstable. On the other hand, the American response to this part of the proposal would have an important bearing on how firm the French would feel they could be in negotiating the other conditions of an armistice.

While recognizing the amorphous nature of the proposals, and the risks to the United States they involved, the Under Secretary of State felt there was more to lose than gain by not supporting them at this stage of the negotiations. Among other things, the United States would probably be in a better position to win Britain, Australia, and New Zealand over to a more active role in a southeast Asian defense.[14]

The Joint Strategic Survey Committee displayed little enthusiasm for the French proposals. They observed that there were no provisions or safeguards to remove or reduce hazards to United States security interests involved in the acceptance of any armistice with the Communists that was not preceded by a satisfactory political settlement. If there were good faith on both sides, the French terms, subject to the addition of certain safeguards, appeared to constitute a satisfactory basis for negotiation. But there was every reason to expect the characteristic bad faith of the Communists. Hence, in the absence of subsequent strong and positive action by the Western Powers, an armistice would almost certainly lead to the subjugation of Indochina and, eventually, to the loss of all southeast Asia to the Communists. However, in view of the decision of the United States Government to concur in the initiation of negotiations, the committee interposed no further objections, providing the French incorporated provisions for international control machinery, to be established,

---

14. (S) Msg, Smith SECTO 155, to SecState, 9 May 54. (S) Msg, Smith SECTO 157 to SecState, 9 May 54.

in place, and ready to function prior to actual cease-fire, and a provision that representatives of the international control commission be guaranteed unrestricted movement in, and free access to, all Indochina.[15]

The recommendations of the Joint Strategic Survey Committee appeared at the head of the list of principles furnished the American delegate to guide him in evaluating proposals offered to the conference. At this time, these principles were considered basic to any acceptable settlement of the Indochinese question:

    1. The establishment of international control machinery in place and ready to function prior to an actual cease-fire.
    2. Representatives of the international control commission should be guaranteed unrestricted movement in, and free access to, all of Indochina.
    3. Such a commission should have sufficient military personnel and logistic support to discharge its responsibilities in connection with the armistice terms.
    4. Provision for UN assumption of responsibility for supervision of the international control commission. (Some other form of effective international control might well be a satisfactory substitute for UN supervision.)
    5. Measures to provide for the security of troops and populations, and guarantees against abuses of the cease-fire by either party.
    6. Provisions for the humane and orderly liberation of POW's and internees.
    7. Evacuation of Viet Minh forces from Laos and Cambodia.
    8. Provision for the examination of political and economic problems following an armistice agreement.

---

    15. (TS) Memo, Col Thackston for JSSC to JCS, "Negotiations with Respect to Indochina," 8 May 54, CCS 092 Asia (6-25-48) sec 65. Official records do not indicate that JCS approved these JSSC recommendations. However, their substance seems to have been provided to, and accepted by, the Department of State.

9. No provisions in the armistice of a political nature, such as for early elections, or for troop withdrawals that would clearly lead to a Communist take-over.[16]

United States acquiescence in armistice negotiations represented abandonment of the demand for a political settlement first. It was a self-inflicted defeat. The United States had taken too extreme a stand in the beginning by insisting that the French hold out for a political settlement before considering an armistice. On 6 May, Admiral Davis had cabled, "General Smith requests I make clear to you his conviction that it is now certain French will not take any negotiating position, even initially, as strong as persistence in Navarre plan."[17] Since the Berlin Conference, it had become increasingly apparent that the French people were in no temper to throw themselves into an all-out effort to win the war if conference negotiations failed. And, in essence, the United States position had been a deliberate invitation to such failure, in order to give free scope for vigorous prosecution of the war. This approach was based on American strength and confidence and good will; it was incomprehensible to the Americans that the French should lack all three.

In addition to the specific principles governing armistice negotiations, the Under Secretary of State, as head of the United States delegation, was provided with a set of basic instructions, approved by the President. General Smith was instructed not to deal with delegates of the Chinese Communist regime, or any other regime not then recognized diplomatically by the United States, on any terms that implied political recognition or which conceded to that regime any status other than that of a regime with which it was necessary to deal on a *de facto*

---

16. (S) Msg, SecState TOSEC 152 to AmCon (Geneva), 13 May 54, DA-IN-58225 (14 May 54).
17 (TS) Msg, Adm Davis (Geneva) to OASD(ISA), 060905Z May 54, DA-IN 56296 (6 May 54), CCS 092 Asia (6-25-48) sec 64.

basis in order to end aggression, and to obtain peace. The position of the United States in the Indochinese phase of the conference was defined as that of an interested nation which, however, was neither a belligerent nor a principal in the negotiation. The United States was participating in the conference to assist in arriving at decisions that would help the nations of that area peacefully to enjoy territorial integrity and political independence under stable and free governments, with the opportunity to expand their economies, to realize their legitimate national aspirations, and to develop security through individual and collective defense against aggression, from within and without. This was meant to imply that these people should not be amalgamated into the Communist bloc of imperialistic dictatorships.

General Smith was informed that the United States was not prepared to give its express or implied approval to any cease-fire, armistice, or other settlement that would have the effect of subverting the existing lawful governments of the three Associated States or of permanently impairing their territorial integrity or of placing in jeopardy the forces of the French Union in Indochina, or that would otherwise contravene the principles under which the United States was participating. If, in the judgment of the U.S. delegate, continued participation in the conference appeared likely to involve the United States in a result inconsistent with the above-stated policy, he was instructed to recommend withdrawal or limitation of the United States' role to that of observer.[18] These instructions had been cleared with the Senate Foreign Relations Committee and the House Foreign Affairs Committee.[19]

The United States delegate was authorized "to support in general terms French initiative looking toward an armistice agreement incorporating effective and

---

18. (C) Msg, SecState TOSEC 138 to USecState, 12 May 54.
19. (C) Msg Dulles TOSEC 137 to USecState, 12 May 54, DA-IN-57085 (13 May 54).

adequate safeguards and under international supervision." He was also to remind the French of the NSC policy concerning the objective of assuring independence and freedom to the Associated States. As far as guarantees were concerned, he was to make it clear that the United States would reserve its position until more was known about the nature of the settlement to be guaranteed and the obligations of the guarantors.[20]

There were few illusions about the nature of any agreement that would come out of Geneva. The United States was just marking time until France realized fully that she was facing virtual surrender.

Conditions for American Intervention

The obvious answer to Geneva was American military intervention, but the French seemed to dread the cure fully as much, if not more, than the complaint. Twice during April the French Government had sought American intervention to save Dien Bien Phu and twice had shown itself unwilling to pay the going price--independence for the Associated States and allied, rather than U.S. unilateral, participation in the war. British unwillingness to take united action had also blocked allied participation. However, in early May Secretary Dulles persuaded the National Security Council and the President that the United States should now concentrate on winning Australian and New Zealand consent for united action, gambling on later British participation.[21] In spite of the need for prompt decisions on internationalizing the war, Secretary Dulles was extremely cautious about imparting to the French the full set of conditions under which the United States would be willing to intervene.

---

20. (S) Msg, SecState TEDUL 49 to USecState, 9 May 54.

21. (TS) Gerhart "Account," p. 63.

He feared that a proposal to internationalize the war would be rejected if the issue were raised before the French were thoroughly convinced that their only choice was between intervention and what amounted to surrender Moreover, the British would be more likely to support, or at least acquiesce in, intervention once Geneva had been shown to offer no prospect of a solution. The Australian Government would almost certainly not take a position until after the elections at the end of May. Nevertheless, it appeared desirable for Premier Laniel to know, in general terms, the American conditions because of their influence on current French military decisions in Indochina and political decisions in Geneva. Accordingly, Mr. Dulles informed Ambassador Dillon that the President would ask Congress for authority to use the armed forces of the United States in the Indochinese area to support friendly and recognized governments against aggression or armed subversion fomented from without, providing he could then state that the following conditions had been, or would be, met:

(a) That US military participation had been formally requested by France and three Associated States;

(b) That Thailand, Philippines, Australia, New Zealand, and United Kingdom also had received similar invitations and that we were satisfied that first two would also accept at once; that next two would probably accept following Australian elections, if US invokes ANZUS Treaty; and that UK would either participate or be acquiescent;

(c) That some aspect of matter would be presented to UN promptly, such as by request from Laos, Cambodia, or Thailand for peace observation commission;

(d) That France guarantees to Associated States complete independence, including an unqualified option to withdraw from French Union at any time;

(e) France would undertake not to withdraw its forces from Indochina during period of united action so that forces from the US - principally air and sea - and others would be supplementary and not in substitution;

(f) That agreement was reached on training of native troops and on command structure for united action.

The United States would require all these conditions to be accepted by the French Cabinet and authorized or endorsed by the French National Assembly, because of the uncertain tenure of any French Government. Once it had agreed to intervene, the United States would be fully committed and would have to be able to rely upon any successor French Government to adhere to the conditions. Mr. Dulles characterized the conditions as "absolutely indispensable as a basis for our /United States/ action."[22]

The Secretary of State authorized the communication of these views, orally, to Premier Laniel unless, in the opinion of the Ambassador, it would result in the immediate resignation of the French Government or hasten its capitulation at Geneva.[23]

On the whole, Premier Laniel and Maurice Schumann appeared to be well pleased by this clarification of the United States position, according to the Ambassador. They were particularly impressed and pleased by the indication that actual participation by the United Kingdom was no longer a prerequisite to action by the United States. They pointed out that France had no control over compliance by Thailand, Australia, etc., with the conditions stipulated for them, and asked to be kept informed of United States progress along those lines.

As was to be expected, the one serious objection was to the condition that France publicly accord to the Associated States the right to withdraw from the French Union. They stressed the fact that even the Viet Minh looked toward the possibility of joining the French Union.[24] When Ambassador Dillon reported that American insistence upon this point might discourage even the strongest supporters of continued French action, Mr. Dulles replied:

---

22. (TS) Msg, SecState to Paris, rptd Geneva as TEDUL 54 (approved by Pres), 11 May 54.
23. (TS) Msg, SecState 4071 to Dillon, 14 May 54.
24. (TS) Msg, Dillon NIACT 4383 to SecState, 14 May 54.

> ... /I/ firmly believe that it is essential
> /to/ remove any taint of colonialism in order to
> attract vital Asian support and forestall opposition
> by other Asian and Middle Eastern countries. . . .
> you should emphasize this concern of ours and our
> belief that the only way to achieve these results
> would be through provision of this right of with-
> drawal.[25]

M. Laniel and Schumann observed that it might be helpful
with Nehru but that French public opinion would never
understand why it was necessary to make such a statement
when it had never been requested by any of the three
Associated States.[26] It also threw into question the
whole concept of the French Union as an association of
free and independent peoples, and cast doubt upon the
honor and veracity of France, who had recently stated
that Viet Nam had been granted independence and had
chosen to remain in the Union.

    It seemed to Ambassador Dillon that the matter of
independence had been taken care of satisfactorily by
the pending treaties between France and Viet Nam, but
that the situation was obscured and complicated by the
existence of a state of war. Much of the difficulty was
caused by the presence of a large French expeditionary
corps on Vietnamese soil, by the necessity for a French
supreme military commander, and by the absence of a
truly powerful Vietnamese national army. Solution of
the problem appeared to hinge on the creation of a real
national army. The Ambassador recalled that Korea, once
regarded as a U.S. puppet, became a demonstrably free
and independent nation as soon as its own army was built
up. Therefore, suggested the Ambassador, the United
States should press for a publicized agreement with
France giving the United States prime responsibility
for training and equipping the Vietnamese army. There
were manifold advantages: Vietnamese independence

---

    25. (TS) Msg, SecState NIACT 4064 to AmEmb (Paris),
13 May 54.
    26. (TS) Msg, Dillon NIACT 4383 to SecState, 14 May
54.

would no longer be questionable; doubts about the ability and good faith of the French military command to accomplish the task would be circumvented; and the French would be able to withdraw the Expeditionary Corps after cessation of hostilities. Withdrawal of non-Asian troops would also most probably have a salutary effect upon the Chinese Communists.[27]

While recognizing the virtues of the foregoing solution, Mr. Dulles rejoined that "We cannot wait for the abolition of all deep-rooted abuses and extra-territorial privileges in times like these." He continued to explore means of obtaining a public, and preferably international, declaration on the subject of Vietnamese independence, and to press for prompt signature of the draft treaties between France and Viet Nam.[28]

Both Ambassador Dillon and Under Secretary Smith were as anxious as Mr. Dulles to see the basic treaties signed. Until that event took place they were forced to occupy an uncomfortably false position at Geneva. Moreover, it was probable that, following signature, Bao Dai would return promptly to Viet Nam and, to the extent his energy and ability permitted, to attempt to assume national leadership.[29]

Premier Laniel and Buu Loc initialled the Franco-Vietnamese treaties of independence and association on 4 June.[30] Mr. Dulles lost no time in cabling the American Ambassador to inform the French that "initialling" the treaties did not conform to the United States condition concerning independence.[31] M. Schumann explained that this initialling was far more important than the usual initialling of a treaty. He may have been referring to the fact that the act permitted Buu Loc to return to

---

27. (TS) Dillon 4402 to SecState, 17 May 54
28. (TS) Msg, SecState 4272 to Dillon, 26 May 54.
29. (TS) Msg, Smith DULTE 109 to SecState, 25 May 54.
30. (C) Msg, Dillon 4723 to SecState, 4 Jun 54.
31. (TS) Msg, SecState 4398 to Dillon, 4 Jun 54.

Viet Nam without the appearance of being empty-handed. Schumann nevertheless gave assurances that the French were ready to sign, but from the Vietnamese Charge it was learned that conclusion and signature of the related convention, to which treaty signature was subordinated, had bogged down.[32] The treaties still had not been signed by the end of the Geneva Conference, and Bao Dai remained in France.

If the French wanted to use the possibility of United States intervention primarily as a card to play at Geneva, it was to their advantage not to come to a firm decision until the conference had run its course. Mr. Dulles tried to impress upon them that, from the point of view of the United States, the practicability of intervention was constantly subject to "consideration in the light of day-to-day developments." While the United States was anxious to bolster the French position, the impression was growing that Laniel might be using the U.S. conditions to create an alibi for himself or his successor. Capitulation could be blamed on the United States for having presented terms so rigorous as to be unacceptable. This suspicion was shared by American representatives at the conference but, as General Smith pointed out, there was good reason to believe the French were as confused about the real intentions of the United States as the Americans were about France's.[33]

Confusion there certainly was. It would be useless to deny that France was loathe to carry out, in any circumstances, the sweeping political changes in Indochina demanded by the United States. France was angling for a United States commitment to intervene, without having to reverse overnight a century of ingrained colonial practices. But confusion also arose from other directions.

---

32. (TS) Msg, Joyce, Paris 4765, to SecState, 9 Jun 54.

33. (TS) Msg, SecState to Amb, Paris, and USecState, 4117, TEDUL 78, 17 May 54; (TS) Msg, Smith DULTE 162 to SecState, 9 Jun 54.

"We make strong statements, and then qualify them," said General Smith. Qualification is always necessary where there is not identity of purpose and intent. And the national interests of the United States and France at Geneva were not the same. The French, beaten, tired, and disgusted, wanted an end to the war, whereas United States security interests were best served by continuation of the war on U.S. terms. Therefore, the attitude of the United States at Geneva was basically negative. The American Government knew precisely what it did **not** want France to do at the conference, because a settlement of any kind represented at least a partial defeat for the United States. Geneva was an impediment to the positive contributions the United States had to offer. From the French point of view, United States support was of a type that would have been a boon to a fighter in the first few rounds. France was in the tenth.

Another likely source of misunderstanding was French unfamiliarity with American constitutional processes. There is a certain amount of evidence that high French officials were not acquainted with the relationships between the President of the United States and the Congress. Moreover, at least partly through their misconceptions about the machinery of American government, the French had a tendency to pay too much attention to the pronouncements of individual Americans, while disregarding the official statements of the Government itself.

French Attempts to Secure Unconditional Intervention

Much confusion stemmed from the fact that the French turned immediately to a detailed consideration of exactly what military support they would receive as a result of intervention, instead of first complying with the political prerequisites upon which intervention itself depended. They thus created the definite impression that they were attempting to "piecemeal us to death" and maneuver the United States into a position where it could be accused of having haggled over minutiae instead of coming to their aid. Once in that position, the United States would have had to enter the war under conditions more suitable to the French, or bear the blame for capitulation.

On the other hand, as a prominent member of the Defense Department observed, it was evident that the French military thought there had already been an agreement, on the governmental level, to the U.S. conditions. Hence, they could not understand why the United States did not proceed with its commitments. For instance, based on the statement of the United States that it would commit principally air and sea forces <u>if it intervened</u>, the French asked for 20,000 Marines, and then raised it to six divisions. When Ambassador Bonnet reported there were not six Marine divisions in existence, Paris replied that there had to be some kind of contribution. And "then they piled it on," commented a State Department representative.34 M. Schumann was "excited and dismayed" when informed that Admiral Radford had said there was no question of using Marines in Indochina. According to the French Ambassador, this answer conflicted with what the French Government had hitherto understood to be the intentions of the United States in this respect.

This imbroglio, coinciding with several other instances of serious misunderstanding, made it very evident how correct General Smith had been when he cabled from Geneva that "the US position is not understood here."35 The Secretary of State attempted to bring the undesirable state of affairs to an abrupt halt. He told the French Ambassador that the U.S. position had been clear from the start, and that the United States was not willing to make in advance a commitment the French could use for internal political maneuvering or for negotiating at Geneva. It would, he said, represent a kind of permanent option on United States intervention, to be used as best suited French purposes. The American stand was "all or nothing." M. Bonnet expressed surprise that the United States thought the French Government had not made up its mind to internationalize the war. He considered

---

34. (TS) Notes of JCS-State Mtg, 9 Jun 54.
35. (TS) Msg, Dillon 4343 to SecState, 13 May 54.

the request had already been made![36] At the same time, Under Secretary Smith, in Europe, was still patiently explaining to MM. Bidault and Chauvel that the President could not ask Congress to sanction intervention until the basic conditions has been fulfilled by France.[37]

A month earlier, when apprising Premier Laniel of the U.S. conditions, Ambassador Dillon had been at pains to make clear that they represented high-level thinking in Washington and did not constitute, at that time, any commitment on the part of the United States Government. This did not deter M. Laniel from requesting definite assurance, preferably in writing, that American aviation would immediately come to the aid of French forces in the Delta if they were attacked by MIGs.[38] In March, General Ely and Admiral Radford had made arrangements for the preparation of plans to cover the eventuality of Chinese air attack, so that there would be no time wasted if an attack came and the United States decided to intervene. Presumably on the basis of those arrangements, it was not long before Premier Laniel, Maurice Schumann, General Ely, and other high French officials were talking as though the Chairman of the Joint Chiefs of Staff had made a commitment of immediate United States retaliation in the event of overt Chinese Communist aggression. The French leaders did seem to realize that any action would require political approval, but they wanted to be sure that assistance would come rapidly. On 1 June, their inquiries were brought to the attention of President Eisenhower, who expressed himself very strongly on the subject. He said that the United States would not intervene in China /sic/ on any basis except united action. He would not be responsible, he asserted, for going into China /sic/ alone unless a joint Congressional resolution ordered him to do so. He made it very plain that united action was a condition related not merely to regional grouping for the defense of Southeast Asia, but also to United

---

36. (TS) Msg, SecState TEDUL 178 to USecState, 9 Jun 54, CCS 092 Asia (6-25-48) sec 71.
37. (TS) Msg, Smith DULTE 165 to SecState, 10 Jun 54.
38. (TS) Msg, Dillon NIACT 4383 to SecState, 14 May 54.

States intervention in response to overt Chinese aggression.[39]

On the day after the President had stated his position, and observed that it did not differ from that of Mr. Dulles, General Valluy asked Admiral Radford whether it would be possible for the President to obtain some sort of "blank check" from the Congress against such a contingency, so that U.S. aid could be provided in a minimum of time. He also wanted to know whether the French could count on U.S. assistance, which might involve the landing of Marines, in case the French were forced to evacuate Hanoi and withdraw to the Haiphong redoubt. The Admiral gave no direct answer to either question. He stated that U.S. intelligence did not indicate the Chinese Communists were making any preparations for air intervention. He also carefully reiterated the U.S. policy of united action. General Valluy was not satisfied. He likened the French situation to that of a man on a sinking ship. Seven or eight destroyers at a distance were little help; what he needed was an airplane to come and rescue him.

Admiral Radford explained that the matter was obviously beyond his control, since it involved a political decision of grave importance. Concerning the Marines, the Admiral reminded General Valluy that any landing could only be pursuant to a political decision to intervene, which in turn depended upon fulfillment of the conditions already transmitted to the French Government. In the event of intervention, the United States force contribution would consist of "principally sea and air forces," although, the Admiral admitted, that would not necessarily rule out the possible use of Marines.

Turning to a survey of other resources, Admiral Radford broached the question of possible use of Korean or Nationalist Chinese troops. General Valluy was quite

---

39. (TS) Memo of Conv, Pres with SpAsst Cutler, 1 Jun 54.

sure the latter would be highly unwelcome in Indochina, where some of the less pleasant aspects of Chinese occupation had not yet been forgotten.[40] It was the opinion of the Joint Chiefs of Staff themselves that, even if the conflict were internationalized, the introduction of Chinese Nationalist troops would be inadvisable. Their ostensible reason was that it would provide such excellent justification for Chinese Communist intervention. Despite their ultimate recommendation that President Rhee's offer of three divisions and essential corps troops be held in abeyance, the Joint Chiefs gave serious consideration to the merits of employing Korean troops. In addition to their fighting qualities, American equipment, organization and training, and relative proximity to Indochina, there were the psychological advantages deriving from the use of Asiatic troops in an Asian war. Unfortunately, Korean troops would have to be accompanied by their American advisers. The presence of the Americans, no matter how few in number, could be construed as an act of overt intervention.[41] The offer was given further study by the Joint Chiefs toward the end of June. They again recommended that, although the offer should not be rejected, no action should be taken on it at that time. Their views were influenced by the fall of the Laniel Government, the election of Mendes-France on a peace platform, and the progress of the Geneva Conference. Furthermore, the initial reaction of the French Government to the suggestion had been adverse.[42]

At the time Admiral Radford first brought the matter up with General Valluy for exploration, the General said the French had never given any thought to using Korean troops and that he would have to think it over. In his report to General Ely, however, he represented Admiral Radford as having *insisted* upon the utility of the Koreans, and as having made the manifestly impossible claim that

---

40. (TS) Memo for Rec, Anderson, 3 Jun 54.
41. (TS) JCS 1992/339, 15 Jun 54, CCS 092 Asia (6-25-48) sec 72.
42. (TS) Memo, CJCS to JCS to SecDef, "ROK Forces for Employment in Indochina," 1 Jul 54, same file, sec 73.

the United States could transport all three divisions from Korea to Indochina in one week![43]

The discussions between Admiral Radford and General Valluy were in the nature of preliminary conversations in anticipation of bilateral staff talks under cover of the Five-Power Military Conference then in session in Washington. General Valluy availed himself of the opportunity to brief Admiral Radford on the military situation in Indochina following the fall of Dien Bien Phu. It was a gloomy report, based on the observations of Generals Ely and Salan after their visit to the theater of operations in May.

Dien Bien Phu, said General Valluy, had left its mark on both civilians and military, particularly in the Tonkin Delta. The troops were tired and their morale visibly low. Effectiveness of the military commands had markedly decreased; there was controversy between Generals Navarre and Cogny, and between their respective staffs; there was no close agreement between higher headquarters and commanders of the mobile groups; there was conflict between General Navarre and the French Air Force; there were differences among the Air Force commanders themselves, and among their staffs. French and Vietnamese troops had lost confidence in one another. Mobilization measures instituted by Bao Dai were a failure. The Vietnamese Government was discredited. The situation in Cochinchina was not good; there was conflict between the Vietnamese troops and the population of the area.

General Valluy admitted that Viet Minh losses at Dien Bien Phu had been considerably less than the French had hoped for. The Viet Minh battle corps was still effective, and within ten days their battle-hardened divisions would reach jump-off positions around the perimeter of the Tonkin Delta. There were prospects of a hard battle for Hanoi toward the end of June.

---

43. (TS) Msg, McClintock 2770 to SecState, 14 Jun 54. (TS) Memo for Rec, RADM G.W. Anderson, Exec to CJCS, 3 Jun 54.

Extraordinary measures were required to make the best of the situation. General Valluy explained that the French were regrouping their forces in order to place the Vietnamese in the static defense of the perimeter, while using French troops as mobile groups. The Viet Minh were capitalizing on the delicacy of the regrouping operation to deal hard blows at some of the Vietnamese units.

The mobile forces were being positioned to retain control of the most useful area of the Delta along the Hanoi-Haiphong axis; there were six "task forces" available in the area. The French hoped to build this force up to nine or ten mobile groups. While each group theoretically consisted of 5,000 men, it was actually maintained at a strength of 3,000 and 4,000. An individual group corresponded roughly to a U.S. regimental combat team, with diminished service and signal support.

Although it was the object of the French to hold the Tonkin redoubt at all costs, they were not assured of success. General Valluy claimed the enemy was building up to a strength of 100 battalions, with high morale, exulting in victory, and with the civilian population leaning more and more in their favor. The French were apprehensive about possible intervention by the Chinese Communist Air Force.

The seriousness of the situation sent General Ely back to Paris begging for reinforcements. According to General Valluy, France was planning to send two more parachute battalions to Indochina during the summer, and a mobile group of Algerian troops was being prepared for shipment. Four additional battalions of colonial troops in North Africa had been alerted for movement in July, September, and October. Three new divisions were being activated in France. Each division, of 12,000 to 13,000 men, would be composed of conscripts and cadres from "couverture" divisions then in Germany. General Valluy did not hide the fact that provision of the cadres would "shatter" the NATO divisions, nor that attempting to send conscripts to Indochina would present the French Government with a very ticklish political problem.[44]

---

44. (TS) Memo for Rec, RAdm G.W. Anderson, Exec to CJCS, 2 Jun 54.

Admiral Radford had already been advised by General Gruenther of the plan to form the new divisions.[45] What General Valluy did not mention was that the United States was going to be asked to equip them. Later, at a meeting between the Joint Chiefs of Staff and the Department of State, it was agreed that the United States ought to do everything possible to help the French, but that the probable initial expenditure of $310,000,000 plus $250,000,000 annually for maintenance, as well as the possible effect on NATO, called for a very careful examination of the whole idea before any commitment should be made.[46]

The State Department was particularly anxious to communicate to the French an agreement in principle, to maintain their will to continue the struggle in Indochina. Moreover, the creation of the new divisions had an important bearing on the forthcoming EDC debates, by providing an example of the flexibility of the European situation, and by demonstrating the ability of the French to withdraw troops as necessary to cope with urgent situations elsewhere in the French Union.[47]

The Joint Chiefs of Staff favored the idea. They recommended that, if a formal request were entered by the French, the United States should agree in principle to equip the three additional divisions, subject to certain provisos. The Joint Chiefs felt that the French should first of all exhibit sufficient determination to implement the plan in time to deploy experienced French Union troops from elsewhere in Indochina to the Tonkin Delta, and prevent its loss. Also, the French ought to implement their conscription decree immediately and accelerate the training of conscripts. Thereafter, the Joint Chiefs wanted the United States to establish an emergency fund

---

45. (TS) Msg, Gruenther exclv for Radford, ALO 481, 011715Z Jun 54, DA-IN-62357.
46. (TS) Notes of JCS-State Dept Mtg, 11 Jun 54.
47. (TS) Ltr, Dep USecState Murphy to Dep SecDef Anderson, 8 Jun 54, App B to Encl to JCS 1992/341, 21 Jun 54, CCS 092 Asia (6-25-48) sec 72.

to assure reimbursement to the service concerned of the cost of the initial equipment, the cost of a year's maintenance in combat, and the cost of a year's ammunition. The same fund would also be used for the replacement of critical major items taken from U.S. Army mobilization reserves and stocks then earmarked for other programs. The rate of production of ammunition would have to be increased immediately. On the fiscal side again, FY 55 Army and/or MDAP funding programs would have to be increased for replacement of equipment and ammunition of the divisions in combat, and for establishing a production rate to support the units.[48]

Available records do not reveal the receipt, before the end of the Geneva Conference, of a formal French request of the type specified by the Joint Chiefs. The United States did concur in a request by the French Minister of Defense to permit movement of the 11th French Infantry Division to Indochina with TO&E equipment.[49] In any event, the whole question became academic following the settlement arrived at through the Geneva Conference.

In the meantime, however, the French military did not hide their desire for American participation, which was the real topic of interest behind the Radford-Valluy talks. On 4 June, three days before his last talk with Admiral Radford, General Valluy had favored the Five-Power Military Conference with his own evaluation of the situation in Indochina.

General Valluy stated that it was not his intention to dramatize, but "only to be realistic among soldiers." The truth, he said, could not be disguised. If the Tonkin were lost, the military line would not be re-established anywhere. The Laos bottleneck or the eighteenth parallel had the tactical characteristics that should permit

---

48. (TS) JCS 1992/345, 22 Jun 54, as amended by Dec On, 24 Jun 54, same file.
49. (TS) Memo for COL Forney, NATO Standing Gp, by LTC C.F. Heasty, 12 Jul 54; (TS) Msg, Jt SD/DD to AmEmb, Paris, MAAG and CINCEUR (note on msg: msg essentially as this dispatched 16 Jun 54). Both in Alden file, OMA.

re-establishment of a line, but General Valluy affirmed that there would be no forces to man that line. He was not speaking of French forces; he meant to indicate that there were no southern Vietnamese who could oppose northern Vietnamese.

Ho Chi Minh's objective was the Tonkin, to be attained either by negotiation at Geneva, or by assault on Hanoi. He wished to entangle the French in negotiations by admitting now, for the first time, that there is a Communist northern state and a non-Communist southern state, and by saying that both might be incorporated in the French Union. Although, admitted General Valluy "among military men," Ho was finding receptive French ears across the negotiating table, he was preparing for military action if it were called for. And his chances of success were good.

"It has been said at this Conference," recalled General Valluy, "that if Tonkin is lost, we will fight in the south." "However," he asserted, "the French will not fight nor will Viet Nam." The General maintained that the conferees would have to provide their own men for the line in the south. Moreover, it would be an artificial line, toward whose defense Laos, Cambodia, and Thailand could contribute nothing. The decisive point was this: if the other conferees did not underwrite the battle for Tonkin, they would fight tomorrow without the French in Saigon and Bangkok. If Tonkin were lost, no Vietnamese would fight against another Vietnamese, and sooner or later (probably sooner) the whole of Viet Nam would become Communist.50

From General Smith in Geneva to Charge McClintock in Saigon, there was no American who chose to contest General Valluy's estimate seriously. McClintock cabled that "General Valluy's appreciation of the situation . . . is exceedingly good--in fact almost too good." It was

---

50. (TS) Msg, SecState TEDUL 171 to AmCon, Geneva, 7 Jun 54.

McClintock's impression that Valluy had made his statement under instructions, less with military considerations in mind than with a political objective; he was probably looking as much at the French Parliament as at the Tonkin Delta. General Ely, announced McClintock, had twice in his presence stated that it was his keenest desire for the United States to enter the war. It was McClintock's belief that the purpose of Valluy's statement was either to bring the United States, and if possible the other powers at the conference, into the conflict or, failing that, to prepare before history an excuse for an armistice the French would then request of the Viet Minh.[51]

General Valluy's presentation of the French plight in Indochina was another in the series of incidents around 9 June that led to emphatic restatement of the United States basic position. To Valluy the answer was the same: fulfill the preliminary conditions and the United States will intervene. Moreover, the United States was well prepared militarily for intervention. The Joint Chiefs of Staff had already drawn up, or were in the process of putting the finishing touches to, plans to cover almost every contingency. They had the strategy worked out, the command structure, the force contributions, plans for training native troops. They waited only the political agreement.

US Military Plans for Intervention

On 20 May, in discussion between the French and the Department of State, the United States had specified that, if intervention were to be undertaken, France would have to agree not to withdraw its forces from Indochina during the period of united action. Thus, the U.S. forces, principally air and sea and other, would be supplementary and not in substitution. An agreement would also have to be reached on the training of native troops and on command structure for united action. In formulating a Department of Defense position on command structure, and on the size

---

51. (TS) Msg, Smith DULTE 161 to SecState, 9 Jun 54; (TS) Msg, McClintock 2714 to SecState, 10 Jun 54.

and composition of United States force contributions, the Joint Chiefs had been guided by several factors: the limited availability of U.S. forces for military action in Indochina; the current numerical advantage of French Union forces over the enemy (approximately 5 to 3); the undesirability of basing large numbers of U.S. troops in Indochina; the primary need for an expanded and intensified training program; the difficulty of superimposing U.S. air forces upon existing facilities in Indochina; the implications of a Chinese Communist reaction to United States intervention; and, finally, the fact that atomic weapons would be used when it was to military advantage.

The Joint Chiefs considered that no command structure was acceptable that did not permit the United States to influence future strategy in Indochina. To solve the problem of over-all strategic guidance, they suggested a Military Representatives Committee, with a steering or standing group along the lines of NATO. The group would be patterned after the U.S. Joint Staff and would be composed primarily of American and French officers. The Committee would draw its membership from those nations contributing the principal forces of the coalition.

Although the Joint Chiefs felt that the Allied Commander in Chief should be French, there also had to be an American Deputy and a U.S. Air Adviser. The Deputy should provide liaison with the French and would coordinate U.S. activities with the over-all operations. The Joint Chiefs were well informed of the complete subordination of the French Air Force to the Army, hence the Air Adviser to see that United States air power was not misused.

The Joint Chiefs of Staff were convinced that the best military course for eventual victory in Indochina lay in the development of effective native armed forces. Therefore, a firm commitment by the French, and firm requests from the governments of the Associated States, for the training and development of those forces were felt to be prerequisites of United States participation.

United States force contributions, as recommended by the Joint Chiefs, would be limited primarily to a fast carrier task force and supporting elements, and to U.S. Air Force units operating from existing bases outside Indochina. It was believed that committing larger naval forces, or basing substantial air forces in Indochina, would reduce readiness to meet probable Chinese Communist reaction elsewhere in the Far East. From the point of view of the United States, with reference to the Far East as a whole, Indochina was devoid of decisive military objectives and the allocation of more than token armed forces to that area would be a serious diversion of limited United States capabilities.

This observation coincided with the Joint Chiefs' central philosophy that the real solution to Far Eastern difficulties lay in the neutralization of Communist China. They noted that the principal sources of Viet Minh support were "outside Indochina," and that the destruction or neutralization of those outside sources would materially reduce French military problems in Indochina.[52]

It was unlikely their strategic thinking in this direction would find acceptance at the political level unless the Chinese Communists intervened overtly in the Indochinese struggle. In that event, the Joint Chiefs' strategic concept and plan of operations called for destroying effective Communist forces and their means of support in the Indochinese action, as well as reducing Chinese Communist capability for further aggression, in order to create conditions under which the forces of the Associated States might assume responsibility for the defense of Indochina. This meant offensive air operations, employing atomic weapons whenever advantageous, as well as other weapons, against military targets in China proper, Hainan, and other islands being used by the Communists in direct support of their operations, or threatening the security of the Allied forces. Simultaneously, French Union forces, augmented by U.S. naval and air units, would exploit whatever success had been achieved as a result of the massive air operations. Should this not suffice to assure victory, the attack against China would have to be stepped up. It would require an enlarged, but highly selective, atomic offensive, in addition to attacks with other weapons systems. The atomic onslaught would

---

52. (TS) Memo for SecDef, CJCS for JCS, 20 May 54, Encl to JCS 1992/316, 18 May 54, CCS 092 Asia (6-25-48), sec 66.

be accompanied by a blockade of the China coast. Consideration was also given to instituting the blockade from the outset, and increasing it steadily, as required. Hainan would be seized or neutralized, and operations against the Chinese mainland would be undertaken by the Chinese Nationalists.

All American forces engaged in these operations would be under the unified command of the Commander in Chief, Pacific. He would insure the coordination of all operations in southeast Asia and provide for the necessary ground-air coordination between French Union forces and U.S. naval and air forces. He would also select targets and conduct air operations against military targets in Indochina and against those in China which directly supported Chinese Communist aggression. The Commander, Strategic Air Command, would support CINCPAC in these operations and would, in addition, conduct air operations as directed by the Joint Chiefs of Staff further to reduce the Chinese Communist war-making capability.

The Joint Chiefs were by no means oblivious to the possible consequences of their strategy. They recommended that it be accompanied by an appropriate degree of mobilization to provide for the greater risk of a general war, so that the United States might be prudently prepared. Immediate action would have to be taken to strengthen America's allies. However, due to the overriding mobilization requirements of U.S. forces, such aid would have to be limited to those allies who could directly support the United States strategic concept of a general war. This aid would further have to be limited to combat-essential materiel, essential replacements, and spare parts beyond the capabilities of the individual countries.

Initially, there would be no requirement for materiel and equipment over and above current MDAP for France and other allied forces in Indochina. Within approximately six months, MDAP would have to be increased to take care of three new ROK-type native divisions, and thereafter would have to be increased as new divisions were developed. But whether or not the United States intervened in Indochina, the Joint Chiefs considered it vital that the war there be financed by methods separate and distinct from the worldwide MDAP.53

---

53. (TS) JCS 1992/321, 20 May 54, as amended by Dec On, 26 May 54, same file, sec 67.

Preparation and involvement on quite such a vast scale would not be necessary, of course, if the Chinese Communists did not project themselves openly into the war. In that case, the Joint Chiefs recommended a more restricted but equally aggressive, hard-hitting plan of operations. This plan assumed that the USSR also would not enter the conflict openly, but that it would defend Soviet-controlled areas, and might covertly supply air and naval forces. The plan further assumed that hostilities in Korea would not be resumed; that French Union forces would continue to resist in Indochina with U.S. military assistance; and that atomics might be used by both sides.

Granted those assumptions, the Joint Chiefs of Staff considered that, regardless of the nationality of the forces engaged, the major courses of action would remain relatively unchanged. Enemy supply lines would have to be interdicted, while sufficient friendly forces were regrouped in the north to conduct coordinated offensive operations in that area. Territory liberated from the enemy would have to be pacified, following which coordinated ground, air and naval operations would be undertaken in central Viet Nam and north Laos to destroy enemy forces therein. Finally, attention would be turned to south Viet Nam and Cambodia to complete the destruction of the enemy. Throughout, psychological and unconventional warfare operations would be carried out. Basic to all these activities was the building-up, training and equipping of regular and guerrilla indigenous forces.

Initial operations would be devoted to the defense of vital areas until sufficient forces were available for an attack out of Tonkin with the prime objective of destroying organized Viet Minh military forces. Their lines of communications would be interdicted, their supply depots destroyed, and their troops prevented from escaping over the Chinese, Thai and Burmese borders. Concurrently, increased support by the natives would have to be developed, to assure effective local leadership in liberated areas, and internal security.[54]

---

54. (TS) JCS 1992/325, 24 May 54, as amended by Dec On, 2 Jun 54, same file, sec 68.

From the military standpoint, the foregoing plan was a good and feasible one for the French themselves to follow, granted continued assistance by the United States as in the past. Could they carry it out without active intervention by American forces?

After a careful estimate of the military situation in the Tonkin Delta, the Joint Chiefs of Staff concluded that the French probably would not be able to hold Hanoi, even though it was within their military capabilities to hold along the Sept Pagodes-Hai Duong-Ninh Giang line for at least sixty days. The Joint Chiefs could see no reason why they could not hold the Haiphong redoubt for the foreseeable future, except for the deterioration of their will to fight.

It was the opinion of the Joint Chiefs of Staff that, in the face of the rapidly crumbling military situation, support by United States air and naval forces, as envisaged, and limited to action within the boundaries of Indochina, would not insure decisive military results. Benefit to the French would be mainly psychological. For the United States, however, it would probably mean that involvement, although initially limited, would continue and expand until it would ultimately require additional naval and air forces, and extensive ground forces to prevent the loss of Indochina. Eventually, this could lead to full United States responsibility for the outcome of the war.

Again the Joint Chiefs warned that involvement in Indochina, even on a limited scale, increased the risk of a general war. Accordingly, if the United States Government decided to intervene, the armed forces should be placed in a more suitable state of readiness to meet such an eventuality. Decisions would have to be made on mobilization and logistic, fiscal and other supporting measures. Although there were no logistic implications that would prevent commitment of the forces envisaged, large-scale diversion of forces, equipment and supplies from the Far East or the United States would necessitate corresponding replacement of units and personnel, and increases in production. For a time, there would be a drain on logistic reserves. Construction of air bases, port and storage facilities, roads, railroads and communications systems in Indochina would be required. A major supply base in south

Indochina, and at least one advanced base near Haiphong would be needed to support United States ground forces. Lift capabilities of MATS and MSTS would have to be expanded and logistical pipelines, separate from those for Korea, would have to be maintained. A major increase in the armed forces, beyond that planned for FY 55, would be required, as well as an expanded draft and recall of some National Guard and Reserve units.[55]

Training of Native Troops

Salient in every American plan for intervention was the stress placed upon the importance of building up the native armies. It is significant that training of indigenous forces, although a military stipulation, appeared in the basic political, as well as military, conditions for intervention presented to France by the United States. Originally, there had been no intention on the part of the United States to conduct the training itself. The language barrier alone would have sufficed to stifle the idea, even if the United States had not sedulously been attempting to restrict its activities entirely to supplying the French with the wherewithal to fight their own war. But as time wore on and the French displayed no more ability than desire to produce an efficient native fighting force, the Americans became more and more impatient. As early as April, 1952, the three Service Secretaries suggested, in a joint memorandum to the Secretary of Defense, that an expanded MAAG undertake the training and equipping of a national army capable at least of preserving internal security, while international support, encouragement and cooperation were sought and brought to bear in developing Indochinese political self-reliance and independence.[56] Nevertheless, almost a year later, the Joint Chiefs, when asked to re-examine the question, rendered the opinion that "in view of their experience and the language difficulties involved, . . .

---

55. (TS) JCS 1992/334, 7 Jun 54 (as amended by Dec On, 23 Jun 54), same file, sec 71.
56. (TS) Memo, Secys Pace, Kimball, Gilpatric to SecDef, "Draft State Department Paper on Indochina dated 27 March 1952," 8 Apr 54, same file, sec 28.

the French are better qualified to conduct the training of the indigenous forces than United States personnel would be." They did suggest, however, that the French might learn some useful techniques from American experience in Korea.57

More time passed, and still no worthwhile results. Reluctantly the Americans came to the conclusion that if the job were ever going to be done, and done properly, they would have to do it themselves. Eventually, they sounded the French out about increased United States assistance in training the Vietnamese army, even though they did not expect the French to receive the suggestion very favorably. Their surmise was justified.

Less than two months before the fall of Dien Bien Phu, General Ely frankly admitted to Admiral Radford that he had been embarrassed by press reports to the effect that he was amenable to such assistance. Basically, he said, the reason for his opposition to the proposal was that increased numbers of Americans in Indochina would jeopardize French prestige in the eyes of the natives and would result in loss of native confidence in the French High Command. In spite of tactful arguments to the contrary advanced by Admiral Radford, General Ely would do no more than grudgingly agree to consider the matter very informally.58 As for General Navarre, the United States missed a fine double opportunity when he threatened to "turn in his suit" if the Americans gained any active part in the training of native troops.59

Ho Chi Minh proved to be considerably more persuasive than the Chairman of the Joint Chiefs of Staff. The harder the battle corps of the Viet Minh surged against the Tonkin perimeter, the more virtue General Ely began to see in

---

57. (TS) Dec On JCS 1992/202, 3 Mar 53, same file, sec 38.
58. (TS) Memo for Rec, Anderson, "Discussions with General Ely, Chairman of the French Chiefs of Staff on Indo-China in the afternoon of 24 March," 24 Mar 54.
59. (TS) Msg, Lacy (Manila) 2670 to SecState, 25 May 54, CCS 092 Asia (6-25-48) sec 68.

American offers of instructor personnel. By July, he had
so succeeded in revising his original opinions that he
was able to complain that "the United States was late
once more."[60]

Repeated American efforts, on the governmental
level, to impress upon the French the necessity of raising
strong native armies have already been recorded. General
O'Daniel's permanent assignment to Indochina in April,
1954, marked the beginning of intensive attempts, on the
military side, to sell the French the notion of requesting
American assistance in the task. And as their military
situation worsened, the French gave ground more and more
before American concepts. Really effective assistance,
however, amounted to nothing less than assuming full
responsibility for all phases of training. Once committed
on that scale, the United States would find itself sharing
the blame if the war turned out badly. Hence, responsibility without some control over combat employment of
native troops and, therefore, a voice in strategy and
operational planning, would be unacceptable. The French
had anticipated this eventuality and feared its consequences, which accounted for much of their reluctance to
ask for American help. By the time American arguments
and the military situation had softened the French to the
point of urgently requesting assistance, the United States
was no longer willing to provide it, unless the French
complied with all the other conditions upon which full
intervention was contingent. By then, it was "all or
nothing."

General O'Daniel had tackled his job with enthusiasm
and optimism. By the middle of May he had won from
Generals Ely and Navarre a considerable degree of acquiescence. General Ely said that he accepted the concept of
American training for the Vietnamese army and he agreed
that United States advisers should be placed in Vietnamese
units. He also said, "The sooner you get into this war,
the better we will like it." On the other hand, he did
not give open assent to General O'Daniel's insistence upon
the necessity of creating light divisions (rather than

---

60. (S) Msg, Ch MAAG IC MG 1566A to CSUSA, 010205Z
Jun 54, DA-IN-62459 (2 Jun 54), same file, sec 69.

battalions), and he emphasized strongly that command would remain in French hands and that there would be no U.S. participation in operational planning.[61] General O'Daniel had indicated that he thought it possible to create nine Vietnamese and three Cambodian divisions by October. The American Charge sounded a note of caution:

> I have the greatest admiration for General O'Daniel's faith, tenacity, and bull-dog courage. I fear, however, he may be over sanguine as to possibilities of making an effective Vietnamese fighting force in 6 months time. Irrespective of General O'Daniel's abundant military virtues, there are many obstacles in his path. Not least of these is complete apathy of Vietnamese populace coupled with increasing tendency of fence-sitters to go over to enemy, absolute break-down of mobilization plan, internecine rivalries between few men capable of showing leadership, and lack of leadership from Bao Dai and his Ministers. I do not say the job cannot be done but that we should take a close look at its dimensions before we come in.[62]

The Assistant Military Attache in Saigon also had his reservations about the advisability of plunging in before looking at the rocks. General Ely was insisting that there be French officers in the training groups. Past experience in Indochina had shown that French pride would not allow them to accept American advice. It was doubtful that these officers would be much more than roadblocks. The Assistant Attache also drew attention to the unsound political base. There was the Mendes-France peace-at-any-price government in France, and Diem, the probable new President of Viet Nam, "did not know the facts of life." The Attache even suggested that French agreement to the training proposal might have the

---

61. (S) Msg, Ch MAAG IC MG 1447A to CSUSA, 191201Z May 54, DA-IN-59456 (19 May 54), same file, sec 67; (S) Msg, McClintock 2468 to SecState, 19 May 54.
62. (TS) Msg, McClintock 2299 to SecState, 9 May 54.

objective of getting the United States into a position where it would share more of the blame, seeing that the French had apparently already decided to give up Indochina.[63]

Undaunted, General O'Daniel had pushed on with his mission and by 24 May he was able to present Secretary of Defense Wilson with a somewhat revised training plan, to a substantial portion of which General Ely had given tacit assent. In brief, the plan called for readying nine divisions in the south, and two in the north, by 1 December. The divisions would be reduced strength (approximately 12,000 men), less heavy equipment. They would be under over-all French command but the United States would have a major voice in their employment and would have counterpart staff representation similar to the Van Fleet solution in Greece. The whole plan could only be brought off if the United States were given a free hand, with full Vietnamese support.[64]

While concurring with the plan as such, the Commander in Chief, Pacific, pointed out that General O'Daniel's hands would be tied if he attempted to arrive at other than preliminary arrangements before firm prior agreements had been concluded on the governmental level. The entire programs for Laos, Cambodia and Viet Nam would have to be completely under U.S. control (although still under French over-all command) to ensure full support of the indigenous authorities. "Nor will present French apathy toward these forces be improved should control of training remain in French hands," added Admiral Stump.[65]

---

63. (TS) Msg, Asst USARMA Saigon NR 1788 to G-2, 20 Jun 54.
64. (TS) Msg, CINCPAC to CNO, 230909Z May 54; (TS) Msg, Lacy, Manila 2670 to SecState, 25 May 54. Both in CCS 092 Asia (6-25-48) sec 68.
65. (TS) Msg, CINCPAC to CNO, 022358Z Jun 54, same file, sec 70.

General Ely had come a long way since March. He now favored the principle of forming native troops into divisional units, although he still felt an American division was not the answer. He also agreed that American advisers should be placed at various levels within a division. On the question of United States participation in operational planning, however, he felt there was need for clarification. There could not be any discussion at that time of the United States sharing responsibility for planning operations. There could be only one commander, and he must be a Frenchman. On the other hand, providing an agreement was reached on intervention, U.S. officers would be integrated into French planning staffs. General Ely was prepared to discuss in Washington the details involved in such integration. Although now actively favoring United States training, his basic position was that questions relating to training were only one part of an over-all plan that would concern itself with fixing the conditions and the nature of United States intervention. They would only become pertinent once an agreement to intervene had been arrived at, and such an agreement would only take place if the Geneva Conference failed.66

General Ely's position was, of course, diametrically opposite that of the United States Government. Nevertheless, acting on his own premises, he summoned General O'Daniel and, through him, requested the United States to organize and supervise the training of Vietnamese divisions, and to do the same for all other Vietnamese training. This request was promptly transmitted to Washington by General O'Daniel on 9 June.67 On the same day there arrived in Washington a cable from General Ely himself, in which he said:

---

66. (TS) Msg, Dillon and Trapnell 4613 to SecState and JCS, 312000Z May 54, DA-IN-62247 (31 May 54), CCS 092 Asia (6-25-48) sec 69. (TS) Msg, Dillon 4662 to SecState, 2 Jun 54.
67. (S) Msg, Ch MAAG IC MG 1651 DA to CSUSA, 091515Z Jun 54, DA-IN-64188 (9 Jun 54), CCS 092 Asia (6-25-48) sec 71.

"I have not yet made a survey of the military situation, especially in Tonkin. However, it seems to me that the decisions I will have to take regarding the operations will rest on the US intentions, in the present situation, as well as those they anticipate in the future.

Therefore, I would very much like to have, either in Paris, where I expect to be possibly on the 19th June, or here in Saigon, as soon as possible, an exchange of view with a qualified representative of Adm RADFORD, in order to know what I can expect on the part of the U.S.A."68

These two messages, the mix-up over the use of Marines, and a number of other incidents indicating the French were ignoring the manner in which the United States had conditioned its offer of intervention, precipitated the crisis of 9 June. Both the Joint Chiefs and the State Department felt it was time to call a halt until the French realized it was "all or nothing." While Mr. Dulles was laying down the law to Ambassador Bonnet, Admiral Radford informed General Valluy that he was not in a position at that time to respond to General Ely's request for conversations on the subject raised in his message. The official position, as communicated to Ambassador Dillon in Paris was:

Prior to French decision to request internationalization, we consider undesirable to start yet another series conversations which would inevitably provoke on French side all kinds hopes and interpretations with regard basic issue US intervention which would only cause further confusion. In other words, it is our feeling that we should not be eased into a series of piecemeal commitments resulting from collateral military conversations in the absence of an understanding with the Fr Gov based on our general proposal /Paris 4023/ described in TEDUL 54 . . . .

---

68. (TS) Msg, Ely to /Valluy?/, Saigon, 9 Jun 54.

With regard to US training Vietnam troops, we feel that situation VN has degenerated to point where any commitments at this time to send over US instructors in near future might expose us to being faced with situation in which it would be contrary to our interests to have to fulfill such commitment. Our position accordingly is that we do not (repeat not) wish to consider US training mission or program separately from over-all operational plans on assumption conditions fulfilled for US participation was Indochina.[69]

To keep him from trying to push more requests for aid, General O'Daniel was informed that any agreement on training would have to be made on a governmental level.[70] However, General Ely had already promised to give him the request in writing. But when it arrived, it turned out to be a statement of agreed principles, not a request for aid, and it came by way of Buu Loc, Vietnamese Prime Minister. General O'Daniel, commenting on the unexpected channel of communication, said:

> Ely gave Bu Loc the copy of the ltr knowing that I had no authority to act. He either misunderstood what I wanted, which is possible, or he may in disappointment failure obtain tng assistance desire show Vietnamese he is trying obtain aid for them and undesiring be placed in asking position himself had suggested Bu Loc ask for tng assistance by US.[71]

A less charitable explanation is also possible.

---

69. (TS) Msg, Murphy TOSEC 392 to AmEmb (Paris), 10 Jun 54.
70. (TS) Notes of JCS-State Mtg, 11 Jun 54.
71. (TS) Msg, Ch MAAG IC MG 1951A to DA, 200915Z Jun 54, DA-IN-66760, CCS 092 Asia (6-25-48) sec 72.

The decision to defer the training program was a drastic one. General O'Daniel protested vigorously: "To wait for a package agreement is sound theoretically but time is running out and no matter what the package deal may be, if action here is delayed any longer nothing short of actual UN-US troop intervention will have a chance of saving the situation."[72] General Smith, viewing the matter in the light of Geneva, advanced some cogent reasons for reconsidering the decision. While fully appreciating the desirability of concluding an agreement on an over-all operational plan for intervention, he pointed out that negotiations at Geneva were reaching a stage where any indication of U.S. support strengthened the French position. A decision to train Vietnamese troops, being a positive action that could be taken during the course of the conference, would be particularly good. French military discussions with the Viet Minh at Geneva had made no appreciable progress, and General Smith thought commitment of a training mission might lend the French negotiators some support. Inasmuch as it looked as though a settlement would result in partition, a national army was going to be needed to protect what was left of Viet Nam. A training mission would still be needed to strengthen the defenders. General Smith also felt that it would not be illogical to treat the matter of training separately from that of over-all intervention because the United States had discussed the possibility of training long before any question of intervention had arisen.[73]

As Ambassador Dillon remarked, the French, too, had always considered training a separate problem, for the same reason. Therefore, if the United States was no longer interested in helping with the training of the Vietnamese Army except within the framework of united action in Indochina, the Ambassador felt that the French should so be informed, to prevent any misunderstanding. He also said, tactfully, that he assumed the State Department had considered the fundamental political psychological importance of the decision. The French

---

72. (TS) Msg, Ch MAAG IC MG 1691 to CSUSA, 130601Z Jun 54, DA-IN-65099 (13 Jun.), CCS 092 Asia (6-25-48) sec 71.
73. (TS) Msg, Smith DULTE 174 to SecState, 12 Jun 54.

Government would most probably consider it meant the definite and final write-off of Indochina by the United States and might therefore use it as an excuse for accepting the Viet Minh's terms. There was also the probability that opponents of the United States in France might, in the future, describe the decision as an attempt to influence the French forcefully to request internationalization of the war. Last, but not least, there was the question of Vietnamese morale.[74]

In replying to Ambassador Dillon, Secretary of State Dulles commented on an apparent discrepancy. The Ambassador had, in one cable, reported General Ely as stating that the question of United States training of native forces was but one part of an over-all plan for intervention. But in his cable protesting the dropping of training, the Ambassador had asserted the French had always considered training as a problem separate from possible united action. Mr. Dulles then continued:

> At the same time, Ely's position seems clear that the French have been opposed to giving US responsibility for training unless US agreed to intervention. It may be that in effort to draw US into conflict without having US conditions on intervention met, French military may now seek US training in advance of US commitment to intervene with own combat forces. . . . we are resolved not to get drawn into training program when due to deteriorating conditions and lack of overall program to reverse situation training program has virtually no chance of success. If French are not going to agree to only kind of armistice which now seems possible at Geneva, but are going to fight for more than protection of expeditionary corps, possibility may exist for development of some program to reverse present downhill trend. But this seems unfortunately most unlikely to us.
>
> Under present circumstances, and particularly in view of three points you make in Emtel 4812, believe you

---

74. (TS) Msg, Dillon 4812 to SecState, 11 Jun 54.

should clarify US position only if you are forced to do so and should in interim reply to French that we are in agreement with Ely's position expressed in Embtel 4662.75

Mr. Dulles' personal opinion was that the United States should try to carry the situation along, avoiding either a formal refusal at that time to train the Vietnamese, or a massive commitment of some two to three thousand MAAG personnel. Such a commitment could not help carrying strong political overtones and might raise Congressional complications. The French "want and in effect have an option on our intervention," said Mr. Dulles, "but they do not want to exercise it and the date of expiry of our option is fast running out."76

Time was running out in Indochina, too. General O'Daniel entered plea after plea for a reversal of the decision on training. While the Chief of Staff, Army, told General O'Daniel it was imperative he comply strictly with his previous orders not to negotiate a training agreement, General Ridgway absolved the armed forces of blame for the delay. In Washington it was apparent that the French military were not completely aware of the situation and were laboring under the misapprehension that governmental agreements had been reached, and that the United States military were responsible for the delay. General Ridgway wanted General O'Daniel to make clear to the French in Indochina that the delays were in no way an indication that the United States was pulling back.77

Unsatisfied, General O'Daniel on 26 June wired an appeal directly to the Joint Chiefs of Staff for permission to go ahead with the training of six divisions. He sketched his outline plan for accomplishing the task, and asked that it be passed along to "the highest authority." The Chairman of

---

75. (TS) Msg, SecState 4551, TEDUL 191, to Amb (Paris), 12 Jun 54.
76. (TS) Msg, SecState TEDUL 197 to AmCon (Geneva), 14 Jun 54.
77. (TS) Msg, CSUSA to Ch MAAG IC, DA-IN-963165, 162246Z Jun 54, CCS 092 Asia (6-25-48) sec 72.

the Joint Chiefs informed him that, regrettably, more positive action was impracticable at that time in view of the obscure situation, but that his message had been passed to the highest authority, as requested.[78]

Thus, at least temporarily, came to an end the concerted effort of the United States to build up the indigenous forces of the Associated States. Frustration of this attempt imperiled more than the immediate future of the Indochinese peninsula; it was a body-blow to one of the salient features of United States strategy toward the Far East as a whole.

United States Strategy in the Far East

In the grand strategy of the United States for developing a position of military strength in the Far East, fostering the growth of the military forces of the Associated States and other non-Communist countries in the Orient was second in importance only to building up the war potential of Japan, Korea and Nationalist China. Indigenous military power was the heart of America's prime objective in the East: to develop the purpose and capability of the non-Communist countries to act collectively and effectively in opposing the threat of Communism. Once this objective had been achieved, the United States might then be able to bring about the establishment of a comprehensive regional security arrangement of these countries, with which the United States, the United Kingdom, and possibly France, would be associated. By the united action of the coalition, the power and influence of the Soviet Union in the Far East could finally be reduced, primarily through the containment and curtailment of Communist China's relative position of power.

This strategy had not existed, as such, in April when the Security Council called upon the Department of Defense to determine means for strengthening the military position of the United States in the Far East. Highly pertinent to an understanding of United States history in this period was the opening comment of the Joint Chiefs in their reply:

---

78. (TS) Msg, Ch MAAG IC MG 1824A to JCS, 260930Z Jun 54, DA-IN-68393 (26 Jun), CCS 092 Asia (6-25-48) sec 73; (TS) Msg, CJCS JCS 963796 to Ch MAAG IC, 302300Z Jun 54.

Since the United States military objectives and programs with respect to a specific country or region stem from approved United States policy as it affects such country or region, the development of United States military objectives toward the Far East should, in the usual course, be within the context of an over-all United States policy respecting that area. Although the United States policy toward Communist China does set forth certain general objectives to be sought in the Far East vis-a-vis that country, <u>the United States has not formulated a comprehensive policy in which the Far East is reviewed as a strategic entity</u> and which would provide definitive direction for the development of a position of military strength in the Far East. Rather, our present policy addresses itself to the individual countries within the area or, as in the case of Southeast Asia, to a segment of the area. . . . Taken in the aggregate, expressions of policy /toward individual countries/ make it clear that the United States, from the standpoint of its security interests, attaches major importance to the Far East area and would be prepared to react with military force against an armed aggression by the USSR or Communist China in that region.[79]

In order to furnish a meaningful answer to the problem posed by the Security Council, the Joint Chiefs were themselves constrained to isolate American objectives in the Far East, relate those objectives to a coherent policy, and then provide courses of action for their attainment. The Joint Chiefs realized that the United States could not play Atlas forever, supporting the entire world. The non-Communist Far East had to stand on its own two feet, with the confidence that comes from solidarity, and the strength that comes from self-reliance. It was the task of the United States to develop the will and the strength to oppose further Communist aggression.

The policy of the Joint Chiefs was essentially political and psychological. The development of native armies was only

---

79. (TS) JCS 1776/452, 9 Apr 54, CCS 383.21 Korea (3-19-45) sec 149. Underlining added.

a means toward the greater end of joining the entire non-Communist Orient into a solid bloc, based upon the very real economic interdependence of the various regions within the area. Recognizing the magnitude of the undertaking, the Joint Chiefs advocated approaching it by easy stages. The grand coalition should be formed out of units that the United States would be able to knit together by bilateral and multilateral treaties as time went on. America should be the integrator and the guide.

The security treaties with Japan, the Philippines, South Korea, Australia, and New Zealand all fitted into the pattern. But this was only a beginning. The impending crisis in Indochina naturally sharpened United States desire to hasten the process. Furthermore, Secretary Dulles hoped that the mere knowledge that multilateral talks on mutual defense were being pursued might tend to moderate Communist demands at Geneva. Beside stressing the necessity for a common stand by all the countries in the area, Mr. Dulles reminded the Foreign Ministers of Australia and New Zealand that no agreement on a position toward the Indochinese phase of the conference existed among the Western Powers. It was, therefore, unclear just what the West would not tolerate from the Communists.[80]

On the basis of the Eden compromise of 5 May, Great Britain had indicated her willingness to participate in a five-power discussion of the subject. There was, however, still serious disagreement over the manner in which the talks should be conducted. The British wished to use the medium of the Five-Power Staff Agency, and widen the discussions to include political and economic problems. Moreover, the British proposal for the talks was couched in terms that involved underwriting the Geneva settlement before it was arrived at.[81]

The United States had no intention of committing itself to defending a settlement that might well be against its own national interests. Furthermore, the Five-Power Staff Agency

---

80. (S) Msg, Dulles, Geneva SECTO 73 to Actg SecState, 3 May 54.
81. (TS) Msg, DULTE 51 to SecState, 5 May 54.

alone or with other nations, was not a satisfactory substitute for a broad political coalition including the Southeast Asian nations to be defended. Even more pertinent, the Staff Agency was composed entirely of Western nations, and the United States could not agree to a "white man's party" to determine the problems of Asian nations.[82]

Accordingly, the United States announced that it would be willing to participate in an examination of the military situation in Southeast Asia, providing the purpose was to explore, through secret and existing channels in Washington, the means by which the United States, Great Britain, France, New Zealand and Australia might assist the countries of Southeast Asia to defend themselves. The United States stressed the fact that this examination was considered supplementary to continue efforts by the United States to organize a regional grouping, and that it was neither a substitute for, nor the nucleus of, such a grouping.[83]

The British accepted the American viewpoint that their two countries should move forward concurrently on parallel lines. They were prepared to start immediately with the military staff talks.[84] Although the United Kingdom yielded to pressure by the United States, as well as by Australia and New Zealand, there were valid reasons for reluctance. Her Majesty's Government were being played upon by Nehru to back his neutralist proposal for what amounted to a sell-out to the Communists at Geneva; the British public was terrified at the thought of the H-Bomb; and there was a widespread feeling in Britain that somehow or other the Geneva Conference was going to settle all the problems of Asia. The British proposal for staff examinations by an already constituted agency was a matter of common prudence, according to Under-Secretary of State Smith. If Geneva succeeded, the talks would not be important but, if Geneva failed, there

---

82. (TS) JCS 1992/324, with Encl, Memo from SpecAsst to Pres Cutler, 7 May, 24 May 54, CCS 092 Asia (6-25-48) sec 68.
83. (TS) Rec of Acts by NSC at 196th Mtg, 8 May 54.
(TS) Gerhart "Account," pp. 63-64.
84. (TS) Msg, Smith DULTE 66 to SecState, 13 May 54.

would be inevitable criticism that staff examinations and long-range planning should have been under way long ago.[85] Presumably, because the talks were secret, the public would not know how long they had been going on.

The United States was not without its own dilemmas. On the one hand, there was the desire to establish a collective defense for Southeast Asia as quickly as possible. On the other hand, there was the desire, apparently not shared by the United Kingdom, to avoid planning during the Geneva Conference, because it would imply that the Associated States had been written off. To counter with the argument that France would speak for the Associated States at Geneva would merely underline the already-present skepticism in Asia about their true independence. The problem of the United States was to move rapidly toward the creation of a minimum coalition to cover the possible loss of Indochina, while avoiding the impression that the Associated States had already been given up as lost.[86]

Secretary Dulles therefore conceived of forming a Southeast Asian community that probably would not include Viet Nam but that might, with luck, embrace Laos and Cambodia. By skirting any discussion of actual inclusion or exclusion of the three states, he hoped to side-step giving the impression they had been written off in advance. Charge d'Affaires McClintock, in Saigon, respectfully but firmly dissented against this course. "Most regrettably," he wrote, "there is no human resource in Cambodia nor Laos, on which to build a bulwark against Communist infiltration or aggression. Furthermore, in the case of Cambodia, there is no geographic barrier against such aggression. Furthermore, once the communists have possession of the complex of modern airfields in Vietnam, there is no barrier to the successful use of airpower against all of Southeast Asia."[87]

---

85. (TS) Msg, Smith DULTE 53 to SecState, 7 May 54.
86. (TS) Msg, Dulles TEDUL 48 to Smith, 9 May 54.
87. (TS) Msg, McClintock 2374 to SecState, 13 May 54.

In discussing the matter of regional grouping with Mr. Dulles, the Chairman of the Joint Chiefs of Staff discovered that the Secretary envisaged making Thailand a position that the Communists could not take either by military action or subversion without triggering off unified action by the coalition against Communist China itself. He was even considering putting token U.S. military forces into Thailand to make the incident absolutely clear, if and when it happened. By coincidence, the United States Ambassador to Thailand on the same day cabled in a suggestion to deploy one F-84G wing to that country to strengthen its defenses. The Joint Chiefs rejected the suggestion as being a fruitless dispersion of air power. On a different occasion, one of the molders of American strategy had referred to Thailand as "the last place in the world" where the United States wanted to become involved with military operation.[88] At this time, however, Admiral Radford remarked only that in his opinion the Thais could not be depended upon. He observed that the Chinese Communists already had a nucleus for a Thai Government, that Thai leadership was at best uncertain, that their recent history showed they would jump to the other side quickly if to their apparent advantage, and that Ambassador Donovan had no confidence in their ability to hold Thailand in the event Indochina were taken over.

The Admiral also felt that there was not much likelihood of an incident in Thailand of the type anticipated by Mr. Dulles. It was more probable, the Admiral thought, that Thailand, Malaya, and Indonesia would be undermined by subversion. Such would probably be the fate also of Laos and Cambodia, even if they were salvaged at Geneva. The Chairman of the Chiefs believed that once the Indochinese incident was settled, there would be no further opportunity to cope with another military adventure on the part of the Chinese, at least until the Communists were ready for the "big show." Admiral Radford pointed out that the United States had not, at the National Security Council level, faced up to the problem of what to do about countries that were taken over

---

88. (TS) Memo for Rec, CJCS, 10 May 54. (TS) Msg, Donovan (Bangkok) 2242 to SecState, 10 May 54, CCS 092 Asia (6-25-48) sec 65; (TS) Notes on JCS-State Mtg, 23 Jul 54.

by the Communists by legal means. The possibility of legal assumption of power by the Communist Party existed in many lands. Because the United States could not use the same tactics for gaining power, its position vis-a-vis the Communists in the Far East would become progressively disadvantageous with the passage of time.

From the purely military standpoint, there were a number of advantages in carrying the action to Communist China itself, but everyone, the Admiral observed, recognized the political disadvantages of such a solution.[89]

Mr. Dulles found himself facing political disadvantages of a different sort in trying to weld Asian and European powers together for concerted action. The issue of colonialism and fear of Communist China acted as a deterrent upon most of the Colombo nations. Although Nehru failed to dominate the conference of Prime Ministers at Colombo in early May, and indeed encountered vigorous opposition from Pakistan in particular, he did succeed in vitiating any strong effect the conference might have had in supporting the stand of the Western Powers at Geneva. The Colombo meeting issued a recommendation that, if Geneva stopped the war, the UK, USSR, China and the United States should agree to prevent resumption of hostilities. Notably, the Colombo conference gave no indication of the intentions, much less of any commitments, on the part of the five south Asian powers as a group, or individually, in regard to future policy toward the Indochinese crisis.[90]

In spite of failing to take any definite and constructive position, the Colombo powers, together with the other countries in south and southeast Asia, displayed growing apprehension that Western attempts to solve the Indochinese problem might lead to World War III. They showed increasing resentment and frustration over the thought that such a development

---

89. (TS) Memo for Rec, CJCS, 10 May 54.
90. (S) Msg, SecState TOSEC 79 to AmCon Geneva, 5 May 54, DA-IN-56239 (6 May).

might be thrust upon them without their having been given an opportunity to express themselves or take collective action. They therefore began to indicate some willingness to help in carrying out an agreed settlement. Mr. Dulles was eager to enlist their services. As the nations most immediately threatened, he felt they should have every opportunity to make their contribution to a settlement. He felt that their participation would help mitigate their fears, nurture their self-confidence, increase their prestige, help to educate them better about Communist intentions, and eventually make them more receptive to the idea of cooperation with the United States and other Western nations. Inasmuch as Communist China could ill-afford to have them united in opposition to it, Mr. Dulles hoped for a more reasonable Chinese attitude at Geneva if the Colombo powers could be organized.[91] But by the end of the Geneva Conference Mr. Dulles had discovered that the East moves in its own inscrutable way. Nor is there any indication that the other half of the "parallel approach," the Five-Power Staff Agency talks in Washington, had the slightest effect upon the tactics or demands of the Communists at Geneva.

The Five-Power military conference lasted from 3 June to 11 June. The conferees agreed that the situation in Indochina was critical, and that retention of the Tonkin Delta was of the greatest importance to the defense of Southeast Asia. They also agreed that stabilization of the situation in the Delta would require outside assistance on the order of three divisions and 300 aircraft. The French representative indicated that "the psychological impact of those reinforcements would be enhanced if they were drawn from the Western Powers." And all five representatives concluded that "the arrival of reinforcements from the Free Nations, other than France, would be an important factor in the restoration of Vietnamese confidence." It had, of course, been understood

---

91. (s) Msg, Dulles (Murphy) TOSEC 240 to AmCon Geneva, 22 May 54.

that the conclusions of the conferees did not in any way imply a commitment of the Governments. And none of the Governments moved to provide the reinforcements that their military representatives had concluded were necessary.

The conference also studied the situation that would occur should the Tonkin Delta be lost to the Viet Minh. The conferees recognized: (a) the necessity of considering the establishment of a recovery line in the south; (b) the fact that land forces immediately available would not be sufficient to hold a Chinese advance, should the Chinese choose to move, and that, therefore, defensive positions in Thailand and Burma should be considered as well as the recovery line in Indochina; and (c) the fact that maintenance of internal security in Southeast Asia depended upon the support of the people therein. The final conclusion related to a possible cease-fire and called for a guarantee by nations other than those directly involved that they would intervene if the agreement were broken.[92] The United States later ignored this conclusion by refusing to do more than "respect" the cease-fire agreement.

United States military thinking was evident in the acceptance by the conference of the conclusion that overall Allied Strategy should be defensive in Southeast Asia in the event of a global war, and that nuclear attacks should be launched against China if war ensued with her. Acceptance of the concept of blockade also reveals United States influence.[93]

The Chief of Staff, Army, after studying the conclusions of the military representatives at the conference, recommended

---

92. (TS) Rpt of the Five Power Military Conference, 11 Jun 54, Encl to (TS) JCS 1992/337, 14 Jun 54, CCS 092 Asia (6-25-58) BP pt 11.
93. (TS) Encl B to (TS) JCS 1992/350, 3 Jul 54, same file, sec 74.

to the Joint Chiefs of Staff that they not accept these
conclusions because they did not conform precisely, in
either language or scope, with previously approved positions
of the Joint Chiefs. Although his recommendation was not
accepted,[94] it does in fact appear that his criticism was
not without foundation.

Consistent with their thinking over a long period of
time, the Joint Chiefs, on 21 May, informed the Secretary of
Defense that they considered a static type of defense for
Southeast Asia unsound from a military viewpoint. The Chiefs
declared there were two basic military concepts for defense
of the area: the static, or Korea, type; or an offensive
against the source of Communist military power being applied
in Southeast Asia. So long as Burma and Thailand were not
under Communist control, the geography of the area and the
lack of Chinese Communist capability for a major
overseas attack rendered Malaya secure from external threat.
Should Burma and Thailand be lost prior to an Allied decision
to hold a line in Southeast Asia, the defensive position
would have to be established in Malaya. A study of the force
requirements and logistic implications of this concept revealed
extensive and damaging weaknesses. It was estimated that it
would take a minimum of twelve months to build up the base
complex and facilities required to support the forces that
would be involved. Those forces would have to remain over an
extended period of time, and the commitment of manpower and
material to maintain them would be unacceptable from the
over-all viewpoint. The presence of large numbers of United
States, Commonwealth, and French troops in the area would
provide the Communists with excellent material for anti-
Western propaganda. Dissipation of Allied strength on such
a scale would be a gift to USSR. Finally, execution of a
static defense plan would result in maldeployment, and less
flexibility in employment of U.S. forces. The capability of
supporting existing war plans logistically would be seriously

---

94. (TS) Memo, CSUSA to JCS, "Final Report of the Five-
Power Military Representatives Conference of June 1954," c.
9 Jul 54, same file, sec 75. Actually, it was not necessary
to approve or disapprove, because the conclusions of the
representatives did not imply commitment by their respective
governments.

jeopardized. The United States should, therefore, adopt the concept of offensive action against Communist China, rather than that of reacting locally at the point of attack.[95]

Neither these plans, nor America's strident efforts to organize a regional grouping, nor the implied threat of the Five-Power Staff meeting served to mar the equanimity of Vyacheslav Molotov, "the smiling log," in Geneva.

The Viet Minh Terms

Molotov could well afford to smile. As an American representative later remarked to an unhappy Vietnamese, "You can expect no more at the conference table than you have won on the field of battle." And there was no doubt about who held victory in the field.

The Viet Minh's terms were victor's terms, and they were hard. Either openly or by implication they demanded every concession the United States had sworn was unacceptable. The Viet Minh presented its proposal for the re-establishment of peace in Indochina at the second plenary session of the Geneva Conference on 11 May. The rest of the conference consisted of the vain thrashings of the hooked victim as the Viet Minh steadily reeled in the line under the skillful coaching of two experts at fishing in troubled waters.

The terms are sufficiently important to be set out in full:

    1. Recognition by France of the sovereignty and independence of Vietnam throughout the territory of Vietnam and also of the sovereignty and independence of Chmer and Pathet Lao.

    2. Conclusion of an agreement on the withdrawal of all foreign troops from the territory of Vietnam, Chmer and Pathet Lao within the time-limits to be

---

    95. (TS) Dec On JCS 1992/312, 21 May 54, same file, sec 65.

agreed upon between the belligerents. Pending the withdrawal of troops the dislocation of French troops in Vietnam shall be agreed upon, particular attention being paid to limit to the minimum the number of their dislocation points. Provision shall be made that the French troops should not interfere in the affairs of local administration in the areas of their dislocation.

3. Holding of free general elections in Vietnam, Chmer and Pathet Lao. Convening of advisory conferences of the representatives of the governments of both sides in Vietnam, Chmer and Pathet Lao, in each of the states separately and under conditions securing freedom of activity for patriotic parties, groups and social organizations in the preparation and the holding of free general elections to establish a unified government in each country; while interference from outside should not be permitted. Local commissions will be set up to supervise the preparation for and the carrying out of the elections.

Prior to the establishment of unified governments in each of the above-mentioned states, the governments of both sides will respectively carry out their administrative functions in the districts which will be under their administration after the settlement had been carried out in accordance with the agreement on the termination of hostilities.

4. The statement by the delegation of the Democratic Republic of Vietnam on the readiness of the government of the Democratic Republic of Vietnam to examine the question of the entry of the Democratic Republic of Vietnam into the French Union in conformity with the principle of free will and on the conditions of this entry. Corresponding statements should be made by the governments of Chmer and Pathet Lao.

5. The recognition by the Democratic Republic of Vietnam as well as by Chmer and Pathet Lao of the economic and cultural interests of France existing in these countries.

After the establishment of unified governments in Vietnam, Chmer, Pathet Lao the economic and cultural relations of these states with France should be subject to the settlement in conformity with the principles of equality and mutual interests. Pending the establishment of the unified governments in the three states the economic and cultural relations of Indochina with France will temporarily remain without a change such as they exist now. However in the areas where communications and trade ties have been broken off they can be reestablished on the basis of understanding between both sides.

The citizens of both sides will enjoy the privileged status to be determined later, in matters pertaining to domicile, movement and business activities on the territory of the other side.

6. The belligerent sides undertake not to prosecute persons who collaborated with the other side during the war.

7. Carrying out mutual exchange of prisoners of war.

8. Implementation of measures referred to in paragraphs 1-7, should be preceded by the cessation of hostilities in Indochina and by the conclusion to this end of appropriate agreements between France and each of the three states which should provide for:

a. Complete and simultaneous cease-fire throughout the whole of the Indochina territory by all armed forces of the belligerent sides:

Ground, naval and air. Both sides in each of the three states of Indochina for the purpose of strengthening the armistice will carry out a necessary settlement of territories and of the areas occupied by them, and it should also be provided that both sides should not hinder each other during the passage, for the purpose of the above mentioned settlement, by the troops of the other side over the territory occupied by the other side.

    b. Complete termination of transportation into Indochina from abroad of new ground, naval and air units or personnel, or any kind of arms and ammunition;

    c. To set up control over the implementation of the terms of agreement on the cessation of hostilities and to establish for this purpose in each of the three states mixed commissions composed of the representatives of the belligerent sides.96

When asked by reporters whether the Viet Minh armistice proposal was acceptable to the United States, Mr. Dulles replied that it was certainly unacceptable in its totality. It followed the same pattern applied in the past to Germany, Austria, and Korea; namely, to compel withdrawal of the forces that sustain free society and to set up a system under which the Communists can grab the whole area.97

To Under Secretary Smith, it seemed that the proposals would result in a rapid turnover to the Communists. Linking of the cease-fire to the other measures was tantamount to rejecting the French proposal, yet because the Viet Minh proposal mentioned conclusion of an agreement on general political questions prior to cessation of hostilities, there could not be an accusation of a demand for immediate cease-fire with no conditions. There was no provision for international control. Elections "without interference" followed the pattern in Korea. The proposals were also cunningly designed to appeal to the French public. The not unfriendly references to the French Union and arrangements for retention of French economic and cultural interests were obviously designed to win French support. There was reason to believe that the Communists might seriously envisage a Communist state within the French Union. It would probably benefit the French as much as the Poles and Czechs benefited from the Soviet accords respecting their cultural and economic interests.

---

    96. (U) Msg, Smith SECTO 162 to SecState, 110525Z May 54. DA-IN-894542 (11 May).
    97. (U) "U. S. Policy in Southeast Asia," news conference statements by Dulles, press releases 241, 244, 245, 11 May 54, State Dept, Bulletin, 24 May 54, pp 781-782.

The entire proposal made it clear that the DRV would determine the question of association with the French Union and would presumably handle other pertinent problems. It was also logical and obvious that the Viet Minh would organize the elections and win them quickly. In any event, it would gradually convert Viet Nam into a Communist state.[98]

Viet Nam, Cambodia and Laos all tabled armistice proposals of their own, to which very little serious attention was paid. The Vietnamese proposed, in effect, that the Viet Minh dissolve their government and army under terms of a general amnesty. Later, Viet Minh soldiers could be integrated into the Vietnamese army, and internationally supervised elections, at an unspecified date in the future, would solve the political questions. The Vietnamese were certainly aware their terms were unacceptable but they were concerned primarily with avoiding loss of territory or any settlement endangering their position as the legal and effective government of Viet Nam. The French objective, on the other hand, was to terminate hostilities with more or less satisfactory guarantees, because of the depth of their military involvement.[99]

Knowledge of the serious military situation in the Delta was just becoming public about the time the Viet Minh offered its proposal. The political situation in the French Cabinet and particularly in Parliment was deteriorating rapidly. There was an increasing desire for peace at any price. The American Ambassador felt that pressure to accept the Viet Minh terms as a basis for negotiation would be irresistible unless some new element entered the picture. It was just at this time, it will be recalled, that the United States insisted upon the right of the Associated States to withdraw from the French Union. The Ambassador was not sure that public retraction of this condition by the United States would stop Parliament from forcing the French Government to accept the

---

98. (S) Msg, Smith SECTO 174 to SecState, 120830Z May 54, DA-IN-57672 (12 May).
99. (U) Msg, Smith SECTO 190 to SecState, 130530Z May 54, DA-IN-895604 (12 May); (S) Msg, Smith SECTO 163 to SecState, 111030Z May 54, DA-IN-57368 (11 May; (S) Msg, Smith SECTO 197 to SecState, 132350Z May 54, DA-IN-58186 (14 May).

Viet Minh terms, but he did think that retraction would greatly help to clarify America's position to the French public and, presumably, to the rest of the world.100

There was really little that could help the Laniel Government. Improved prospects for EDC in this period so stirred up the opposition that it made a concerted effort to overthrow Laniel, using Indochina as a pretext.101 The Government fell on 12 June. The decline of its Radical Socialist support, while also indicating a long-term trend to the left, was due to a grass-roots feeling that more must be done to finish the war. De Gaullist opposition was largely motivated by EDC, plus general opposition tactics and a desire to punish the Government for weakness regarding Indochina. The Ambassador pointed out that the successor Government, no matter what it said, and although Bidault might remain as Foreign Minister, would be under implicit instruction to end the war, even at the cost of major concessions. As far as Geneva was concerned, said the Ambassador, the French bargaining position was so weak, and recently had become still weaker as the United States grew more reluctant to intervene in Indochina, that the fall of the Government actually would not make much difference.102

Pierre Mendes-France accepted the premiership under a four-week "contract" to bring about an honorable settlement of the Indochinese war. In spite of repeated assertions that he would not in any event accept a peace that was a surrender to the Viet Minh, nor even accept a disguised capitulation, Mendes-France was, from the start, identified with peace-at-any-price.

The change in government, for which the United States must bear some of the responsibility, if only through its failure to support sufficiently the previous one, cannot be regarded as advantageous to the United States. Although not advocating outright capitulation, it was a foregone conclusion

---
100. (TS) Msg, Dillon to SecState, 13 May 54.
101. (S) Msg, Dillon 4735 to SecState, 5 Jun 54.
102. (C) Msg, Dillon 4833 to SecState, 14 Jun 54.

that the new Government would not take as strong a stand at Geneva as had Bidault up to that time. Moreover, the new government was opposed to ex-High Commissioner de Jean's coming to Geneva as an advisor. De Jean's removal in Indochina was depicted by Charge McClintock as a serious blow to the furtherance of U.S. policy in that area. "Not only has he been the most courageous French official here," said McClintock, "but also the only one with a clear-eyed view of what stakes we are fighting for, not only in Southeast Asia but likewise in Europe against international Communism." The new Minister of Associated States was reported to be entirely new to the problem. Mendes-France himself was poorly informed. Finally, the composition of the new Cabinet showed an even more far-reaching break in continuity of French governments since the war than had been expected. It had deprived itself to a great extent of the "continuity men", such as Bidault, Pleven, Marie, etc. Some of the new Ministers, such as Koenig, in Defense, boded trouble for the United States. Koenig was expected to open wide the pressure-valve of army opposition to EDC upon which Pleven had been sitting.[103]

However, it has already been observed that there was little that any French government could do at Geneva. It quickly became evident that, in working out the details of cease-fire and regroupment of forces, the negotiators were edging closer and closer toward an inevitable partitioning of Viet Nam. It was also clear that even though the Viet Minh relaxed enough to pay lip service to international supervision of the armistice, the French were in no position to secure a set of controls that would guarantee the effectiveness of such supervision.

---

103. (S) Msg, Johnson SECTO 498 to SecState, 21 Jun 54; (C) Msg, Dillon 4972 to SecState, 21 Jun 54 DA-IN-67069 (22 Jun); (TS) Msg, Johnson SECTO 534 to SecState, 26 Jun 54; (TS) Msg, McClintock 2676 to SecState, 6 Jun 54; (C) Msg, Dillon 4909 to SecState, 18 Jun 54.

Final US Position toward Settlement

On 26 June the United States and the United Kingdom received the following aide-memoire from the French Government:

> . . . Following his conversation with Mr. Chou En-Lai, the head of the French Government has instructed M. Chauvel to approach M. Phan Van Dong with a view to carrying on with him directly negotiations to ascertain whether a basis can be found, in his opinion, for a territorial settlement in Vietnam or not.
>
> The objective of the French Government is to arrive at a regrouping which will assure the State of Vietnam a territory as solid as possible. . . .
>
> It is difficult to predict the result of this negotiation in which the French authorities must face two sorts of difficulties: on the one hand it will be most difficult to obtain concessions from the Viet Minh in the north; and on the other hand the negotiations risk causing, if the agreement is concluded, dangerous reactions by the Vietnamese Government whose citizens are serving at the present time under the orders of the French command, comprising a major portion thereof.

The message continued by noting that the Communists undoubtedly were afraid of the conflict spreading. The French Government, therefore, felt it would be very useful if the British and American Governments, who were at that time conducting talks in Washington, were to issue a final communique from the talks, in which they stated that a serious aggravation of international relations would result, if it were not possible to reach a reasonable settlement at Geneva. The French also strongly hoped they could count on the United States to counsel wisdom and self-control to the Vietnamese, to dissuade them from refusing an agreement. Conversely, the United States was begged not to do anything that might even implicitly encourage a Vietnamese outburst.[104]

---

104. (TS) Msg, Dulles 4852 to Amb (Paris), 28 Jun 54.

The British and American Governments drafted an answer to the aide-memoire in the hope of stiffening the French position. The two governments informed the French that they would be willing to respect an <u>agreement</u> that:

1. preserves the integrity and independence of Laos and Cambodia and assures the withdrawal of Vietminh forces therefrom;

2. preserves at least the southern half of Vietnam, and if possible an enclave in the Delta; in this connection we would be unwilling to see the line of division of responsibility drawn further south than a line running generally west from Dong Hoi;

3. does not impose on Laos, Cambodia or retained Vietnam any restrictions materially impairing their capacity to maintain stable non-Communist regimes; and especially restrictions impairing their right to maintain adequate forces for internal security, to import arms and to employ foreign advisers;

4. does not contain political provisions which would risk loss of the retained area to Communist control;

5. does not exclude the possibility of the ultimate unification of Vietnam by peaceful means;

6. provides for the peaceful and humane transfer, under international supervision, of those people desiring to be moved from one zone to another of Vietnam; and

7. provides effective machinery for international supervision of the agreement.[105]

Besides pointing out that the fourth and fifth paragraphs of the joint statement seemed to contradict each other, the French inquired about the meaning of "respect" which struck them as a very weak and unclear word.[106]

---

105. (S) Msg, Dulles 4853 to Amb (Paris), 28 Jun 54.
106. (S) Msg, Dillon 50 to SecState, 6 Jul 54.

Secretary Dulles explained that the United States realized that even an agreement seeming to meet all seven points could not guarantee that Indochina would not one day pass into Communist hands. The apparent contradiction was merely an attempt to get the best conditions under the circumstances. He further explained that "respecting" the agreement meant that the United States would not oppose a settlement that conformed to the seven points. It did not, of course, mean that the settlement would be guaranteed or necessarily supported in public. "Respect" also meant that the United States would not seek directly or indirectly to upset the settlement by force.[107] Mr. Dulles hastened to add that M. Mendes-France should be under no illusion that observance of the seven points would in itself suffice to elicit a public statement by the United States that it would respect the agreement, unless the Associated States had assented to the settlement.[108]

In a personal message to M. Mendes-France, Secretary Dulles himself gave an excellent analysis of the United States position, and of the Geneva Conference as a whole, up to that time:

> . . . We doubt very much that the Communists will in fact accept this seven-point position unless they realize that the alternative is some common action upon which we have all agreed. So far, there is no such alternative.
> Under these circumstances, we greatly fear that the seven-points which constitute a minimum as far as the US is concerned will constitute merely an optimum solution so far as your Government and perhaps the UK are concerned, and that an armistice might be concluded on terms substantially less favorable than those we could respect.
> We gather that there is already considerable French thinking in terms of the acceptability of departures from certain of the seven-points. For example: Allowing Communist forces to remain in

---

107. (S) Msg, Dulles 77 to Amb (Paris), 7 Jul 54.
108. (S) Msg, Dulles to Amb (Paris), no. unk, 8 Jul 54.

Northern Laos; accepting a Vietnam line of military demarcation considerably south of Donghoi; neutralizing and demilitarizing Laos, Cambodia and Vietnam so as to impair their capacity to maintain stable, non-Communist regimes; accepting elections so early and so ill-prepared and ill supervised as to risk the loss of the entire area to Communism; accepting international supervision by a body which cannot be effective because it includes a Communist state which has veto power.
    These are but illustrations of a whittling-away process, each stroke of which may in itself seem unessential, but which cumulatively could produce a result quite different from that envisaged by the seven-points. . . .[109]

The possibility of complete United States disassociation from the final stages of the conference so deeply disturbed M. Mendes-France that Secretary Dulles found it expedient to confer with him personally in Paris on 13 July. The most immediate problem for the French Premier was the refusal of the United States to renew its representation at the conference on the ministerial level. The five Foreign Ministers recessed on 19 June, leaving the working out of armistice details to the military negotiators. The American delegation was reduced in size and concept, and reverted to an advisory or observer role. Its basic instructions were withdrawn and it proceeded to function on an ad hoc basis, in order to be more responsive to "realities as we see them, not only at Geneva but also in US and Indochina."[110]

M. Mendes-France pointed out that this would be the first time since the war that the United States had not been represented at a level equal to that of other powers at an important conference. He felt certain it would have catastrophic effects in the Far East and Europe. There would be no one to take a strong personal position with Molotov.

---

109. (TS) Msg, Dulles 127 to Amb (Paris), 10 Jul 54.
110. (TS) Msg, SecState, TOSEC 480 to AmCon (Geneva), 25 Jun 54.

The Communists would surely increase their pressure to deepen the obvious rift between the Western powers, whereas, with the Secretary present, the United States would in effect have a veto power on the decisions of the conference.[111]

In spite of the Premier's arguments, Mr. Dulles was more impressed by the probably disastrous effect of a sudden and dramatic severance from the conference at the last moment. Nevertheless, after consultation with President Eisenhower, he went to Paris to thrash the matter out with M. Mendes-France. From their meeting came an agreed Franco-American position on Indochina:

    1. France and the Associated States of Vietnam, Laos and Cambodia are recognized to be those which, on the non-Communist side, are primarily interested in the Indochina phase of the Geneva Conference. The United States is interested primarily as a friendly nation which desires to assist, when desired, in arriving at a just settlement, but who will not seek, or be expected, to impose its views in any way upon those primarily interested.

    2. The attached seven-points constitute a result which France believes to be obtainable by negotiation at Geneva and which would be acceptable to France and, France believes, to the Associated States. The United States, while recognizing the right of those primarily interested to accept different terms, will itself be prepared to respect terms conforming to the attached. The United States will not be asked or expected by France to respect terms which in its opinion differ materially from the attached and it may publicly disassociate itself from such differing terms.

    3. If the settlement is one which the United States is prepared to "respect," its position will be expressed unilaterally or in association only with non-Communist states in terms which apply to the situation the principles of non-use of forces which are embodied in Article 2 (4) & (6) of the Charter of the United Nations.

    4. The United States is prepared to seek, with other interested nations, a collective defense

---

111. (TS) Msg, Dillon 134 to SecState, 11 Jul 54.

association designed to preserve, against direct and indirect aggression, the integrity of the non-Communist areas of Southeast Asia following any settlement.

    5. If there is no settlement, the United States and French Governments will consult together on the measures to be taken. This will not preclude the United States, if it so desires, bringing the matter before the United Nations as involving a threat to peace as dealt with by Chapter VII of the Charter of the United Nations.

    6. France reaffirms the principle of independence for the Associated States in equal and voluntary association as members of the French Union.[112]

The seven points referred to were those of the joint British-American reply to the French aide-memoire, previously discussed. Following the issuance of the position paper, an exchange of letters took place between Mr. Dulles and M. Mendes-France, in the course of which the French Premier refuted the pro-abstention arguments. "In a situation as difficult as this," he wrote in part, "only the unity of the western diplomatic front, supported by the immense potential which we have in common, can bring about the very military and strategic unity which we should seek eventually to establish in that part of the world. It is in this spirit that the French Government envisages, aside from the assurances which the conference itself could furnish, the establishment of a collective guarantee by virtue of which the signatories would declare themselves prepared to intervene if, in Indochina, one of the three states was a victim of aggression."[113]

Whether or not, as he claimed, M. Mendes-France was responsible for changing Mr. Dulles' mind,[114] the decision

---

    112. (S) Agreed Fr-US position paper on IC, following mtg Sec Dulles and Mendes-France, included in (S) Msg, Dulles (Paris) 179, to SecState, 14 Jul 54.
    113. (S) Ltr, Mendes-France to Dulles, in (S) Msg, Dulles (Paris) 179, to SecState, 14 Jul 54; (S) Ltr, Dulles to Mendes-France, in (S) Msg, Dulles (Paris) 179 to SecState.
    114. Speech of Mendes-France to Nat Assem, 22 Jul 54, in *Journal Officiel, Assem Nat*, p. 3536.

to resume participation at the ministerial level was taken, following talks with Britain's Anthony Eden and consultation with President Eisenhower. Under Secretary of State Smith left for Geneva on 16 July.

The United States performed another service requested by France in the 28 June aide-memoire. Ambassador Heath, in Saigon, was instructed to inform the Vietnamese Premier, Diem, of the probability of a compromise at Geneva that would slice his country in half. It was Ambassador Heath's unhappy task to make Diem see the futility of resisting the settlement. He was to tell the Premier that President Eisenhower and Mr. Dulles, in conference with Prime Minister Churchill and Mr. Eden, had made clear their strong opposition to any settlement that might be made on terms leading to permanent division of his country. The Ambassador was also to advise Diem of the seven-point British-American note to France. Finally, still speaking in Mr. Dulles' name, he was to state that "while we recognize that settlement along these lines imposes hardships on Vietnam, we fear that deteriorating military situation and separate negotiations in progress with Vietminh and Chinese Communists could lead to something still worse."[115] The intent of this demarche was not entirely altruistic. The United States had established the fact that the French were not keeping the Vietnamese adequately informed. Beside trying to avert a violent reaction by the bitterly disappointed Vietnamese, the United States wished to place its relations with Diem on a more realistic and confidential basis, if it were later to play a more useful role in Viet Nam.[116]

The 26 June aide-memoire from the French had also asked that the final communique from the British-American conversations in Washington contain a statement to the effect that the issuing governments would take a serious view of unacceptable Communist demands at Geneva. President Eisenhower and Sir Winston Churchill who headed the British delegation,

---

115. (S) Msg, SecState TOSEC 529, to AmCon (Geneva), 10 Jul 54.
116. Ibid.

obliged by inserting, at the end of the press release covering their discussions, a statement that, "We are both convinced that if at Geneva the French Government is confronted with demands which prevent an acceptable agreement regarding Indochina, the international situation will be seriously aggravated."[117]

Anglo-American Discussions

The Anglo-American discussions were carried on in Washington from 25 to 29 June by President Eisenhower, Mr. Dulles, Sir Winston, and Mr. Eden. There was no formal agenda but among the topics covered was that of Indochina and the Geneva Conference. Sir Winston had indicated previously his preoccupation with the need to establish a firm front in Southeast Asia. He favored a Southeast Asia Treaty Organization and a Middle East Treaty Organization to match NATO.[118] The Americans were less convinced that the answer, at least for the time being, was a NATO-type entente. Diversity of opinion did not stop here. It appears that the main reason for these extraordinarily high-level talks was that divergence between American and British basic policies in a number of spheres was reaching serious proportions. Certainly the concept of regional grouping, and attitude toward acceptable conditions at Geneva were two such areas. Moreover, the French were not the only ones to be bewildered by America's schizo-diplomatia. "Sometimes it is awfully difficult," said Mr. Attlee, "to understand what the American line is, as between what members of the Government say and what Senators say, and sometimes what generals and admirals say."[119] In spite of bland assurance of solidarity and "intimate comradeship," the 29 June declaration issued by the White House gives no real indication of how much true mutual understanding had been achieved.

---

117. Eisenhower & Churchill, "Anglo-American Discussions on International Situation," WH press release of 28 Jun 54, State Dept, Bulletin, 12 Jul 54, p. 49.
118. (TS) Notes of JCS-State Mtg, 25 Jun 54.
119. (C) Msg, Butterworth (London) 5939, to SecState, 24 Jun 54.

As a follow-up to the Eisenhower-Churchill meeting, a United States-United Kingdom Study Group on Southeast Asia was established. Three sessions had been held by 16 July and some of the main lines of thought were beginning to emerge. The British view was that a collective security arrangement for Southeast Asia should be considered in two contexts: (1) on the basis of a settlement in Indochina, and (2) on the basis of no settlement. In the event of a settlement that posed no immediate military problem, the British preferred a generalized arrangement, designed to bring in as many states as possible, including the Colombo powers. On the other hand, if there were no settlement at Geneva, the British agreed to the immediate establishment of an organization to meet the military threat. This organization, presumably, was to be limited to the powers making military commitments.

One thing was clear: the British had no intention of pressing forward with any kind of security organization until the Indochina phase of the Geneva Conference had terminated. The United Kingdom considered that the principal problem in dealing with Southeast Asia after an Indochinese settlement would be large-scale economic assistance. Although there was no discussion of support for this program, there was little doubt who the chief contributor would be.

On a number of occasions, the British representative referred to military force to repel overt Communist aggression, but his attitude about countering subversion and infiltration remained vague. The Americans pointed out that the principal danger in the future would probably come about through infiltration and subversion, and that the security organization should be in a position to deal with the situation effectively. Also, the organization should be established immediately, to deal with the probable adverse military and political repercussions of an unsatisfactory settlement at Geneva.[120] Even if a pact were signed within a month or so, there would be a time-lag of six to twelve months for ratification by the various

---

120. (TS) JCS 1992/358, 16 Jul 54, CCS 092 Asia (6-25-48) sec 75.

countries. There had, therefore, to be some kind of interim machinery.

The Americans felt that it was too early to set up machinery like NATO, because it was not yet known whether a NATO-type organization was what was wanted. Instead, they were toying with the idea of an interim council. By making the American Ambassador the U.S. representative, and supplementing his staff with political and military advisers, day-to-day business could be conducted without large, and possibly unnecessary, staffs. The biggest problem still remained that of deciding upon the nature of the basic treaty organization.

General Bedell Smith, echoing the Joint Chiefs of Staff position, argued strongly for viewing the matter in the light of the whole Far East, and not just Southeast Asia. Any organization sponsored by the United States should make room for the inclusion of Japan, the Philippines, and other Asian allies of America. As long as she remained "neutral" and, to a large extent unpredictable, United States military men were leery of including India. They feared, and probably with much reason, that India would wreck more military plans than ever she abetted. Indian obstructionism could be especially effective in the type of organization the British favored, composed of three elements: a council including all participants; an economic and political council, with as many members as possible; and a military organization. Luckily, India would unquestionably not wish to participate in the military aspects, per se, but would still be able to do much harm in the other councils.[121]

---

121. (TS) Notes of JCS-State Mtg, 23 Jul 54, (TS JCS 1992/358, 16 Jul 54, CCS 092 Asia (6-25-48) sec 75; (TS) Notes of JCS-SD Mtg, 9 Jul 54. (TS) Ann 15, "Policy with Respect to the Colombo Powers," to Memo, CSUSA, "JCS Positions in Connection with the Meeting between President Eisenhower & Prime Minister Churchill," CCS 337 (7-23-48) sec 5.

A side issue of note on the military organization was that the British were reported to be thinking of proposing that the entire command structure in the Pacific, including Southeast Asia, be American. In return, however, they would suggest complete British control in the east Atlantic, including IBERLANT; unqualified assignment of U.S. fleet strike forces to CINCEASTLANT; the assignment of Strike Force South to CINCAFMED; and probably, in due time, the appointment of a British officer as SACLANT. From the United States point of view, there would be certain disadvantages to such an arrangement.[122]

When the Colombo powers were sounded out by the British on their attitude toward the proposed organization, Indonesia replied that its position was one of strict neutrality. Burma also protested neutrality, but let it be known that she was not adverse to the idea. Ceylon took a very similar stand. The Indian attitude was assumed to be negative, but it was thought that if the others took a reasonable approach with time, India might not care to be left in an isolated position.

Although the Joint Chiefs of Staff had pressed hard, for a long time, for some type of Southeast Asian security organization that could be tied in with other Far Eastern alliances with the United States, it was the military who sounded a note of caution just after the signing of the Geneva settlement. The situation had now changed radically. In April, it had been assumed that the power of Viet Nam would be a factor. But as the situation was developing, it appeared that there was much talk of a military defensive arrangement where there were no military forces to speak of. Except for the British police in Malaya, and negligible Thai and Burmese forces, the only military power available was in Korea and Formosa. The cost of developing military might in the area would be tremendous.

It was one thing to make promises, and quite another to carry them out. Consequently, the armed forces wished to subject the undertaking to very close scrutiny to make sure that a great mistake was not being made. With limited

---

122. (TS) Memo, CNO to CJCS, 8 May 54.

funds for defense and MDAP programs, commitment of huge sums of money in Southeast Asia would mean cutting somewhere else, without generating any real strength. Thailand, for example, had produced a plan for an 81,000-man force which would cost the United States 400 million dollars. Adequate for internal security, this force would contribute nothing to real mutual defense. The Burmese had a similar plan. Led along to think in these terms, Asian peoples would only end up disappointed and the United States would have enemies instead of friends. Military aggression would not be counteracted by the United States in Thailand; it would be cut off at the roots, in China, to the north. Aid and materiel poured into Thailand would only weaken the places where the United States might actually have to fight.

For this reason, consideration had to be given to the type of defense the countries of Southeast Asia would be asked to engage themselves to. A NATO-type of defense was out of the question; each country could not be guaranteed one hundred per cent protection. Moreover, that would require building up the armed forces of each country in the area, a task of staggering proportions and of dubious military value. As it was, military aid programs were bleeding the United States heavily. Turkey received 100 million dollars; the Thais, 25 million dollars; the Philippines were asking for six destroyers and five wings of jets; and so it went on. The aid programs were beginning to get out of hand.[123]

One of the worst features of aiding weak or indefensible nations was the very great possibility of ending up aiding the enemy instead. Indochina itself was an excellent case in point. In April, the Joint Chiefs of Staff, anticipating an unsatisfactory settlement at Geneva, advised the National Security Council that shipments of military materiel should be suspended if fighting halted before a controlled armistice could be put into effect. They also suggested that an attempt should be made to

---

123. (TS) Notes of JCS-SD Mtg, 23 Jul 54.

recover or destroy equipment already in Indochina.[124] They followed up this suggestion by pointing out that the United States would be justified, despite the fact that the French legally held title to the equipment, in insisting upon its return if no longer employed in the defense of Indochina. They recommended, however, that in the event of partition, units suited to guerrilla operations should not be disarmed.[125] CINCPAC was directed to prepare plans for salvaging or destroying American materiel. He, in turn, assigned the responsibility for these operations to MAAG Indochina.[126]

When the diplomats at Geneva formally agreed on 21 July to partition Viet Nam, the Defense Department immediately suspended all shipments of materiel to Indochina, and diverted all shipments en route to Indochina to Japan and Title III countries.[127] Although within two days France gave her assurance that American equipment would be evacuated to South Viet Nam, CINCPAC and MAAG continued to collaborate on measures to safeguard the materiel. At the instigation of the State Department, however, MAAG was directed not to press plans for recovery and destruction until France had been given sufficient time to determine her course of action in Indochina.[128] Since the French were already engaged in evacuating equipment and personnel from the Hanoi area to South Viet Nam, American concern was primarily confined to U.S. Air Force personnel and B-26 and C-119 aircraft on loan to the French Air Force.

---

124. (TS) JCS 1992/301, 28 Apr 54 /as amended by Dec On, 30 Apr 54/, CCS 092 Asia (6-25-48) sec 64; (TS) JCS 1992/302, 29 Apr 54, same file; (TS) Note to Holder of JCS 1992/301, 17 May 54, same file.
125. (TS) JCS 1992/336, 8 Jun 54 /as amended by Dec on, 16 Jun 54/, same file, sec 71.
126. (TS) Msg, JCS 963958 to CINCPAC, 021338Z Jul 54, same file, sec 74; (TS) Msg, AMINO, CINCPAC 6871 to MATS Andrews AFB, COMSTS, CINCFE, 070255Z Jul 54, same file.
127. (C) Msg, Dulles 261 to AmAmb (Paris), 21 Jul 54.
128. (S) Encl, Memo, Asst SecDef, ISA to USecys Army, Navy, AF, "Suspension of Shipments of Military Aid to Indochina," 2 Aug 54, to (S) JCS 1992/373, 6 Aug 54, CCS 092 Asia (6-25-48) sec 77A.

The Commander, Far East Air Force, had been concerned throughout the spring and summer for the safety of the American Air Force mechanics in Indochina. Early in July he stated that the French C-47 capability was sufficient to meet operational requirements and recommended that the sixteen C-119's and supporting personnel be withdrawn by 10 July. General O'Daniel opposed this suggestion, and instead recommended that half of the C-119's and Air Force mechanics be withdrawn on 10 July and the remainder at a later date. The Joint Chiefs of Staff supported General O'Daniel's viewpoint, and eight C-119's with maintenance support crews were retained in Indochina.[129]

The American desire to withdraw the cargo planes on loan irritated General Ely, who protested that C-119's were needed more than ever in view of the redeployment from the Delta to South Viet Nam. General O'Daniel reported that General Ely interpreted the United States action as an expression of displeasure with French agreement to a cease-fire. General Ely remarked that France was not alone in suffering reverses, as the United States knew from its own experiences in China and Korea. To dispel this impression, General O'Daniel advised that the B-26's be withdrawn on 11 August and the C-119's within thirty days thereafter. This would permit the French to retain the use of the planes during the peak of the redeployment.[130] The Joint Chiefs considered the question on 6 August, and as a result COMFEAF was directed to withdraw the B-26's on 11 August and the remaining C-119's on 1 September. The American maintenance personnel were to be withdrawn as no longer needed to support the aircraft.[131]

Subsequent to Geneva, the United States adopted an interim policy on aid to the Associated States and to the French in Indochina. Pending further examination of the

---

129. (S) JCS 1992/352, 7 Jul 54, same file, sec 74.
130. (TS) Msg, Ch MAAG Indochina MG 2079A to CINCPAC, 200835Z Jul 54, DA-IN-75488, same file, sec 76.
131. (TS) JCS 1992/337, 6 Aug 54, same file, sec 77A.

problem, only common-use items directly alleviating suffering, preventing disease, and assisting in the evacuation of military forces and refugees from north Viet Nam were to be programmed for Indochina. Each case was to be considered individually, as it arose, on its own merits.[132]

It was the American intention to use as much as possible of the materiel rescued from northern Viet Nam to help equip the native forces of the Associated States. This disposition of the equipment was in line with the idea that the non-Communist nations in the area would have to build up their own forces for internal security, while leaving the main fighting to the United States and its more powerful allies. Corollary to that idea was, of course, the conception that the significant fighting would take place elsewhere. If at all possible, United States strategists wished to avoid becoming involved deeply in the militarily unimportant area of Southeast Asia. Hence, they tended to oppose the British, who, for economic and political reasons, preferred a NATO-type of security organization, with its implications of limited area defense. Viewed realistically, as undoubtedly the British did view it, such an organization was greatly to their benefit, provided they could induce the United States to pay for it. By late July they had not yet succeeded in doing so, either through the Eisenhower-Churchill conversations nor the subsequent U.S.-U.K. Study Group.

US Unilateral Declaration on Geneva

Although there was still much ground to cover in smoothing out the difficulties standing in the way of a security organization the Study Group accomplished its second purpose more quickly. It had been charged also with preparing recommendations on "the terms on which our two countries /Great Britain and the United States/ might be willing to be associated with an agreement which might be reached in Geneva."[133] In non-diplomatic language, the task of the

---

132. (S) Memo, AsstSecDef, ISA to USecys Army, Navy, AF, "Suspension of Shipments of Military Aid to Indochina," 2 Aug 54, Encl to (S) JCS 1992/373, 6 Aug 54, CCS 092 Asia (6-25-48) sec 77A.
133. (S) Msg, Dulles 125 to Paris, Geneva 530, 10 Jul 54.

Study Group was to find a satisfactory solution to the vexing question of a declaration in the event of a settlement. It has already been pointed out that the policy of Great Britain was much more flexible than that of the United States in this respect. Although both countries had subscribed to the seven criteria for an acceptable settlement, the United Kingdom had all along been willing to associate itself with terms falling considerably short of the ideal established by the criteria. Moreover, Great Britain preferred a multilateral declaration including Australia, New Zealand, and, if possible, India and other interested nations in the area. Nor did Britain exclude the possibility of the declaration's bearing Communist signatures. The United States made it plain that it would not participate in any declaration that included Communist China, and that it would not compromise with the seven-point statement.[134] President Eisenhower accordingly announced publicly that the United States had not itself been a party to, nor was bound by, the decisions taken by the conference, and that the United States was, therefore, issuing a statement to the effect that it was not prepared to join in the conference declaration.[135] Instead, the following unilateral declaration was presented by Under Secretary Smith to the last plenary session of the conference on 21 July:

> The Government of the United States being resolved to devote its efforts to the strengthening of peace in accordance with the principles and purposes of the United Nations takes note of the agreements concluded at Geneva on July 20 and 21, 1954 between (a) the Franco-Laotian Command and the Command of the Peoples Army of Viet-Nam; (b) the Royal Khmer Army Command and the Command of the Peoples Army of Viet-Nam; (c) Franco-Vietnamese Command and the Command of the Peoples Army of Viet-Nam and of paragraphs 1 to 12 inclusive of the declaration presented to the Geneva Conference on

---
134. (TS) JCS 1992/358, 16 Jul 54, CCS 092 Asia (6-25-48) sec 75.
135. Statement by President, WH Press Release, 21 Jul 54, State Dept, Bulletin, 2 Aug 54, p. 163.

July 21, 1954 declares with regard to the aforesaid agreements and paragraphs that (i) it will refrain from the threat or the use of force to disturb them, in accordance with Article 2 (4) of the Charter of the United Nations dealing with the obligation of members to refrain in their international relations from the threat or use of force; and (ii) it would view any renewal of the aggression in violation of the aforesaid agreements with grave concern and as seriously threatening international peace and security.

In connection with the statement in the declaration concerning free elections in Viet-Nam my Government wishes to make clear its position which it has expressed in a declaration made in Washington on June 29, 1954, as follows:

'In the case of nations now divided against their will, we shall continue to seek to achieve unity through free elections supervised by the United Nations to insure that they are conducted fairly.'

With respect to the statement made by the representative of the State of Viet-Nam, the United States reiterates its traditional position that peoples are entitled to determine their own future and that it will not join in an arrangement which would hinder this. Nothing in its declaration just made is intended to or does indicate any departure from this traditional position.

We share the hope that the agreements will permit Cambodia, Laos and Viet-Nam to play their part, in full independence and sovereignty, in the peaceful community of nations, and will enable the peoples of that area to determine their own future.[136]

Secretary Dulles, in a statement two days after the conference, did not let the French go unscathed. Without naming names, he maintained that one of the lessons of Geneva was that resistance to Communism needs popular support, and that this in turn meant the people should feel they are defending their own national institutions.

---

136. "U.S. Declaration on Indochina," USecState W. B. Smith, 21 Jul 54, State Dept, Bulletin, 2 Aug 54, pp. 162-163.

One of the good aspects of Geneva, claimed Mr. Dulles, was that it advanced the independent status of the Associated States. He had been assured by the President of France that French representatives in Viet Nam had been instructed to complete by 30 July precise projects for the transfer of authority that would give reality to the independence France had promised.[137]

Both Mr. Dulles and President Eisenhower had admitted that the Geneva settlement contained undesirable features. The President philosophically observed, however, that a great deal would depend upon how they worked out.[138] It was not long before the Planning Board produced an estimate of how they probably would work out, and what it would mean to the United States.

The board pointed out that, regardless of the fate of South Viet Nam, Laos and Cambodia, the Communists had secured possession of a salient in Viet Nam from which military and non-military pressures could be mounted against adjacent and more remote non-Communist areas. The board predicted that the loss of prestige in Asia suffered by the United States, as backer of France and the Bao Dai government, would raise further doubts about United States leadership and about the ability of the United States to check future Communist expansion in Asia. Also, United States prestige would inescapably be associated with subsequent developments in Southeast Asia. The Communists, on the other hand, had increased their military and political prestige, and with it, their capacity for extending Communist influence without resorting to armed attack. They were now in an even better position to exploit the economic and political instability of the free countries of Asia.

The Planning Board also brought out the fact that the Communists were in a better position for propaganda attacks on the United States. By having adopted an appearance of moderation

---

137. Statement by Secy Dulles, 23 Jul 54, Press Release 400, State Dept. Bulletin, 2 Aug 54, p. 163.
138. Statement by President, WH press release, 21 Jul 54, State Dept, Bulletin, 2 Aug 54, p. 163.

at Geneva, and by having taken credit for the cessation of hostilities in Indochina, they could exploit their political strategy of imputing to the United States motives of extremism, belligerency, and opposition to co-existence. The Communists thus had a basis for accentuating sharply their peace propaganda and peace program in Asia to allay fears of Communist expansionist policies. They now had a better opportunity to alienate the United States from its Asian friends and allies, while at the same time establishing for themselves closer ties with the free nations of Asia.

One very alarming feature of the loss of Southeast Asia, the board warned, was that it would imperil the retention of Japan as a key element of the off-shore island chain. In this connection High Commissioner de Jean, of Indochina, who had once been the French Ambassador to Tokyo, had predicted back in May that a Communist victory would so enhance the prestige of Communist China that the whole balance of power in the Pacific would be affected, and the Japanese policy would tend toward rapprochement with a new and powerful Peiping.[139]

The situation was serious, yet, in the words of the Department of Defense representative at Geneva, it was no better or no worse than could be expected "under existing circumstances wherein French unable and/or unwilling pursue war to military conclusion, and in light of United States decision apparently made some time ago that it would not intervene militarily to save Indochina from Communist encroachment. . . ."[140]

As Anthony Eden remarked in the House of Commons, "I think everyone will agree that the proceedings of this Conference have been of unparalleled complexity."[141] They were also of momentous long-range significance to the world at large.

---

139. (TS) NSC 5429, "Review of U.S. Policy in the Far East, 4 Aug 54, CCS 092 Asia (6-25-48) sec 77A; (S) Msg, McClintock 2356 to SecState, 12 May 54.
140. (TS) Msg, Lt. Col. J. E. Dwan to OSD, c. 21 Jul 54, quoted in (TS) Gerhart "Account," p. 71.
141. Statement by Eden before House of Commons, 22 Jul 54, U.S. News and World Report, 30 Jul 54, pp 88-89.

CONCLUSIONS

Why was it that a small and seemingly insignificant insurgent movement was able to defeat a major power of Western Europe? One obvious reason was the formidable fighting qualities of the Viet Minh soldier, combined with the ability and ruthlessness of his leadership. But a number of other factors played equal or more important parts in thwarting France's postwar ambitions in Indochina.

For example, it would be fair to say that France's gross mishandling of the political side of the conflict played directly into the hands of the communists. The French Government and its representatives in Vietnam never conceded to that country the political sovereignty upon which a viable national government could be based. Had the French at any time between 1946 and 1951 conferred upon a noncommunist Vietnamese Government the degree of independence contemplated in the treaty negotiations of early 1954, the outcome might have been entirely different. But any Vietnamese regime depended upon the sufferance and support of French colonial administrators could not satisfy the aspirations of Vietnamese nationalism. Political concessions came "too little and too late," and leadership of the independence movement passed into the hands of Ho Chi Minh and his communist colleagues.

An observer can hadly fail to be struck by the contrast between the colonial policies of France and of the United Kingdom after World War II. The one country sought to regain its postwar position, the other came to terms with rising nationalism. Even as French leaders were attempting to turn back the clock in Indochina, a neighboring British colony--Burma--assumed a position of full independence, departing the Empire with the blessing of Whitehall. Other imperial dependencies--notably India, once turbulent and rife with anti-British feelings--became partners in a commonwealth of sovereign equals.

The US role in the dispute between France and her Indochinese colonies blended sentimental and practical considerations. Their own history and tradition disposed Americans to a ready sympathy for Indochina's aspirations to independence; at the same time, US self-interest would be served by the creation of stable, democratic governments in Indochina, linked with France by ties of friendship and serving as a source of strength rather than a drain on French military and economic resources. Moreover, observing the Stalinist regimes in Eastern Europe and in North Korea, US policymakers saw no reason to believe that the peoples of Indochina would improve their lot if Marxist dictatorship were substituted for French colonial rule. These considerations guided the decisions of President Truman and of his successor, President Eisenhower.

It might be asserted that the United States could have sought its objectives in a more forceful manner. Such criticism amounts to stating that the United States should have made stronger efforts to induce France to grant political concessions that would have undermined the appeal of the communist movement in Vietnam. Several considerations led the United States Government to pull its punches, so to speak, in dealing with France. Extreme pressure might have led to the fall of any one of the shaky French Cabinets, besides possibly alienating French public opinion. Either effect would have seriously handicapped the attempt to build a coordinated Western European defense--a major objective of US foreign policy.

Another important factor in the Viet Minh victory in 1954 was the conquest of China by the communists under Mao Tse-Tung. The insurgents in Vietnam thus acquired a powerful base of support--an "inviolable sanctuary," such as has proved necessary for the success of most (though not all) guerrilla movements in modern times. Chinese assistance in materiel and training aided the conversion of guerrilla units into an army able to fight French regulars on equal terms. Moreover, the constant threat of overt Chinese intervention, though it never materialized, helped to paralyze the French high command.

Still another important element of defeat was the general weakness--political, economic, and military--of France after World War II. Unstable governments lacked the strength and self-confidence to make the concessions necessary to grant independence to the Associated States. The constant turnover of cabinets precluded long-range, well-considered planning for victory in Indochina. After committing itself to reconquest, the nation lacked the resources in men, money, and materiel that were necessary for victory. The inadequacy of France's military leadership--so glaringly evident in World War II--was demonstrated anew by the nation's inability to find aggressive and competent generals to conduct the war; the sole exception--General de Lattre--stands out conspicuously. Finally, the deterioration of public support for the war, becoming evident in 1952, assured the eventual outcome.

Beginning in 1950 the United States, through the MDAP, undertook to supply France with materiel resources that, it was hoped, would provide the margin of victory. The aid program for Indochina had to compete with those for other countries (especially Western Europe) and with the demands of the Korean War. Nevertheless the flow of US supplies contributed in no small degree to the success enjoyed by Franco-Vietnamese forces while de Lattre was in command. Thus by early 1952 the military situation in Indochina seemed favorable for a decisive stroke against the Viet Minh. But de Lattre was removed by an untimely death, and his successor, reverting to defensive warfare, forfeited whatever opportunity existed.

By the time the Eisenhower Administration came into office, the deterioration of the Indochina situation was obvious. Unless the military stalemate could be broken, growing French disgust for the war would force France to seek a settlement on almost any terms. For the first time, US intervention began to be seriously considered. The Joint Chiefs of Staff pressed for a decision on the matter, but for the moment, the Administration merely enlarged the scale of the aid program.

By the time of the Berlin Foreign Ministers' Conference in 1954, it was clear that the public demand for a peace settlement could no longer be resisted by the French Government. The United States still sought to induce France to carry the war to victory. But it was clear that undue pressure on France might alienate public opinion in that country and jeopardize the status of negotiations for the European Defense Community. Necessarily, therefore, the United States agreed to the convening of the Geneva Conference.

During the weeks that followed the Berlin meeting, the French political and military situation continued to deteriorate. Viet Minh forces, seeking to improve their bargaining position, opened an attack against the exposed French outpost of Dien Bien Phu, which had attained a symbolic importance out of all proportion to its military value. The fall of this bastion, on the eve of the discussion of Indochina at Geneva, was a shattering blow to France's diplomatic position.

The one remaining hope of retrieving the situation was through the use of US military forces in Indochina. This grave step was weighed both before the Geneva Conference and while it was in session, by the President and the National Security Council. President Eisenhower proceeded with great caution, making it clear that if any intervention were to take place, it must be based on a sound political foundation, including international support. When it became evident that this support would not be forthcoming, there was no choice for the United States but to acquiesce in the peace terms worked out at Geneva. Given these conditions, one can accept as final the judgment pronounced by General Walter Bedell Smith, that the results of the conference were "the best that we could possibly have obtained in the circumstances."

APPENDIX I

SUMMARY OF THE AID PROGRAM

Between the outbreak of the Indochinese war in 1946 and the close of the Geneva Conference in the summer of 1954 France spent a total of 7 billion dollars to prosecute the war. The American contribution to the French war effort, begun in the spring of 1950 with an allocation of 15 million dollars, had mounted to a total of 2.7 billion dollars by July 1954. Almost half of this amount was spent in Fiscal Year 1954 alone. After the Pau Conference in December 1950 the Associated States began providing financial support to the extent of their abilities, and by the end of the fighting had expended 250 million dollars. Thus the financial cost of the Indochinese war from 1946 to 1954 amounted to almost 10 billion dollars.[1]

Throughout the course of the war the United States had administered several types of aid programs that contributed directly or indirectly to combating the Viet Minh. The most important in terms of results was the program of military assistance. French Union Forces fighting in Indochina received under MDAP large quantities of military end-items, components and spare parts. The Defense Department programmed this material for Indochina, and the United States bore the cost not only of the equipment itself but also of delivery and distribution. The cumulative program for Fiscal Years 1950-1953 amounted to 773 million dollars. The Fiscal Year 1954 program, with its supplemental allocations necessitated by the Dien Bien Phu crisis, totalled 535 million dollars. Thus under the Fiscal Years 1950-1954 MDA Material Program an aggregate of 1.3 billion dollars was made available to the Defense Department to program equipment for Indochina.[2]

---

[1]. (TS) "Congressional Presentation FY 1955 Indochina MDA Material Program," sec, "Questions and Answers," Alden Files, OMA.
[2]. The summary figures used in this section are based primarily upon (TS) "Congressional Presentation FY 1955 Indochina MDA Material Program," sec, "Questions and Answers," Alden Files, OMA. Since the "Congressional Presentation"

Closely approaching the military assistance expenditure was the total of 1.29 billion dollars made available to France in financial support (Direct Forces Support Program). This program began with the grant of 200 million dollars made to France at Lisbon in February 1952, and hence it has generally been defined as Lisbon-type aid. The main vehicle for expenditure in financial support was the Offshore Procurement Program (OSP). By purchasing items in France for Indochina the United States helped alleviate the French dollar shortage, underwrote military expenditures that otherwise would have seriously damaged the French budget, and enabled France to meet her NATO obligations more readily. The United States appropriated 500 million dollars in Lisbon-type grants in Fiscal Years 1952-1953 and subsequently agreed to support the French budget to the extent of 785 million dollars in Fiscal Year 1954.

---

was prepared early in 1954, some of the figures for that year are only tentative; others are rounded off in such a manner that the cumulative effect is not in the interest of close accuracy. The sums given in the present study are computed from several sources but do not differ materially from the summary figures given in the Alden Files. Throughout the course of the aid story, the figures given by various sources reveal serious conflict. Great difficulty was encountered in attempting to reconcile these differing views to obtain an accurate year-by-year record of allocations, as distinct from general summaries. Other sources used in arriving at the totals in this study follow: (TS) Encl, Memo, SecDef to Secys Army, AF, Nav, "Adjustment of FY 1953 Programs for Indochina, Formosa, and France," 7 Mar 52, to (TS) JCS 2099/179, 11 Mar 52, CCS 092 (8-22-46) sec 70; (TS) NSC 148, 6 Apr 53, CCS 092 Asia (6-25-48) sec 40; (C) App, "Estimated Expenditures in Connection with U.S. Courses of Action in Southeast Asia," to (TS) NSC 5405, 16 Jan 54, same file, sec 55; (C) JCS 2099/369, 21 Apr 54, CCS 092 (8-22-46) sec 110; (S) GI D-30a, "Geneva Conference, April 1954, Indochinese Phase - Background Paper, Summary of US Aid Program for Indochina," 25 Mar 54 CCS 092 Asia (6-25-48) sec 60.

The Fiscal Year 1954 program, however, was interrupted by the Geneva settlement. Processing of OSP contracts was suspended in August until the problem could be re-examined. At this point 200 million dollars had already been covered by contract, 300 million dollars was in the pipeline, and an unencumbered balance of 285 million dollars remained.[3]

In 1953 the Military Support Program (MSP or Milsup) was initiated. Funds allocated to this account were used to provide so-called "common-use" items inadmissible under MDAP screening criteria. Examples of this kind were roads, transport facilities, communications centers, water supply systems, and machine tools that contributed directly to the war effort but could not be classified as military equipment. An initial sum of 30 million dollars was set aside for use in Fiscal Year 1953, and the total Fiscal Year 1953-1954 MSP expenditure amounted to 75 million dollars.

Under the Defense Support Program (DSP) almost the same purposes were accomplished. Funds appropriated for economic aid to the Associated States were administered under DSP, and in Fiscal Years 1951-1954 totalled 95 million dollars. Expenditure of DSP funds was supervised by MSA, and its successor FOA, through STEM in Indochina. DSP was designed to help stabilize the economies of the Associated States, but in so doing it assisted greatly in supporting the military effort. Examples of STEM projects were power developments, introduction of advanced agricultural techniques, and expansion and improvement of transportation networks.

The monetary contribution of the United States to the war against the Viet Minh over the four-year period aggregated 2.753 billion dollars and may be summarized as follows:

---

[3]. (S) Memo, MG G. C. Stewart, Dir OMA, to Radford, "Status of the $785 million FY 1954 Direct Forces Support Program for Indochina," 24 Sep 54.

Military Assistance	$1,308 million
Financial Support of French Budget	1,285 million
Military Support Program	75 million
Defense Support Program	95 million
Total Cost to U.S. of Indochina War	2,763 million

Perhaps a better conception of the magnitude of American help to France and the Associated States can be obtained from a survey of equipment actually delivered in the four years during which MDAP operated in Indochina. When the United States entered the picture in 1950 French Union Forces were indifferently armed with largely obsolescent World War II equipment. Long and hard usage in the humid climate of Indochina, together with improper and inadequate maintenance, had made much of this equipment nearly unserviceable. Between 1950 and 1954 the French and native troops were almost completely re-equipped with modern weapons and vehicles.

During this period French Union ground troops received under MDAP 1,280 tanks and combat vehicles, 30,887 motor transport vehicles, 361,522 small arms and machine guns, and 5,045 artillery pieces. Spare parts and maintenance apparatus for these items were likewise supplied. The United States also furnished a continuing supply of ammunition, and during the four-year period shipped over 500 million rounds of small arms ammunition, and over 10 million artillery shells. The French Navy received 438 vessels, mostly small patrol craft and landing ships, together with seventy naval aircraft. Two World War II aircraft carriers (CVL) were transferred to the French Navy for Indochina service. The French Air Force, flying a few worn-out World War II planes in 1950, was developed into a comparatively strong, modern Air Force. A total of 394 Hellcat fighters, B-26 bombers, and C-47 cargo planes were transported to the French Air Force in Indochina. By July 1954 over one and a half million measurement tons of military end-items had been dispatched to Indochina, not including aircraft and vessels delivered under their own power. Seventy-two per cent of the material was lifted by American commercial shipping.[4]

---

4. (S) MDAP Status Report for the Month of July 1954.

The Fiscal Years 1950-1952 programs alone provided equipment for three French infantry divisions, six Vietnamese divisions, four Laotian and five Cambodian infantry battalions. By the middle of 1952 the French Air Force had made important gains in the process of expansion and modernization. It already operated four fighter squadrons equipped with F8F and F6F naval fighter planes, two light bombardment squadrons flying B-26 bombers, and three squadrons of transport planes. The latter as yet had not been completely modernized, and consisted of mixed C-47 and German JU-52 transports.[5]

By the spring of 1954, however, the French Army in Indochina consisted of fifty infantry battalions, eighteen AAA battalions, and four armored battalions largely equipped by the United States. The new and growing Vietnamese native army had twenty-nine infantry battalions, twenty-seven light infantry battalions, and two AAA battalions almost entirely equipped through MDAP. The French Air Force now possessed 140 F8F fighters, fifty-five B-26 bombers, 106 C-47 cargo planes, and 164 MO500 light liaison planes for observation and medical evacuation, all furnished through American aid. The French naval air arm operated sixteen F8F fighters, twelve SB2C Helldivers, twenty-five Corsair fighters, eight Privateers for reconnaissance work, and nine Grumman Goose scout planes. Added to this were twenty-four C-119 cargo planes and twenty-five B-26 bombers loaned by the American Far East Air Force (FEAF) during the defense of Dien Bien Phu. Almost three hundred USAF maintenance personnel were temporarily assigned to Indochina to provide maintenance support for the C-119's, C-47's, and B-26's.[6]

---

5. (S) Memo for Rec, "Status of Major Items as of 31 December 1951 Based on Preliminary Data. Indo-China," nd (c. Feb 52), Indo-China 2a (1952), Alden Files, OMA; (TS) Encl, Ltr, Col J. S. Driscol, USAF, to LTG L. C. Craigie, DCS/D, USAF, 9 Oct 52, same file.
6. (TS) Encl B, Intel Data, "The Current French Capability of Holding Hanoi and the Tonkin Delta with Forces Available to Them," to (TS) JCS 1992/334, 7 Jun 54, CCS 092 Asia (6-25-48) sec 71.

Conclusions on Aid Program

Despite the great quantity of arms the United States provided from 1950 through 1954, the aid program never functioned entirely to the satisfaction either of France or the United States.

Defense Department officials recognized a basic fallacy in the use of MDAP to support an active war. Combat operations require a smooth flow of material and the immediate availability of equipment to meet unforeseen contingencies. MDAP simply could not meet these requirements. It had been designed to build up the defensive forces of free world nations over a long period of time and was never intended to supply armies engaged in actual fighting.

Supply procedures called for the French to submit requisitions to MAAG for screening. MAAG officials eliminated all items not meeting JCS screening criteria and considered the remainder in light of their own knowledge of whether the French actually needed the items, whether they could employ them efficiently, and whether they could maintain them properly. MAAG then forwarded the revised list to Washington for screening by the military services. The services further revised the list on the basis of funds available for Indochina support. By the time the material had been programmed, procured, and delivered to Indochina, the need may have passed and some other type of equipment might be in urgent demand to meet the current situation.

Defense authorities concerned with the Indochinese program recognized this fault. In presenting the Fiscal Year 1955 Indochina program to Congress, OMA officials repeatedly stressed the fact that MDAP was being used to support a war, a purpose for which it was never intended.[7] The Joint Chiefs of Staff studied the problem in January 1954 and concluded: "The furnishing of material and other types of aid to France through the medium of MDAP has proved to be too time-consuming and cumbersome because of all the criteria and administrative procedures involved. Experience

---

7. (TS) "Congressional Presentation FY 1955 Indochina MDA Material Program," Sec, "Questions and Answers," Alden Files, OMA.

indicates that MDAP is not adaptable to or effective in providing support to our Allies during an active war." The Chiefs recommended that a special fund for Indochina be placed under the direct supervision of the Secretary of Defense. Within this framework, they declared, "criteria and procedures can be developed to satisfy the particular needs involved in supporting the French effort in the war."[8] Sentiment in favor of a solution of this type was growing, but the Geneva settlement in July made further discussion pointless.

Despite the drawbacks inherent in employment of MDAP in wartime the program undoubtedly would have operated more smoothly had the French command and staff functioned efficiently. The High Command, however, was burdened by pre-World War II staff thinking and a cumbersome logistics apparatus that resulted in waste of material and unrealistic equipment requests. MAAG officers found that the French supply organization lacked an efficient and centralized stock control system and hence had no provision for lateral redistribution. The French would submit requisitions for a given item on the basis of a shortage existing at one installation. Investigation would reveal an oversupply of the same item at another installation. These operating procedures placed a heavy burden on the American logistics system.[9]

The whole problem was concisely summarized in February 1954 by the Army attache in Saigon:

> Fact possibly not apparent to those who do not have daily contact with French military here is that their staff thinking and procedure is vintage 1935-1939. Although Navarre demands that his requirements (for United States logistical support) be filled without further screening fact that his staff not capable of accurately generating and evaluating these requirements. Acceptance these requests without detailed screening by United States military supply agencies would result waste millions of dollars.

---

8. (TS) Encl B to (TS) JCS 1992/270, 12 Jan 54, CCS 092 Asia (6-25-48) sec 54.
9. (TS) "Congressional Presentation FY 1955 Indochina MDA Material Program," Sec, "Questions and Answers," Alden Files, OMA.

Staff action are often uncoordinated and there
is no rpt no evidence of detailed long range planning.
Striking examples of this is the continuing request
for additional aircraft without making a coordinated
effort to obtain maximum utilization of those already
available. French seem to unconsciously feel that
the arrival of large quantities of new type equipment
. . . will somehow allow them to conduct operations
without commitment of manpower. In their planning
they completely overlook requirements for operation,
maintenance and storage of these items.[10]

Often MAAG's refusal to approve certain French requests was based upon the fact, known to MAAG but rarely recognized by the French, that the desired items could not be properly maintained or utilized with existing facilities and personnel. The French were wasteful and haphazard in their maintenance practices and were sensitive to criticism and offers of technial advice. Although MAAG was charged with insuring proper care of equipment supplied by the United States, French commanders barely concealed their reluctance to accept MAAG inspection, and they carefully controlled the conditions under which MAAG officers were permitted to examine their units. The French Air Force was a particularly consistent offender. Rarely did American inspectors find proper maintenance of aircraft or utilization rates approaching those of the USAF. As an OMA official told Congressmen, "The problem of supporting French units in Indochina with U.S. equipment is not concerned so much with procurement and delivery of equipment as it is with the ability of the French to support it after it is placed in their hands. . . ."

Further complicating the situation was a lack of coordination between the French High Command in Indochina and the General Staff in Paris. Never throughout the war did Paris support the armies in Indochina properly, and successive French commanders found it impossible to get personnel from

---

10. (S) Msg, USARMA Saigon Vietnam MG 39-54, to CSUSA for G-2, 032355Z Feb 54, DA-IN-37222 (4 Feb 54), CCS 092 Asia (6-25-48) sec 57.
11. (TS) "Congressional Presentation FY 1955 Indochina MDA Material Program," Sec, "Questions and Answers," Alden Files, OMA.

Metropolitan France in sufficient numbers to maintain American material received. Further, authorities in Paris frequently submitted requests through diplomatic channels or the Paris MAAG for material that French Union Forces could not use or support and, indeed, did not want.

The use of MDAP to support a war, together with inefficient French staff and supply practices, inevitably resulted in what came to be known as "crash basis supply," a type of operation that reached its peak during the Dien Bien Phu crisis. Equipment vitally needed for projected combat operations became the subject of urgent requests for immediate delivery. American programming, procurement, and shipping agencies were consequently placed under an intolerable strain, and it was frequently necessary to divert funds from the programs of other countries to the Indochina program in order to meet the increased financial demands. The occasional inability of the United States to comply with these requests led to criticism by the French that the United States was not properly supporting the war effort.

Another problem that developed, partly from American difficulty in meeting recurring crash basis requests, was that of out-of-channel communications. When the United States did not produce needed equipment promptly, or when MAAG eliminated items particularly desired, the French resorted to channels other than MAAG to obtain results. The situation was aggravated by high American officials leading the French to expect more than MAAG or the Defense Department felt could be efficiently used. When an item deemed essential was deleted from a program, the French protested through diplomatic channels. These agencies were entirely unacquainted with the merits of the argument and basis for the MAAG decision, but they generally transmitted the protest anyhow. The United States repeatedly asked France to confine MDAP business to liaison with MAAG, but the French discovered that they normally got what they wanted by using improper channels and continued to do so throughout the war.

These various factors combined to interfere with an expeditious flow of material throughout the four years during which the French received American aid in Indochina.

The demands for American aid arising from the Dien Bien Phu battle brought the whole problem into focus. It demonstrated the need for a thorough modernization of French supply organization, a more cooperative and understanding French attitude toward MAAG, and an American aid structure geared to the specific situation in Indochina. The Geneva Accords in July 1954, however, obviated the need for such a reappraisal.

APPENDIX II

TEXT OF FINAL DECLARATION - GENEVA CONFERENCE

(Unofficial translation)

Final declaration, dated July 21, 1954, of the Geneva Conference on the problem of restoring peace in Indochina, in which the representatives of Cambodia, the Democratic Republic of Viet-Nam, France, Laos, the People's Republic of China, the State of Viet-Nam, the Union of Soviet Socialist Republics, the United Kingdom and the United States of American took part.

1. The Conference takes note of the agreements ending hostilities in Cambodia, Laos, and Viet-Nam and organizing international control and the supervision of the execution of the provisions of these agreements.

2. The Conference expresses satisfaction at the ending of hostilities in Cambodia, Laos, and Viet-Nam. The Conference expresses its conviction that the execution of the provisions set out in the present declaration and in the agreements on the cessation of hostilities will permit Cambodia, Laos, and Viet-Nam henceforth to play their part, in full independence and sovereignty in the peaceful community of nations.

3. The Conference takes note of the declarations made by the Governments of Cambodia and of Laos of their intention to adopt measures permitting all citizens to take their place in the national community, in particular by participating in the next general elections, which, in conformity with the constitution of each of these countries, shall take place in the course of the year 1955, by secret ballot and in conditions of respect for fundamental freedoms.

4. The Conference takes note of the clauses in the agreement on the cessation of hostilities in Viet-Nam prohibiting the introduction into Viet-Nam of foreign troops and military personnel as well as of all kinds of arms and munitions. The Conference also takes note of the declarations made by the Governments of Cambodia and Laos of their resolution not to request foreign aid, whether in war material, in personnel, or in instructors except for

the purpose of effective defense of their territory and, in the case of Laos, to the extent defined by the agreements on the cessation of hostilities in Laos.

5. The Conference takes note of the clauses in the agreement on the cessation of hostilities in Viet-Nam to the effect that no military base at the disposition of a foreign state may be established in the regrouping zones of the two parties, the latter having the obligation to see that the zones allotted to them shall not constitute part of any military alliance and shall not be utilized for the resumption of hostilities or in the service of an aggressive policy. The Conference also takes note of the declarations of the Governments of Cambodia and Laos to the effect that they will not join in any agreement with other states if this agreement includes the obligation to participate in a military alliance not in conformity with the principles of the charter of the United Nations or, in the case of Laos, with the principles of the agreement on the cessation of hostilities in Laos or, so long as their security is not threatened, the obligation to establish bases on Cambodian or Laotian territory for the military forces of foreign powers.

6. The Conference recognizes that the essential purpose of the agreement relating to Viet-Nam is to settle military questions with a view to ending hostilities and that the military demarcation line should not in any way be interpreted as constituting a political or territorial boundary. The Conference expresses its conviction that the execution of the provisions set out in the present declaration and in the agreement on the cessation of hostilities creates the necessary basis for the achievement in the near future of a political settlement in Viet-Nam.

7. The Conference declares that, so far as Viet-Nam is concerned, the settlement of political problems, effected on the basis of respect for the principles of independence, unity, and territorial integrity, shall permit the Vietnamese people to enjoy the fundamental freedoms, guaranteed by democratic institutions established as a result of free general elections by secret ballot.